2nd Workshop on Knowledge Extraction and Integration for Deep Learning Architectures (DeeLIO 2021)

Deep Learning Inside Out

Online
10 June 2021

ISBN: 978-1-7138-3022-1

Printed from e-media with permission by:

Curran Associates, Inc.
57 Morehouse Lane
Red Hook, NY 12571

Some format issues inherent in the e-media version may also appear in this print version.

Association for Computational Linguistics
209 N. Eighth Street
Stroudsburg, Pennsylvania 18360

Phone: 1-570-476-8006
Fax: 1-570-476-0860

acl@aclweb.org

Additional copies of this publication are available from:

Curran Associates, Inc.
57 Morehouse Lane
Red Hook, NY 12571 USA
Phone: 845-758-0400
Fax: 845-758-2633
Email: curran@proceedings.com
Web: www.proceedings.com

NAACL-HLT 2021

Deep Learning Inside Out (DeeLIO): The 2nd Workshop on Knowledge Extraction and Integration for Deep Learning Architectures

Proceedings of the Workshop

June 10 2021

Introduction

Welcome to the Second Workshop on Knowledge Extraction and Integration for Deep Learning Architectures (DeeLIO)! Following the first successful edition of the workshop at EMNLP 2020, DeeLIO 2021 continues to bring together the knowledge interpretation, extraction and integration lines of research in deep learning, and to cover the area in between. Now in its second year, DeeLIO has already been established as a forum for the exchange of ideas on these topics, fostering collaboration within these research fields.

This volume includes the 14 papers presented at the workshop. DeeLIO 2021 was co-located with the Annual Conference of the North American Chapter of the Association for Computational Linguistics (NAACL-HLT 2021) and was held on June 10, 2021 as an online workshop.

We received an exceptional batch of high-quality research papers, and decided to finally accept 14 out of 22 submissions (acceptance rate 63.6%), which were presented at the workshop. It is again great to see that the accepted papers cover both thematic aspects of DeeLIO: the extraction of linguistic knowledge from deep neural models as well as the integration of knowledge from external resources, and all this for different languages and applications. All papers were presented as posters during several online poster sessions with live interactions and Q&A sessions.

We take this opportunity to thank the DeeLIO program committee for their help and thorough reviews. We also thank the authors who presented their work at DeeLIO, and the workshop participants for the valuable feedback and discussions. Encouraged by the great research presented at the workshop and all the positive feedback received, we hope to continue with the DeeLIO organization in the years to come. Finally, we are deeply honored to have three excellent talks from our invited speakers Sebastian Riedel, Vered Shwartz, and Lena Voita.

The DeeLIO workshop organizers,
Eneko Agirre, Marianna Apidianaki, and Ivan Vulić

Organizers:

Eneko Agirre (University of the Basque Country)
Marianna Apidianaki (University of Helsinki)
Ivan Vulić (University of Cambridge)

Invited Speakers:

Sebastian Riedel (Facebook AI Research and University College London)
Vered Shwartz (Allen Institute for AI and University of Washington)
Lena Voita (University of Edinburgh and University of Amsterdam)

Program Committee:

Mohit Bansal (UNC Chapel Hill)
Davide Buscaldi (Université Paris 13)
Ilias Chalkidis (University of Copenhagen)
Anne Cocos (Ask Iggy)
Valeria de Paiva (Topos Institute)
Luis Espinosa-Anke (University of Cardiff)
Francis Ferraro (University of Maryland Baltimore County)
Goran Glavaš (University of Mannheim)
Eduard Hovy (Carnegie Mellon Institute)
Aishwarya Kamath (New York University)
Giannis Karamanolakis (Columbia University)
Anne Lauscher (University of Mannheim)
Carolin Lawrence (NEC Labs)
Qianchu Liu (University of Cambridge)
Olga Majewska (University of Cambridge)
Prodromos Malakasiotis (Athens University of Economics and Business)
Stephen Mayhew (Duolingo)
Sebastian Padó (University of Stuttgart)
Simone Paolo Ponzetto (University of Mannheim)
Roi Reichart (Technion, IIT)
Steven Schockaert (University of Cardiff)
Sabine Schulte im Walde (University of Stuttgart)
Aitor Soroa (University of the Basque Country)
Tim Van de Cruys (KU Leuven)
John Wieting (Carnegie Mellon University)
Deyi Xiong (Tianjin University)
Dian Yu (Tencent AI Lab)

Table of Contents

Transformer visualization via dictionary learning: contextualized embedding as a linear superposition of transformer factors
Zeyu Yun, Yubei Chen, Bruno Olshausen and Yann LeCun 1

Reconstructing Implicit Knowledge with Language Models
Maria Becker, Siting Liang and Anette Frank 11

Investigating the Effect of Background Knowledge on Natural Questions
Vidhisha Balachandran, Bhuwan Dhingra, Haitian Sun, Michael Collins and William Cohen . . . 25

Augmenting Topic Aware Knowledge-Grounded Conversations with Dynamic Built Knowledge Graphs
Junjie Wu and Hao Zhou 31

What Makes My Model Perplexed? A Linguistic Investigation on Neural Language Models Perplexity
Alessio Miaschi, Dominique Brunato, Felice Dell'Orletta and Giulia Venturi 40

How Do BERT Embeddings Organize Linguistic Knowledge?
Giovanni Puccetti, Alessio Miaschi and Felice Dell'Orletta 48

ERNIE-NLI: Analyzing the Impact of Domain-Specific External Knowledge on Enhanced Representations for NLI
Lisa Bauer, Lingjia Deng and Mohit Bansal 58

Enhancing Multiple-Choice Question Answering with Causal Knowledge
Dhairya Dalal, Mihael Arcan and Paul Buitelaar 70

Low Anisotropy Sense Retrofitting (LASeR) : Towards Isotropic and Sense Enriched Representations
Geetanjali Bihani and Julia Rayz 81

KW-ATTN: Knowledge Infused Attention for Accurate and Interpretable Text Classification
Hyeju Jang, Seojin Bang, Wen Xiao, Giuseppe Carenini, Raymond Ng and Young ji Lee 96

Multi-input Recurrent Independent Mechanisms for leveraging knowledge sources: Case studies on sentiment analysis and health text mining
Parsa Bagherzadeh and Sabine Bergler 108

What BERTs and GPTs know about your brand? Probing contextual language models for affect associations
Vivek Srivastava, Stephen Pilli, Savita Bhat, Niranjan Pedanekar and Shirish Karande 119

Attention vs non-attention for a Shapley-based explanation method
Tom Kersten, Hugh Mee Wong, Jaap Jumelet and Dieuwke Hupkes 129

Predicting Numerals in Natural Language Text Using a Language Model Considering the Quantitative Aspects of Numerals
Taku Sakamoto and Akiko Aizawa 140

Transformer visualization via dictionary learning: contextualized embedding as a linear superposition of transformer factors

Zeyu Yun[*2] **Yubei Chen**[* 1,2] **Bruno A Olshausen**[2,4] **Yann LeCun**[1,3]

[1] Facebook AI Research
[2] Berkeley AI Research (BAIR), UC Berkeley
[3] New York University
[4] Redwood Center for Theoretical Neuroscience, UC Berkeley

Abstract

Transformer networks have revolutionized NLP representation learning since they were introduced. Though a great effort has been made to explain the representation in transformers, it is widely recognized that our understanding is not sufficient. One important reason is that there lack enough visualization tools for detailed analysis. In this paper, we propose to use dictionary learning to open up these 'black boxes' as linear superpositions of transformer factors. Through visualization, we demonstrate the hierarchical semantic structures captured by the transformer factors, e.g., word-level polysemy disambiguation, sentence-level pattern formation, and long-range dependency. While some of these patterns confirm the conventional prior linguistic knowledge, the rest are relatively unexpected, which may provide new insights. We hope this visualization tool can bring further knowledge and a better understanding of how transformer networks work. The code is available at `https://github.com/zeyuyun1/TransformerVis`.

1 Introduction

Though the transformer networks (Vaswani et al., 2017; Devlin et al., 2018) have achieved great success, our understanding of how they work is still fairly limited. This has triggered increasing efforts to visualize and analyze these "black boxes". Besides a direct visualization of the attention weights, most of the current efforts to interpret transformer models involve "probing tasks". They are achieved by attaching a light-weighted auxiliary classifier at the output of the target transformer layer. Then only the auxiliary classifier is trained for well-known NLP tasks like part-of-speech (POS) Tagging, Named-entity recognition (NER) Tagging, Syntactic Dependency, etc. Tenney et al. (2019) and Liu et al. (2019) show transformer models have excellent performance in those probing tasks. These results indicate that transformer models have learned the language representation related to the probing tasks. Though the probing tasks are great tools for interpreting language models, their limitation is explained in Rogers et al. (2020). We summarize the limitation into three major points:

- Most probing tasks, like POS and NER tagging, are too simple. A model that performs well in those probing tasks does not reflect the model's true capacity.
- Probing tasks can only verify whether a certain prior structure is learned in a language model. They can not reveal the structures beyond our prior knowledge.
- It's hard to locate where exactly the related linguistic representation is learned in the transformer.

Efforts are made to remove those limitations and make probing tasks more diverse. For instance, Hewitt and Manning (2019) proposes "structural probe", which is a much more intricate probing task. Jiang et al. (2020) proposes to generate specific probing tasks automatically. Non-probing methods are also explored to relieve the last two limitations. For example, Reif et al. (2019) visualizes embedding from BERT using UMAP and shows that the embeddings of the same word under different contexts are separated into different clusters. Ethayarajh (2019) analyzes the similarity between embeddings of the same word in different contexts. Both of these works show transformers provide a context-specific representation.

Faruqui et al. (2015); Arora et al. (2018); Zhang et al. (2019) demonstrate how to use dictionary learning to explain, improve, and visualize the uncontextualized word embedding representations. In

* equal contribution. Correspondence to: Zeyu Yun <chobitstian@berkeley.edu>, Yubei Chen <yubeic@{fb.com, berkeley.edu}>

Proceedings of Deep Learning Inside Out (DeeLIO): The 2nd Workshop on Knowledge Extraction and Integration for Deep Learning Architectures, pages 1–10
Online, June 10, 2021.

this work, we propose to use dictionary learning to alleviate the limitations of the other transformer interpretation techniques. Our results show that dictionary learning provides a powerful visualization tool, leading to some surprising new knowledge.

2 Method

Hypothesis: contextualized word embedding as a sparse linear superposition of transformer factors. It is shown that word embedding vectors can be factorized into a sparse linear combination of word factors (Arora et al., 2018; Zhang et al., 2019), which correspond to elementary semantic meanings. An example is:

$$\text{apple} = 0.09\text{“dessert”} + 0.11\text{“organism”} + 0.16\text{“fruit”} + 0.22\text{“mobile\&IT”} + 0.42\text{“other”}.$$

We view the latent representation of words in a transformer as contextualized word embedding. Similarly, we hypothesize that a contextualized word embedding vector can also be factorized as a sparse linear superposition of a set of elementary elements, which we call *transformer factors*. The exact definition will be presented later in this section.

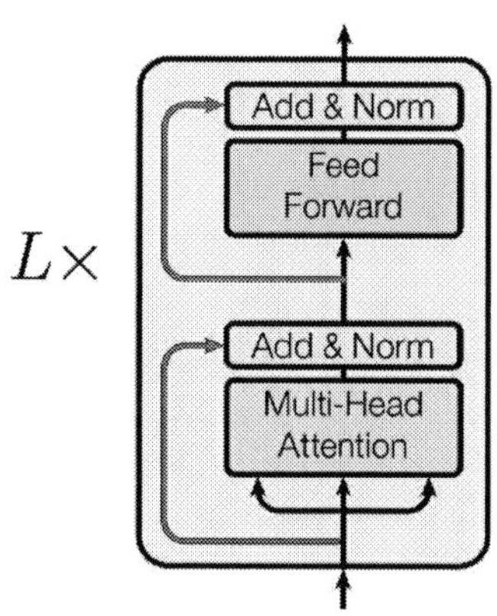

Figure 1: Building block (layer) of transformer

Due to the skip connections in each of the transformer blocks, we hypothesize that the representation in any layer would be a superposition of the hierarchical representations in all of the lower layers. As a result, the output of a particular transformer block would be the sum of all of the modifications along the way. Indeed, we verify this intuition with the experiments. Based on the above observation, we propose to learn a single dictionary for the contextualized word vectors from different layers' output.

To learn a dictionary of transformer factors with non-negative sparse coding.

Given a set of tokenized text sequences, we collect the contextualized embedding of every word using a transformer model. We define the set of all word embedding vectors from lth layer of transformer model as $X^{(l)}$. Furthermore, we collect the embeddings across all layers into a single set $X = X^{(1)} \cup X^{(2)} \cup \cdots \cup X^{(L)}$.

By our hypothesis, we assume each embedding vector $x \in X$ is a sparse linear superposition of *transformer factors*:

$$x = \Phi\alpha + \epsilon,\ s.t.\ \alpha \succeq 0, \tag{1}$$

where $\Phi \in \mathbb{R}^{d\times m}$ is a dictionary matrix with columns $\Phi_{:,c}$, $\boldsymbol{\alpha} \in \mathbb{R}^m$ is a sparse vector of coefficients to be inferred and $\boldsymbol{\epsilon}$ is a vector containing independent Gaussian noise samples, which are assumed to be small relative to $\boldsymbol{x}$. Typically $m > d$ so that the representation is *overcomplete*. This inverse problem can be efficiently solved by FISTA algorithm (Beck and Teboulle, 2009). The dictionary matrix Φ can be learned in an iterative fashion by using non-negative sparse coding, which we leave to the appendix section C. Each column $\Phi_{:,c}$ of Φ is a *transformer factor* and its corresponding sparse coefficient $\boldsymbol{\alpha}_c$ is its activation level.

Visualization by top activation and LIME interpretation. An important empirical method to visualize a feature in deep learning is to use the input samples, which trigger the top activation of the feature (Zeiler and Fergus, 2014). We adopt this convention. As a starting point, we try to visualize each of the dimensions of a particular layer, $X^{(l)}$. Unfortunately, the hidden dimensions of transformers are not semantically meaningful, which is similar to the uncontextualized word embeddings (Zhang et al., 2019).

Instead, we can try to visualize the transformer factors. For a transformer factor $\Phi_{:,c}$ and for a layer-l, we denote the 1000 contextualized word vectors with the largest sparse coefficients $\alpha_c^{(l)}$ as $X_c^{(l)} \subset X^{(l)}$, which correspond to 1000 different sequences. For example, Figure 3 shows the top 5 words that activated transformer factor-17 $\Phi_{:,17}$ at layer-0, layer-2, and layer-6 respectively. Since a contextualized word vector is generally affected by many tokens in the sequence, we can use LIME (Ribeiro et al., 2016) to assign a weight to each token in the sequence to identify their relative importance to α_c. The detailed method is left to Section 3.

To determine low-, mid-, and high-level transformer factors with importance score. As we build a single dictionary for all of the transformer layers, the semantic meaning of the transformer factors has different levels. While some of the factors appear in lower layers and continue to be used in the later stages, the rest of the factors may only be activated in the higher layers of the transformer network. A central question in representation learning is: "where does the network learn certain information?" To answer this question, we can compute an "importance score" for each transformer factor $\Phi_{:,c}$ at layer-l as $I_c^{(l)}$. $I_c^{(l)}$ is the average of the largest 1000 sparse coefficients $\alpha_c^{(l)}$'s, which correspond to $X_c^{(l)}$. We plot the importance scores for each transformer factor as a curve is shown in Figure 2. We then use these importance score (IS) curves to identify which layer a transformer factor emerges. Figure 2a shows an IS curve peak in the earlier layer. The corresponding transformer factor emerges in the earlier stage, which may capture lower-level semantic meanings. In contrast, Figure 2b shows a peak in the higher layers, which indicates the transformer factor emerges much later and may correspond to mid- or high-level semantic structures. More subtleties are involved when distinguishing between mid-level and high-level factors, which will be discussed later.

An important characteristic is that the IS curve for each transformer factor is relatively smooth. This indicates if a vital feature is learned in the beginning layers, it won't disappear in later stages. Instead, it will be carried all the way to the end with gradually decayed weight since many more features would join along the way. Similarly, abstract information learned in higher layers is slowly developed from the early layers. Figure 3 and 5 confirm this idea, which will be explained in the next section.

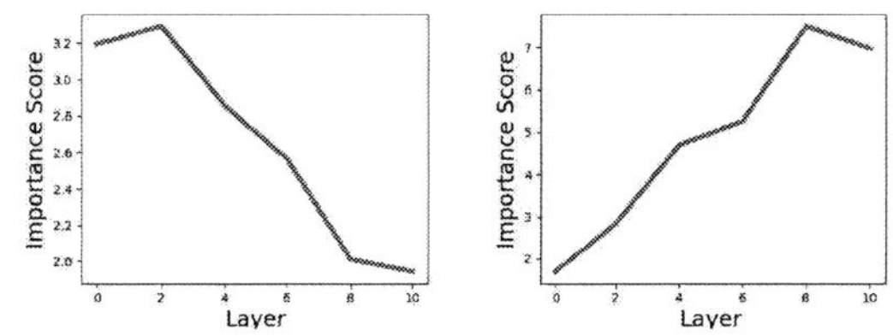

(a) (b)

Figure 2: Importance score (IS) across all layers for two different transformer factors. (a) This figure shows a typical IS curve of a transformer factor corresponding to low-level information. (b) This figure shows a typical IS curve of a transformer factor corresponds to mid-level information.

3 Experiments and Discoveries

We use a 12-layer pre-trained BERT model (Pre; Devlin et al., 2018) and freeze the weights. Since we learn a single dictionary of transformer factors for all of the layers in the transformer, we show that these transformer factors correspond to different levels of semantic or syntactic patterns. The patterns can be roughly divided into three categories: word-level disambiguation, sentence-level pattern formation, and long-range dependency. In the following, we provide detailed visualization for each pattern category. Due to the space limit, only a small amount of the factors are demonstrated in the paper. To alleviate the "cherry-picking" bias, we also build a website for the interested readers to play with these results.

Low-level: word-level polysemy disambiguation. While the input embedding of a token contains polysemy, we find transformer factors with early IS curve peaks usually correspond to a specific word-level meaning. By visualizing the top activation sequences, we can see how word-level disambiguation is gradually developed in a transformer.

We show how the disambiguation effect develops progressively through each layer in Figure 3. In Figure 3, the top 5 activated words and their contexts for transformer factor $\Phi_{:,30}$ in different layers are listed. The top activated words in layer 0 contain the word "left" varying senses, which is being mostly disambiguated in layer 2 albeit not completely. In layer 4, the word "left" is fully disambiguated since the top-activated word contains only "left" with the word sense "leaving, exiting." We also show more examples of those types of transformer factors in Table 1: for each transformer factor, we list out the top 3 activated words and their contexts in layer 4. As shown in the table, nearly all top-activated words are disambiguated into a single sense.

Further, we can quantify the quality of the disambiguation ability of the transformer model. In the example above, since the top 1000 activated words

- he< unk> shortly to returne to italy where he left his family
- banks who bet big in assisting gulf to defeat mesa only to be left broke when gulf backed out.
- with huggins at the helm, roundly defeated the rump left wing of the reform party to begin 28 years of unint
- l level; the robe is held at the right thigh by the left hand, and the legs are shapeless.
- end), howard felver(quarterback), caley(left halfback), gustave ferbert(right halfback

(a) layer 0

- in from oklahoma and northeast texas, dissipating what was left of this tropical depression by september 2.
- learning to fly and had completed nearly 250 hours by the time he left america.
- years later, in 1967, lefty is incorrectly told that that year' s detroit riots were
- ang told reporters from nature that about a dozen of the fossils had left china illegally.
- allegiance; the ten who refused were taken to newgate prison and left to starve.

(b) layer 2

- in getting the naval officers into his house, and the mob eventually left.
- all of the federal troops had left at this point, except totten who had stayed behind to
- saying that he has left the outsiders, kovu asks simba to let him join
- eventually, all boycott' s employees left, forcing him to run the estate without help.
- story concerned the attempts of a scientist to photograph the soul as it left the body.

(c) layer 6

Figure 3: Visualization of a low-level transformer factor, $\Phi_{:,30}$ at different layers. (a), (b) and (c) are the top-activated words and contexts for $\Phi_{:,30}$ in layer-0, 2 and 4 respectively. We can see that at layer-0, this transformer factor corresponds to word vectors that encode the word "left" with different senses. In layer-2, a majority of the top activated words "left" correspond to a single sense, "leaving, exiting." In layer 4, all of the top-activated words "left" have corresponded to the same sense, "leaving, exiting." Due to space limitations, we invite the readers to use our website to see more of those disambiguation effects.

	Top 3 activated words and their contexts	Explanation
$\Phi_{:,2}$	• that snare shot sounded like somebody' d kicked open the door to your mind". • i became very frustrated with that and finally made up my mind to start getting back into things." • when evita asked for more time so she could make up her mind, the crowd demanded," ¡ ahora, evita,<	• Word "mind" • Noun • Definition: the element of a person that enables them to be aware of the world and their experiences.
$\Phi_{:,16}$	•nington joined the five members xero and the band was renamed to linkin park. • times about his feelings about gordon, and the price family even sat away from park' s supporters during the trial itself. • on 25 january 2010, the morning of park' s 66th birthday, he was found hanged and unconscious in his	• Word "park" • Noun • Definition: a common first and last name
$\Phi_{:,30}$	• saying that he has left the outsiders, kovu asks simba to let him join his pride • eventually, all boycott' s employees left, forcing him to run the estate without help. • the story concerned the attempts of a scientist to photograph the soul as it left the body.	• Word "left" • Verb • Definition: leaving, exiting
$\Phi_{:,33}$	• forced to visit the sarajevo television station at night and to film with as little light as possible to avoid the attention of snipers and bombers. • by the modest, cream@-@ colored attire in the airy, light@-@ filled clip. • the man asked her to help him carry the case to his car, a light@-@ brown volkswagen beetle.	• Word "light" • Noun • Definition: the natural agent that stimulates sight and makes things visible

Table 1: Several examples of low-level transformer factors. Their top-activated words in layer 4 are marked blue, and the corresponding contexts are shown as examples for each transformer factor. As shown in the table, nearly all of the top-activated words are disambiguated into a single sense. Please note the last example of $\Phi_{:,33}$ is a rare exception, the reader may check the appendix to see a more complete list. More examples, top-activated words and contexts are provided in Appendix.

and contexts are "left" with only the word sense "leave, exiting", we can assume "left" when used as a verb, triggers higher activation in $\Phi_{:,30}$ than "left" used as other sense of speech. We can verify this hypothesis using a human-annotated corpus: Brown corpus (Francis and Kucera, 1979). In this corpus, each word is annotated with its corresponding part-of-speech. We collect all the sentences contains the word "left" annotated as a verb in one set and sentences contains "left" annotated as other part-of-speech. As shown in Figure 4a, in layer 0, the average activation of $\Phi_{:,30}$ for the word "left" marked as a verb is no different from "left" as other senses. However, at layer 2, "left" marked as a verb triggers a higher activation of $\Phi_{:,30}$. In layer 4, this difference further increases, indicating disambiguation develops progressively across layers. In fact, we plot the activation of "left" marked as verb and the activation of other "left" in Figure 4b. In layer 4, they are nearly linearly separable by this

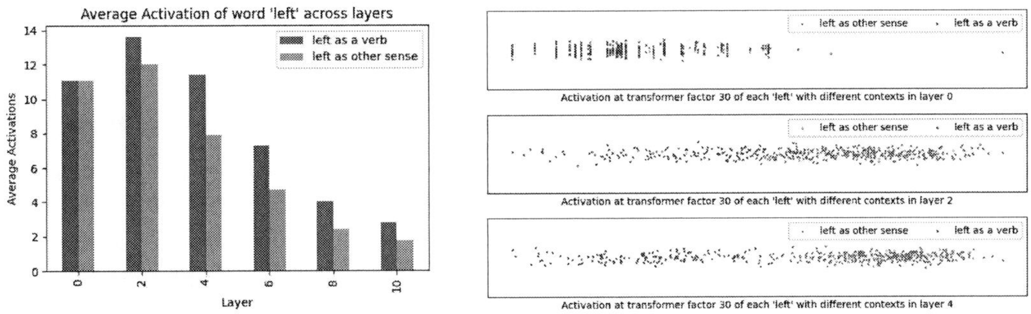

(a) (b)

Figure 4: (a) Average activation of $\Phi_{:,30}$ for word vector "left" across different layers. (b) Instead of averaging, we plot the activation of all "left" with different contexts in layer-0, 2, and 4. Random noise is added to the y-axis to prevent overplotting. The activation of $\Phi_{:,30}$ for two different word senses of "left" is blended together in layer-0. They disentangle to a great extent in layer-2 and nearly separable in layer-4 by this single dimension.

(a) layer 4

- wrote that" stankonia reeks of artful ambition rendered with impeccable skill"
- stated similar pros, describing the soundtrack as" suspenseful, dynamic and always adrenaline charged."
- with guest performances from vocalists frances maya and susan calloway, among others. the concert premiered several
- . it was an attitude of mind which tempered the sternness of his approach with an engaging humour and
- " all very effectively done, creepily atmospheric and splendidly gruesome"

(b) layer 6

- a film that' s stylish, breezily entertaining, and surprisingly sweet." on metacritic
- consensus reads" charming, audacious, and timely, wall@-@ e' s light
- .@ 1 out of 10, as being" beautiful, charismatic, engaging and one of the most
- that sinatra is" simply superb, comical, pitiful, childishly brave,
- everything madonna has been denounced for being — meticulous, calculated, domineering and artificial.

(c) layer 8

- new york times called it a" zany, lively, uninhibited, sexual odyssey
- she stated that the show was" breezy and entertaining and reasonably clever, at least when its sherlock
- of five stars, called it" a dark and delicious delight[and] a must@-@
- episodes, saying," it ' s smart, entertaining, and has moments so shocking that you '
- " full of exhilarating, ecstatic, thrilling, fun and sometimes downright silly songs"

Figure 5: Visualization of a mid-level transformer factor. (a), (b), (c) are the top 5 activated words and contexts for this transformer factor in layer-4, 6, and 8 respectively. Again, the position of the word vector is marked blue. Please notice that sometimes only a part of a word is marked blue. This is due to that BERT uses word-piece tokenizer instead of whole word tokenizer. This transformer factor corresponds to the pattern of "consecutive adjective". As shown in the figure, this feature starts to develop at layer-4 and fully develops at layer-8.

	Precision (%)	Recall (%)	F1 score (%)
Average perceptron POS tagger	92.7	95.5	94.1
Finetuned BERT base model for POS task	97.5	95.2	96.3
Logistic regression classifier with activation of $\Phi_{:,30}$ at layer 4	97.2	**95.8**	**96.5**

Table 2: Evaluation of binary POS tagging task: predict whether or not "left" in a given context is a verb.

single feature. Since each word "left" corresponds to an activation value, we can perform a logistic regression classification to differentiate those two types of "left". From the result shown in Figure 4a, it is pretty fascinating to see that the disambiguation ability of just $\Phi_{:,30}$ is better than the other two classifiers trained with supervised data. This result confirms that disambiguation is indeed done in the early part of pre-trained transformer model and we are able to detect it via dictionary learning.

Mid level: sentence-level pattern formation. We find most of the transformer factors, with an IS curve peak after layer 6, capture mid-level or high-level semantic meanings. In particular, the mid-level ones correspond to semantic patterns like phrases and sentences pattern.

We first show two detailed examples of mid-level transformer factors. Figure 5 shows a transformer factor that detects the pattern of consecutive usage of adjectives. This pattern starts to emerge at layer 4, develops at layer 6, and becomes quite reliable at layer 8. Figure 6 shows a transformer factor, which corresponds to a pretty unexpected pattern: "unit exchange", e.g., 56 inches (140 cm). Although this exact pattern only starts to appear at layer 8, the sub-structures that make this pattern, e.g., parenthesis and numbers, appear to trigger this factor in layers 4 and 6. Thus this transformer factor is also

• – 1 at home to end york' s three@-@ match run without a win, with all the team' s goals coming in the first half from carson, fletcher and brobbel(2).
• football league second division(2): 1932 – 33, 1962 – 63
• the journal of modern history 33(2): 148 – 156@.
• football league first division runner@-@ up(1): 1955 – 56
• the journal of modern history 40(2): 155 – 165@.

(a) layer 4

• the spy next door(larry(lucas till))
• hannah montana: the movie(travis brody(lucas till))
• percy jackson& the olympians: the lightning thief(percy jackson(logan lerman))
• charlie and the chocolate factory(willy wonka(johnny depp))
• harry potter film series(percy weasley(chris rankin))

(b) layer 6

•-@ 16 hand(56 to 64 inches(140 to 160 cm)) war horse is that it was a matter of pride
• moving above 83 ° f(28 ° c) sea surface temperatures, kathleen quickly strengthened.
• at prudhoe bay was more than 120 ° f(49 ° c) degrees, and there was a danger that if it
•@ 3@-@ inch(160 mm) calibre steel barrel.
• outdoor seating area(4@,@ 300 square feet(400 m2)) and a 2@,@ 500@-@

(c) layer 8

Figure 6: Another example of a mid-level transformer factor visualized at layer-4, 6, and 8. The pattern that corresponds to this transformer factor is "unit exchange". Such a pattern is somewhat unexpected based on linguistic prior knowledge.

	2 example words and their contexts with high activation	Patterns	L4 (%)	L6 (%)	L8 (%)	L10 (%)
$\Phi_{:,13}$	• the steel pipeline was about 20 ° f(- 7 ° c) degrees. • hand(56 to 64 inches(140 to 160 cm)) war horse is that it was a	Unit exchange with parentheses	0	0	64.5	95.5
$\Phi_{:,42}$	• he died at the hospice of lancaster county from heart • holly' s drummer carl bunch suffered frostbite to his toes(while aboard the ailments on 23 june 2007.	Something unfortunate happened	94.0	100	100	100
$\Phi_{:,50}$	• hurricane pack 1 was a revamped version of story mode; • in 1998, the categories were retitled best short form music video, and best	Doing something again, or making something new again	74.5	100	100	100
$\Phi_{:,86}$	• he finished the 2005 – 06 season with 21 appearances and seven goals. • of an offensive game, finishing off the 2001 – 02 season with 58 points in the 47 games	Consecutive years, used in foodball season naming	0	100	85.0	95.5
$\Phi_{:,102}$	• the most prominent of which was bishop abel muzorewa' s united african national council • ralambo' s father, andriamanelo, had established rules of succession by	African names	99.0	100	100	100
$\Phi_{:,125}$	• music writer jeff weiss of pitchfork describes the" enduring image" • club reviewer erik adams wrote that the episode was a perfect mix	Describing someone in a paraphrasing style. Name, Career	15.5	99.0	100	98.5
$\Phi_{:,184}$	• the world wide fund for nature(wwf) announced in 2010 that a biodiversity study from • fm) was halted by the federal communications commission(fcc) due to a complaint that the company buying	Institution with abbreviation	0	15.5	39.0	63.0
$\Phi_{:,193}$	• 74, 22@,@ 500 vietnamese during 1979 – 92, over 2@,@ 500 bosnian •, the russo@-@ turkish war of 1877 – 88 and the first balkan war in 1913.	Time span in years	97.0	95.5	96.5	95.5
$\Phi_{:,195}$	•s, hares, badgers, foxes, weasels, ground squirrels, mice, hamsters •-@ watching, boxing, chess, cycling, drama, languages, geography, jazz and other music	Consecutive of noun (Enumerating)	8.0	98.5	100	100
$\Phi_{:,225}$	• technologist at the united states marine hospital in key west, florida who developed a morbid obsession for • 00°,11", w, near smith valley, nevada.	Places in US, followings the convention "city, state"	51.5	91.5	91.0	77.5

Table 3: A list of typical mid-level transformer factors. The top-activation words and their context sequences for each transformer factor at layer-8 are shown in the second column. We summarize the patterns of each transformer factor in the third column. The last 4 columns are the percentage of the top 200 activated words and sequences that contain the summarized patterns in layer-4,6,8, and 10 respectively.

gradually developed through several layers.

While some mid-level transformer factors verify common semantic or syntactic patterns, there are also many surprising mid-level transformer factors. We list a few in Table 3 with quantitative analysis.

For each listed transformer factor, we analyze the top 200 activating words and their contexts in each layer. We record the percentage of those words and contexts that correspond to the factors' semantic pattern in Table 3. From the table, we see that large

	Adversarial Text	Explaination	α_{35}
(o)	album as "full of exhilarating, ecstatic, thrilling, fun and sometimes downright silly songs"	The original top-activated word and its context sentence for transformer factor $\Phi_{:,35}$ (not an adversarial text)	9.5
(a)	album as "full of delightful, lively, exciting, interesting and sometimes downright silly songs"	Replace the adjectives in sentence (o) with different adjectives.	9.2
(b)	album as "full of unfortunate, heartbroken, annoying, boring and sometimes downright silly songs"	Replace the adjectives in sentence (o) with negative adjectives.	8.2
(c)	album as "full of [UNK], [UNK], thrilling, [UNK] and sometimes downright silly songs"	Mask the adjectives in sentence (o) with unknown tokens.	5.3
(d)	album as "full of thrilling and sometimes downright silly songs"	Remove the first three adjectives in sentence (o).	7.8
(e)	album as "full of natural, smooth, rock, electronic and sometimes downright silly songs"	Replace the adjectives in sentence (o) with neutral adjectives.	6.2
(f)	each participant starts the battle with one balloon. these can be re@-@ inflated up to four	Use a random sentence.	0.0
(g)	The book is described as "innovative, beautiful and brilliant". It receive the highest opinion from James Wood	We create this sentence that contain the pattern of consecutive adjective.	7.9

Table 4: We construct adversarial texts similar but different to the pattern "Consecutive adjective". The last column shows the activation of $\Phi_{:,35}$, or $\alpha_{35}^{(8)}$, w.r.t. the blue-marked word in layer 8.

percentages of top-activated words and contexts do corresponds to the pattern we describe. It also shows most of these mid-level patterns start to develop at layer 4 or 6. More detailed examples are provided in the appendix section F. Though it's still mysterious why the transformer network develops representations for these surprising patterns, we believe such a direct visualization can provide additional insights, which complements the "probing tasks".

To further confirm a transformer factor does correspond to a specific pattern, we can use constructed example words and context to probe their activation. In Table 4, we construct several text sequences that are similar to the patterns corresponding to a particular transformer factor but with subtle differences. The result confirms that the context that strictly follows the pattern represented by that transformer factor triggers a high activation. On the other hand, the closer the adversarial example to this pattern, the higher activation it receives at this transformer factor.

High-level: long-range dependency. High-level transformer factors correspond to those linguistic patterns that span an extended range in the text. Since the IS curves of mid-level and high-level transformer factors are similar, it is difficult to distinguish those transformer factors based on their IS cures. Thus, we have to manually examine the top-activation words and contexts for each transformer factor to differentiate between mid-level and high-level transformer factors. To ease the process, we choose to use the black-box interpretation algorithm *LIME* (Ribeiro et al., 2016) to identify the contribution of each token in a sequence. There also exist interpretation tools that specifically leverage the transformer architecture (Chefer et al., 2021, 2020). In the future, one could adapt those interpretation tools, which may potentially provide better visualization.

Given a sequence $s \in S$, we can treat $\alpha_{c,i}^{(l)}$, the activation of $\Phi_{:,c}$ in layer-l at location i, as a scalar function of s, $f_{c,i}^{(l)}(s)$. Assume a sequence s triggers a high activation $\alpha_{c,i}^{(l)}$, i.e. $f_{c,i}^{(l)}(s)$ is large. We want to know how much each token (or equivalently each position) in s contributes to $f_{c,i}^{(l)}(s)$. To do so, we generated a sequence set $\mathcal{S}(s)$, where each $s' \in \mathcal{S}(s)$ is the same as s except for that several random positions in s' are masked by ['UNK'] (the unknown token). Then we learns a linear model $g_w(s')$ with weights $w \in \mathbb{R}^T$ to approximate $f(s')$, where T is the length of sentence s. This can be solved as a ridge regression:

$$\min_{w \in \mathbb{R}^T} \mathcal{L}(f, w, \mathcal{S}(s)) + \sigma \|w\|_2^2.$$

The learned weights w can serve as a saliency map that reflects the "contribution" of each token in the sequence s. Like in Figure 7, the color reflects the weights w at each position. Red means the given position has positive weight and green means negative weight. The magnitude of weight is represented by the intensity. The redder a token is, the more it contributions to the activation of the transformer factor. We leave more implementation and mathematical formulation details of LIME algorithm in the appendix.

We provide detailed visualization for two different transformer factors that show long-range dependency in Figure 7, 8. Since visualization of high-level information requires more extended context, we only offer the top two activated words and their contexts for each such transformer factor. Many more will be provided in the appendix section G.

We name the pattern for transformer factor $\Phi_{:,297}$ in Figure 7 as "repetitive pattern detector". All top activated contexts for $\Phi_{:,297}$ contain an obvious repetitive structure. Specifically, the text snippet "can't get you out of my head" appears twice in the first example, and the text snippet "xxx class passenger, star alliance" appears three times in the second example. Compared to the patterns we found in the mid-level [6], the high-level patterns like "repetitive pattern detector" are much more abstract. In some sense, the transformer detects if there are two (or multiple) almost identical embedding vectors at layer-10 without caring what they are. Such behavior might be highly related to the concept proposed in the capsule networks (Sabour et al., 2017; Hinton, 2021). To further understand this behavior and study how the self-attention mechanism helps model the relationships between the features outlines an interesting future research direction.

Figure 8 shown another high-level factor, which detects text snippets related to "the beginning of a biography". The necessary components, day of birth as month and four-digit years, first name and last name, familial relation, and career, are all mid-level information. In Figure 8, we see that all the information relates to biography has a high weight in the saliency map. Thus, they are all together combined to detect the high-level pattern.

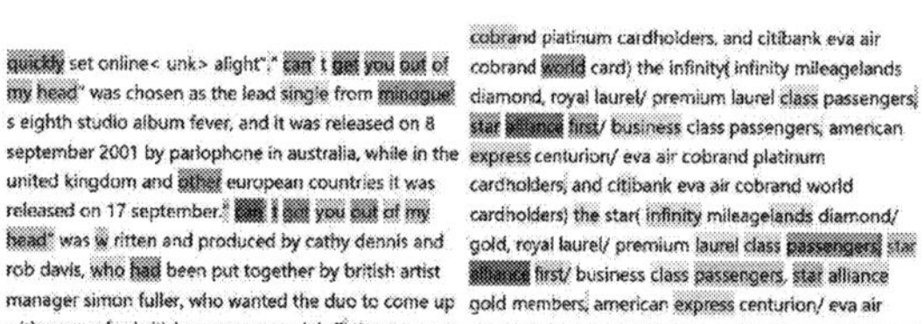

Figure 7: Two examples of the high activated words and their contexts for transformer factor $\Phi_{:,297}$. We also provide the saliency map of the tokens generated using LIME. This transformer factor corresponds to the concept: "repetitive pattern detector". In other words, repetitive text sequences will trigger high activation of $\Phi_{:,297}$.

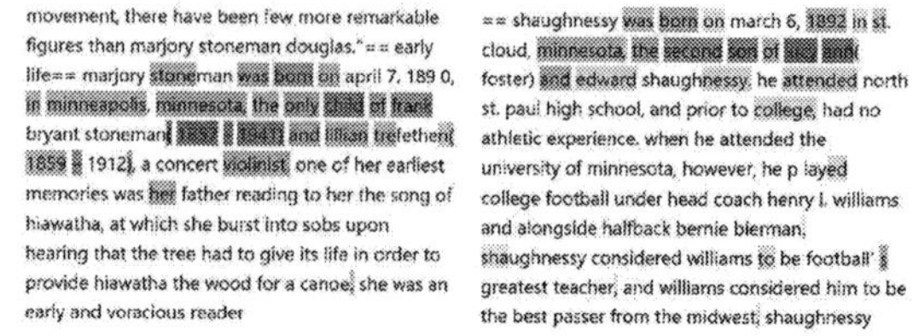

Figure 8: Visualization of $\Phi_{:,322}$. This transformer factor corresponds to the concept: "some born in some year" in biography. All of the high-activation contexts contain the beginning of a biography. As shown in the figure, the attributes of someone, name, age, career, and familial relation all have high saliency weights.

4 Discussion

Dictionary learning has been successfully used to visualize the classical word embeddings (Arora et al., 2018; Zhang et al., 2019). In this paper, we propose to use this simple method to visualize the representation learned in transformer networks to supplement the implicit "probing-tasks" methods. Our results show that the learned transformer factors are relatively reliable and can even provide many surprising insights into the linguistic structures. This simple tool can open up the transformer networks and show the hierarchical semantic or syntactic representation learned at different stages. In short, we find word-level disambiguation, sentence-level pattern formation, and long-range dependency. The idea of a neural network learns low-level features in early layers, and abstract concepts in the later stages are very similar to the visualization in CNN (Zeiler and Fergus, 2014). Dictionary learning can be a convenient tool to help visualize a broad category of neural networks with skip connections, like ResNet (He et al., 2016), ViT models (Dosovitskiy et al., 2020), etc. For more interested readers, we provide an interactive website[1] for the readers to gain some further insights.

Acknowledgements

We thank our reviewers for their detailed and insightful comments. We also thank Yuhao Zhang for his suggestions during the preparation of this paper.

References

Pretrained bert base model (12 layers). `https://huggingface.co/bert-base-uncased`,

[1] https://transformervis.github.io/transformervis/

last accessed on 03/11/2021.

Sanjeev Arora, Yuanzhi Li, Yingyu Liang, Tengyu Ma, and Andrej Risteski. 2018. Linear algebraic structure of word senses, with applications to polysemy. *Transactions of the Association for Computational Linguistics*, 6:483–495.

Amir Beck and Marc Teboulle. 2009. A fast iterative shrinkage-thresholding algorithm for linear inverse problems. *SIAM journal on imaging sciences*, 2(1):183–202.

Hila Chefer, Shir Gur, and Lior Wolf. 2020. Transformer interpretability beyond attention visualization. *CoRR*, abs/2012.09838.

Hila Chefer, Shir Gur, and Lior Wolf. 2021. Generic attention-model explainability for interpreting bimodal and encoder-decoder transformers. *CoRR*, abs/2103.15679.

Jacob Devlin, Ming-Wei Chang, Kenton Lee, and Kristina Toutanova. 2018. BERT: pre-training of deep bidirectional transformers for language understanding. *CoRR*, abs/1810.04805.

Alexey Dosovitskiy, Lucas Beyer, Alexander Kolesnikov, Dirk Weissenborn, Xiaohua Zhai, Thomas Unterthiner, Mostafa Dehghani, Matthias Minderer, Georg Heigold, Sylvain Gelly, et al. 2020. An image is worth 16x16 words: Transformers for image recognition at scale. *arXiv preprint arXiv:2010.11929*.

John Duchi, Elad Hazan, and Yoram Singer. 2011. Adaptive subgradient methods for online learning and stochastic optimization. *Journal of Machine Learning Research*, 12(Jul):2121–2159.

Kawin Ethayarajh. 2019. How contextual are contextualized word representations? comparing the geometry of bert, elmo, and GPT-2 embeddings. In *Proceedings of the 2019 Conference on Empirical Methods in Natural Language Processing and the 9th International Joint Conference on Natural Language Processing, EMNLP-IJCNLP*, pages 55–65. Association for Computational Linguistics.

Manaal Faruqui, Yulia Tsvetkov, Dani Yogatama, Chris Dyer, and Noah A. Smith. 2015. Sparse overcomplete word vector representations. In *Proceedings of the 53rd Annual Meeting of the Association for Computational Linguistics and the 7th International Joint Conference on Natural Language Processing (Volume 1: Long Papers)*. Association for Computational Linguistics.

W. N. Francis and H. Kucera. 1979. Brown corpus manual. Technical report, Department of Linguistics, Brown University, Providence, Rhode Island, US.

Kaiming He, Xiangyu Zhang, Shaoqing Ren, and Jian Sun. 2016. Deep residual learning for image recognition. In *Proceedings of the IEEE conference on computer vision and pattern recognition*, pages 770–778.

John Hewitt and Christopher D. Manning. 2019. A structural probe for finding syntax in word representations. In *Proceedings of the 2019 Conference of the North American Chapter of the Association for Computational Linguistics: Human Language Technologies, Volume 1 (Long and Short Papers)*.

Geoffrey Hinton. 2021. How to represent part-whole hierarchies in a neural network. *arXiv preprint arXiv:2102.12627*.

Zhengbao Jiang, Frank F. Xu, Jun Araki, and Graham Neubig. 2020. How can we know what language models know. *Trans. Assoc. Comput. Linguistics*, 8:423–438.

Nelson F. Liu, Matt Gardner, Yonatan Belinkov, Matthew E. Peters, and Noah A. Smith. 2019. Linguistic knowledge and transferability of contextual representations. In *Proceedings of the 2019 Conference of the North American Chapter of the Association for Computational Linguistics: Human Language Technologies, Volume 1 (Long and Short Papers)*. Association for Computational Linguistics.

Emily Reif, Ann Yuan, Martin Wattenberg, Fernanda B. Viégas, Andy Coenen, Adam Pearce, and Been Kim. 2019. Visualizing and measuring the geometry of BERT. In *Advances in Neural Information Processing Systems 32: Annual Conference on Neural Information Processing Systems, (NeurIPS)*, pages 8592–8600.

Marco Túlio Ribeiro, Sameer Singh, and Carlos Guestrin. 2016. "why should I trust you?": Explaining the predictions of any classifier. *CoRR*, abs/1602.04938.

Anna Rogers, Olga Kovaleva, and Anna Rumshisky. 2020. A primer in bertology: What we know about how BERT works. *Trans. Assoc. Comput. Linguistics*, 8:842–866.

Sara Sabour, Nicholas Frosst, and Geoffrey E Hinton. 2017. Dynamic routing between capsules. *arXiv preprint arXiv:1710.09829*.

Ian Tenney, Patrick Xia, Berlin Chen, Alex Wang, Adam Poliak, R Thomas McCoy, Najoung Kim, Benjamin Van Durme, Samuel R Bowman, Dipanjan Das, et al. 2019. What do you learn from context? probing for sentence structure in contextualized word representations. *arXiv preprint arXiv:1905.06316*.

Ashish Vaswani, Noam Shazeer, Niki Parmar, Jakob Uszkoreit, Llion Jones, Aidan N Gomez, Lukasz Kaiser, and Illia Polosukhin. 2017. Attention is all you need. *arXiv preprint arXiv:1706.03762*.

Matthew D Zeiler and Rob Fergus. 2014. Visualizing and understanding convolutional networks. In *European conference on computer vision*, pages 818–833. Springer.

Juexiao Zhang, Yubei Chen, Brian Cheung, and Bruno A Olshausen. 2019. Word embedding visualization via dictionary learning. *arXiv preprint arXiv:1910.03833*.

Reconstructing Implicit Knowledge with Language Models

Maria Becker, Siting Liang, Anette Frank
Department of Computational Linguistics, Heidelberg University
mbecker|liang|frank@cl.uni-heidelberg.de

Abstract

In this work we propose an approach for generating statements that explicate implicit knowledge connecting sentences in text. We make use of pre-trained language models which we refine by fine-tuning them on specifically prepared corpora that we enriched with implicit information, and by constraining them with relevant concepts and connecting commonsense knowledge paths. Manual and automatic evaluation of the generations shows that by refining language models as proposed, we can generate coherent and grammatically sound sentences that explicate implicit knowledge which connects sentence pairs in texts – on both in-domain and out-of-domain test data.

1 Introduction

In everyday communication and in texts people usually omit information that seems clear and evident, such that only part of the message needs to be expressed in words. In the following sentence:

(1-i) *Students should be allowed to use computers during the lectures,* (1-ii) *even though that bears the risk that they are writing emails instead of listening to the teacher.*

in order to understand the connection between (i) and (ii) we must know that *Computers are used for sending emails*, or that *Lectures are given by teachers*. Such **implicit** knowledge can easily be inferred by humans, since it is part of their background knowledge. By contrast, for computational systems implicitness in texts represents a challenge.

In this work we propose an approach for generating implicit knowledge sentences *in-between* contiguous sentences, which explicate their logical connection, utilizing pre-trained language models (LMs) that we refine as follows: i) we inject 'explanatory' knowledge by fine-tuning LMs on specifically prepared corpora, and (ii) condition text generation through constraints in form of relevant concepts and knowledge paths. Our work is inspired by the recent success of pre-trained LMs (Devlin et al., 2018; Radford et al., 2019; Yang et al., 2019a) in various downstream NLP tasks, including text generation and NL inference (Wang et al., 2018). However, for the task of *reconstructing implicit knowledge*, such LMs need to be carefully guided, not only to yield coherent statements, but to also ensure that they convey the missing, implicit information that connects given sentences in a text. To this end we create corpora with sentence pairs enriched with implicit information based on on Generics-KB (Bhakthavatsalam et al., 2020) and e-SNLI (Camburu et al., 2018), which we use for LM **fine-tuning**. For improved performance we explore methods of **constrained** language generation, guiding the model by way of relevant concepts and connecting commonsense knowledge paths.

We aim to build a system that is not limited to specific text genres or knowledge domains, and thus evaluate our models **in-domain** – on testsets from our fine-tuning corpora; and **out-of-domain** – using IKAT (Becker et al., 2020), an argumentative corpus which offers sentence pairs annotated with implicit knowledge that connects them.

A central contribution of this work is an **in-depth evaluation** of the quality of generations delivered by different model variants, and their ability of expressing implicitly conveyed knowledge. We propose a **manual** evaluation setup covering four dimensions – grammaticality, coherence, content, and comparison to gold references –, and compare these to various **automatic** evaluation metrics. Our experiments show that with our proposed approach we can generate coherent sentences that explicate implicit knowledge that connects given sentence pairs; and that current text generation metrics are not sufficient to evaluate this challenging task.

Our **contributions** are: (i) We empirically compare different types of LMs, exploring which model is best suited for the task of generating sentences that express implicit information between sen-

Proceedings of Deep Learning Inside Out (DeeLIO): The 2nd Workshop on Knowledge Extraction and Integration for Deep Learning Architectures, pages 11–24
Online, June 10, 2021.

tences. (ii) We create datasets that include implicit information holding between sentence pairs, which we use for fine-tuning our LMs, and which can be used for general commonsense reasoning tasks. (iii) We propose a method for constrained generation by injecting concepts or commonsense knowledge paths as language modeling constraints, and show that key concepts, and even more, knowledge paths improve the quality of generations. (iv) We carefully evaluate the quality of the generated implicit knowledge sentences, both manually and automatically, and discuss strengths and limitations of automatic similarity metrics.[1]

2 Related Work

Recent progress in **pretraining LMs** on large text corpora led to improvements for various downstream NLP tasks. It has also been shown that knowledge acquired during pre-training can be leveraged by **fine-tuning** these models to advanced semantic inference or NL generation tasks (Wang et al. 2018). Recently, pre-trained LMs have been augmented with **external knowledge** from commonsense knowledge bases such as ConceptNet, which provides more explicit knowledge grounding and improves their performance on downstream tasks that require reasoning abilities. Wang et al. (2020b), for example, retrieve multi-hop knowledge paths from ConceptNet for fine-tuning LMs for multiple choice question answering. Chang et al. (2020) and Bosselut et al. (2021) incorporate knowledge paths from ConceptNet into pre-trained LMs for solving the SocialIQA task (Sap et al., 2019). However, all these approaches evaluate the effectiveness of integrating commonsense knowledge *indirectly* on downstream tasks, and do not explicitly evaluate the impact and relevance of knowledge for a specific system prediction. We address this shortcoming by generating and carefully evaluating statements that connect pairs of sentences as *explanations* of their underlying, *implicit knowledge* link. Closest to this aim is the task of **explanation generation**, which has received attention very recently. Wang et al. (2020a) propose the SemEval-2020 Task 4 (Subtask C), which is to generate an explanation for why a statement does not make sense, by way of a natural language statement. A comparison of the participating systems (cf. Perumal et al./Jon et al. 2020) shows that **pre-trained LMs** play a central role in the success of the top-performing systems, demonstrating that they contain commonsense information to a good extent. The success of models enriched with **knowledge from external sources** such as ConceptNet furthermore shows that additional knowledge supports the generation of commonsense explanations. However, there is still a large gap between systems and human performance.

Pre-trained LMs enhanced with commonsense knowledge have also been the models of choice for other **text generation** tasks, e.g. dialogue generation (Zhou et al., 2018), story ending generation (Guan et al., 2020), or abductive NLI (Ji et al., 2020b). While these models aim at generating explanations for a *single* statement, or *completing* a given sequence of sentences, we investigate how to make use of LMs to generate a sentence that fills in implicit knowledge *between* two sentences.

Constraining LMs. Recent work addresses how to control content in LM text generation, while maintaining fluency, coherence and plausibility of the generated text. Lin et al. (2020) explore how to generate a coherent and plausible situation description given an unordered **set of concepts** as input, and find that even pre-trained LMs (BART, T5) fine-tuned to this task cannot solve it: the generated sentences are grammatical, but highly implausible, lacking commonsense. This suggests that either the underlying LMs, or input constraints for generation need to incorporate commonsense knowledge. Orbach and Goldberg (2020) attempt to control the content when generating longer stories by **specifying facts** the story needs to include. They propose a plan-and-cloze model that first creates a cloze template, placing input facts at fixed positions in the output. In the cloze step, the system expands the fact tokens into complex sentences that complete the story. While uni-directional LMs such as GPT-2 or BART generate fluent text but do not well adhere to the desired content, the fine-tuned multi-directional XLNet outputs coherent text and adheres to the facts.

While none of the above works incorporate external knowledge to guide generation, Ji et al. (2020a) perform explanation generation for *single statements*, using ConceptNet background knowledge. The model selects concepts from the statement, retrieves connecting paths from ConceptNet, and selects **bridge concepts** from a subgraph. A pre-

[1]The code for our proposed approach can be found here: `https://github.com/Heidelberg-NLP/LMs4Implicit-Knowledge-Generation`.

trained decoder generates the explanation, using as input the statement and top-ranked concepts from the subgraph. In our work we also select concepts from texts, but *dynamically* generate commonsense knowledge paths as constraints. Importantly, we aim to generate coherent explanations *in-between* sentences – a challenge for uni-directional LMs.

3 Knowledge-constrained text generation

3.1 Task Definition and Approach

The task we tackle in this work is: given two contiguous sentences (*source sentences* S_1, S_2), generate an explanatory sentence (*target sentence* T) that explains the underlying, implicit information that connects them. We explore **different types of LMs** and their aptness for solving this task. We **fine-tune** them on existing or adapted datasets to inject relevant knowledge, and add *key concepts* or *connecting knowledge-paths* as **constraints** to achieve coherent and informative explanations.

3.2 Types of Language Models

We compare three types of LMs: **GPT-2** (Radford et al., 2019), an autoregressive model which generates the output sequence from left to right; **XLNet** (Yang et al., 2019b), a bidirectional generalized autoregressive LM; and **BART** (Lewis et al., 2019), a seq2seq model with a bidirectional masked encoder and a left-to-right decoder. While GPT-2 and BART generate the next tokens seeing only the left (previous) context, XLNet predicts the next tokens based on the left *and* right context, in a random order. GPT-2 is pre-trained on web pages from CommonCrawl, XLNet on CommonCrawl+ClueWeb (Callan et al., 2009), and BART on the CNN/DM summarization dataset (Hermann et al., 2015).

3.3 Fine-tuning LMs

Task-adapted Datasets for LM Fine-tuning. All chosen LMs are pre-trained on information that is *explicit* in text. To condition them to generate *implicit* information that connects sentences, we fine-tune them on datasets that include knowledge statements connecting contiguous sentence pairs. We create two such corpora, one based on Generics-KB (Bhakthavatsalam et al., 2020), which offers statements expressing generic knowledge; the other on e-SNLI (Camburu et al., 2018), which comprises explanations of inferential commonsense knowledge. Each data instance contains two source sentences S_1, S_2, a target sentence T, and two key concepts c_1, c_2 which we extract from the original data as described below. For examples see Table 1.

Generics-KB contains naturally occurring generic sentences crawled from the web using linguistic rules and BERT-based scoring. It is rich in high-quality statements that express generic knowledge. Each generic sentence occurs in its surrounding context (1-5 sents before/after), hence each instance forms a triple consisting of the context before (C_b), the generic sentence (GS) and the context after (C_a). We collect all instances where a phrase p_1 (NP, VP, ADJP or ADVP) from GS also occurs in C_b, and another phrase p_2 from GS occurs in C_a. For each instance we extract the sentence containing p_1 and the one containing p_2 as our source sentences S_1, S_2; GS as our target sentence T; and p_1 and p_2 as key concepts c_1, c_2.

e-SNLI is an extension of the SNLI dataset (Bowman et al., 2015), additionally annotated with explanations: Given a premise-hypothesis pair and the relation between them (entailment, contradiction, or neutral), annotators added natural language sentences that explain why the pair is in the relation. Annotators had to mark essential key phrases for the relation in premise and hypothesis, and had to formulate explanations that employ these key phrases. For fine-tuning and testing our models, we consider all instances labelled with entailment and contradiction relations (but do not include the labels in fine-tuning). We interpret premise and hypothesis as our source sentences S_1 and S_2, the explanation as our target sentence T, and the marked key phrases as our key concepts c_1 and c_2.

In- and Out-Of-Domain Test Sets. We test the resulting models *in-domain* – on testsets from our fine-tuning corpora; and *out-of-domain* – on the **IKAT** dataset (Becker et al., 2020), which is based on the argumentative Microtexts Corpus (Peldszus and Stede, 2015). For all sentence pairs S_1 and S_2 that are adjacent or argumentatively related, annotators added the implicit knowledge that connects them, using simple sentences, which we use as targets T. They also marked two key phrases in each implicit knowledge sentence, where in most cases one key phrase appears in the first source sentence, and the other in the second – which we interpret as key concepts c_1 and c_2 in our approach.

3.4 Constraining Explanation Generation

Our hypothesis is that *unconditioned* generation may not be sufficient to produce statements carry-

Dataset	Source Sentence 1	Source Sentence 2	Target Sentence	Key Concepts	Paths
G-KB	The patient is assessed for pain every 4 hours.	Combination of treatments are needed for effective pain management.	Pain management is provided for patients in pain.	pain management, patients	pain management USEDFOR patients
eSNLI	The city has a lot of people in it.	It is busy city that looks like New York City	A city that is busy has a lot of people in it.	a lot of people, busy city	busy city HASPROPERTY a lot of people
IKAT	Education and training are fundamental rights which the state must provide.	If a university lacks the fundings, sponsors must be found.	Education and training must be funded.	education and training, fundings	education and training HAS PREREQUISITE fundings

Table 1: **Source sentence pairs** and **target sentences** (reference) from our three datasets, with marked **key concepts** and automatically predicted knowledge **paths** between them.

Gen-KB	BL	*Patients often report back to the clinic with a worsening pain condition within one to two hours of first assessment.*
	+c	*Patients often have few if any symptoms at first, but pain becomes less intense and less frequent in coming hours.*
	+p	*Patients are admitted to the hospital with moderate to high intensity pain.*
e-SNLI	BL	*A busy city that looks like new york city has a lot of people in it, so the city has to have a lot to people in the city.*
	+c	*The city has a lot of people in it because it is a busy city.*
	+p	*A busy city implies that there are a lot of people in the city.*
IKAT	BL	*The state and society must be found if a university lacks the funds to provide education and training.*
	+c	*The state and the society must pay for education and training if the university lacks the funds.*
	+p	*If a university lacks the funds, it can not be providing education and training to its students.*

Table 2: **Example generations** for pairs from Tab. 1, from **BART**: w/o constraints or **constrained** w/ concepts (c) or paths (p).

ing relevant knowledge which explains the connection between two sentences. Hence we experiment with direct injection of constraints or triggers to guide the generation to emit meaningful and coherent implicit knowledge statements: We include (i) **key concepts** as offered by each dataset, since we expect them to direct the model towards concepts that are relevant for explaining how the two sentences are related. We also include (ii) relational knowledge between the key concepts as constraints, by establishing **multi-hop knowledge paths** between them. To this end we combine relation classification and target prediction models specifically adapted to ConceptNet. The two respective models are based on LMs fine-tuned on ConceptNet (Speer et al., 2017), a large network that represents commonsense facts.[2] We generate single- and multihop paths between key concepts from a sentence pair, and use these paths as constraints when generating target sentences. We expect the generated paths to provide useful relational information for the model. Example paths appear in Table 1.

4 Data and Experimental Setup

Datasets. We use the data from GenericsKB and e-SLNI for fine-tuning and testing models (in-domain), and IKAT for testing out-of-domain.[3] For statistics see Table 3. All instances contain two source sentences $S_{1,2}$, a target sentence T, and two key concepts $c_{1,2}$, where $c_1 \in S_1$, $c_2 \in S_2$, and $c_{1,2} \in T$. We experiment with $c_{1,2}$, and with paths p generated between c_1 and c_2 as constraints, which we establish as explained above.

Input Sequences. We build the input sequences by concatenating the source sentences S_1 and S_2, separated by a SEP token. When including key concepts $c_{1,2}$ or knowledge paths p as constraints, we append them to the input sequence right after S_1 and S_2, separated by a SEP token. Thus, the concepts and paths we use as constraints are encoded by the tokenizer of each language model together with the rest of the input sequence. Accordingly, our input sequences are structured as follows: S_1 <SEP> S_2 <SEP> $(c_1, c_2|p)$ <EOT> T.

Fine-tuning LMs. For LM fine-tuning, we append the target sentence to the input sequence, separated from the rest of the input by an EOT tag. GPT-2 and XLNet are trained to reconstruct the target sentence T. During inference, the models only see the source sentences, and constraints if

[2] Details about the models appear in the Appendix.

[3] In preliminary experiments we also tried to fine-tune our LMs on GenericsKB *and* e-SNLI together, which did not improve results compared to when using these datasets separately for fine-tuning – most likely because the datasets are very different from each other in terms of linguistic characteristics (e.g. sentence lengths and structure) and the covered topics.

	train	dev	test	eval-1	eval-2
G-KB	21,644	6,184	3,091	10	30
e-SNLI	18,160	2,028	1,002	10	30
IKAT	-	-	719	10	40

Table 3: Datasets: Nb. of **source sentence pairs** with associated implicit knowledge sentences, used for fine-tuning and testing; and subsets from test used in evaluations.

given, and they complete the input sequence by generating T. In contrast, BART encodes S_1 and S_2, and its decoder is trained to predict T based on the encoded source sentences.

We use the pre-trained models from HuggingFace Transformers (Wolf et al., 2019) and adapt them for fine-tuning on our customized training data. In order to generate compact sentences capturing the relevant implicit knowledge (instead of long explanations), we set a length limitation of 20 tokens for each generation. More details about our models are listed in the Appendix.

5 Evaluation and Results

This section presents an **in-depth evaluation** of the quality of generations from different model variants, and their ability of expressing implicitly conveyed knowledge. We design a **manual** evaluation setup covering various dimensions, and compare the results to several **automatic** evaluation metrics. We conduct evaluation *in-domain* on our customized test data; and *out-of-domain* on IKAT.

5.1 Manual Evaluation

Questions to Annotators.[4] To filter out source sentence pairs between which no implicit information is missing, we first ask the annotators for each source sentence pair if they are **implicitly connected** by some (unexpressed) piece of knowledge (*yes/no*). The annotators are then guided through follow-up questions covering four dimensions:
(1) **Grammaticality** – we ask if the generated sentence is grammatically correct, given the choices *correct, almost correct* (minor grammatical errors), and *incorrect* (major grammatical errors);
(2) **Coherence** – we ask if the generated sentence is logically and semantically consistent with respect to the two source sentences, given the choices *fully coherent, partly coherent*, or *incoherent*;
(3) **Content** – we ask if the generated sentence gives an **explanation** of the connection between the two source sentences, given the choices *yes, neutral* (if the generated sentence is related to the source sentences, but not in a clear logical relation), and *no* (if the sentence is misleading or contradictory in the context of the source sentences);[5] (4) **Comparison** to the annotated reference sentence [6] – we ask if the generated sentence is similar in meaning to the reference, given the choices *similar, partly similar*, or *not similar*. In addition, we ask if the reference sentence or the generated sentence is a more meaningful explanation of the implicit knowledge that connects the source sentences, or if both are equally meaningful explanations.

Annotation Setup. Our goal is to investigate which model variant is best suited for generating grammatically sound, coherent and meaningful explanations. We approach this question with two annotation rounds: In a first round we aim to determine which **model** is best suited for generating implicitly conveyed knowledge, and which **dataset** is best suited for fine-tuning the model for generating statements on *out-of-domain* test sets. In a second annotation round we aim to determine which types of **constraints** yield best results, now restricted to the best performing model and training setup, as determined in round one.

Annotator Agreement. Annotation was performed by two annotators with a background in computational linguistics. We measure IAA using Cohen's Kappa, combined over round one and two, and achieve an agreement of 95% on dimension 1, 80% on 2, 77% on 3, and on dimension 4 82% for the first and 78% for the second question. Remaining conflicts were resolved by an expert annotator.

5.1.1 Best Model Type and Fine-Tuning Data

For the first annotation round we sample 10 source sentence pairs from each testset, hence 30 pairs overall, and the sentences generated by GPT-2, XLNet and BART for each instance, using concepts as

[4]The annotation manual together with example annotations can be found here: `https://github.com/Heidelberg-NLP/LMs4Implicit-Knowledge-Generation/blob/main/manual.pdf`

[5]The difference between dimension 2 and 3 is that with dimension 2 (*coherence*), we want to explore if the generated sentence semantically fits to the two given source sentences. We understand coherence together with Hobbs (1979) as the existence of specific knowledge relations that hold between concepts in a text (or discourse), such as *Cause-Effect, Condition*, or *Temporal Sequence*, cf. Wolf and Gibson (2004). These relations make the texts interpretable and informative and are motivated ultimately by the speaker's or writer's need to be understood (Hobbs, 1979). In contrast, when evaluating the *content* of the generated sentence in dimension 3, we want to discover if the sentence really *explains* the connection between the two source sentences.

[6]The reference sentence is *only* provided for Question 4.

S1: Germany's aging society is undergoing demographic change,
S2 thus social security and pension costs are increasing.
T: Germany's aging society causes increased costs for social security and pension.
Concepts: increasing costs; Germany's aging society
Path: Germany's aging society; Causes; increasing costs

GPT-2	Concepts	eSNLI	the cost of a social security and pension is not the same as the cost of a social security and pensions.
		G-KB	Pension costs are rising faster than wages for everyone, and the elderly are being priced out of the pension plans of millions of their working-age population.
	Paths	eSNLI	the cost of a social security and pensions is not the same as the cost of a social security and pensions.
		G-KB	Pension costs are rising faster than wages in Germany.
BART	Concepts	eSNLI	the social security and pension costs are being paid for by the people of germany.
		G-KB	social security and pension costs are rising in a country like germany.
	Paths	eSNLI	Social security and pension costs are rising because more pension is needed for elderly people in Germany.
		G-KB	More pension is needed to pay for Germany's aging society's social security and pension costs are on the rise.
XLNet	Concepts	eSNLI	more pension is a form of paying for the elderly social security and pensions.
		G-KB	More is being paid for social security and pension costs in Germany.
	Paths	eSNLI	More pension is needed for elderly people in Germany's pension system than for the working population.
		G-KB	Social security and pension costs are rising because the level of pension is rising and the level of pension is.

S1: Besides it should be in the interest of the health insurers to recognize alternative medicine as treatment,
S2: since both methods can lead to the prevention, mitigation or cure of an illness.
T: Alternative medicine can lead to the prevention of an illness.
Concepts: alternative medicine; prevent illness
Path: alternative medicine; CapableOf; prevent illness

GPT-2	Concepts	eSNLI	alternative medicine is a form of treatment.
		G-KB	Alternative medicine is an effective way to treat many kinds of illnesses.
	Paths	eSNLI	alternative medicine is used for the purpose of avoiding an illness.
		G-KB	Alternative medicine is an effective way to treat many kinds of illnesses.
BART	Concepts	eSNLI	alternative medicine can be used to prevent an illness or cure it.
		G-KB	Alternative medicine is an effective way to reduce the symptoms of an illness.
	Paths	eSNLI	alternative medicine can be used to prevent or cure an illness.
		G-KB	Alternative medicine is an effective way to treat many kinds of illnesses that are common.
XLNet	Concepts	eSNLI	alternative medicine is a form of treatment.
		G-KB	Alternative medicine is a form of complementary medicine that uses traditional medical methods
	Paths	eSNLI	the medical device used to prevent an illness is a medical device that is used for treating.
		G-KB	Alternative medicine is a very popular approach to treating illness in the United States.

Figure 1: Example generations for the IKAT test set, for all three models, fine-tuned on e-SNLI vs. GenericsKB, with concepts vs. paths as constraints.

constraints. For IKAT, we consider the sentences generated by each model fine-tuned on e-SNLI vs. GenericsKB. This sums up to 120 annotation samples (generated sentences).[7] In Fig. 1 we give example generations for IKAT, for all three model types, comparing fine-tuning on e-SNLI vs. GenericsKB; and constraining with concepts vs. with paths. More examples appear in the Appendix.

Results. For all 30 sentence pairs the annotators agreed that there is some implicit information connecting them. Table 4 displays the results of the first annotation round for the four dimensions described above. All three models are able to generate **grammatically correct** sentences (col. 1), with BART's generations scored as correct most often. BART also generates the most **coherent** sentences (col. 2), in-domain (e-SNLI and GenericsKB) and out-of-domain (IKAT), followed by XLNet. For dimension 3, which evaluates whether the generations are **meaningful explanations** of implicit knowledge connecting the source sentences (col. 3), only BART fine-tuned on e-SNLI gives satisfactory results (in-domain, when fine-tuned and tested on e-SNLI; *and* out-of domain, when fine-tuned on e-SNLI and tested on IKAT). Many of the generations from GPT-2 are judged as neutral (orange in Table 4) or misleading (red). The last two columns reflect the **comparison** of the generated vs. annotated **reference sentence** (dimension 4). BART's generations are overall rated as most similar to the reference sentence, especially when fine-tuned on e-SNLI (in- and out-of-domain), and are judged as better or equally good explanations compared to the reference sentences in 70% (e-SNLI, in-domain) and 50% (IKAT–e-SNLI, out-of-domain).

To summarize, according to our first round of evaluation, the BART model generates the most grammatical and coherent statements that are found to explain the connection between the source sentences best. They are also judged to be most similar to the reference sentence. When applied on out-of-domain testsets, BART performs best when fine-tuned on e-SNLI.

5.1.2 Best Constraints

While the first round of annotations used a relatively small set of 120 generated target sentences that helped us to determine BART as the best-suited model type, we now aim to deeper investigate the generations of BART to study the **effect of different types of constraints** on the quality of expla-

[7] 30 generated sents for e-SNLI and GenericsKB, resp. (10 source sents x 3 models), and 60 generated sents for IKAT (10 source sents x 3 models x 2 different fine-tuning datasets).

	DIMENSION	Grammaticality	Coherence	Explanation	Sim. to Reference	Gen. vs. Ref.
	CHOICES	Yes/Almost/No	Yes/Partly/No	Yes/Neutral/No	Yes/Partly/No	GS/Both/RS
GPT-2	e-SNLI	60/30/10	30/20/50	60/20/20	40/20/40	20/20/60
	G-KB	100/0/0	40/50/10	30/70/0	20/40/40	0/20/80
	IKAT - e-SNLI	70/10/20	20/30/50	20/80/0	20/60/20	0/40/60
	IKAT - G-KB	100/0/0	40/50/10	20/60/20	20/20/60	10/10/80
XLNet	e-SNLI	90/10/0	60/20/20	60/20/20	60/20/20	30/30/40
	G-KB	90/10/0	40/50/10	50/50/0	0/60/40	20/10/70
	IKAT - e-SNLI	80/20/0	60/20/20	50/40/10	30/60/10	0/40/60
	IKAT - G-KB	90/0/10	20/80/0	50/30/20	10/20/70	0/10/90
BART	e-SNLI	100/0/0	100/0/0	100/0/0	80/20/0	40/30/30
	G-KB	100/0/0	40/60/0	40/60/0	20/80/0	20/10/70
	IKAT - e-SNLI	90/0/0	60/40/0	70/20/10	60/30/10	20/30/50
	IKAT - G-KB	100/0/0	50/50/0	50/40/10	50/40/10	40/0/60

Table 4: Results of the 1st manual evaluation (in %). For all 10 source sentence pairs, each model generates a target sentence when fine-tuned and tested *in-domain* on (i) e-SNLI and (ii) GenericsKB; or *out-of-domain* testing on IKAT, when fine-tuned on (iii) e-SNLI or (iv) GenericsKB; with marked best/worst scores for in- and out-of domain testing.

nations. We provide our annotators with 70 new source sentence pairs (20 from e-SNLI, 20 from GenericsKB, 30 from IKAT), and three different targets per pair, generated by three model variants of BART: (i) a baseline fine-tuned *without* any knowledge constraints; (ii) BART fine-tuned using the *key concepts* as constraints; and (iii) BART fine-tuned using an automatically generated *commonsense knowledge path* between the key concepts as constraint. Since fine-tuning on e-SNLI has been determined as best suited for out-of-domain testing, we consider only generations from BART fine-tuned on e-SNLI for testing on IKAT. In our evaluation we consider the 70 sentence pairs and the respective sentence generations from Round 2, and the generations for the 30 source sentence pairs from the best performing model BART from Round 1, resulting in 100 sentence pairs, with three generations per pair.

Results. Similar to Round 1, for 98% of the source sentence pairs the annotators agreed that there is some implicit information connecting them.

Fig. 2 shows the results of the second round of evaluations, example generations appear in Table 2. We find that using **knowledge constraints improves the quality** of generations compared to the baseline without constraints, on all four dimensions: on each of our three test sets, generations are rated as more grammatical when constrained with concepts and paths (with GenericsKB as only exception); they are annotated as more coherent, and rated as better explanations of implicit knowledge. Knowledge constraints also lead to a higher similarity to the reference sentence on all three datasets, and sentences generated with knowledge constraints are more often rated as better explanations than the reference sentences. Overall we find that *knowledge paths* improve scores over the baseline *more than concepts* (a plus of 2–15 pp). The improvements are most significant for IKAT, where adding concepts boosts evaluation scores between 18 (Grammaticality) and 53 pp (Coherence), and adding paths by 20 (Grammaticality) and 55 pp (Coherence). The generations of BART, fine-tuned on e-SNLI, as shown in the first example in Fig. 1, demonstrate how the integration of paths as constraints can improve text generation even more than when only injecting key concepts. The path used as constraint is *Germany's aging society* CAUSES *increasing costs*. When constraining BART with key concepts, it generates *The social security and pension costs are being paid for by the people of Germany*, while the generation with the knowledge path as constraint is *Social security and pension costs are rising because more pension is needed for elderly people in Germany*). This shows that the relation CAUSES gives our model an important hint about the causal relation that is needed to explain the connection between the two given sentences.

To summarize, the results from our second evaluation round clearly show that constraints in form of relevant concepts and knowledge paths can help LMs for generating grammatically sound, coherent and meaningful explanations of the missing knowledge between sentences, especially when applied on out-of-domain test sets.

5.2 Automatic Evaluation

In our automatic evaluation setup, we apply a range of different evaluation metrics commonly applied in text generation tasks, which either measure the *similarity* to a reference sentence (in our case, the

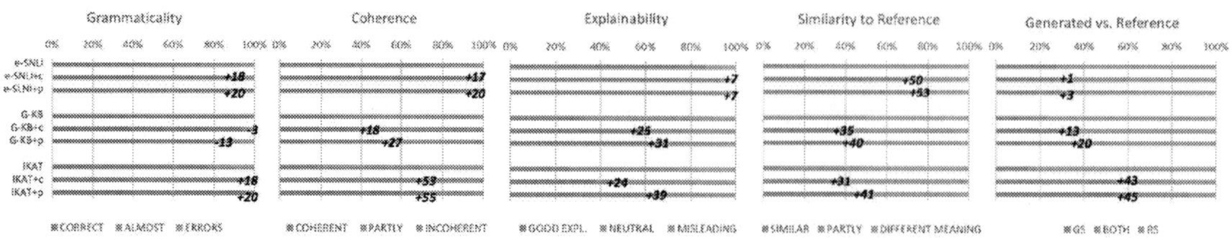

Figure 2: Results of 2nd manual evaluation: comparing models constrained with concepts (+c) or paths (+p) against a baseline without constraints. We display improvements in percentage points (pp) for the best option (blue bar) per dimension.

generic sentences in GenericsKB, inference explanations in e-SNLI, or implicit knowledge statements in IKAT); or the *linguistic quality and diversity* of the generated sentence.

(i) **BLEU** (Papineni et al., 2002) and **ROUGE** (Lin, 2004) measure token overlap using ngrams. We apply BLEU-1 to measure precision and ROUGE-1 to measure recall based on unigrams;

(ii) **BERT-Score** (Zhang* et al., 2020) and **Sentence-BERT** (Reimers and Gurevych, 2019) compute semantic similarity scores for text sequences based on word or sentence representations. BERT-Score uses BERT's contextualized word embeddings to calculate a cross similarity score for each token in the generation with each token in the reference, while Sentence-BERT is fine-tuned on NLI and STS to predict the similarity of two sequences. For BERT-Score we report F1 scores; for Sentence-BERT we average the similarity scores obtained for the generated vs. reference sentences.

(iii) **S2Match** (Opitz et al., 2020) is an AMR graph matching metric, which measures the overlap of the AMR semantic graphs that we construct from the reference and generated sentence using Cai and Lam (2020)'s parser, and reports accuracy;

(iv) **Distinct-N** (Li et al., 2015) and **GRUEN** (Zhu and Bhat, 2020) are *reference-free* metrics that only consider properties of the generated sentence. Distinct-N measures the diversity of a sentence by focusing on the number of distinct unigrams (Distinct-1) and bigrams (Distinct-2); GRUEN evaluates the linguistic quality of a sentence in terms of grammaticality, non-redundancy, and structure.

In a **preliminary experiment** based on the *complete test sets* of Generics-KB, e-SNLI and IKAT (cf. Table 3) we first investigate which **model** generates sentences that are most similar to the reference sentence (using reference-based metrics), or which show highest linguistic quality and diversity (using reference-free metrics); and which **dataset** is best suited for fine-tuning the models for generating statements on *out-of-domain* test sets (here, IKAT). Results and detailed analysis of this experiment appear in our Appendix. We find that deciding which **model** performs best depends a lot on the chosen similarity metric, but overall we don't see the clear superiority of the BART model (nor the inferiority of GPT-2) that we determined through manual evaluation. While in Dimension 4 of the manual evaluation setup (where annotators judged whether generated and reference sentence express the same or similar meaning), BART was clearly rated as the best performing model, this is not reflected in the automatic evaluation scores. Among all metrics only **SentenceBERT**, giving highest scores to BART, followed by XLNet, aligns with our observations from manual evaluation. However, our other observation from manual evaluation – that **e-SNLI** is the most appropriate dataset for fine-tuing LMs for out-of-domain testing — aligns with the scores obtained by automatic evaluation metrics (for details, cf. Appendix).

	BLEU-1	ROU-1	S2M	BERT	S-BERT	dist1	dist2	GRUEN
e-SNLI	7.27	0.4	0.34	0.89	0.56	0.72	0.58	0.63
e-SNLI+c	12.71	0.47	0.38	0.90	0.63	0.75	0.66	0.63
e-SNLI+p	9.51	0.48	0.39	0.89	0.65	0.76	0.67	0.66
G-KB	1.22	0.15	0.31	0.88	0.53	0.71	0.62	0.82
G-KB+c	1.58	0.18	0.32	0.88	0.54	0.72	0.66	0.83
G-KB+p	1.14	0.17	0.31	0.89	0.56	0.73	0.67	0.80
IKAT	4.6	0.22	0.33	0.88	0.49	0.70	0.64	0.66
IKAT+c	6.06	0.31	0.42	0.90	0.63	0.72	0.67	0.71
IKAT+p	7.23	0.33	0.46	0.91	0.64	0.74	0.70	0.76

Table 5: Automatic similarity scores for generations of best performing model BART, w/o constraints or with concepts/paths as constraints. Adding concepts and paths improves scores *in-domain* (e-SNLI and Generics-KB), and *out-of-domain* (IKAT finetuned on e-SLNI).

We next analyse which types of **constraints** improve generation, focusing on the *BART* model, which has shown to be best for generating implicit knowledge statements in our manual evaluation setup. Our automatic evaluation is based on the same *subset* of source sentence pairs used for the second round of manual annotations (cf. Table 3), and we again compare generations without constraints to conditioning on key concepts or knowledge paths.[8] Results are displayed in Table 5. We observe that for all metrics, scores increase when constraining LMs with concepts or knowledge paths, with BLEU and S2Match scores for GenericsKB as only exceptions. As in manual evaluation (Fig. 1), we find that improvements are most significant for IKAT. The observed improvements may in part be traced back to increased word overlap due to key concepts being used as constraints. Yet we also observe that automatically generated knowledge paths between these concepts improve scores additionally – according to reference-based metrics (showing that generations become more similar to references), and reference-free metrics (showing improvement of the linguistic quality and diversity of generations). This points to the fact that constraining LMs with automatically generated relational knowledge is a promising step towards generating grammatically correct and meaningful implicit knowledge statements.

6 Discussion

Limitations of Automatic Evaluation Metrics for Text Generations. Concluding, we pinpoint two important limitations of automatic text generations metrics – especially reference-based ones: Besides well-known issues regarding the reliability, interpretability and biases of such metrics (Callison-Burch et al., 2006), scores are mostly obtained by comparing generations against a single reference, which is – here, as in other generation tasks – often only *one* among *several* valid options. For the task of reconstructing implicit information, Becker et al. (2017) show that annotators often propose different valid sentences for filling knowledge gaps in argumentative texts. For our setting this means that a generated sentence may be a relevant explicitation of implicit information, even if *not* similar to the reference. Such cases are poorly or not at all captured by automatic similarity metrics. An exception we found is SentenceBERT, which is based on sentence representations, and which aligned reasonably well with insights from our manual evaluation. Still, automatic evaluation of text generations needs to be considered with caution, and should always be accompanied by manual evaluation.

Our Implicitness Assumption. Our experiments are based on the underlying assumption that usually some information between pairs of sentences stays implicit, which has been confirmed empirically for our datasets: Our annotators stated for 100% (first round) and 98% (second round) of all sentence pairs that they are implicitly connected by some unexpressed piece of knowledge. However, we did not specifically address the cases of sentence pairs between which no implicit information is missing (even though these cases are rare), nor did we investigate how our models would perform when provided with sentence pairs that are *not* related (arbitrary pairs). For a real-world application, both aspects would be considerable.

7 Conclusion

In this work we propose an approach for generating statements that explicate implicit knowledge connecting sentences in text, using pre-trained LMs. We show that despite their great success in many NLP downstream tasks, LMs need to be well equipped and carefully guided for the challenging task of reconstructing implicit knowledge, to ensure that they convey the missing, implicit information that connects sentences in text. We refine different pre-trained LMs by fine-tuning on specifically prepared corpora that we enrich with implicit information, filled in between sentences, and explore methods of constrained language generation, guiding the models by way of relevant concepts and connecting commonsense knowledge paths.

While most current automatic NLG metrics are not sufficient to evaluate this challenging task, our in-depth evaluation of the quality of generations from different model variants shows that the BART model, which attends over its full input when generating text, yields most informative and relevant explanations. We also establish that e-SNLI, being focused on the NLI task, is best suited for conditioning LMs for our task, especially for out-of domain settings. Finally, by providing the LMs with relevant connecting key concepts as constraints, and further by connecting commonsense knowledge paths, we achieve generation of coherent and grammatically sound sentences that – according to manual evaluation – can explicate the implicit knowledge that connects sentence pairs in texts – for in-domain and out-of-domain test data.

[8]The automatic evaluation scores for the complete test sets, which confirm our findings from the subset of the second annotation round, appear in the Appendix.

References

Maria Becker, Katharina Korfhage, and Anette Frank. 2020. Implicit Knowledge in Argumentative Texts: An Annotated Corpus. In *Proceedings of the 12th Conference on Language Resources and Evaluation (LREC)*, pages 2316–2324, Marseille, France.

Maria Becker, Michael Staniek, Vivi Nastase, and Anette Frank. 2017. Enriching Argumentative Texts with Implicit Knowledge. In *Applications of Natural Language to Data Bases (NLDB) - Natural Language Processing and Information Systems*, Lecture Notes in Computer Science. Springer.

Maria Becker, Michael Staniek, Vivi Nastase, and Anette Frank. 2019. Assessing the difficulty of classifying ConceptNet relations in a multi-label classification setting. In *RELATIONS - Workshop on meaning relations between phrases and sentences*, Gothenburg, Sweden. Association for Computational Linguistics.

Sumithra Bhakthavatsalam, Chloe Anastasiades, and Peter Clark. 2020. GenericsKB: A Knowledge Base of Generic Statements. In *Arxiv Preprint.*

Antoine Bosselut, Ronan Le Bras, , and Yejin Choi. 2021. Dynamic neuro-symbolic knowledge graph construction for zero-shot commonsense question answering. In *Proceedings of the 35th AAAI Conference on Artificial Intelligence (AAAI).*

Antoine Bosselut, Hannah Rashkin, Maarten Sap, Chaitanya Malaviya, Celikyilmaz Asli, and Choi Yejin. 2019. Comet: Commonsense transformers for automatic knowledge graph construction. In *ACL*, pages 4762–4779.

Samuel R. Bowman, Gabor Angeli, Christopher Potts, and Christopher D. Manning. 2015. A large annotated corpus for learning natural language inference. In *Proceedings of the 2015 Conference on Empirical Methods in Natural Language Processing*, pages 632–642, Lisbon, Portugal. Association for Computational Linguistics.

Deng Cai and Wai Lam. 2020. Amr parsing via graph-sequence iterative inference.

Jamie Callan, Mark Hoy, Changkuk Yoo, and Le Zhao. 2009. Clueweb09 data set.

Chris Callison-Burch, Miles Osborne, and Philipp Koehn. 2006. Re-evaluating the role of Bleu in machine translation research. In *11th Conference of the European Chapter of the Association for Computational Linguistics*, Trento, Italy. Association for Computational Linguistics.

Oana-Maria Camburu, Tim Rocktäschel, Thomas Lukasiewicz, and Phil Blunsom. 2018. e-snli: Natural language inference with natural language explanations. In *Advances in Neural Information Processing Systems*, volume 31, pages 9539–9549. Curran Associates, Inc.

Ting-Yun Chang, Yang Liu, Karthik Gopalakrishnan, Behnam Hedayatnia, Pei Zhou, and Dilek Hakkani-Tur. 2020. Incorporating commonsense knowledge graph in pretrained models for social commonsense tasks. In *Proceedings of Deep Learning Inside Out (DeeLIO): The First Workshop on Knowledge Extraction and Integration for Deep Learning Architectures*, pages 74–79, Online. Association for Computational Linguistics.

Jacob Devlin, Ming-Wei Chang, Kenton Lee, and Kristina Toutanova. 2018. Bert: Pre-training of deep bidirectional transformers for language understanding.

Jian Guan, Fei Huang, Zhihao Zhao, Xiaoyan Zhu, and Minlie Huang. 2020. A knowledge-enhanced pre-training model for commonsense story generation. *Transactions of the Association for Computational Linguistics*, 8:93–108.

Karl Moritz Hermann, Tomas Kocisky, Edward Grefenstette, Lasse Espeholt, Will Kay, Mustafa Suleyman, and Phil Blunsom. 2015. Teaching machines to read and comprehend. In *NIPS.*

Jerry R. Hobbs. 1979. Coherence and coreference*. *Cognitive Science*, 3(1):67–90.

Haozhe Ji, Pei Ke, Shaohan Huang, Furu Wei, and Minlie Huang. 2020a. Generating commonsense explanation by extracting bridge concepts from reasoning paths. In *Proceedings of the 1st Conference of the Asia-Pacific Chapter of the Association for Computational Linguistics and the 10th International Joint Conference on Natural Language Processing*, pages 248–257, Suzhou, China. Association for Computational Linguistics.

Haozhe Ji, Pei Ke, Shaohan Huang, Furu Wei, Xiaoyan Zhu, and Minlie Huang. 2020b. Language generation with multi-hop reasoning on commonsense knowledge graph. In *Proceedings of the 2020 Conference on Empirical Methods in Natural Language Processing (EMNLP)*, pages 725–736, Online. Association for Computational Linguistics.

Josef Jon, Martin Fajcik, Martin Docekal, and Pavel Smrz. 2020. BUT-FIT at SemEval-2020 task 4: Multilingual commonsense. In *Proceedings of the Fourteenth Workshop on Semantic Evaluation*, pages 374–390, Barcelona (online). International Committee for Computational Linguistics.

Mike Lewis, Yinhan Liu, Naman Goyal, Marjan Ghazvininejad, Abdelrahman Mohamed, Omer Levy, Veselin Stoyanov, and Luke Zettlemoyer. 2019. Bart: Denoising sequence-to-sequence pre-training for natural language generation, translation, and comprehension. *arXiv preprint arXiv:1910.13461.*

Jiwei Li, Michel Galley, Chris Brockett, Jianfeng Gao, and Bill Dolan. 2015. A diversity-promoting objective function for neural conversation models. *CoRR*, abs/1510.03055.

Bill Yuchen Lin, Wangchunshu Zhou, Ming Shen, Pei Zhou, Chandra Bhagavatula, Yejin Choi, and Xiang Ren. 2020. CommonGen: A constrained text generation challenge for generative commonsense reasoning. In *Findings of the Association for Computational Linguistics: EMNLP 2020*, pages 1823–1840, Online. Association for Computational Linguistics.

Chin-Yew Lin. 2004. ROUGE: A package for automatic evaluation of summaries. In *Text Summarization Branches Out*, pages 74–81, Barcelona, Spain. Association for Computational Linguistics.

Juri Opitz, Anette Frank, and Letitia Parcalabescu. 2020. Amr similarity metrics from principles. *Transactions of the Association for Computational Linguistics*, 8(0):522–538.

Eyal Orbach and Yoav Goldberg. 2020. Facts2Story: Controlling text generation by key facts. In *Proceedings of the 28th International Conference on Computational Linguistics*, pages 2329–2345, Barcelona, Spain (Online). International Committee on Computational Linguistics.

Kishore Papineni, Salim Roukos, Todd Ward, and Wei jing Zhu. 2002. Bleu: a method for automatic evaluation of machine translation. pages 311–318.

Andreas Peldszus and Manfred Stede. 2015. An annotated corpus of argumentative microtexts. In *Proceedings of the First European Conference on Argumentation*.

Anandh Perumal, Chenyang Huang, Amine Trabelsi, and Osmar Zaïane. 2020. Ana at semeval-2020 task 4: multi-task learning for commonsense reasoning (union).

Alec Radford, Jeff Wu, Rewon Child, David Luan, Dario Amodei, and Ilya Sutskever. 2019. Language models are unsupervised multitask learners.

Nils Reimers and Iryna Gurevych. 2019. Sentence-bert: Sentence embeddings using siamese bert-networks. *CoRR*, abs/1908.10084.

Maarten Sap, Hannah Rashkin, Derek Chen, Ronan LeBras, and Yejin Choi. 2019. Socialiqa: Commonsense reasoning about social interactions. *ArXiv*, abs/1904.09728.

Robyn Speer, Joshua Chin, and Catherine Havasi. 2017. ConceptNet 5.5: An Open Multilingual Graph of General Knowledge. In *AAAI*.

Alex Wang, Amanpreet Singh, Julian Michael, Felix Hill, Omer Levy, and Samuel R. Bowman. 2018. GLUE: A multi-task benchmark and analysis platform for natural language understanding. In *ICLR*.

Cunxiang Wang, Shuailong Liang, Yili Jin, Yilong Wang, Xiaodan Zhu, and Yue Zhang. 2020a. SemEval-2020 task 4: Commonsense validation and explanation. In *Proceedings of the Fourteenth Workshop on Semantic Evaluation*, pages 307–321, Barcelona (online). International Committee for Computational Linguistics.

Peifeng Wang, Nanyun Peng, Filip Ilievski, Pedro Szekely, and Xiang Ren. 2020b. Connecting the dots: A knowledgeable path generator for commonsense question answering. *Findings of the Association for Computational Linguistics: EMNLP 2020*, pages 4129–4140.

Florian Wolf and Edward Gibson. 2004. Representing discourse coherence: A corpus-based analysis. In *COLING 2004: Proceedings of the 20th International Conference on Computational Linguistics*, pages 134–140, Geneva, Switzerland. COLING.

Thomas Wolf, Lysandre Debut, Victor Sanh, Julien Chaumond, Clement Delangue, Anthony Moi, Pierric Cistac, Tim Rault, Rémi Louf, Morgan Funtowicz, and Jamie Brew. 2019. Huggingface's transformers: State-of-the-art natural language processing. *CoRR*, abs/1910.03771.

Zhilin Yang, Zihang Dai, Yiming Yang, Jaime Carbonell, Russ R Salakhutdinov, and Quoc V Le. 2019a. Xlnet: Generalized autoregressive pretraining for language understanding. In *Advances in Neural Information Processing Systems*, volume 32. Curran Associates, Inc.

Zhilin Yang, Zihang Dai, Yiming Yang, Jaime G. Carbonell, Ruslan Salakhutdinov, and Quoc V. Le. 2019b. Xlnet: Generalized autoregressive pretraining for language understanding. *CoRR*, abs/1906.08237.

Tianyi Zhang*, Varsha Kishore*, Felix Wu*, Kilian Q. Weinberger, and Yoav Artzi. 2020. Bertscore: Evaluating text generation with bert. In *International Conference on Learning Representations*.

Hao Zhou, Tom Young, Minlie Huang, Haizhou Zhao, J. Xu, and Xiaoyan Zhu. 2018. Commonsense knowledge aware conversation generation with graph attention. In *IJCAI*.

Wanzheng Zhu and Suma Bhat. 2020. GRUEN for evaluating linguistic quality of generated text. In *Findings of the Association for Computational Linguistics: EMNLP 2020*, pages 94–108, Online. Association for Computational Linguistics.

A Training Details

Finetuning Language Models. Details about the models and fine-tuning procedure as well as the running time for one batch are listed in Table 6. We fine-tuned all models with 2 GPUs on 3 epochs. Our training batch size is 8 as suggested by the HuggingFace's Transformers framework (Wolf et al., 2019). GPT-2 is the lightest one of our three models and takes 4 hours for fine-tuning on our e-SNLI and

GenericsKB datasets, respectively, while BART requires 8 hours, and XLNet around 20 hours (due to its permutation procedure) for the same data.

Limiting Length of Generations. In order to generate compact sentences capturing the relevant implicit knowledge (instead of long explanations), we set a length limitation of 20 tokens for each generation. In the left-to-right decoding procedure of GPT-2 and BART, the generation can be stopped earlier than 20 tokens, when the model predicts an EoT token. Thus, both GPT-2 and BART models can predict complete sentences of up to 20 tokens due to the autoregressive decoder. In contrast, XLNet has a permutation language modeling mechanism and predicts the next tokens based on the previous and next tokens. Its generations usually don't contain a significant EoT token. predicted target sequence of tokens in a post-processing step by cutting it after a generated comma (,).

Maximum Sequence Lengths. Our customized train sets have different maximum sequence lengths: e-SNLI has a maximum sequence length of 80 tokens including the target sentence, while GenericsKB has up to 140 tokens per sequence.

B Establishing Knowledge Paths for Constraining Text Generation

For dynamically establishing connections between the key concepts from two source sentences, we combine two model types: COREC-LM (Becker et al., 2019), an open-world multi-label relation classifier enhanced with a pretrained language model, that predicts *relation types* between two given concepts – for establishing direct connections between concepts; and COMET (Bosselut et al., 2019), a pretrained transformer model that learns to generate *target concepts* given a source concept and a relation, for generating multihop paths. By combining the generations of these models, we generate single- and multihop paths between key concepts c_1, c_2 from a sentence pair, and use these paths as constraints when generating target sentences. We are able to retrieve paths for 86.2% of all key concept pairs from GenericsKB, respectively, for 30.2% from e-SNLI and for 44.2% from IKAT. The differences can be explained by the fact that while the key concepts in GenericsKB are extracted phrases (NPs, VPs, ADJPs and ADVPs), the key concepts in e-SNLI and IKAT are manually labelled, and thus are often very specific and contain nested phrases (e.g. *leans over a pickup truck* (e-SNLI)). Therefore, it is more difficult to predict a relation or path between them. When we experiment with paths as constraints; for all instances where no path could be established between the key concepts, we only use the key concepts as constraints.

C Automatic Evaluation of the Complete Test Sets

As mentioned in Section 5.2 of our main paper, in a preliminary study based on the **complete test sets** of Generics-KB, e-SNLI and IKAT, we investigate which **model** generated sentences that are most similar to the reference sentence, or which show highest linguistic quality and diversity; and which **dataset** is best suited for finetuning the models for generating statements on *out-of-domain* test sets (here, IKAT). Results for this first analysis appear in Table 7. For metrics that measure token overlap (**BLEU** and **ROUGE**), highest scores are obtained when finetuning and testing on e-SNLI, which can be traced back to frequently used linguistic patterns (e.g., *x implies y*, or *x is the same as y*) that occur in train and test sets of e-SNLI. The reference-free metrics **Distinct** and **GRUEN** that measure diversity and non-redundancy, therefore yield higher scores when models are finetuned on the more diverse GenericsKB data, for both in- and out-of-domain testing. The AMR metric **S2Match** gives higher scores on e-SNLI than GenericsKB in in-domain testing, and finetuning on e-SNLI yields higher S2Match scores for out-of-domain testing on IKAT. This also aligns with the sentence representation based metric **SentenceBERT**. **BertScore**, finally, is not at all discriminative – it yields uniformly high scores for each model and configuration, ranging only between .88 and .9.

We also find that the scores differ considerably for **in-domain** vs. **out-of-domain** testing: results on IKAT are lower compared to testing on e-SNLI or GenericsKB according to all reference-based metrics, while we observe the opposite for the reference-free metrics.

We next analyse on the complete test set which types of **constraints** improve generation, focusing on the *BART* model, which has shown to be best for generating implicit knowledge statements in our manual evaluation setup. The automatic evaluation scores for the complete test sets are displayed in Table 8 and confirm our findings from the subset of the second annotation round, as presented in

Pretrained model ID	Model details	Parameters	Time in s (seq length = 80)	Time in s (seq length = 140)
gpt2	12-layer, 768-hidden, 12-heads	117M	0.039	0.056
xlnet-large-case	24-layer, 1024-hidden, 16-heads	340M	0.166	0.297
facebook/bart-large-cnn	24-layer, 1024-hidden, 16-heads	406M	0.075	0.116

Table 6: Benchmarks of the used pre-trained models.

Section 5.2 of our main paper.

D Example Generations

In addition to the examples shown in our main paper, in Fig. 1 we give some more example generations for the IKAT test set, for all three model types, comparing finetuning on e-SNLI vs. GenericsKB; and constraining with concepts vs. with paths.

TEST	TRAIN	BLEU-1	ROU-1	S2M	BERT	S-BERT	dist1	dist2	GRUEN
GPT-2									
G-KB	G-KB	5.3	.2	.33	.88	.5	.95	.89	.79
e-SNLI	e-SNLI	14.9	.46	.44	.89	.58	.91	.86	.52
IKAT	G-KB	2.9	.19	.3	.88	.45	.96	.85	.78
IKAT	e-SNLI	4.7	.26	.37	.89	.51	.88	.86	.64
XLNet									
G-KB	G-KB	6.6	.27	.36	.89	.53	.92	.87	.74
e-SNLI	e-SNLI	10.7	.43	.38	.89	.59	.88	.85	.58
IKAT	G-KB	4.2	.22	.34	.9	.48	.97	.88	.79
IKAT	e-SNLI	10.5	.33	.42	.9	.56	.9	.85	.69
BART									
G-KB	G-KB	5.2	.27	.35	.89	.57	.86	.93	.75
e-SNLI	e-SNLI	10.7	.44	.42	.89	.61	.81	.91	.59
IKAT	G-KB	2.37	.22	.3	.88	.53	.88	.93	.80
IKAT	e-SNLI	3.92	.29	.38	.9	.58	.87	.93	.71

Table 7: Automatic Similarity scores computed for the generations of all models, on the *complete test sets*. We compare the impact of (i) model types and (ii) data used for finetuning (train), in-domain (GenericsKB and e-SNLI) and out-of-domain (IKAT).

	BLEU-1	ROU-1	S2M	BERT	S-BERT	dist1	dist2	GRUEN
e-SNLI	7.36	0.37	0.36	0.88	0.54	0.77	0.89	0.59
e-SNLI+c	10.73	0.44	0.42	0.89	0.61	0.81	0.91	0.59
e-SNLI+p	11.71	0.44	0.43	0.89	0.62	0.84	0.92	0.59
G-KB	5.21	0.23	0.32	0.88	0.55	0.86	0.93	0.75
G-KB+c	5.2	0.27	0.35	0.89	0.57	0.86	0.93	0.75
G-KB+p	5.4	0.28	0.35	0.89	0.58	0.87	0.93	0.75
IKAT	2,74	0.19	0.29	0.87	0.43	0.86	0.92	0.67
IKAT+c	3.92	0.28	0.38	0.89	0.56	0.87	0.92	0.7
IKAT+p	4.84	0.3	0.4	0.9	0.57	0.9	0.93	0.72

Table 8: Automatic similarity scores for generations of best performing model BART on the *complete test sets*, w/o constraints or with concepts/paths as constraints. Adding concepts and paths improves scores *in-domain* (e-SNLI and GenericsKB), and *out-of-domain* (IKAT finetuned on e-SLNI).

S_1: Rent prices should be limited by a cap when there's a change of tenant.
S_2: Landlords may want to earn as much as possible.
T: The landlord may increase the rent in the event of a change of tenant.
Concepts: landlord; increase rent
Path: landlord; capable of; increase rent

MODEL	CONSTRAINT	TRAIN	GENERATION
GPT-2	Concepts	eSNLI	the landlord can not be both raising the rent and simultaneously lowering the price.
		G-KB	Landlords can use a variety of mechanisms to reduce their rent payments.
	Paths	eSNLI	the landlord can not be preparing to pay the higher rents if he is preparing to pay the higher rents.
		G-KB	Landlords sometimes collect a rent increase without giving a lease.
BART	Concepts	eSNLI	landlord can't be trying to increase the rent if they are just trying to earn as much as possible.
		G-KB	Landlords are entitled to raise the rent without violating the terms of the rent control provisions .
	Paths	eSNLI	the landlord can't raise the rent if the tenants are prepared to pay higher rents.
		G-KB	Landlords know what they want from tenants and are prepared to accept less rent.
XLNet	Concepts	eSNLI	landlords are a type of landlord.
		G-KB	Landlords can raise rent to cover the cost of a new tenant's moving expenses.
	Paths	eSNLI	a landlord is a type of landlord.
		G-KB	Rents are not set to increase unless the landlord decides to raise the rent.

S1: There should be much higher fines for dog dirt left on pavements.
S2: Besides, the fines for public urination by a human are higher than for leaving behind dog dirt on the pavement, which is disproportionate.
T: Dog dirt is a greater offense as public urination.
Concepts: dog dirt; public urination
Path: dog dirt; IsA; public urination

MODEL	CONSTRAINT	TRAIN	GENERATION
GPT-2	Concepts	eSNLI	a dog dirt is a greater offense than public urination.
		G-KB	Public urination is a misdemeanor, and therefore a violation of the law.
	Paths	eSNLI	the people are either leaving behind dog dirt on the pavement or they are not.
		G-KB	worse offense than
BART	Concepts	eSNLI	dog dirt is not the same as public urination by a human, therefore the fines are not equal.
		G-KB	Dog dirt is an offense more serious than public urination.
	Paths	eSNLI	the fines are higher for public urination than for dog dirt.
		G-KB	Dog dirt is a greater offense than public urination, but people are no so much more likely to report dog poo on the streets than they are to cite a public urinate.
XLNet	Concepts	eSNLI	public urination is a form of dog dirt.
		G-KB	Dog dirt is a misdemeanor.
	Paths	eSNLI	public urination is a more serious offense than dog dirt.
		G-KB	Dog scat is a serious offense.

Figure 3: Example generations for IKAT, for all three models, finetuned on e-SNLI vs. GenericsKB, with concepts vs. paths as constraints.

Investigating the Effect of Background Knowledge on Natural Questions

Vidhisha Balachandran[1*] **Bhuwan Dhingra**[2] **Haitian Sun**[1*]
Michael Collins[2] **William W. Cohen**[2]
[1] Language Technologies Institute, Carnegie Mellon University
[2] Google Research
{vbalacha, haitians}@cs.cmu.edu
{bdhingra, mjcollins, wcohen}@google.com

Abstract

Existing work shows the benefits of integrating KBs with textual evidence for QA only on questions that are answerable by KBs alone (Sun et al., 2019). In contrast, real world QA systems often have to deal with questions that might not be directly answerable by KBs. Here, we investigate the effect of integrating background knowledge from KBs for the Natural Questions (NQ) task. We create a subset of the NQ data, Factual Questions (FQ), where the questions have evidence in the KB in the form of paths that link question entities to answer entities but still must be answered using text, to facilitate further research into KB integration methods. We propose and analyze a simple, model-agnostic approach for incorporating KB paths into text-based QA systems and establish a strong upper bound on FQ for our method using an oracle retriever. We show that several variants of Personalized PageRank based fact retrievers lead to a low recall of answer entities and consequently fail to improve QA performance. Our results suggest that fact retrieval is a bottleneck for integrating KBs into real world QA datasets[1].

1 Introduction

Prior work has shown the benefit of retrieving paths of related entities (Sun et al., 2018; Wang and Jiang, 2019; Sun et al., 2019) and learning relevant knowledge graph embeddings (Sawant et al., 2018; Bordes et al., 2014; Luo et al., 2018) for answering questions on KBQA datasets such as WebQuestions (Berant et al., 2013) and MetaQA (Zhang et al., 2018). But such datasets are often curated to questions with KB paths that contain the right path to the answer and hence are directly answerable via KB. An open question remains whether such approaches are useful for questions not specifically designed to be answerable by KBs. In this paper, we aim to evaluate KB integration for real-world QA settings in the context of the Natural Questions (NQ) dataset (Kwiatkowski et al., 2019) which consists of questions naturally posed by users of a search engine. NQ is one of the common benchmarks that is used to test the real-world QA applicability of models, hence motivating our choice.

To study the effect of augmenting KB knowledge, we construct a subset of NQ - *Factual Questions* (FQ). In FQ, answer entities are connected to question entities via short paths (up to 3 steps) in the Wikidata KB (Vrandečić and Krötzsch, 2014). Using FQ, we analyze a simple but effective approach to incorporating KB knowledge into a textual QA system. We convert KB paths to text (using surface forms of entities and relation) and append it to the textual passage as additional context for a BERT-based (Devlin et al., 2019) QA system.

We first establish an upper bound oracle setting by building a retriever that provides the shortest path to an answer. We show that, in the presence of such knowledge, our approach leads to significant gains (up to 6 F1 for short-answers, 8-9 F1 for multi-hop questions). We experiment with several variants of KB path-retrieval methods and show that retrieving good paths is difficult: previously-used Personalized PageRank (Haveliwala, 2003) (PPR)-based methods find answer entities less than 30% of the time, and even our weakly-supervised improvements recall answer entities no more than 40% of the time. As a consequence injecting retrieved KB paths in a realistic QA setting like NQ yields only small, inconsistent improvements.

To summarize our contributions, we (1) identify a new experimental subset of NQ that supports (2) the study of effectiveness of KB path-retrieval approaches. We also (3) describe a simple, model-agnostic method to using oracle KB paths that can significantly improve QA performance and evaluate PPR based path-retrieval methods. To our

[1]Data and Code available at: https://github.com/vidhishanair/fact_augmented_text
*Work done at Google Research

Proceedings of Deep Learning Inside Out (DeeLIO): The 2nd Workshop on Knowledge Extraction and Integration for Deep Learning Architectures, pages 25–30
Online, June 10, 2021.

knowledge this is the first study of such approaches on a QA dataset not curated for KBQA.

2 Dataset

The Natural Questions (NQ) dataset (Kwiatkowski et al., 2019) is a large scale QA dataset containing 307,373 training, 7,830 dev, and 7,842 test examples. Each example is a user query paired with Wikipedia documents annotated with a passage (long answer) answering the question and one or more short spans (short answer) containing the answer. The questions in NQ are not artificially constructed, making the NQ task more difficult (Lee et al., 2019). We use Sling (Ringgaard et al., 2017) (which uses an NP chunker and phrase table for linking entities to Wikidata) to entity link the questions and documents.

To focus on knowledge-driven factoid question answering, we create a subset of NQ having relevant knowledge in the KB. Shortest paths between entities in KB is very often used as a proxy for gold knowledge linking questions to answer (Sun et al., 2019) and we use the same proxy in our setting. Specifically, we select questions whose short answers are entities in the KB and have a short path (up to 3 steps) from a question entity to an answer entity. These paths contain knowledge relevant to the question but are not necessarily the right path to answer the question. We call this subset *Factual Questions (FQ)* containing 6977 training, 775 dev and 264 (83 1-hop, 97 2-hop and 84 3-hop) test samples. FQ being an entity centric subset of NQ, provides a setting to investigate augmenting KB paths for real-world factoid question for which relevant knowledge exists in the KB. Examples of the dataset are provided in Table 4.

3 Model

Given a question Q, our knowledge retriever extracts top facts from a KB. We represent them in natural language form and augment it to a standard BERT model for reading comprehension as additional context along with the passage P.

3.1 Knowledge Retriever

The Knowledge Retriever (KR) uses the input question Q to retrieve relevant facts for augmentation. We use the entities in the question as the set of seed entities denoted as E and use the Personalized PageRank (PPR) algorithm to perform a random walk over the KB to assign relevance scores to other entities around the seed entities.

The *Traditional PPR* algorithm takes the seed entities and iteratively jumps from and expands the seed entities until convergence. At each iteration, a transition with probability γ is made to a new entity in the KB (with all outgoing edges having equal weight) and a transition with probability $1-\gamma$ is made to the start seed entities. The stationary distribution of this walk gives the relevance scores (PPR weights) of entities (nodes) w.r.t seed entities. Sun et al. (2018) present an improved PPR version, *Question Informed (QI) PPR*, to weigh relations which are semantically closer to the question higher. Specifically, they average the GLOVE (Pennington et al., 2014) embeddings to compute a relation vector $v(R)$ from the relation surface form, and a question vector $v(Q)$ from the question text, and use cosine similarity between them as edge-weights for PPR. For every node, the γ probability is multiplied by the edge-score to weigh entities along relevant paths higher.

We improve on this setting by introducing *Weakly Supervised (WS) PPR*, which uses weak supervision from the QA pairs to train a classifier to discriminate relevant relations from irrelevant ones. We create a classification dataset of questions aligned with relations along the shortest KB path connecting question entities and answer entities as positive relevant examples. Other random relations connected to the question entities form negative examples. We train a simple BERT based classifier to classify relations as relevant or irrelevant conditioned on the question. The trained classifier is used to score relations for every question and used as edge-weights for PPR similar to QI PPR. Examples of the facts retrieved from WS PPR are provided in Table 4.

After running PPR we retain the top-K entities $e_1, \ldots, e_K$ by PPR score, along with any edges between them. To further rank the facts, we compute entity scores as the sum of the PPR score and frequency of the entity in the text and aggregate the subject and object entity scores by taking the maximum score between them.

Oracle Setting: In this upper bound setting for the Knowledge Retriever, the answer entities are known. The facts along the shortest path connecting the question entities and the answer entities are considered as gold or relevant facts to the question and are shuffled and augmented to the input of the

	Factual NQ		Hop 1		Hop 2		Hop 3	
	Short F1	Long F1	Short F1	Long F1	Short F1	Long F1	Short F1	Long F1
Text Only	68.2	77.3	77.3	82.2	60.0	74.3	60.2	73.4
Text + PPR(Q) facts	68.1	77.8	78.3	83.7	57.9	72.8	61.9	75.7
Text + QI PPR(Q) facts	68.2	77.5	79.2	83.9	55.2	72.0	58.9	74.4
Text + WS PPR(Q) facts	67.8	76.3	76.9	81.7	58.1	72.5	60.2	72.1
Text + Clean Oracle	74.9	80.8	79.5	83.0	69.1	80.2	72.4	77.2
Text + Noisy Oracle	75.3	81.3	80.7	84.4	69.7	80.2	71.9	77.2

Table 1: Results on FQ data compared to Alberti et al. (2019). Both Clean and Noisy Oracle setting improve over only text baseline setting. Variants of PPR do not improve over the text only baseline.

	Shortest Path Fact R	Ans R
BM25	19.1	29.8
PPR(Q)	33.0	28.8
QI PPR(Q)	31.2	25.2
WS PPR(Q)	**51.0**	**40.0**

Table 2: Answer Recall and Shortest Path Fact Recall metrics for the different Retrieval Methods. Traditional and QI PPR methods have very low recall and WS PPR method improves the recall significantly.

	Long F1	Short F1
DecAtt + DocReader	54.8	31.4
$\text{BERT}_{\text{joint}}$	64.7	52.7
$\text{BERT}_{\text{joint}}$ *	**68.1**	54.0
Traditional PPR	66.7	54.3
QI PPR	65.8	53.6
WS PPR	67.5	**54.4**

Table 3: Results on Full NQ. Baselines: DecAtt (Parikh et al., 2016), DocReader (Chen et al., 2017), and $\text{Bert}_{\text{Joint}}$ (Alberti et al., 2019). *- our reimplementation. WS PPR improves over previous baseline on Short F1 and has comparable performance to $\text{Bert}_{\text{Joint}}$ on Long F1.

QA model in place of the KB retrieved facts. As the oracle setting uses gold KB links, this setting is tested on the FQ subset where such links exist and is called the Clean Oracle. To establish a harder upper bound setting, random facts about the question are added in addition to the oracle shortest path facts using PPR, forming a Noisy Oracle setting.

3.2 Knowledge Augmented Text for QA

Given a ranked set of triples from the retriever, a natural language statement is constructed from each fact using the surface form of the entities e_s and e_o and the natural language description of R (e.g. "Washington D.C capital of United States") similar to Lauscher et al. (2020). These form the background knowledge to be injected F. We then tokenize them using the standard BERT tokenizers and augment them to the input of QA model as X = "`[CLS]` Question tokens `[SEP]` Passage tokens `[SEP]` Fact tokens".

Following Alberti et al. (2019), we use a simple BERT architecture by training two linear classifiers independently on top of the output representations of X for predicting the answer span boundary (start and end). We assume that the answer, if present, is contained only in the given passage, P, and do not consider potential mentions of the answer in the background F. For instances which do not contain the answer, we simply set the answer span to be the special token `[CLS]`. We use a fixed Transformer input window size of 512, and use a sliding window with a stride of 128 tokens to handle longer documents. We use 256 tokens each for document passage input and KB facts.

4 Experiments and Results

Setup: As every passage that doesn't contain the answer is a potential negative, we sample a subset of negatives to balance the dataset. For the Factual NQ subset, we sample 2% of the negatives as in Alberti et al. (2019) to enable faster training. We find that increasing the negatives to 10% improves results by $\sim$2 points and hence for a fair comparison, we sample 10% of the negatives for our models and the reimplemented baseline on the Full NQ dataset. We use the same preprocessing steps and all other hyperparameter settings as in Alberti et al. (2019).

4.1 Retriever Results

While the KB retriever's effect can be measured in the downstream QA model, it is beneficial to

Question	Hops	Clean Oracle Facts	WS PPR Facts
Who is the existing prime minister of pakistan ?	1	Prime Minister of Pakistan *officeholder* Imran Khan .	Pakistan *office held by head of government* Prime Minister of Pakistan . Imran Khan *position held* Prime Minister of Pakistan . Pakistan *head of government* Imran Khan . Prime Minister of Pakistan *officeholder* Imran Khan . Imran Khan *instance of* human . Pakistan *instance of* country .
What emperor took over france after the reign of terror	3	Reign of Terror *part of* French Revolution . French Revolution *significant event* 18 Brumaire . 18 Brumaire *participant* Napoleon .	Napoleon *participant of* French Revolution . Absolute Monarchy *subclass of* Monarchy . First French Empire *head of state* Napoleon . Seven years ' war *instance of* war .
Who plays the bad guy in looney tunes back in action ?	1	Looney Tunes: Back in Action *cast member* Steve Martin .	Heather Locklear *instance of* human . Heather Locklear *occupation* actor . Looney Tunes: Back in Action *cast member* Heather Locklear . Stan Freberg *occupation* actor . Looney Tunes: Back in Action *cast member* Stan Freberg . Looney Tunes: Back in Action *cast member* Steve Martin . Steve Martin *instance of* human . Steve Martin *sex or gender* male .
Where does the book of daniel take place	2	The Burning Fiery Furnace *narrative location* Babylon. Book of Daniel *derivative work* The Burning Fiery Furnace .	The Burning Fiery Furnace *based on* Book of Daniel . Book of Daniel *derivative work* The Burning Fiery Furnace . Belshazzar's Feast *based on* Book of Daniel . Book of Daniel *derivative work* Belshazzar's Feast . Suzanne bathing *based on* Book of Daniel . Belshazzar's Feast *based on* Book of Daniel . Book of Daniel *derivative work* Suzanne bathing .

Table 4: Examples of Clean Oracle facts and WS PPR retrieved facts. Relations are highlighted in *Italics*.

directly measure the quality of the top retrieved facts. As we consider the shortest path between the question and answer entities as gold facts, we evaluate our retriever using recall of answer entities and shortest path facts in a set of 200 questions from FQ. We compare our retriever with BM25 (Robertson and Zaragoza, 2009), traditional PPR and QI PPR (Sun et al., 2018) as baselines. Table 2 shows the retriever recall results. BM25, traditional PPR and the QI PPR have very poor recall of answers and facts. The low recall of QI PPR shows that questions in NQ do not have similar predicates to relations in the KB, and hence do not benefit from pretrained word vectors. In WS PPR answer entity recall improves by 15 points and Shortest Path fact recall improves by 20 points showing significant improvement. This shows that retrieval methods need question supervision to work in real-world settings and that heuristic methods do not adapt well to it. We show qualitative examples of oracle and retrieved facts in the Appendix.

Additionally, Table 5 (Top) shows that the question independent knowledge (passage entities as seeds PPR(P)) version is slightly worse than question dependent knowledge (question entities as seeds PPR(Q)), showing the benefit of a question dependent factual knowledge retriever.

	Text Only	PPR(Q)	PPR(P)
Short F1	68.2	68.1	67.6
Long F1	77.3	77.8	76.8

	Text Only	Aug Facts	Sep Facts
Short F1	52.7	54.4	52.3
Long F1	64.7	67.5	62.5

Table 5: Top: Comparing different seeds for PPR on FQ. Using question entities as starting seeds is better than passage specific entities. Bottom: Comparing Facts as Augmented Input (Aug Facts) v/s as Separate Input (Sep Facts) on NQ. Augmenting Facts as additional context is significantly better than embedding them via an independent module.

4.2 QA Performance

Factual Questions: Table 1 shows the results of our Knowledge Augmented QA system on the FQ subset[2]. The clean oracle setting improves over the text only baseline and when segregated along the number of hops in the gold shortest path, it has significantly large gains for 2 and 3 hop questions. These questions are generally more complex involving multiple steps of reasoning and augmenting gold facts linking the question to the answer entities significantly helps in the model's performance.

[2]As NQ and FQ rely on span based evaluation, we do not consider KB only baselines for fair comparison.

The noisy oracle setting which has additional facts with oracle facts maintains the QA performance showing that random facts with oracle are still useful to the QA model. This shows that the presence of relevant knowledge from the KB helps QA performance and establishes a strong upper bound for our KB integration. The performance drops when the QA model is given only the PPR facts, without the oracle facts. Both Short and Long answer F1 are similar to the text only setting showing that the retrieved facts are not providing any relevant knowledge to the QA model. Though the weakly supervised setting improves recall of answer entities and shortest path facts, it doesn't improve on the downstream QA task showing that this improved recall is still insufficient for the model to leverage. Comparing the oracle and no-oracle settings, we believe that better KB retrieval methods that have bery high recall of answer entities and relevant facts could lead to improved QA performance, even in real-world complex questions.

We also validate that our performance gains in oracle settings were not due to trivial entity overlap between the text and retrieved facts. We measure the entity overlap in the entire dev set and found that on average, correct predictions had 3.67 entities in common while incorrect predictions had 3.28, and the overall dev set had about 3.54. The small difference in overlap indicates that the oracle setting doesn't leverage any hidden bias.

Natural Questions: Table 3 show the performance of incorporating KB facts in the Full NQ task. Though we see improvements to previously published results, careful ablations reveal that the baseline achieves similar results with more (10%) negative examples. This confirms that even in the full dataset PPR methods fail to retrieve relevant knowledge for the model to leverage for QA.

Facts as Augmented Input: To understand the benefit of augmenting facts as input, we compare against a baseline where the retrieved facts are separately represented by a Transformer. We use a stacked Transformer with the same architecture as BERT as a fact encoder. We feed top retrieved facts in natural language form to it, use a multi-head attention layer between the text only BERT representation and the fact representation and use the new fact-attended text representation for prediction similar to Section 3.2. Results on NQ in Table 5 shows that the separate fact representation has lower performance than our approach showing the benefit of our augmented input approach.

4.3 Qualitative Examples:

Table 4 shows examples of facts from clean oracle and retrieved facts from WS PPR for questions of varying difficulty. The first two examples shows a question where the oracle KB path (shortest path connecting question entities to answer entities) is the correct reasoning path for answering the question. The third and fourth examples shows a case where the oracle KB path contains relevant knowledge for the question but is not the right path for answering the question. WS PPR in all cases retrieves relevant facts about the question entity, and some oracle KB facts. For the first and the third examples, WS PPR retrieves the entire KB path. In the second and last example, WS PPR retrieves part of the oracle KB path but not the entire path.

5 Conclusion

We investigate incorporating KB facts into a real-world QA - Natural Questions. We create a subset of NQ, Factual Questions, to facilitate evaluation of KB integration. We present an oracle setting, where the gold KB path is provided and establish a strong upper-bound. We experimentally show that PPR based retrievers have low recall of answer entities and do not improve downstream QA showing that path-retrieval is a bottleneck for KB integration.

Acknowledgements

We thank the anonymous reviewers for their feedback and suggestions. We are grateful to Mandar Joshi for detailed regular discussions and feedback during the course of this work. We thank Chris Alberti, Kenton Lee and Matthew Siegler for feedback and help with implementation.

References

Chris Alberti, Kenton Lee, and Michael Collins. 2019. A bert baseline for the natural questions. *arXiv preprint arXiv:1901.08634*.

Jonathan Berant, Andrew Chou, Roy Frostig, and Percy Liang. 2013. Semantic parsing on freebase from question-answer pairs. In *Proceedings of the 2013 conference on empirical methods in natural language processing*, pages 1533–1544.

A. Bordes, S. Chopra, and J. Weston. 2014. Question answering with subgraph embeddings. In *EMNLP*.

Danqi Chen, Adam Fisch, Jason Weston, and Antoine Bordes. 2017. Reading wikipedia to answer open-domain questions. In *ACL*.

Jacob Devlin, Ming-Wei Chang, Kenton Lee, and Kristina Toutanova. 2019. BERT: Pre-training of deep bidirectional transformers for language understanding. In *Proceedings of the 2019 Conference of the North American Chapter of the Association for Computational Linguistics: Human Language Technologies, Volume 1 (Long and Short Papers)*, pages 4171–4186, Minneapolis, Minnesota. Association for Computational Linguistics.

Taher H Haveliwala. 2003. Topic-sensitive pagerank: A context-sensitive ranking algorithm for web search. *IEEE transactions on knowledge and data engineering*, 15(4):784–796.

Tom Kwiatkowski, Jennimaria Palomaki, Olivia Redfield, Michael Collins, Ankur Parikh, Chris Alberti, Danielle Epstein, Illia Polosukhin, Jacob Devlin, Kenton Lee, et al. 2019. Natural questions: a benchmark for question answering research. *Transactions of the Association for Computational Linguistics*, 7:453–466.

Anne Lauscher, Olga Majewska, Leonardo F. R. Ribeiro, Iryna Gurevych, Nikolai Rozanov, and Goran Glavaš. 2020. Common sense or world knowledge? investigating adapter-based knowledge injection into pretrained transformers. In *Proceedings of Deep Learning Inside Out (DeeLIO): The First Workshop on Knowledge Extraction and Integration for Deep Learning Architectures*, pages 43–49, Online. Association for Computational Linguistics.

Kenton Lee, Ming-Wei Chang, and Kristina Toutanova. 2019. Latent retrieval for weakly supervised open domain question answering. In *ACL*.

Kangqi Luo, F. Lin, Xusheng Luo, and K. Q. Zhu. 2018. Knowledge base question answering via encoding of complex query graphs. In *EMNLP*.

Ankur Parikh, Oscar Täckström, Dipanjan Das, and Jakob Uszkoreit. 2016. A decomposable attention model for natural language inference. In *Proceedings of the 2016 Conference on Empirical Methods in Natural Language Processing*, pages 2249–2255, Austin, Texas. Association for Computational Linguistics.

Jeffrey Pennington, Richard Socher, and Christopher D. Manning. 2014. Glove: Global vectors for word representation. In *Empirical Methods in Natural Language Processing (EMNLP)*, pages 1532–1543.

Michael Ringgaard, Rahul Gupta, and Fernando CN Pereira. 2017. Sling: A framework for frame semantic parsing. *arXiv preprint arXiv:1710.07032*.

Stephen Robertson and Hugo Zaragoza. 2009. The probabilistic relevance framework: Bm25 and beyond. *Found. Trends Inf. Retr.*, 3:333–389.

U. Sawant, S. Garg, S. Chakrabarti, and G. Ramakrishnan. 2018. Neural architecture for question answering using a knowledge graph and web corpus. *Information Retrieval Journal*, 22:324–349.

Haitian Sun, Tania Bedrax-Weiss, and William W. Cohen. 2019. Pullnet: Open domain question answering with iterative retrieval on knowledge bases and text. In *EMNLP/IJCNLP*.

Haitian Sun, Bhuwan Dhingra, Manzil Zaheer, Kathryn Mazaitis, Ruslan Salakhutdinov, and William W. Cohen. 2018. Open domain question answering using early fusion of knowledge bases and text. In *EMNLP*.

Denny Vrandečić and Markus Krötzsch. 2014. Wikidata: a free collaborative knowledgebase. *Communications of the ACM*, 57(10):78–85.

Chao Wang and Hui Jiang. 2019. Explicit utilization of general knowledge in machine reading comprehension. In *ACL*.

Y. Zhang, Hanjun Dai, Zornitsa Kozareva, A. Smola, and L. Song. 2018. Variational reasoning for question answering with knowledge graph. In *AAAI*.

Augmenting Topic Aware Knowledge-Grounded Conversations with Dynamic Built Knowledge Graphs

Junjie Wu[♠,♣] **Hao Zhou**[◇]
[♠]AI Thrust, Information Hub, HKUST
[♣]Department of Computer Science and Technology, HKUST
[◇]Department of Computer Science, Tsinghua University
junjie.wu@connect.ust.hk
zhouhao16@mails.tsinghua.edu.cn

Abstract

Dialog topic management and background knowledge selection are essential factors for the success of knowledge-grounded open-domain conversations. However, existing models are primarily performed with symmetric knowledge bases or stylized with pre-defined roles between conversational partners, while people usually have their own knowledge before a real chit-chat. To address this problem, we propose a dynamic knowledge graph-based topical conversation model (DKGT). Given a dialog history context, our model first builds knowledge graphs from the context as an imitation of human's ability to form logical relationships between known and unknown topics during a conversation. This logical information will be fed into a topic predictor to promote topic management, then facilitate background knowledge selection and response generation. To the best of our knowledge, this is the first attempt to dynamically form knowledge graphs between chatting topics to assist dialog topic management during a conversation. Experimental results manifest that our model can properly schedule conversational topics and pick suitable knowledge to generate informative responses comparing to several strong baselines.

1 Introduction

Conversational AI, especially the open-domain dialog system, is an essential and challenging problem that leads to a variety of applications (Vinyals and Le, 2015; Serban et al., 2017). Previous works introduce external background knowledge to help their systems generate more informative responses (Li et al., 2016b; Dinan et al., 2018; Ghazvininejad et al., 2018; Young et al., 2018). However, these systems are facing a main issue that they tend to only utilize dialog utterances as queries to match appropriate knowledge sentences. Table 1 shows two responses corresponding to the same post. As can be seen, response1 changes the chatting topic abruptly and thus becomes incoherent. By contrast, response2 first manages to deepen the current topic "William Shakespeare", then picks a suitable knowledge candidate to generate an engaging response. Therefore, a good topic managing strategy is also very crucial to dialog generation.

Chatting topics: William Shakespeare; Sun; Jane Austen **Knowledge:** ...... Shakespeare invented the names Miranda, Jessica, and Olivia. ......
Dialog ...... **A**: Do you like shakespeare? **B**: Yes a little bit. He is often called england' s national poet and the "bard of avon". **A**: He is a great dramatist that influenced a lot of people, like Joenesbo.
Response 1: Did you know that Ronald Reagan was rejected for a movie role because an entertainment executive didn' t look presidential enough? **Response 2:** I love shakespeare' s works. Did you know that he invented the names Miranda, Jessica, and Olivia ?

Table 1: Example responses generated by two models.

To solve this problem, some papers propose to plan a set of conversational topics as chatting goals in advance to boost knowledge matching and response generation (Wu et al., 2019; Xu et al., 2020). However, it is difficult to schedule an appropriate topic transition route beforehand since topics are switching dynamically during a chit-chat based on many real-time factors, especially when two partners have different personal knowledge. Hence, these methods could not pre-schedule a topic at each turn properly and thus becoming non-attractive.

Another problem these knowledge-grounded or topic-enhanced models might encounter is that they are typically tested under symmetric knowledge settings (Young et al., 2018), or asymmetric settings with pre-defined roles (Dinan et al., 2018). Yet people usually have unequal personal knowledge prior to real-world conversations. Hence, such models cannot reflect the effect of information transferring

Proceedings of Deep Learning Inside Out (DeeLIO):
The 2nd Workshop on Knowledge Extraction and Integration for Deep Learning Architectures, pages 31–39
Online, June 10, 2021. ©2021 Association for Computational Linguistics

and learning between two strangers, which is crucial to an engaging conversation. This issue will matter more when there are no pre-defined roles between two conversation partners.

To solve these problems, in this paper, we study the problem of topic transitions in open-domain conversations under both symmetric and asymmetric settings. To this end, we propose a dynamic knowledge graph-based topical conversation model (DKGT). Given a dialogue context and a corresponding knowledge base, we first extract knowledge triples from each utterance and then jointly combine those triples through a static graph attention mechanism. Such logical information will then be fed into a topic predictor to predict the next chatting topic, which assists background knowledge selection and dialog generation. We further demonstrate the effectiveness of our method on Topical-Chat (Gopalakrishnan et al., 2019), comparing to several baselines. The main contributions of this paper can be wrapped as follows:

- To the best of our knowledge, this is the first attempt to dynamically mine logical relationships between chatting topics during a conversation to assist topic management, in the form of knowledge graphs.
- The proposed model has two benefits: 1. The dynamic built KG can automatically form logical information between chatting topics during a conversation, which helps our system to learn from its conversational partner especially when they have different prior knowledge. 2. Such logical information can be used to facilitate topic transition and background knowledge selection, then prompts coherent dialog generation.
- Experimental results demonstrate that our method is capable of scheduling appropriate topics and picking suitable background knowledge to generate informative and diverse responses.

2 Related Work

Knowledge-Grounded Open-Domain Dialog Systems Since traditional end-to-end architectures (Li et al., 2015; Serban et al., 2017) often generate generic and dull responses, several works introduce external background knowledge to produce diverse context (Ghazvininejad et al., 2018; Dinan et al., 2018; Li et al., 2019). Although these methods have obtained promising results, they are facing two main issues. First, such models are agnostic to internal topic coherence, which usually leads to less logical conversations. Second, their conversation partners often have pre-defined roles or the external knowledge provided for these partners is usually symmetric, which could not reflect real-world chit-chats.

Topic-aware Conversational models A variety of approaches proposed to leverage topic information by recognizing topic words inside or outside the previous utterances (Xing et al., 2017; Wang et al., 2018; Dziri et al., 2019). However, simply fusing topic words into text representations makes these models ignore logical relationships between topics and thus fail to perform smooth topic transitions. Except for applying attention mechanism on topic words, researchers have also investigated proactive conversation, whose topic transition and conversation development are conditioned on pre-scheduled chatting goals (Li et al., 2018; Wu et al., 2019; Xu et al., 2020). Nevertheless, these models are limited by pre-defined topic and goal sequences, hence not applicable to open-domain and open-topic conversations.

Graph-enhanced Conversational Models Structured knowledge has been studied to improve dialog generation for a long time (Hixon et al., 2015; Zhou et al., 2018; Moon et al., 2019; Tuan et al., 2019). However, these models are mainly based on pre-defined knowledge graphs, which restrict their ability under symmetric knowledge settings. By contrast, our dynamic knowledge graphs enable our system to learn logical information through the conversation like humans, which facilitates both topic management and dialog generation.

3 Model

3.1 Task Definition and Overview

Formally, let $D = [x_1, x_2, ..., x_k]$ be a conversation history including k utterances, where $x_i (1 \leq i \leq k)$ stands for the ith utterance. Each x_i is associated with its speaker's background knowledge set K, which has been segmented into several sentences $[k_1, k_2, ..., k_j]$. Given such information, our goal is to predict the chatting topic at each turn and make good use of knowledge set K to generate a coherent response x_{i+1}.

Figure 1 shows the overview architecture of our proposed DKGT. Given a conversation history D,

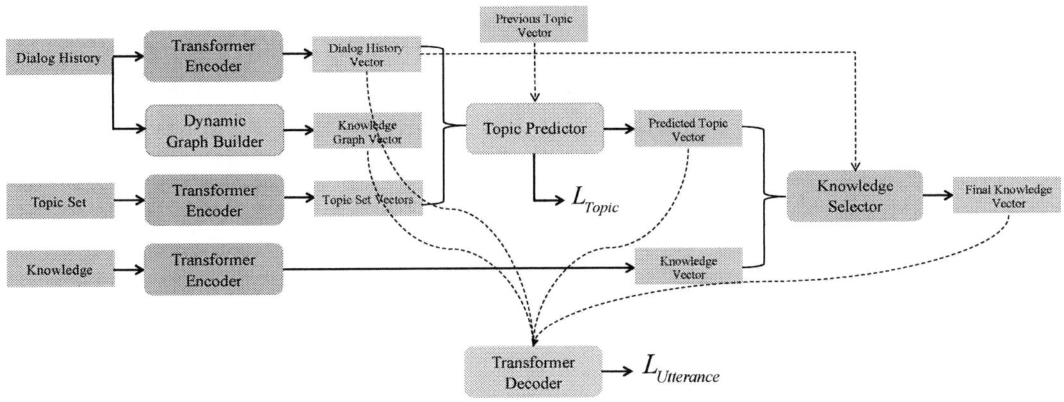

Figure 1: Overview of our proposed DKGT model.

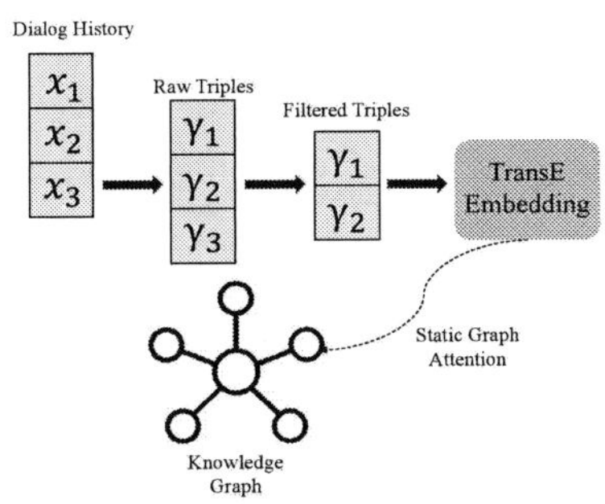

Figure 2: Structure of the Dynamic Graph Builder.

the dynamic graph builder first extracts knowledge triples across specified entities to construct a knowledge graph $G = [\gamma_1, \gamma_2, ..., \gamma_m]$, where each triple is denoted as $\gamma = (h, r, t)$ (head entity, relation, tail entity). We then adopt TransE (Bordes et al., 2013) to obtain vector representation $\boldsymbol{G}$ of knowledge graph G. Next, the topic predictor takes encoded representation $\boldsymbol{D}$ and $\boldsymbol{G}$ as input and applies a MLP-based module to predict the topic label T. The assigned T enables our model to decrease knowledge set K to a smaller one $\boldsymbol{K}$ and thus facilitates further knowledge acquisition. Afterward, the knowledge retriever adopts another attention mechanism to obtain a cumulative knowledge representation $\boldsymbol{K}$ of the decreased knowledge set K. Finally, dialog context $\boldsymbol{D}$, accumulated knowledge $\boldsymbol{K}$, topic vector $\boldsymbol{T}$ and graph vector $\boldsymbol{G}$ are concatenated orderly and fed into a transformer decoder. Our transformer decoder will then attentively read the concatenated vector and generates an informative response.

3.2 Dynamic Graph Builder

As shown in Figure 2, at each turn, the model first extracts knowledge triples from all individual sentences that are longer than three words using an open-source relation extraction tool OpenNRE (Han et al., 2019) [1]. With preassigned entities, OpenNRE can provide a relation between the head and tail entity along with a confidential probability score. In this work, the scope of graph entities is limited to two categories: topic entities provided by the Topical-Chat dataset and named entities (except numerical entities like date and time). To confirm the quality of generated triples, we manually set 0.7 as a threshold probability score to perform filtering. When a new utterance x_{i+1} comes in, the knowledge graph G will be updated dynamically following the above procedure. This strategy enables our system to learn knowledge and form new logical relationships in real-time.

For each triple $\gamma = (h, r, t)$ in graph G, we adopt TransE (Bordes et al., 2013) to obtain its low-dimension representation. Moreover, to fill in the representation gap between raw utterances and triples, we employ an MLP layer on those triple embeddings. Therefore, a triple vector $\boldsymbol{\gamma}$ can be further denoted as $\boldsymbol{\gamma} = (\boldsymbol{h}, \boldsymbol{r}, \boldsymbol{t})$, where $\boldsymbol{h}$, $\boldsymbol{r}$, $\boldsymbol{t}$ are the transformed TransE embeddings of h, r, t respectively.

The static graph attention mechanism (Zhou et al., 2018) is then applied to capture semantic information from entities and their relations. All the knowledge triple vectors $[\boldsymbol{\gamma_1}, \boldsymbol{\gamma_2}, ..., \boldsymbol{\gamma_m}]$ are jointly computed to generate a graph vector $\boldsymbol{G}$:

[1] https://github.com/thunlp/OpenNRE

$$\mu_i = (\boldsymbol{W_r r_i})^\top tanh(\boldsymbol{W_h h_i} + \boldsymbol{W_t t_i}), \quad (1)$$

$$\eta_i = \frac{exp(\mu_i)}{\sum_{j=1}^{m} exp(\mu_j)}, \quad (2)$$

$$\boldsymbol{G} = \sum_{i=1}^{m} \eta_i [\boldsymbol{h_i}; \boldsymbol{t_i}], \quad (3)$$

where $\boldsymbol{W_h}$, $\boldsymbol{W_r}$, $\boldsymbol{W_t}$ are weight matrices for $\boldsymbol{h}$, $\boldsymbol{r}$, $\boldsymbol{t}$, and $[\boldsymbol{h_i}; \boldsymbol{t_i}]$ denotes the concatenated vector of $\boldsymbol{h_i}$ and $\boldsymbol{t_i}$.

3.3 Encoder

A shared transformer-based (Vaswani et al., 2017) encoder is employed to encode dialog utterances, knowledge sentences and topic labels. In this task, the topic label T_i of each utterance x_i is a word or phrase that refers to an entity in the pre-defined topic entity set [2]. To better capture the structural information between utterances, the dialog history input at turn i is defined as the concatenation of previous utterances $D_i = [x_1; x_2; ...; x_i]$. We use $\boldsymbol{D_i}, \boldsymbol{k_i}, \boldsymbol{T_i}, \boldsymbol{T_s}$ to symbol the encoded counterparts, where $\boldsymbol{T_s}$ is the encoded representation for all topic entities in the pre-defined set.

3.4 Topic Predictor

At each turn i, upon obtaining knowledge graph vector $\boldsymbol{G}$, dialog history vector $\boldsymbol{D_i}$,topic vector $\boldsymbol{T_i}$ and $\boldsymbol{T_s}$, a three-layer MLP-based module is applied to predict the topic label of the next utterance. We concatenate the first token's (the [CLS] token) hidden state from both dialog context vector $\boldsymbol{D_i}$, topic vectors $\boldsymbol{T_i}$ and $\boldsymbol{T_s}$ as input to attain a probability distribution of the next topic label T_{i+1}:

$$T_{i+1} = Softmax(\boldsymbol{MLP}([\boldsymbol{D_{i_{first}}}; \boldsymbol{T_{s_{first}}}; \boldsymbol{T_{i_{first}}}; \boldsymbol{G}])), \quad (4)$$

where $\boldsymbol{D_{i_{first}}}$, $\boldsymbol{T_{s_{first}}}$ and $\boldsymbol{T_{i_{first}}}$ are the first token's hidden states for $\boldsymbol{D_i}$,$\boldsymbol{T_i}$ and $\boldsymbol{T_s}$.

3.5 Knowledge Retriever

During the whole chat, each speaker has access to a specific knowledge set K that includes dozens of candidates k_i. However, it is challenging for existing models to handle large knowledge bases at once. Hence, we operate a general attention mechanism between dialog context and knowledge candidates to get an informative knowledge representation. A sentence embedding layer (Cer et al., 2018) will first obtain sentence-level representations of $\boldsymbol{D_i}$ and knowledge representation $\boldsymbol{k_i}$ as $\boldsymbol{D_i^s}$ and $\boldsymbol{k_i^s}$. Next, given the predicted topic T_{i+1}, we can pick T_{i+1} related knowledge from the original knowledge set to form K_{small}. Our model then orderly attends on each knowledge candidate in K_{small} to generate a knowledge representation for the next turn as below:

$$\alpha_m = \boldsymbol{k_m^{s\top} W_{D_i^s} D_i^s}, \quad (5)$$

$$\beta_m = \frac{exp(\alpha_m)}{\sum_{j=1}^{N_{K_{small}}} exp(\alpha_j)}, \quad (6)$$

$$\boldsymbol{K_{i+1}} = \sum_{m=1}^{N_{K_{small}}} \beta_m \boldsymbol{k_m^s}, \quad (7)$$

where $\boldsymbol{W_{D_i^s}}$ is the weight matrix for $\boldsymbol{D_i^s}$ and $N_{K_{small}}$ is the number of candidates in K_{small}. $\boldsymbol{K_{i+1}}$ is the final knowledge representation to be used in the decoding part.

3.6 Decoder and Loss Function

As illustrated in Figure 1, we adopt another transformer as a decoder to generate coherent responses, whose structure is the same as the encoder. Our decoder generates responses with the following procedure:

Formally, let the gold token distribution be Γ_k and the predicted token distribution be Δ_k, we optimize our model's parameters by minimizing the cross entropy error between these two distributions. Besides, we employ supervised signals on the topic predictor to teacher-force the model to predict a suitable topic. Finally, the loss function between generated sequence $\boldsymbol{Y}$ and ground truth $\boldsymbol{X}$ ($\boldsymbol{X} = (x_1, x_2, ..., x_n)$, $\boldsymbol{Y} = (y_1, y_2, ..., y_m)$) at turn i is formulated as:

$$L(\theta) = -\lambda_1 \sum_{k=1}^{m} \Gamma_k log(\Delta_k) - \lambda_2 \sum_{j=1}^{N_{set}} T_{i+1_j}^{g} log(\boldsymbol{T_{i+1_j}^{p}}), \quad (8)$$

where $T_{i+1_j}^{g}$ and $\boldsymbol{T_{i+1_j}^{p}}$ are the ground truth label and predicted probability distribution at turn $i+1$ respectively. λ_1 and λ_2 stand for the weights of our two loss terms, and N_{set} is the number of topic labels in the pre-defined topic set. In our experiments, λ_1 and λ_2 are set to 1 and 20.

[2]Topical-chat provides three topic entities for each conversation, which consists of our topic set.

	Config	Train	Valid Freq	Valid Rare	Test Freq	Test Rare
Dialogs	A	1181	62	73	44	70
	B	1144	54	75	34	78
	C	1298	58	78	31	72
	D	1205	54	80	122	85
	Total	4828	228	306	231	305
Utterances	A	24,609	1,272	1,531	934	1,466
	B	23,888	1,118	1,548	699	1,632
	C	27,151	1,225	1,624	647	1,488
	D	25,199	1,137	1,654	2,579	1,816
	Total	100,847	4,752	6,357	4,859	6,402

Table 2: Statistics of the dataset.

Set	Total Number	Averaged per Dialog
Train	52829	10.9
Valid Freq	2210	9.7
Valid Rare	3070	10.0
Test Freq	2139	9.3
Test Rare	3115	10.2

Table 3: Statistics of extracted triples on different sets.

4 Experiments

4.1 Dataset

In this work, we use a public released dataset Topical-Chat [3], which contains thousands of knowledge-grounded conversations spanning 300 specific topics. [4] To enhance the effect of knowledge graphs on this dataset, we firstly used OpenNRE to extract triples for every utterance, then filtered out conversations with less than 5 triples. The statistics of our downsampled dataset and extracted triples are shown in Table 2 and Table 3 respectively.

4.2 Obtaining Topic Labels

Although Topical-Chat does not provide topic annotation for each utterance directly, workers have attached their choice of knowledge scope at each turn during crowd-sourcing, which can then be converted into topic labels automatically. Hence, we first obtained ground truth topic labels in the following steps:

1. If a given knowledge source is solely related to a fun fact under one of the topic entities, this topic entity will become the topic label.
2. If a given knowledge source is solely related to an article sentence, the topic which appears most frequently will become the topic label.
3. While an utterance equips multiple knowledge sources, we take its closest utterance(e.g. $i+1$ and $i-1$ given i) 's topic as the topic label.
4. If "Personal Knowledge" appears in the knowledge source, we ignore it for simplicity. When "Personal Knowledge" is the only knowledge source, the strategy in step3 will be performed to generate a topic label.

Although step3 acts as an estimate of the current chatting topic and might bring some biases, our topic annotation is still effective in two ways: **First**, the accurate annotation step1 and step2 have covered most of the utterances in the dataset (e.g. 82.3 % in the training corpus); **Second**, topic transition in a dialog usually happens after several turns, which means the topic label at turn i is often the same as turn $i-1$ and turn $i+1$. More importantly, the above strategy highly reduces human efforts when annotating data.

4.3 Baselines

To make an empirical comparison, we choose the following baseline models:

Seq2Seq-TF: A simple sequence to sequence architecture (Vinyals and Le, 2015) that applies transformer-based encoder and decoder. We also add a topic classifier at the top of each utterance representation to perform topic prediction for further comparison.

Wizard-TF is a transformer-based memory network for document-grounded open-domain dialog generation (Dinan et al., 2018). It takes context

[3] https://github.com/alexa/alexa-prize-topical-chat-dataset

[4] We recommend readers to read (Gopalakrishnan et al., 2019)

vectors as queries to match a single knowledge candidate to generate responses. A topic predictor is also added for our evaluation.

For our proposed **DKGT** model, we further devise two variants for comparison and ablation study:

DKGT w/ all Know is used to evaluate the effect of the topic predictor. After predicting a topic for the next turn, the size of the knowledge set will not be decreased by the predicted topic and the model needs to match background knowledge from the raw knowledge base.

DKGT w/o Graph: A variant without the dynamic graph module. This setup aims to check the effectiveness of our proposed dynamic graph builder.

4.4 Implementation Details

We apply PyTorch [5] to perform all the experiments. During data preprocessing, the max sequence length is 128 for dialog history utterances, 50 for responses, 64 for knowledge candidates, and 10 for topic entities respectively. For Wizard Transformer, we follow their original hyperparameter settings. For other transformer-based models, their hidden size is 512. The number of layers of encoder and decoder is set to 3 while the number of attention heads in multi-head attention is 4. All the transformer modules are based on Hugging Face's framework [6]. In the dynamic graph builder, we adopt TransE (Bordes et al., 2013) to generate entity and relation representations, and the embedding size of both entities and relations is set to 100. For decoding, we apply the Top-p sampling strategy proposed by (Holtzman et al., 2019) with a temperature of 0.7, and the threshold of the cumulative probability is 0.9. During training, we use the AdamW optimizer with a batch size of 64. The gradient clip is limited to 0.1. We take the first two training epochs as a warm-up process and the learning rate is set to 0.0001(except Wizard-TF). All the models are trained for at most 30 epochs and the training stops when the perplexity on the validation freq set starts to increase. The training stage of each model took about two and a half days on a Titan X GPU machine.

4.5 Automatic Evaluation

Metrics: In our experiments, we use perplexity (PPL) and BLEU 1-gram to evaluate our system at the content level. We also adopt distinct 1-gram (Li et al., 2016a) to assess the diversity of generated responses. To evaluate our models at the topic level, we calculate the accuracy between the predicted topic label and the ground truth topic label.

Model	PPL	BLEU-1%	Dist-1%	Acc
Seq2Seq-TF	36.82	23.03	1.37	0.395
Wizard-TF	37.67	22.41	1.41	0.307
DKGT *w/all Know*	36.54	23.44	**1.49**	**0.782**
DKGT w/o *Graph*	**35.97**	23.41	1.42	0.765
DKGT	36.08	**23.58**	1.46	0.780

Table 4: Automatic evaluation results.

Results: Table 3 shows the automatic evaluation results for all the models. As can be seen, DKGT outperforms Wizard-TF and Seq2Seq-TF on all the metrics, demonstrating that our model can generate more fluent and informative responses with the help of all the proposed strategies. Moreover, the topic accuracy scores of Seq2Seq-TF and Wizard-TF are extremely low. This is due to their lack of additional supervision signals on topic labels during training.

To examine the influence of different modules, we also perform an ablation study using two variant models. As we can see, after removing the dynamic kg module, topic accuracy drops a lot, proving that the dynamic kg module augments our system's ability to manage dialog topics since it stores logical information between topic entities. Although DKGT *w/o Graph* attains the lowest perplexity score, our model not only achieves a similar perplexity score but also obtains the highest BLEU-1 value, showing that it can perform proper topic management without sacrificing content fluency. In practice, topic accuracy is more important than perplexity in consideration of the generated responses are already fluent with the perplexity of 36.82. Besides, comparing to DKGT *w/all Know*, our model performs better on both perplexity and BLEU-1. This is because proper topic prediction highly reduces the difficulty of picking suitable knowledge, thus facilitate response generation. Note that it is reasonable for DKGT *w/all Know* to get the highest Dist-1 score since it encounters the whole knowledge base.

4.6 Manual Evaluation

To better evaluate the generated responses, we further perform a manual evaluation. We randomly sampled 200 posts from the test frequent and rare set (50 posts for each knowledge setting) respec-

[5] https://pytorch.org/
[6] https://huggingface.co/

Opponent	Win	Loss	Tie
DKGT vs. Seq2Seq-TF***	**39.0%**	22.5%	38.5%
DKGT vs. Wizard-TF*	**36.0%**	30.0%	34.0%
DKGT vs. DKGT w/*all Know****	**35.5%**	21.0%	43.5%
DKGT vs. DKGT w/o *Graph****	**42.0%**	17.0%	41.0%

Table 5: Manual evaluation results. We conducted two-tailed binomial test to obtain the p-value. * refers to $p < 0.05$, ** refers to $p < 0.01$ and ** refers to $p < 0.001$ respectively.

tively to conduct a pair-wise comparison between DKGT and one of the other four baselines.

Annotation settings: Three annotators are asked to evaluate these 800 pairs independently with the following rules: (1) Given a post and relevant topics, annotators are required to rate among 'win', 'lose' and 'tie' (response1 versus response2) on two generated responses. (2) Model identifiers are masked during annotation. (3) If three annotators give three distinct answers, the result will be counted as 'tie'. Before the annotation starts, annotators were trained with a few examples to understand three criteria comprehensively:

- **Topic appropriateness:** whether a generated response appropriately deepens or widens the current conversation topic smoothly.
- **Content coherency:** whether a response is relevant and fluent to the given dialog history and the knowledge base.
- **Response informativeness:** whether a response is diverse and informative like produced by humans.

Annotators attained a Krippendorff's α of 0.469 on 200 mutually-labeled pairs, indicating moderate agreement.

Results: The results are shown in Table 4. It can be seen that our proposed model outperforms all the other baselines significantly. Besides, both the knowledge retriever and the dynamic graph builder boost the generated responses to become more acceptable to humans with a percentage of 14.5% and 25%, indicating that our model can better perform topic management and response generation with these proposed strategies.

It is worth noting that when comparing to DKGT *w/o Graph*, DKGT got the highest "Win" rate (42.0%) and the lowest "Lose" rate (17%), yet automatic evaluation results show that they have similar perplexity scores. By checking the annotation examples, we found that in most cases, though DKGT

Model	Config	PPL	Acc
Wizard-TF	A	36.37	0.290
	B	37.81	0.312
	C	33.24	0.344
	D	40.63	0.295
DKGT w/o *Graph*	A	34.91	0.778
	B	36.36	0.770
	C	31.92	0.759
	D	38.47	0.758
DKGT	A	34.94	0.786
	B	36.37	0.776
	C	32.18	0.768
	D	38.60	0.781

Table 6: Automatic evaluation results under different knowledge settings. Config A and B are asymmetric settings while C and D are symmetric settings.

Opponent	Config	Win	Loss	Tie
DKGT vs. Wizard-TF	A	42%	28%	30%
	B	44%	20%	36%
	C	30%	26%	44%
	D	32%	42%	26%
DKGT vs. DKGT w/o *Graph*	A	40%	20%	40%
	B	52%	12%	36%
	C	38%	14%	48%
	D	38%	22%	40%

Table 7: Manual evaluation results under different knowledge settings.

w/o Graph could predict the correct topic label for the next turn, it fails to pick a suitable knowledge candidate from the decreased knowledge base since it does not store relationships between topic entities. Moreover, DKGT *w/o Graph* tends to explore topics abruptly, while coherent transitions usually appear in DKGT's responses, which further proves the effectiveness of the dynamic graph module.

4.7 Analysis of results under different knowledge settings

To examine our model's ability to conduct conversations under asymmetric knowledge settings, we further perform experiments under different configs between three representative models. Topical-Chat equips four types of prior knowledge settings between two conversational partners naming config A, B, C and D, where config A and config B represent asymmetric in entity-level fun facts and entity-level Wikipedia descriptions respectively. For automatic evaluation, we split the test set based on different configs and calculate corresponding perplexity and topic accuracy scores. For manual evaluation, we directly obtain the "win", "lose" and "tie" rates from our annotation results.

As shown in Table 5, DKGT and DKGT *w/o Graph* beats Wizard-TF on perplexity steadily under the four different knowledge settings, indicating that the topic predictor, as well as knowledge retriever can help with picking suitable knowledge to generate responses regardless of the symmetry of knowledge between two partners. Although DKGT has higher perplexity scores than DKGT *w/o Graph* with all the configs due to its consideration on topic accuracy, the gaps under config A and config B are much smaller, demonstrating that our system can use dynamic graphs to capture semantic information from the dialog history, then facilitates context generation. Moreover, our model still keeps the highest topic accuracy under all knowledge settings with a relatively high score on the two asymmetric datasets, which further proves that logical information stored in dynamic graphs can assist our model to manage chatting topics more appropriately.

Manual evaluation results in Table 6 also clarify the importance of the dynamic graph module when handling asymmetric knowledge bases. Comparing to DKGT *w/o Graph*, DKGT has an average "win" rate of 46% on asymmetric sets, while the value drops to 38% on the other two sets. Also, the average "loss" and "tie" rates on asymmetric sets decrease correspondingly (16% versus 18% and 38% versus 44%). These results further illustrate that our proposed dynamic graph module could facilitate the model to perform topic transition smoothly then generates more human-like responses, especially when the prior knowledge between two partners is not equal.

5 Conclusion and Future Work

In this paper, we propose a dynamic knowledge graph-based topical conversation model (DKGT) to perform coherent topic transitions under both symmetric and asymmetric knowledge settings. Specifically, a dynamic graph builder that constructs knowledge graphs from the context to form logical relationships between known and unknown topics is introduced to assist topic management. Automatic and manual evaluation results show that DKGT can not only schedule dialog topics properly but also generate informative responses preferred by humans.

In the future, we will further explore the usage of our proposed dynamic knowledge graph strategy to improve chatbot's interpretability, which may depend on some inferential methods like multi-hop reasoning. We release our codes at `https://github.com/wujunjie1998/DKGT`.

References

Antoine Bordes, Nicolas Usunier, Alberto Garcia-Duran, Jason Weston, and Oksana Yakhnenko. 2013. Translating embeddings for modeling multi-relational data. In *Advances in neural information processing systems*, pages 2787–2795.

Daniel Cer, Yinfei Yang, Sheng-yi Kong, Nan Hua, Nicole Limtiaco, Rhomni St John, Noah Constant, Mario Guajardo-Céspedes, Steve Yuan, Chris Tar, et al. 2018. Universal sentence encoder. *arXiv preprint arXiv:1803.11175*.

Emily Dinan, Stephen Roller, Kurt Shuster, Angela Fan, Michael Auli, and Jason Weston. 2018. Wizard of wikipedia: Knowledge-powered conversational agents. *arXiv preprint arXiv:1811.01241*.

Nouha Dziri, Ehsan Kamalloo, Kory Mathewson, and Osmar R Zaiane. 2019. Augmenting neural response generation with context-aware topical attention. In *Proceedings of the First Workshop on NLP for Conversational AI*, pages 18–31.

Marjan Ghazvininejad, Chris Brockett, Ming-Wei Chang, Bill Dolan, Jianfeng Gao, Wen-tau Yih, and Michel Galley. 2018. A knowledge-grounded neural conversation model. In *Thirty-Second AAAI Conference on Artificial Intelligence*.

Karthik Gopalakrishnan, Behnam Hedayatnia, Qinglang Chen, Anna Gottardi, Sanjeev Kwatra, Anu Venkatesh, Raefer Gabriel, Dilek Hakkani-Tür, and Amazon Alexa AI. 2019. Topical-chat: Towards knowledge-grounded open-domain conversations. In *INTERSPEECH*, pages 1891–1895.

Xu Han, Tianyu Gao, Yuan Yao, Deming Ye, Zhiyuan Liu, and Maosong Sun. 2019. OpenNRE: An open and extensible toolkit for neural relation extraction. In *Proceedings of EMNLP-IJCNLP: System Demonstrations*, pages 169–174.

Ben Hixon, Peter Clark, and Hannaneh Hajishirzi. 2015. Learning knowledge graphs for question answering through conversational dialog. In *Proceedings of the 2015 Conference of the North American Chapter of the Association for Computational Linguistics: Human Language Technologies*, pages 851–861.

Ari Holtzman, Jan Buys, Li Du, Maxwell Forbes, and Yejin Choi. 2019. The curious case of neural text degeneration. *arXiv preprint arXiv:1904.09751*.

Jiwei Li, Michel Galley, Chris Brockett, Jianfeng Gao, and Bill Dolan. 2015. A diversity-promoting objective function for neural conversation models. *arXiv preprint arXiv:1510.03055*.

Jiwei Li, Michel Galley, Chris Brockett, Jianfeng Gao, and Bill Dolan. 2016a. A diversity-promoting objective function for neural conversation models. In *Proceedings of the 2016 Conference of the North American Chapter of the Association for Computational Linguistics: Human Language Technologies*, pages 110–119.

Jiwei Li, Michel Galley, Chris Brockett, Georgios Spithourakis, Jianfeng Gao, and Bill Dolan. 2016b. A persona-based neural conversation model. In *Proceedings of the 54th Annual Meeting of the Association for Computational Linguistics (Volume 1: Long Papers)*, pages 994–1003.

Raymond Li, Samira Ebrahimi Kahou, Hannes Schulz, Vincent Michalski, Laurent Charlin, and Chris Pal. 2018. Towards deep conversational recommendations. In *Advances in neural information processing systems*, pages 9725–9735.

Zekang Li, Cheng Niu, Fandong Meng, Yang Feng, Qian Li, and Jie Zhou. 2019. Incremental transformer with deliberation decoder for document grounded conversations. In *Proceedings of the 57th Annual Meeting of the Association for Computational Linguistics*, pages 12–21.

Seungwhan Moon, Pararth Shah, Anuj Kumar, and Rajen Subba. 2019. Opendialkg: Explainable conversational reasoning with attention-based walks over knowledge graphs. In *Proceedings of the 57th Annual Meeting of the Association for Computational Linguistics*, pages 845–854.

Iulian Vlad Serban, Alessandro Sordoni, Ryan Lowe, Laurent Charlin, Joelle Pineau, Aaron Courville, and Yoshua Bengio. 2017. A hierarchical latent variable encoder-decoder model for generating dialogues. In *Thirty-First AAAI Conference on Artificial Intelligence*.

Yi-Lin Tuan, Yun-Nung Chen, and Hung-yi Lee. 2019. Dykgchat: Benchmarking dialogue generation grounding on dynamic knowledge graphs. *arXiv preprint arXiv:1910.00610*.

Ashish Vaswani, Noam Shazeer, Niki Parmar, Jakob Uszkoreit, Llion Jones, Aidan N Gomez, Łukasz Kaiser, and Illia Polosukhin. 2017. Attention is all you need. In *Advances in neural information processing systems*, pages 5998–6008.

Oriol Vinyals and Quoc Le. 2015. A neural conversational model. *arXiv preprint arXiv:1506.05869*.

Wenjie Wang, Minlie Huang, Xin-Shun Xu, Fumin Shen, and Liqiang Nie. 2018. Chat more: Deepening and widening the chatting topic via a deep model. In *The 41st International ACM SIGIR Conference on Research & Development in Information Retrieval*, pages 255–264.

Wenquan Wu, Zhen Guo, Xiangyang Zhou, Hua Wu, Xiyuan Zhang, Rongzhong Lian, and Haifeng Wang. 2019. Proactive human-machine conversation with explicit conversation goal. In *Proceedings of the 57th Annual Meeting of the Association for Computational Linguistics*, pages 3794–3804.

Chen Xing, Wei Wu, Yu Wu, Jie Liu, Yalou Huang, Ming Zhou, and Wei-Ying Ma. 2017. Topic aware neural response generation. In *Thirty-First AAAI Conference on Artificial Intelligence*.

Jun Xu, Haifeng Wang, Zhengyu Niu, Hua Wu, and Wanxiang Che. 2020. Knowledge graph grounded goal planning for open-domain conversation generation. In *Proceedings of the AAAI Conference on Artificial Intelligence*, volume 34, pages 9338–9345.

Tom Young, Erik Cambria, Iti Chaturvedi, Hao Zhou, Subham Biswas, and Minlie Huang. 2018. Augmenting end-to-end dialogue systems with commonsense knowledge. In *Thirty-Second AAAI Conference on Artificial Intelligence*.

Hao Zhou, Tom Young, Minlie Huang, Haizhou Zhao, Jingfang Xu, and Xiaoyan Zhu. 2018. Commonsense knowledge aware conversation generation with graph attention. In *IJCAI*, pages 4623–4629.

What Makes My Model Perplexed?
A Linguistic Investigation on Neural Language Models Perplexity

Alessio Miaschi[⋆ ◇], **Dominique Brunato**[◇], **Felice Dell'Orletta**[◇], **Giulia Venturi**[◇]
[⋆]Department of Computer Science, University of Pisa
[◇]Istituto di Linguistica Computazionale "Antonio Zampolli", Pisa
ItaliaNLP Lab – *www.italianlp.it*
alessio.miaschi@phd.unipi.it, {name.surname}@ilc.cnr.it

Abstract

This paper presents an investigation aimed at studying how the linguistic structure of a sentence affects the perplexity of two of the most popular Neural Language Models (NLMs), BERT and GPT-2. We first compare the sentence–level likelihood computed with BERT and the GPT-2's perplexity showing that the two metrics are correlated. In addition, we exploit linguistic features capturing a wide set of morpho-syntactic and syntactic phenomena showing how they contribute to predict the perplexity of the two NLMs.

1 Introduction and Motivation

Perplexity is one of the most standard metrics to assess the quality of a language model. It is also used in different scenarios, such as to classify formal and colloquial tweets (González, 2015), to detect the boundaries between varieties belonging to the same language family (Gamallo et al., 2017), to identify speech samples produced by subjects with cognitive and/or language diseases e.g. dementia, (Cohen and Pakhomov, 2020) or to assess whether it matches various human behavioural measures, such as gaze duration during reading (Demberg and Keller, 2008; Goodkind and Bicknell, 2018). With the recent success gained by Neural Language Models (NLMs) across a variety of NLP tasks, the notion of perplexity has started being investigated also to dig into issues related to the interpretability of contextual word representations, with the aim of understanding whether there is a relationship between this metric and the grammatical abilities implicitly encoded by a NLM (Gulordava et al., 2018; Marvin and Linzen, 2018; Kuncoro et al., 2019). In this context, Hu et al. (2020) and Warstadt et al. (2020) observed a dissociation between the perplexity of a NLM and its performance on targeted syntactic assessments probing the model's ability to encode a range of subtle syntactic phenomena. These findings seem to be valid for models tested across languages (Mueller et al., 2020).

In this paper, we address this scenario but from a different perspective. Rather than studying the relation between the NLM's perplexity and its linguistic competences assessed on sentences undergoing controlled syntactic modifications, we focus on sentences representative of real usage. Our purpose indeed is to understand which linguistic phenomena of the input sentence may make perplexed a NLM and whether they can effectively predict the assigned perplexity score. To have a in-depth understanding of the relation between linguistic structure and perplexity, we rely on a wide spectrum of linguistic features modeling a variety of phenomena, specifically morpho-syntactic and syntactic ones. As we also intend to evaluate the possible influence of the NLM architecture on this relation, in all our experiments we consider two of the most popular NLMs, a traditional unidirectional one, i.e. GPT-2 (Radford et al., 2019), and a bidirectional model such as BERT (Devlin et al., 2019).

Contributions In this paper: (i) we showed that a sentence-level likelihood computed by masking each word sequentially for the BERT model has a robust correlation with GPT-2's perplexity scores; (ii) we verified whether it is possible to predict NLMs' perplexities using a wide set of linguistic features extracted by a sentence; (iii) we identified the linguistic properties of a sentence that mostly cause perplexity, reporting differences and similarities between the two models.

2 Our Approach

We defined two sets of experiments. The first consists in investigating the relationship between BERT and GPT-2 sentence-level perplexity (*PPL*) scores. To do so, we first computed BERT and GPT-2 *PPL* scores for sentences contained in the English Universal Dependencies (UD) treebank (Nivre et al., 2016) and we assessed their corre-

Proceedings of Deep Learning Inside Out (DeeLIO): The 2nd Workshop on Knowledge Extraction and Integration for Deep Learning Architectures, pages 40–47
Online, June 10, 2021.

lation. In the second set of experiments, we studied whether a simple regression model that takes as input a wide range of linguistic features automatically extracted from each UD sentence is able to predict the two NLMs sentence-level perplexities.

To understand which linguistic phenomena contribute to the prediction of BERT and GPT-2 PPLs, and how these features differ between them, we performed an in-depth investigation training the regression model with one feature at a time.

2.1 Linguistic Features

The set of considered linguistic features is based on the ones described in Brunato et al. (2020) which are acquired from raw, morpho-syntactic and syntactic levels of annotation for a total of 78 features that can be categorised in 9 groups corresponding to different linguistic phenomena. A summary of the linguistic features is reported in Table 1, while the whole list is provided in Appendix A.

As shown in Table, these features model linguistic phenomena ranging from raw text one, to morpho–syntactic information and inflectional properties of verbs, to more complex aspects of sentence structure modeling global and local properties of the whole parsed tree and of specific subtrees, such as the order of subjects and objects with respect to the verb, the distribution of UD syntactic relations, also including features referring to the use of subordination and to the structure of verbal predicates.

All these features have been shown to play a highly predictive role when leveraged by traditional learning models on a variety of classification problems, also including the development of probes as reported by Miaschi et al. (2020), who showed that these features can be effectively used to profile the knowledge encoded in the language representations of a pretrained NLM.

Linguistic Feature
Raw Text Properties
Sentence Length
Word Length
Vocabulary Richness
Type/Token Ratio for words and lemmas
Morphosyntactic information
Distibution of UD and language–specific POS
Lexical density
Inflectional morphology
Inflectional morphology of auxiliary verbs
Verbal Predicate Structure
Distribution of verbal heads and verbal roots
Verb arity and distribution of verbs by arity
Global and Local Syntactic Tree Structures
Depth of the whole syntactic tree
Average length of dependency links and of the longest link
Average length of prepositional chains and distribution by depth
Clause length
Relative order of elements
Order of subject and object
Syntactic Relations
Distribution of dependency relations
Use of Subordination
Distribution of subordinate and principal clauses
Average length of subordination chains and distribution by depth
Relative order of subordinate clauses

Table 1: Linguistic Features used in the experiments.

2.2 Models and Data

For our experiments, we rely on the pre-trained version of the two NLMs previously defined. BERT (Devlin et al., 2019) is a Transformer-based masked language model, pretrained on BookCorpus (Zhu et al., 2015) and English Wikipedia. GPT-2 (Radford et al., 2018) is a large transformer-based language model trained using the language modeling task (LM) on 8 million documents for a total of 40 GB of text.

We first computed GPT-2's sentence-level perplexities by dividing the sum of all sub-word conditional log-probabilities by the total number of words for each sentence in the UD dataset. On the other hand, since BERT masked language modeling task does not allow to compute well-formed probability distributions over sentences, we measure BERT sentence-level likelihood by masking each word sequentially and computing the probability as follows:

$$p(S) \approx \prod_{i=1}^{k} p(w_i|context)$$

where *context*, given the deep bidirectionality of the model, corresponds to $w_1, ..., w_{i-1}, w_{i+1}, ..., w_k$. The perplexity is then computed as follows:

$$PPL_S = e^{(\frac{p(S)}{N})}$$

where *N* correspond to the length of sentence *S*. In order to uniform the terminology, in what follows we will refer to the BERT sentence-level likelihood as perplexity.

In order to evaluate our approach on gold annotated sentences, we relied on the three English Universal Dependencies (UD) treebanks: the English version of ParTUT (Sanguinetti and Bosco, 2015), the UD version of the GUM corpus (Zeldes, 2017) and of the English Web Treebank (EWT) (Silveira et al., 2014). Overall, the final dataset consists of 22,505 sentences.

Lengths	ρ score	# samples
All	0.63	22,505
n=10	0.66	847
n=15	0.60	793
n=20	0.64	643
n=25	0.53	422
n=30	0.54	277

Table 2: Spearman correlations between BERT and GPT-2 perplexities computed for all UD sentences (*All*) and sentences with fixed-length *n*.

3 A Linguistic Investigation on Perplexity

As a first step, we assessed whether there is a relationship between the perplexity of a traditional NLM and of a masked NLM. We thus calculated BERT and GPT-2 perplexity scores for each UD sentence and measured the correlation between them. Since *PPL* scores are highly affected by the length of the input sequence, we computed ρ correlation coefficients also considering groups of sentences with fixed length. Specifically, we relied on Spearman correlation because we were interested in measuring how the variations in perplexity scores relate each other, rather than focusing on the actual *PPL* values. Results are reported in Table 2. As we can notice, even considering samples with fixed length, the two NLMs' perplexities exhibit moderate to substantial correlation (with $p < 0.001$), thus showing that BERT an GPT-2 do not diverge excessively in their ability of predicting the likelihood of the input sentences. Moreover, this allows us to confirm that, although the deep bidirectional structure of BERT does not permit to compute a well-formed probability distribution over a sentence (see Section 2.2), this metric could be considered as a valid approximation of the perplexity computed with a unidirectional NLM.

Once established the correlation between the perplexities of the two NLMs, we performed a second experiment to investigate (i) if the considered set of linguistic features plays a role in predicting their perplexity and (ii) which are the features that contribute more to the prediction task. To do so, we trained a LinearSVR model that predicts perplexity's scores using our set of linguistic properties as input features. Since most of them refer to syntactic properties of sentence that are strongly correlated with its length, we considered as a baseline a SVR model that takes sentence length as input and outputs BERT/GPT-2 sentence's perplexity. Regression results deriving by considering both the whole set (*All*) and each of the 9 groups of linguistic features separately are reported in Figure 1. As a general remark, for the whole UD dataset, we can observe that the results considering both all and the 9 groups of linguistic features outperform the results obtained by the baseline, i.e. ρ=0.38 for BERT and 0.22 for GPT-2 respectively. This demonstrates that the considered features are able to model aspects involved in NLM's perplexity that go beyond the simple length of sentence. This is particularly the case of GPT-2, suggesting that the probability assigned to a sentence by a traditional NLM is more explainable in terms of linguistic phenomena mainly affecting morpho-syntactic and syntactic structure. Consequently, the baseline score is higher for BERT. If we consider the scores obtained for each group of sentences with fixed length, we can see that higher scores are obtained for groups containing shorter sentences, for both NLMs. This is quite expected since in these sentences the possible output space is smaller for almost all features,

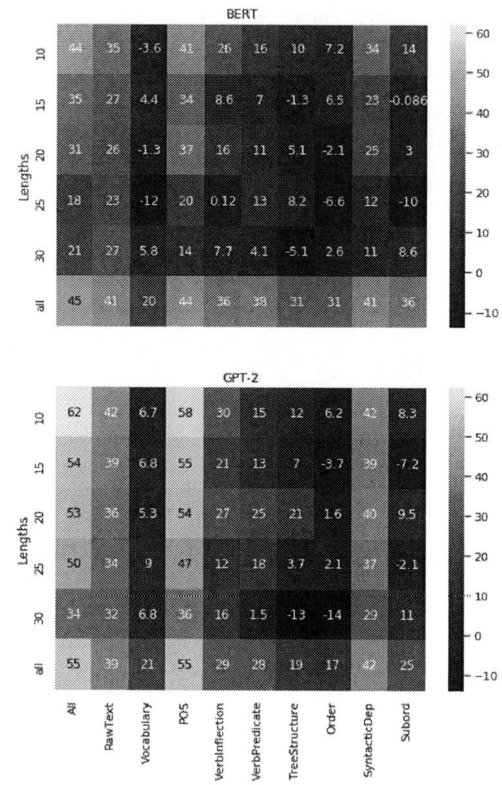

Figure 1: BERT and GPT-2 ρ scores (multiplied by 100) obtained with the LinearSVR model using linguistic features, for the whole UD dataset and groups of sentences with fixed length.

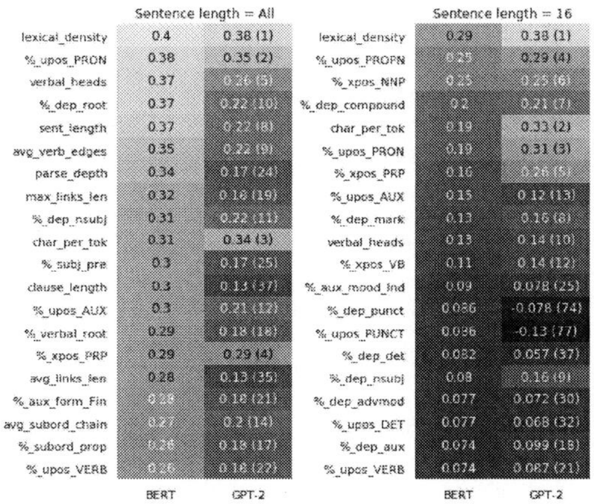

Figure 2: BERT and GPT-2 ρ scores obtained with the LinearSVR model, for the whole UD dataset and 16 token-long sentences. Scores are reported for the 20 top-ranked features for BERT. Numbers in brackets correspond to the relative in the GPT-2 ranking.

thus making them more predictive. Also in this case, the impact of the linguistic features is always higher for the prediction of GPT-2's perplexity.

A more in-depth analysis of these results shows that the distribution of the morpho-syntactic characteristics of a sentence (*POS*) and of the syntactic dependency relations (*SyntacticDep*) are the two most predictive sources of linguistic information. As Figure 1 reports, this holds for the two NLM models and it remains constant throughout all the groups of sentences with fixed lengths. Interestingly, if we consider the whole set of sentences, the effect of the morpho-syntactic information on the prediction of GPT-2's perplexity is exactly the same of that of the whole set of linguistic features. For some sentence lengths (15, 20, 30) the scores obtained using only this type of information outperform even those obtained considering the whole set of features. Note that this last remark is true also in the prediction of BERT's perplexity. As expected the other most predictive group is the one (*RawText*) that includes the length of sentence.

3.1 Focus on the contribution of individual features

To investigate more in depth which linguistic phenomena are more involved in the perplexity of the two models, we trained the LinearSVR model using each individual feature at a time. This was done for both the whole dataset and the subset of sentences (i.e. 758 sentences) having a length of 16 tokens, which corresponds to the mean sentence length of the UD dataset. A subset of results is reported in Figure 2, while the whole results are provided in Appendix B. As we can see in the left-side of the heatmap, the two models share many features in the first ten positions, thus showing that the two NLM architectures are made perplexed by similar linguistic characteristics of a sentence. In particular, for both of them, the two most predictive features correspond to the lexical density and the presence of pronouns confirming the highly predictive power of morpho-syntactic information. They are followed by features related to the presence of verbs and to their internal structure (i.e. *verbal_heads* and *avg_verb_edges*), and, as it was expected, by the length of the sentence. Despite these similarities, we can see that the scores obtained by the regression model to predict BERT's perplexity are on average higher than GPT-2's scores. Considering that we obtained higher scores using all (or groups of) features in the prediction of GPT-2' perplexity (see Figure 1), this latter result may suggest that the interaction among features is less relevant in the prediction of BERT's perplexity. Differences among the two models concern features that are highly sensitive to sentence length, which result to be more predictive of BERT's perplexity. This is the case of syntactic features capturing global and local aspects of sentence structure, i.e. the depth of the whole syntactic tree (*parse_depth*), the maximum length of dependency links (*max_links_len*) and the length of verbal clauses (*clause_length*). Also, the canonical order of nuclear sentence elements such as pre-verbal subjects contribute more to predict BERT's than GPT-2's perplexity. Instead, the distribution of proper nouns (*%_upos_PROPN*), in particular in their singular form (*%_xpos_NNP*), the length of token (*char_per_tok*) and vocabulary richness are more predictive of GPT-2's perplexity. Although we cannot say from ranking results whether features highly ranked are positively or negatively correlated with perplexity, we can hypothesize that knowing the distribution of tokens belonging to open lexical categories (e.g. proper nouns vs determiners) make the perplexity easier to identify.

The right-side heatmap shows the top-ranked features used to predict the two models perplexity for sentences 16-token long. As expected, when sentence length is controlled, the role of other features less related to length becomes predominant.

In particular, morpho-syntactic information is still highly predictive for the two models, with lexical parts-of-speech showing to be relevant not only for GPT-2's but also of BERT's perplexity.

4 Conclusion

In this paper we proposed an investigation of the linguistic phenomena characterizing the perplexity of a undirectional and a bidirectional Neural Language Model, GPT-2 and BERT. We first reported robust correlations between GPT-2's perplexity and the sentence-level likelihood computed with BERT. This is a quite prominent result, especially considering that these two metrics are differently computed as a consequence of the two NLMs architectures.

Interestingly, we found the effectiveness of linguistic features modelling a wide set of morpho-syntactic and syntactic phenomena in predicting the perplexity of the two NLMs, especially for shorter sentences. Despite similar trends, we observed some differences between the two NLMs both at the level of regression accuracy and in the rankings of the features exploited in the prediction of perplexity. GPT-2's perplexity is better captured by the considered features and it resulted to be more affected by lexical parts-of-speech and features capturing the vocabulary richness of a sentence. On the contrary, BERT's perplexity seems to be best predicted by syntactic features highly sensitive to sentence length.

References

Dominique Brunato, Andrea Cimino, Felice Dell'Orletta, Giulia Venturi, and Simonetta Montemagni. 2020. Profiling-ud: a tool for linguistic profiling of texts. In *Proceedings of The 12th Language Resources and Evaluation Conference*, pages 7147–7153, Marseille, France. European Language Resources Association.

Trevor Cohen and Serguei Pakhomov. 2020. A tale of two perplexities: Sensitivity of neural language models to lexical retrieval deficits in dementia of the Alzheimer's type. In *Proceedings of the 58th Annual Meeting of the Association for Computational Linguistics*, pages 1946–1957, Online. Association for Computational Linguistics.

V. Demberg and Frank Keller. 2008. Data from eye-tracking corpora as evidence for theories of syntactic processing complexity. *Cognition*, 109:193–210.

Jacob Devlin, Ming-Wei Chang, Kenton Lee, and Kristina Toutanova. 2019. Bert: Pre-training of deep bidirectional transformers for language understanding. In *Proceedings of the 2019 Conference of the North American Chapter of the Association for Computational Linguistics: Human Language Technologies, Volume 1 (Long and Short Papers)*, pages 4171–4186.

Pablo Gamallo, Jose Ramom Pichel, and Iñaki Alegria. 2017. A perplexity-based method for similar languages discrimination. In *VarDial2017 workshop at EACL 2017. Proceedings of the Fourth Workshop on NLP for Similar Languages, Varieties and Dialects, pages 109–114,Valencia, Spain, April 3, 2017. c©2017 Association for Computational Linguistics (http://web.science.mq.edu.au/ smalmasi/vardial4/index.html)*.

M. González. 2015. An analysis of twitter corpora and the differences between formal and colloquial tweets. In *TweetMT@SEPLN*.

Adam Goodkind and Klinton Bicknell. 2018. Predictive power of word surprisal for reading times is a linear function of language model quality. In *Proceedings of the 8th Workshop on Cognitive Modeling and Computational Linguistics, CMCL 2018, Salt Lake City, Utah, USA, January 7, 2018*, pages 10–18. Association for Computational Linguistics.

Kristina Gulordava, Piotr Bojanowski, Edouard Grave, Tal Linzen, and Marco Baroni. 2018. Colorless green recurrent networks dream hierarchically. In *Proceedings of the 2018 Conference of the North American Chapter of the Association for Computational Linguistics: Human Language Technologies, Volume 1 (Long Papers)*, pages 1195–1205, New Orleans, Louisiana. Association for Computational Linguistics.

Jennifer Hu, Jon Gauthier, Peng Qian, Ethan Wilcox, and Roger Levy. 2020. A systematic assessment of syntactic generalization in neural language models. In *Proceedings of the 58th Annual Meeting of the Association for Computational Linguistics*, pages 1725–1744, Online. Association for Computational Linguistics.

Adhiguna Kuncoro, Chris Dyer, Laura Rimell, Stephen Clark, and Phil Blunsom. 2019. Scalable syntax-aware language models using knowledge distillation. In *Proceedings of the 57th Annual Meeting of the Association for Computational Linguistics*, pages 3472–3484, Florence, Italy. Association for Computational Linguistics.

Rebecca Marvin and Tal Linzen. 2018. Targeted syntactic evaluation of language models. In *Proceedings of the 2018 Conference on Empirical Methods in Natural Language Processing*, pages 1192–1202.

Alessio Miaschi, Dominique Brunato, Felice Dell'Orletta, and Giulia Venturi. 2020. Linguistic profiling of a neural language model. In *Proceedings of the 28th International Conference on Computational Linguistics*, pages 745–756,

Barcelona, Spain (Online). International Committee on Computational Linguistics.

Aaron Mueller, Garrett Nicolai, Panayiota Petrou-Zeniou, Natalia Talmina, and Tal Linzen. 2020. Cross-linguistic syntactic evaluation of word prediction models. In *Proceedings of the 58th Annual Meeting of the Association for Computational Linguistics*, pages 5523–5539, Online. Association for Computational Linguistics.

Joakim Nivre, Marie-Catherine De Marneffe, Filip Ginter, Yoav Goldberg, Jan Hajic, Christopher D Manning, Ryan McDonald, Slav Petrov, Sampo Pyysalo, Natalia Silveira, et al. 2016. Universal dependencies v1: A multilingual treebank collection. In *Proceedings of the Tenth International Conference on Language Resources and Evaluation (LREC'16)*, pages 1659–1666.

Alec Radford, Karthik Narasimhan, Tim Salimans, and Ilya Sutskever. 2018. Improving language understanding by generative pre-training.

Alec Radford, Jeffrey Wu, Rewon Child, David Luan, Dario Amodei, and Ilya Sutskever. 2019. Language models are unsupervised multitask learners. *Technical report.*

Manuela Sanguinetti and Cristina Bosco. 2015. Parttut: The turin university parallel treebank. In *Harmonization and Development of Resources and Tools for Italian Natural Language Processing within the PARLI Project*, pages 51–69. Springer.

Natalia Silveira, Timothy Dozat, Marie-Catherine De Marneffe, Samuel R Bowman, Miriam Connor, John Bauer, and Christopher D Manning. 2014. A gold standard dependency corpus for english. In *LREC*, pages 2897–2904.

Alex Warstadt, Alicia Parrish, Haokun Liu, Anhad Mohananey, Wei Peng, Sheng-Fu Wang, and Samuel R. Bowman. 2020. BLiMP: The benchmark of linguistic minimal pairs for english. *Transactions of the Association for Computational Linguistics*, 8:377–392.

Amir Zeldes. 2017. The GUM corpus: Creating multilayer resources in the classroom. *Language Resources and Evaluation*, 51(3):581–612.

Yukun Zhu, Ryan Kiros, Rich Zemel, Ruslan Salakhutdinov, Raquel Urtasun, Antonio Torralba, and Sanja Fidler. 2015. Aligning books and movies: Towards story-like visual explanations by watching movies and reading books. In *The IEEE International Conference on Computer Vision (ICCV).*

A Appendix A

fRaw Text Properties
[sent_length]: average length of sentences in a document, calculated in terms of the number of words per sentence
[char_per_tok]: average number of characters per word (excluded punctuation)
Vocabulary Richness
[ttr_lemma]: Type/Token Ratio (TTR) calculated with respect to the lemmata in a sentence. It ranges between 1 (high lexical variety) and 0 (low vocabulary richness)
[ttr_form]: Type/Token Ratio (TTR) calculated with respect to the word forms in a sentence. It ranges between 1 (high lexical variety) and 0 (low vocabulary richness)
Morphosyntactic information
[%_upos_*]: distribution of the part-of-speech categories defined in the Universal POS tags, as detailed at the following link: `https://universaldependencies.org/u/pos/index.html`
[%_xpos_*]: distribution of the part-of-speech categories defined in the Penn Treebank POS tags, as detailed at the following link: `https://www.ling.upenn.edu/courses/Fall_2003/ling001/penn_treebank_pos.html`
[lexical_density]: the value corresponds to the ratio between content words (nouns, proper nouns, verbs, adjectives, adverbs) over the total number of words in a sentence
Inflectional morphology
[%_aux_tense_*]: distribution of auxiliary verbs according to their tense: `https://universaldependencies.org/u/feat/Tense.html`
[%_aux_mood_dist_*]: distribution of auxiliary verbs according to their moods: `https://universaldependencies.org/u/feat/Mood.html`
[%_aux_form_*]: distribution of auxiliary verbs according to their forms: `https://universaldependencies.org/u/feat/VerbForm.html`
[verbs_gender_dist_*]: distribution of verbs according to the gender of participle forms, for the languages that have this features: `https://universaldependencies.org/u/feat/Gender.html`
[%_aux_num_pers_*]: distribution of auxiliary verbs according to their number and person: `https://universaldependencies.org/u/feat/Person.html`
Verbal Predicate Structure
[verbal_head]: average distribution of verbal heads in the document, out ot the total of heads.
[%_verbal_roo]: average distribution of roots headed by a lemma tagged as verb, out of the total of sentence roots;
[avg_verb_edges]: verbal arity, calculated as the average number of instantiated dependency links (covering both arguments and modifiers) sharing the same verbal head, excluding punctuation and auxiliaries bearing the syntactic role of copula according to the UD scheme
[verbal_arity*]: distribution of verbs for arity class (e.g. verbs with arity 1, 2, ...)
Global and Local Syntactic Tree Structures
[parse_depth]: mean of the maximum tree depths of the sentence. The maximum depth is calculated as the longest path (in terms of occurring dependency links) from the root of the dependency tree to some leaf
[clause_length]: average clause length, calculated in terms of the average number of tokens per clause, where a clause is defined as the ratio between the number of tokens in a sentence and the number of either verbal or copular head
[avg_links_len]: average number of words occurring linearly between each syntactic head and its dependent (excluding punctuation dependencies)
[max_links_len]: the value of the longest dependency link in the document, calculated in number of tokens
[prep_1]: distribution of prepositional chains 1-complement long. A prepositional chain is calculated as the number of embedded prepositional complements dependent on a noun
Relative order of elements
[%_obj_post]: distribution of objects following the verb
[%_subj_pre]: distribution of subjects preceding the verb
Syntactic Relations
[%_dep_*]: average distribution of the 37 universal syntactic relations used in UD (`https://universaldependencies.org/u/dep/index.html`)
Use of Subordination
[principal_prop_dist]: distribution of principal clauses
[%_subord_prop]: distribution of subordinate clauses, as defined in the UD scheme: `https://universaldependencies.org/u/overview/complex-syntax.html#subordination`
[subord_post]: distribution of subordinate clauses following the main clause
[avg_subord_chain]: average length of subordinate chains, where a subordinate 'chain' is calculated as the number of subordinate clauses embedded on a first subordinate clause
[subord_1]: distribution of subordinate chains 1-clause long

Table 3: Linguistic features used in the experiments.

B Appendix B

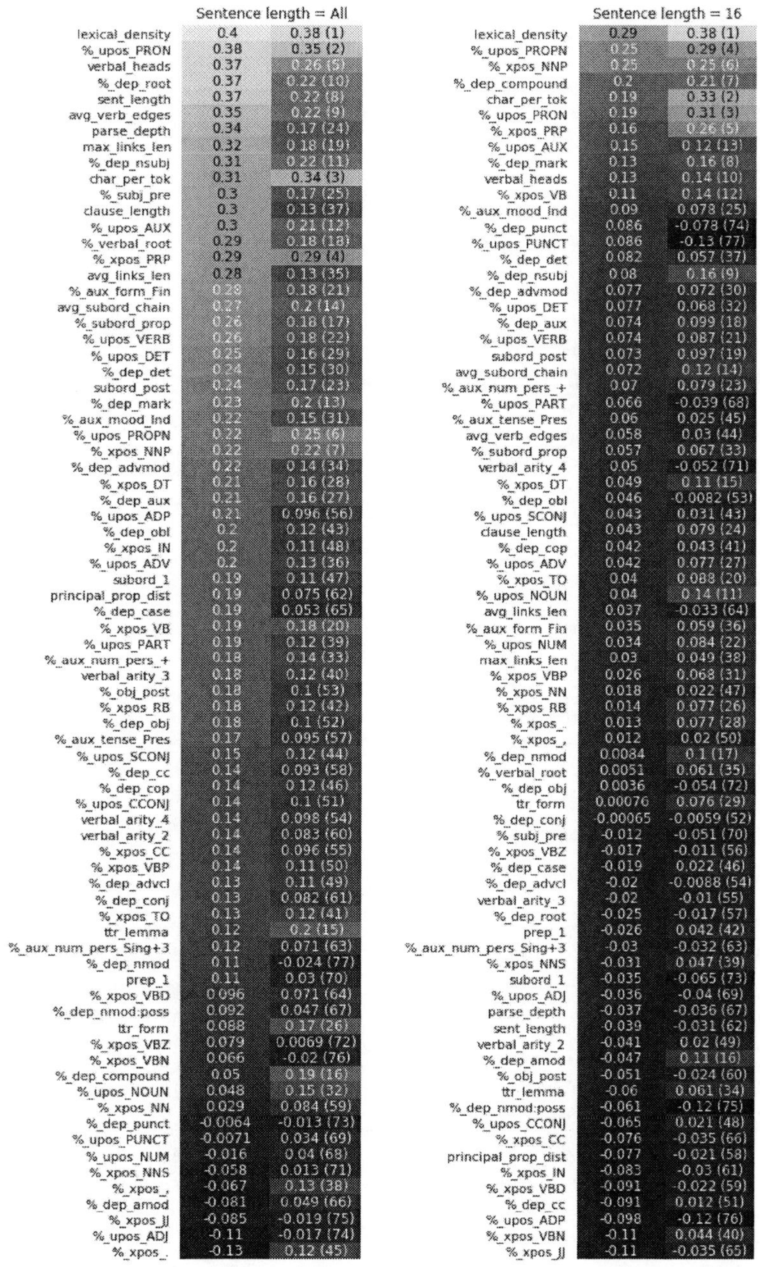

Figure 3: BERT and GPT-2 ρ scores obtained with the LinearSVR model using one feature at a time, for the whole UD dataset and sentences with lengths = 16.

How Do BERT Embeddings Organize Linguistic Knowledge?

Giovanni Puccetti[†◇], **Alessio Miaschi**[⋆◇], **Felice Dell'Orletta**[◇]
[†] Scuola Normale Superiore, Pisa
[⋆]Department of Computer Science, University of Pisa
[◇]Istituto di Linguistica Computazionale "Antonio Zampolli", Pisa
ItaliaNLP Lab – *www.italianlp.it*
giovanni.puccetti@sns.it, alessio.miaschi@phd.unipi.it, felice.dellorletta@ilc.cnr.it

Abstract

Several studies investigated the linguistic information implicitly encoded in Neural Language Models. Most of these works focused on quantifying the amount and type of information available within their internal representations and across their layers. In line with this scenario, we proposed a different study, based on Lasso regression, aimed at understanding how the information encoded by BERT sentence-level representations is arranged within its hidden units. Using a suite of several probing tasks, we showed the existence of a relationship between the implicit knowledge learned by the model and the number of individual units involved in the encodings of this competence. Moreover, we found that it is possible to identify groups of hidden units more relevant for specific linguistic properties.

1 Introduction

The rise of contextualized word representations (Peters et al., 2018; Devlin et al., 2019) has led to significant improvement in several (if not every) NLP tasks. The main drawback of these approaches, despite the outstanding performances, is the lack of interpretability. In fact, high dimensional representations do not allow for any insight of the type of linguistic properties encoded in these models. Therefore this implicit knowledge can only be determined a posteriori, by designing tasks that require a specific linguistic skill to be tackled (Linzen and Baroni, 2020) or by investigating to what extent certain information is encoded within contextualized internal representations, e.g. defining probing classifier trained to predict a variety of language phenomena (Conneau et al., 2018a; Hewitt and Manning, 2019; Tenney et al., 2019a).

In line with this latter approach and with recent works aimed at investigating how the information is arranged within neural models representations (Baan et al., 2019; Dalvi et al., 2019; Lakretz et al., 2019), we proposed an in-depth investigation aimed at understanding how the information encoded by BERT is arranged within its internal representation. In particular, we defined two research questions, aimed at: (i) investigating the relationship between the sentence-level linguistic knowledge encoded in a pre-trained version of BERT and the number of individual units involved in the encoding of such knowledge; (ii) understanding how these sentence-level properties are organized within the internal representations of BERT, identifying groups of units more relevant for specific linguistic tasks. We defined a suite of probing tasks based on a variable selection approach, in order to identify which units in the internal representations of BERT are involved in the encoding of similar linguistic properties. Specifically, we relied on a wide range of linguistic tasks, which resulted to successfully model different typology of sentence complexity (Brunato et al., 2020), from very simple features (such as sentence length) to more complex properties related to the morphosyntactic and syntactic structure of a sentence (such as the distribution of specific dependency relations).

The paper is organized as follows. In Sec. 2 we present related work, then we describe our approach (Sec. 3), with a focus on the model and the data used for the experiments (Sec. 3.1) and the set of probing tasks (Sec. 3.2). Experiments and results are discussed in Sec. 4 and 5. To conclude, we summarize the main findings of our work in Sec. 6.

2 Related work

In the last few years, a number of recent works have explored the inner mechanism and the linguistic knowledge implicitly encoded in Neural Language Models (NLMs) (Belinkov and Glass, 2019). The most common approach is based on

Proceedings of Deep Learning Inside Out (DeeLIO): The 2nd Workshop on Knowledge Extraction and Integration for Deep Learning Architectures, pages 48–57
Online, June 10, 2021.

the development of *probes*, i.e. supervised models trained to predict simple linguistic properties using the contextual word/sentence embeddings of a pre-trained model as training features (Conneau et al., 2018b; Zhang and Bowman, 2018; Miaschi et al., 2020). These latter studies demonstrated that NLMs are able to encode a wide range of linguistic information in a hierarchical manner (Blevins et al., 2018; Jawahar et al., 2019; Tenney et al., 2019b) and even to support the extraction of dependency parse trees (Hewitt and Manning, 2019). For instance, Liu et al. (2019) quantified differences in the transferability of individual layers between different models, showing that higher layers of RNNs (ELMo) are more task-specific (less general), while transformer layers (BERT) do not exhibit this increase in task-specificity.

Other works also investigated the importance of individual neurons within models representations (Qian et al., 2016; Bau et al., 2019; Baan et al., 2019). Dalvi et al. (2019) proposed two methods, *Linguistic Correlations Analysis* and *Cross-model correlation analysis*, to study whether specific dimensions learned by end-to-end neural models are responsible for specific properties. For instance, they showed that open class categories such as verbs and location are much more distributed across the network compared to closed class categories (e.g. coordinating conjunction) and also that the model recognizes a hierarchy of linguistic proprieties and distributes neurons based on it. Lakretz et al. (2019), instead, proposed a detailed study of the inner mechanism of number tracking in LSTMs at single neuron level, showing that long distance number information (from the subject to the verb) is largely managed by two specific units.

Differently from those latter work, our aim was to combine previous approaches based on probes and on the study on individual units in order to propose an in-depth investigation on the organization of linguistic competence within NLM contextualized representations.

3 Approach

To study how the information used by BERT to implicitly encode linguistic properties is arranged within its internal representations, we relied on a variable selection approach based on Lasso regression (Tibshirani, 1996), which aims at keeping as few non-zero coefficients as possible when solving specific regression tasks. Our aim was to identify which weights within sentence-level BERT internal representations can be set to zero, in order to understand the relationship between hidden units and linguistic competence and whether the information needed to perform similar linguistic tasks is encoded in similar positions. We relied on a suite of 68 sentence-level probing tasks, each of which corresponds to a specific linguistic feature capturing characteristics of a sentence at different levels of granularity. In particular, we defined a Lasso regression model that takes as input layer-wise BERT representations for each sentence of a gold standard Universal Dependencies (UD) (Nivre et al., 2016) English dataset and predicts the actual value of a given sentence-level feature. Lasso regression consists in adding an L_1 penalization to the usual ordinary least square loss. To do so, one of the most relevant parameters is λ, which tunes how relevant the L_1 penalization is for the loss function. We performed a grid search with cross validation for each feature-layer pair, in order to identify the best suited value for λ according to each task. Specifically, our goal was to find the most suited value for seeking the best performance when having as few non-zero coefficients as possible.

3.1 Model and data

We used a pre-trained version of BERT (BERT-base uncased, 12 layers). In order to obtain the representations for our sentence-level tasks we experimented with the activation of the first input token (*[CLS]*) and the mean of all the word embeddings for each sentence (*Mean-pooling*).

With regard to the data used for the regression experiments, we relied on the Universal Dependencies (UD) English dataset. The dataset includes three UD English treebanks: UD_English-ParTUT, a conversion of a multilingual parallel treebank consisting of a variety of text genres, including talks, legal texts and Wikipedia articles (Sanguinetti and Bosco, 2015); the Universal Dependencies version annotation from the GUM corpus (Zeldes, 2017); the English Web Treebank (EWT), a gold standard universal dependencies corpus for English (Silveira et al., 2014). Overall, the final dataset consists of 23,943 sentences.

3.2 Linguistic features

As already mentioned, we defined a suite of probing tasks relying on a wide set of sentence-level linguistic features automatically extracted from the parsed sentences in the UD dataset. The set of

Level of Annotation	Linguistic Feature	Label
	Raw Text Properties	
Raw Text	Sentence Length	sent_length
	Word Length	char_per_tok
	Vocabulary Richness	
Vocabulary	Type/Token Ratio for words and lemmas	ttr_form, ttr_lemma
	Morphosyntactic information	
POS tagging	Distibution of UD and language–specific POS	upos_dist_*, xpos_dist_*
	Lexical density	lexical_density
	Inflectional morphology	
	Inflectional morphology of lexical verbs and auxiliaries	xpos_VB-VBD-VBP-VBZ, aux_*
	Verbal Predicate Structure	
Dependency Parsing	Distribution of verbal heads and verbal roots	verbal_head_dist, verbal_root_perc
	Verb arity and distribution of verbs by arity	avg_verb_edges, verbal_arity_*
	Global and Local Parsed Tree Structures	
	Depth of the whole syntactic tree	parse_depth
	Average length of dependency links and of the longest link	avg_links_len, max_links_len
	Average length of prepositional chains and distribution by depth	avg_prep_chain_len, prep_dist_*
	Clause length	avg_token_per_clause
	Order of elements	
	Order of subject and object	subj_pre, obj_post
	Syntactic Relations	
	Distribution of dependency relations	dep_dist_*
	Use of Subordination	
	Distribution of subordinate and principal clauses	principal_prop_dist, subordinate_prop_dist
	Average length of subordination chains and distribution by depth	avg_subord_chain_len, subordinate_dist_1
	Relative order of subordinate clauses	subordinate_post

Table 1: Linguistic Features used in the experiments.

features is based on the ones described in Brunato et al. (2020) which are acquired from raw, morpho-syntactic and syntactic levels of annotation and can be categorised in 9 groups corresponding to different linguistic phenomena. As shown in Table 1, these features model linguistic phenomena ranging from raw text one, to morpho–syntactic information and inflectional properties of verbs, to more complex aspects of sentence structure modeling global and local properties of the whole parsed tree and of specific subtrees, such as the order of subjects and objects with respect to the verb, the distribution of UD syntactic relations, also including features referring to the use of subordination and to the structure of verbal predicates.

4 Linguistic competence and BERT units

As a first analysis, we investigated the relationship between the implicit linguistic properties encoded in the internal representations of BERT and the number of individual units involved in the encoding of these properties. Figure 1 and 2 report layerwise R^2 results for all the probing tasks along with the number of non-zero coefficients obtained with the sentence representations computed with the *[CLS]* token and the *Mean-pooling* strategy respectively. As a first remark, we can notice that the *Mean-pooling* method proved to be the best one for almost all the probing features across the 12 layers. Moreover, in line with Hewitt and Manning (2019), we noticed that there is high variability among different tasks, whereas less variation occurs among the model layers. In general, we observe that best scores are related to features belonging to raw text and vocabulary proprieties, such as sentence length and Type/Token Ratio. Nevertheless, BERT representations implicitly encode information also related to more complex syntactic features, such as the order of the subject (*subj_pre*) or the distribution of several dependency relations (e.g. *dep_dist_det*, *dep_dist_punct*). Interestingly, the knowledge about POS differs when we consider more granular distinctions. For instance, within the broad categories of verbs and nouns, worse predictions were obtained by sub-specific classes of verbs based on tense, person and mood features (see especially past participle, *xpos_dist_VBN*). Similarly, within the verb predicate structure properties, we observe that lower R^2 scores were obtained by features related to sub-categorization information about verbal predicates, such as the distribution of verbs by arity (*verbal_arity_**).

Focusing instead on the relationship between R^2 scores and number of non-zero coefficients, we can notice that although best scores are achieved at lower layers (between layers 12 and 8 for both configurations), the highest number of non-zero coefficients occurs instead at layers closer to the output. This is particularly evident for the results achieved using the *[CLS]* token, for which we observe a continuous increase across the 12 layers in the number of units used by the the probing models.

For both configurations, features more related to the structure of the whole syntactic tree are

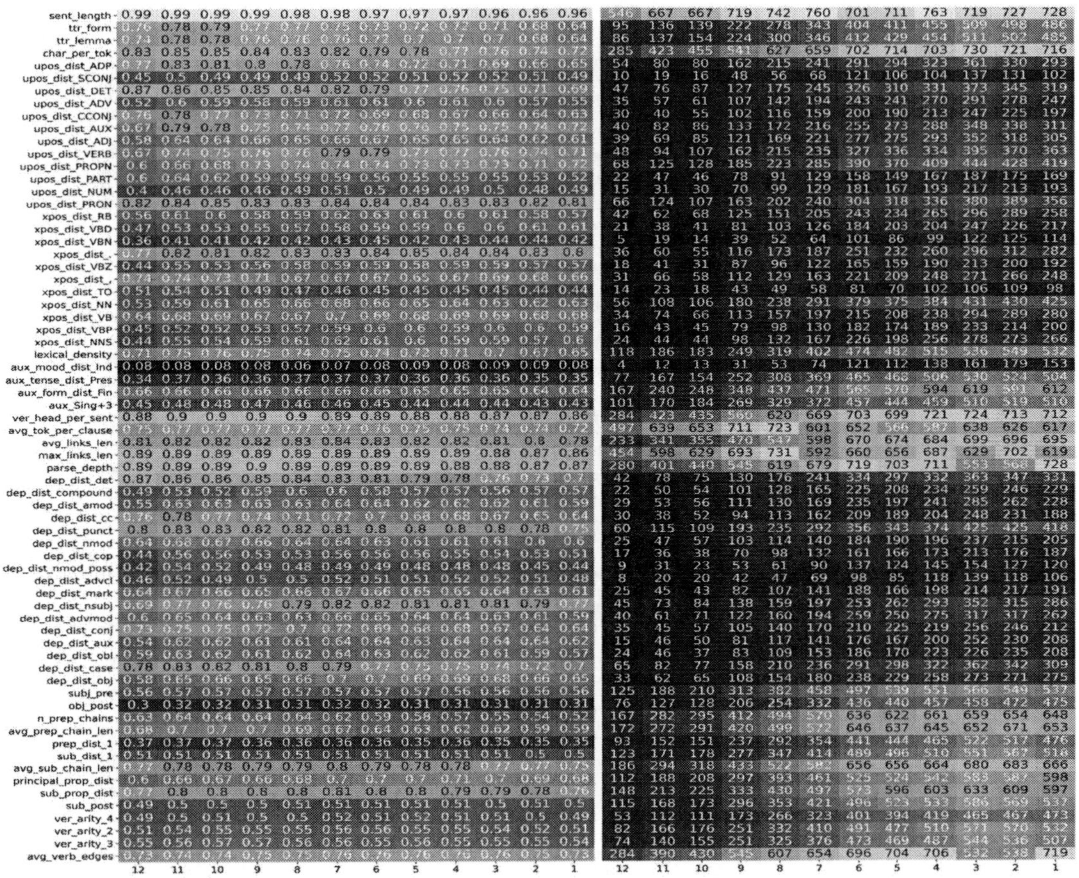

Figure 1: Layerwise R^2 results for all the probing tasks (*left heatmap*) along with the number of non-zero coefficients (*right heatmap*) obtained with the sentence representations computed using the *[CLS]* token.

those for which less units were set to zero during regression (e.g. *max_links_len*, *parse_depth*, *n_prepositional_chains*), while properties belonging to word–based properties (i.e. features related to POS and dependency labels) were predicted relying on less units. Moreover, we can clearly notice that features related to specific POS and dependency relationships are also those that gained less units through the 12 layers (e. g. *xpos_dist_.*, *xpos_dist_AUX*). On the contrary, features belonging to the structure of the syntactic tree tend to acquire more non-zero units as the output layer is approached. This is particularly evident for the linguistic features predicted using sentence representations computed using the *[CLS]* token (e.g. *subj_pre*, *parse_depth*, *n_prepositional_chains*). We believe this is due to the fact that the interdependence between different units in each representation tend to increase across layers, thus making the information less localized especially for those features that belong to the whole structure of the syntactic tree. This is coherent with the fact that using the *Mean-pooling* strategy a higher number of non-zero coefficients was preserved also in the very first input layers, suggesting that this strategy increases the interdependence between each unit and makes the extraction of localized information more complex.

In order to focus more closely on the relationship between R^2 scores and non-zero units, we reported in Figures 3a and 3b average R^2 scores versus average number of non-zero coefficients, along with the line of best fit, for each layer and according to the *[CLS]* token and to the *Mean-pooling* strategy respectively. Interestingly, for both *[CLS]* and *Mean-pooling* representations, R^2 scores tend to improve as the number of non-zero coefficients increases. Moreover, when considering sentence representations computed with the *[CLS]* token, this behaviour becomes more pronounced as the output

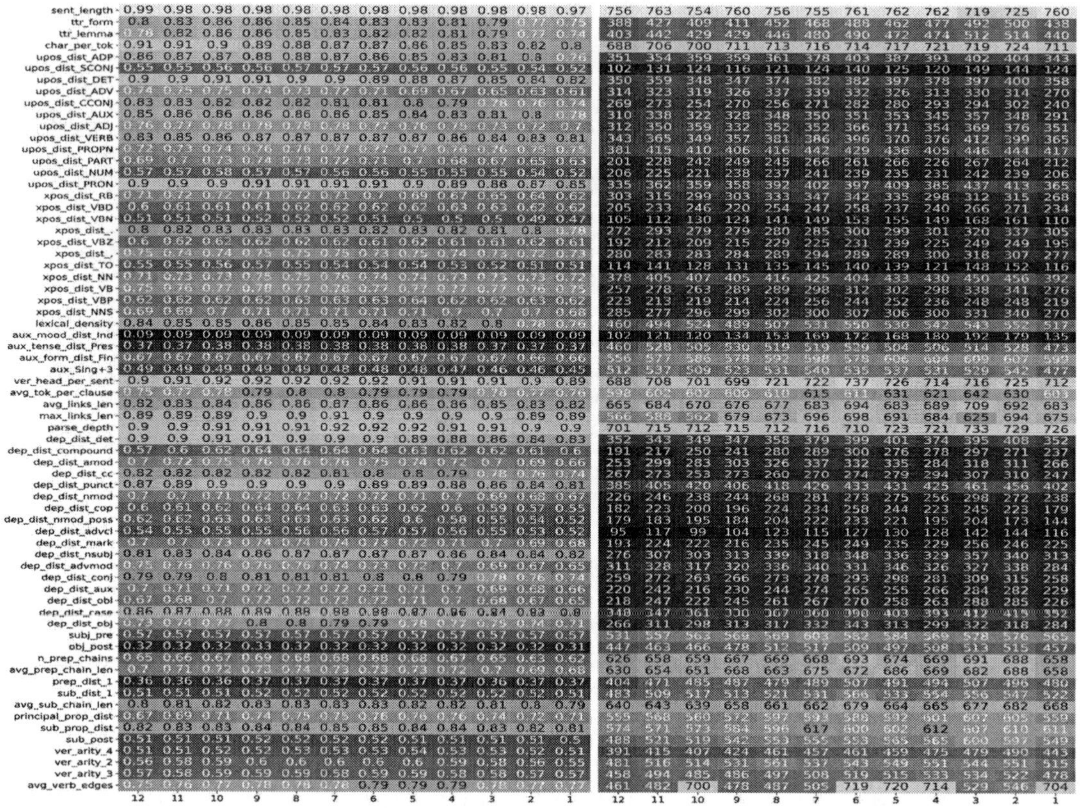

Figure 2: Layerwise R^2 results for all the probing tasks (*left heatmap*) along with the number of non-zero coefficients (*right heatmap*) obtained with the sentence representations computed with the *Mean-pooling* strategy.

layer is reached. This is in line with what we already noticed, namely that the interdependence between different units tend to increase across layers, especially when taking into account representations extracted without using a mean-pooling strategy.

In order to investigate more in depth the behaviour of BERT hidden units when solving the probing tasks, we focused more closely at how the different units in the internal representations are kept and lost across subsequent layers. Figure 4 reports the average number of non-zero coefficients in a layer that are set to zero in the following one (4a), the average number of zero coefficients in a layer that are set to non-zero in the following one (4b) and the average value of the difference between the number of non-zero coefficients at pairs of consecutive layers (4c). As it can be observed, there is high coherence between each layer and its subsequent one, meaning that the variation in the number of selected coefficient is stable (4c). However, the first two plots also show that there is a higher variation when considering non-zero coefficients in the same positions between pairs of layers. This underlines the fact that the information is not localized within BERT's internal representations, since the algorithm shows a degree of freedom in which units can be zeroed and which cannot.

In Figure 5 we report instead how many times each individual unit in the *[CLS]* (5a) and *Mean-pooling* (5b) internal representations has been kept non-zero when solving the 68 probing tasks for all the 12 BERT layers (816 regression task). In general, we can observe that the regression tasks performed using sentence-level representations obtained with the *Mean-pooling* strategy tend to use more hidden units with respect to the *[CLS]* ones. It is also interesting to notice that there is a highly irregular unit (number 308) that has been kept different from zero in a number of tasks and layers much higher than the average. This could suggest that this unit is particularly relevant for encoding almost all the linguistic properties devised in our probing tasks.

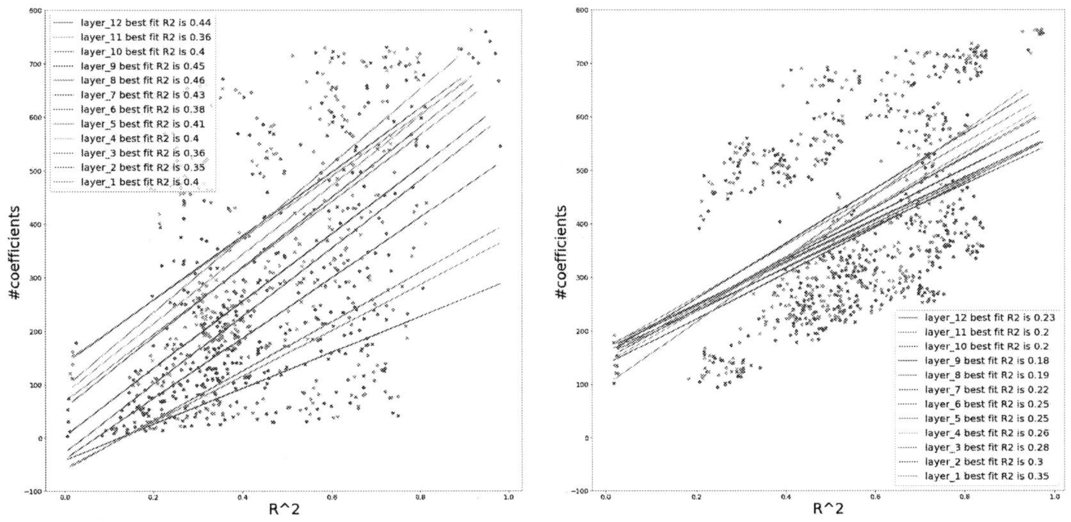

(a) (b)

Figure 3: Average R^2 scores versus average number of non-zero coefficients, along with the line of best fit, for each layer and according to *[CLS]* (a) and *Mean-pooling* (b) strategy.

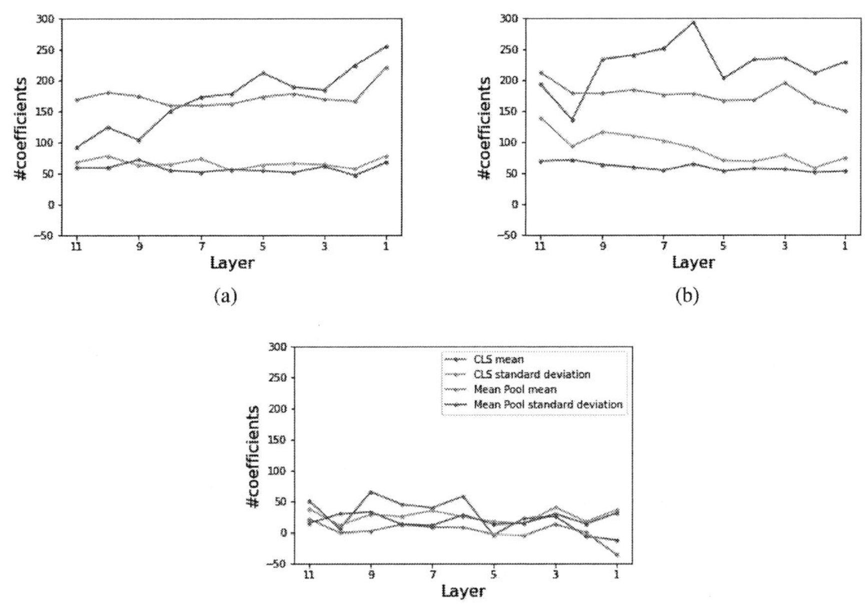

(c)

Figure 4: In (a) the average number of non-zero coefficients in a layer that are set to zero in the following one (*average number of dropped coefficients*), in (b) the average number of zero coefficients in a layer that are set to non-zero in the following one (*average number of gained coefficients*) and in (c) the value of the difference between the number of non-zero coefficients at pairs of consecutive layers (*average number of changed coefficients*).

5 Is information linguistically arranged within BERT representations?

Once we have investigated the relationship between the linguistic knowledge implicitly encoded by BERT and the number of individual units involved in it, we verified whether we can identify groups of units particularly relevant for specific probing tasks. To this end, we clustered the 68 probing features according to the weights assigned by the regression

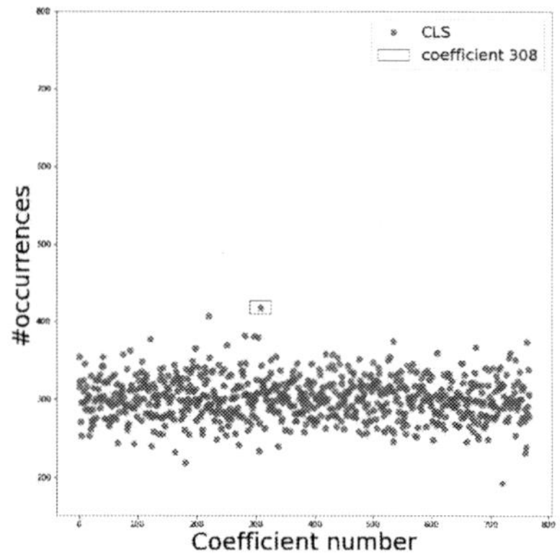

(a)

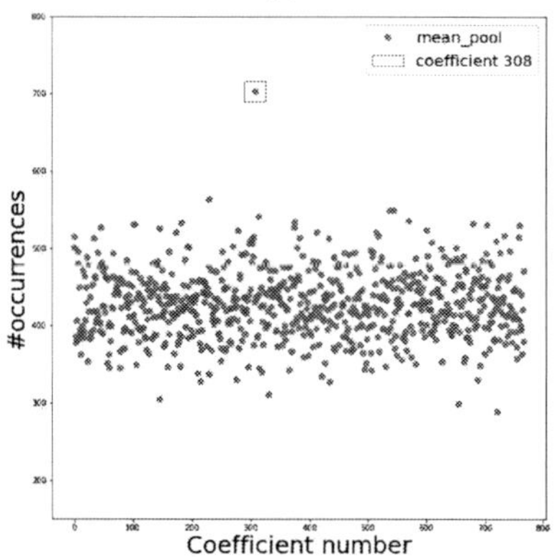

(b)

Figure 5: Number of times in which each BERT individual unit (computed with *[CLS]* token in (a) and with *Mean-pooing* aggregation strategy in (b)) has been kept as non-zero when solving all the probing tasks for all the 12 layers.

models to each BERT hidden unit. Specifically, we perform hierarchical clustering using correlation distance as distance metric. Figure 6 and 7 report the hierarchical clustering obtained with the *[CLS]* and *Mean-pooling* internal representations at layers 12, 8 and 1. We chose layers 12 and 1 in order to study differences of the clustering of linguistic features taking into account the representations that were more distant and more closer to the language modeling task respectively, while layer 8 was chosen since it was the layer after which BERT's representations tend to lose their precision in encoding our set of linguistic properties.

As a general remark, we can notice that, despite some variations, the linguistic features are organized in a similar manner across the tree layers and for both the configuration. This is to say that, despite the number of non-zero coefficients varies significantly between layers and according to the strategy for extracting the internal representations, the way in which linguistic properties are arranged within BERT embeddings is quite consistent. This suggests that there is a coherent organization of linguistic features according to non-zero coefficients that is independent from the layer and the aggregation techniques taken into account.

Focusing on specific groups of features, we observe that, even if the traditional division with respect to the linguistic annotation levels (see Table 1) has not been completely maintained, it is possible to identify different clusters of features referable to the same linguistic phenomena for all the 3 layers taken into account and for both configurations. In particular, we can clearly observe groups of features related to the length of dependency links and prepositional chains (e.g. *max_links_len*, *avg_links_len*, *n_prepositional_chains*), to vocabulary richness (*ttr_form*, *ttr_lemma*), to properties related to verbal predicate structure and inflectional morphology of auxiliaries (e.g. *xpos_dist_VBD*, *xpos_dist_VBN aux_form_dist_Fin*, *aux_tense_dist_pres*) and to the use of punctuation (*xpos_dist_.*, *xpos_dist_,*, *dep_dist_punct*) and subordination (e.g. *subordinate_dist_1*, *subordinate_post*). Interestingly enough, BERT representations also tend to put together features related to each other but not necessarily belonging to the same linguistic macro-category. This is the case, for instance, of characteristics corresponding to functional properties (e.g. *upos_dist_ADP*, *dep_dist_det*).

6 Conclusions

In this paper we proposed an in-depth investigation aimed at understanding how BERT embeddings encode and organize linguistic competence. Relying on a variable selection approach applied on a suite of 68 probing tasks, we showed the existence of a relationship between the implicit linguistic knowledge encoded by the NLM and the number of individual units involved in the encoding of this knowledge. We found that, according to the strategy for obtaining sentence-level representations, the amount of hidden units devised to encode linguistic properties varies differently across BERT layers: while the number of non-zero units used in the *Mean-pooling* strategy remains more or less constant across layers, the *[CLS]* representations show a continuous increase in the number of

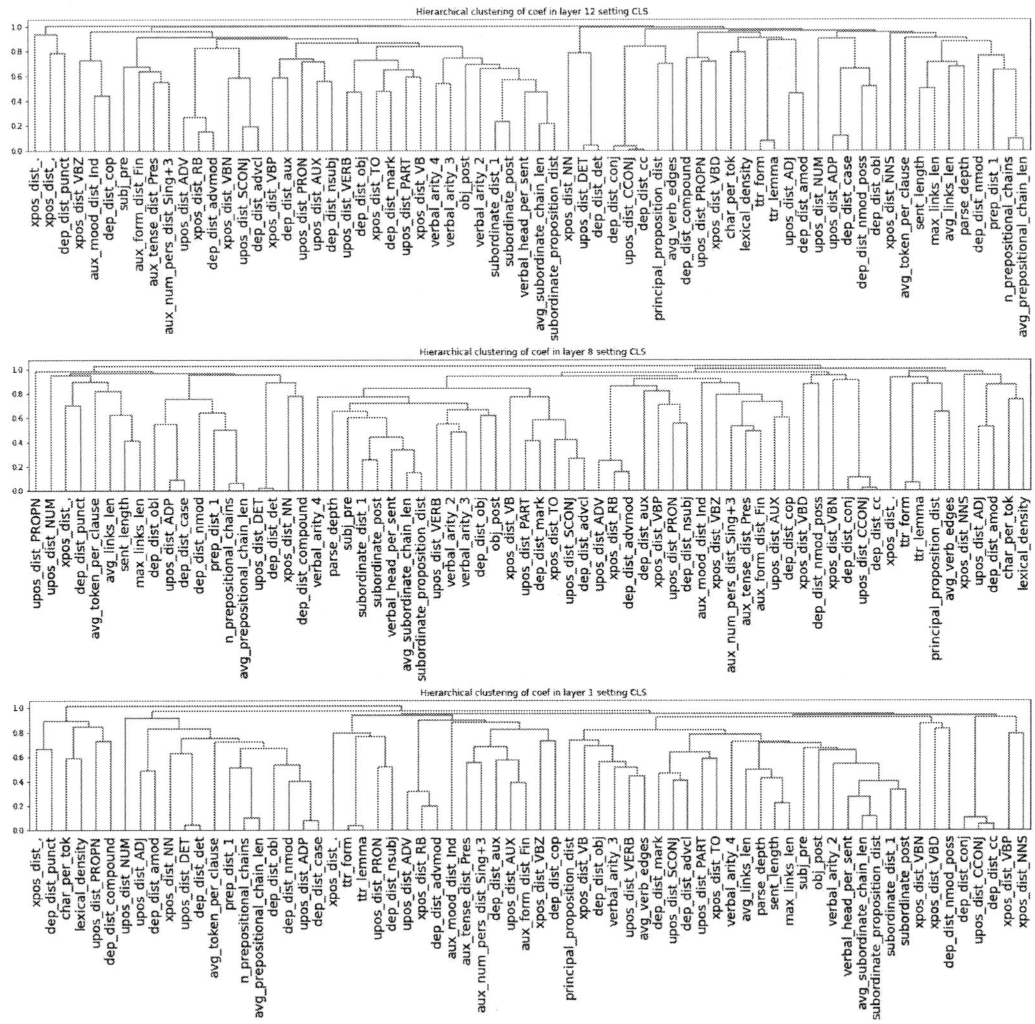

Figure 6: From top to bottom, the hierarchical clustering for the *[CLS]* setting of all the tasks respectively at layers 12, 8 and 1.

used coefficients. Moreover, we noticed that this behaviour is particularly significant for linguistic properties related to the whole structure of the syntactic tree, while features belonging to POS and dependency tags tend to acquire less non-zero units across layers.

Finally, we found that it is possible to identify groups of units more relevant for specific linguistic tasks. In particular, we showed that clustering our set of sentence-level properties according to the weights assigned by the regression models to each BERT unit we can identify clusters of features referable to the same linguistic phenomena and this, despite some variations, is true for both the configurations and for all the BERT layers.

References

Joris Baan, Jana Leible, Mitja Nikolaus, David Rau, Dennis Ulmer, Tim Baumgärtner, Dieuwke Hupkes, and Elia Bruni. 2019. On the realization of compositionality in neural networks. In *Proceedings of the 2019 ACL Workshop BlackboxNLP: Analyzing and Interpreting Neural Networks for NLP*, pages 127–137, Florence, Italy. Association for Computational Linguistics.

Anthony Bau, Yonatan Belinkov, Hassan Sajjad, Nadir Durrani, Fahim Dalvi, and James Glass. 2019. Identifying and controlling important neurons in neural machine translation. In *International Conference on Learning Representations*.

Yonatan Belinkov and James Glass. 2019. Analysis methods in neural language processing: A survey.

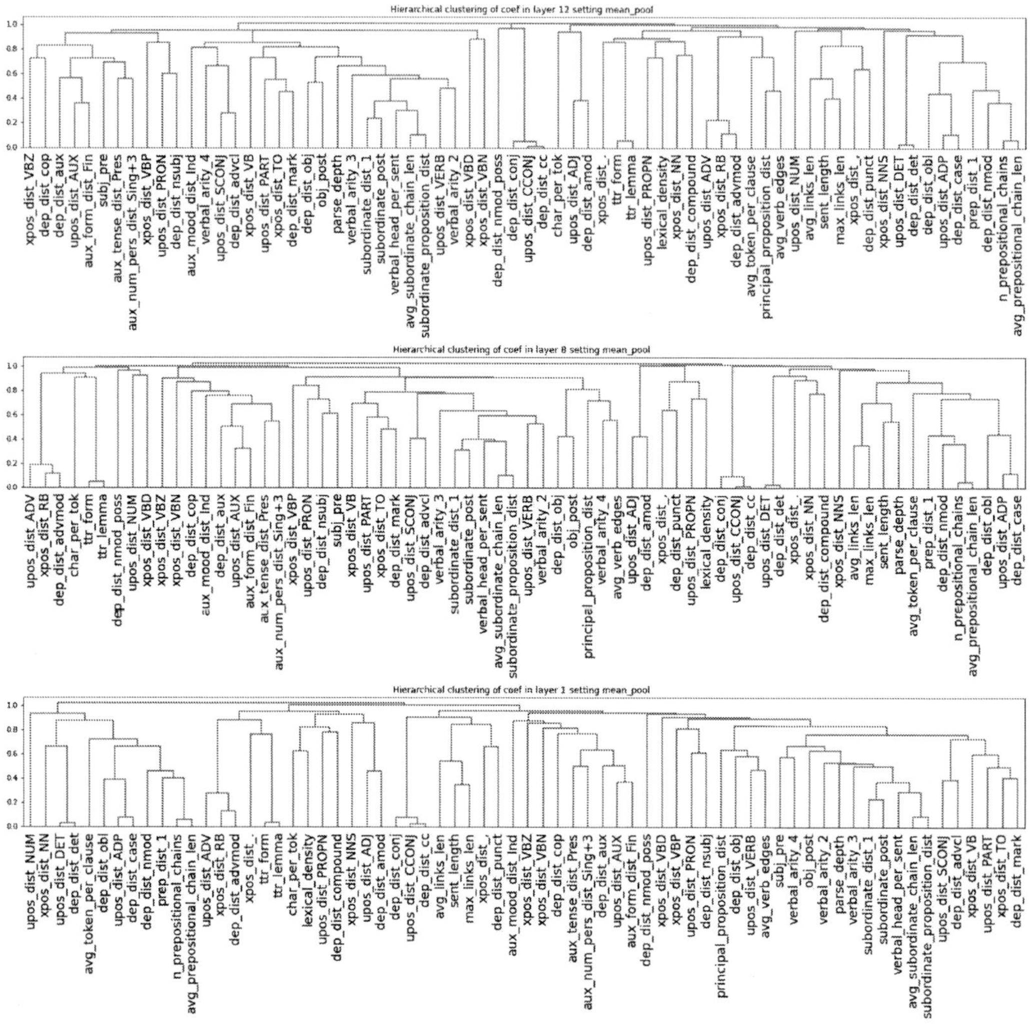

Figure 7: From top to bottom, the hierarchical clustering for the *Mean-pooling* setting of all the tasks respectively at layers 12, 8 and 1.

Transactions of the Association for Computational Linguistics, 7:49–72.

Terra Blevins, Omer Levy, and Luke Zettlemoyer. 2018. Deep rnns encode soft hierarchical syntax. In *Proceedings of the 56th Annual Meeting of the Association for Computational Linguistics (Volume 2: Short Papers)*, pages 14–19.

Dominique Brunato, Andrea Cimino, Felice Dell'Orletta, Giulia Venturi, and Simonetta Montemagni. 2020. Profiling-ud: a tool for linguistic profiling of texts. In *Proceedings of The 12th Language Resources and Evaluation Conference*, pages 7147–7153, Marseille, France. European Language Resources Association.

Alexis Conneau, German Kruszewski, Guillaume Lample, Loïc Barrault, and Marco Baroni. 2018a. What you can cram into a single $&!#* vector: Probing sentence embeddings for linguistic properties. In *Proceedings of the 56th Annual Meeting of the Association for Computational Linguistics (Volume 1: Long Papers)*, pages 2126–2136, Melbourne, Australia. Association for Computational Linguistics.

Alexis Conneau, Germán Kruszewski, Guillaume Lample, Loïc Barrault, and Marco Baroni. 2018b. What you can cram into a single $&!#* vector: Probing sentence embeddings for linguistic properties. In *Proceedings of the 56th Annual Meeting of the Association for Computational Linguistics (Volume 1: Long Papers)*, pages 2126–2136.

Fahim Dalvi, Nadir Durrani, Hassan Sajjad, Yonatan Belinkov, Anthony Bau, and James Glass. 2019. What is one grain of sand in the desert? analyzing individual neurons in deep nlp models. In *Proceedings of the AAAI Conference on Artificial Intelligence*, volume 33, pages 6309–6317.

Jacob Devlin, Ming-Wei Chang, Kenton Lee, and Kristina Toutanova. 2019. Bert: Pre-training of deep bidirectional transformers for language understanding. In *Proceedings of the 2019 Conference of the North American Chapter of the Association for Computational Linguistics: Human Language Technologies, Volume 1 (Long and Short Papers)*, pages 4171–4186.

John Hewitt and Christopher D Manning. 2019. A structural probe for finding syntax in word representations. In *Proceedings of the 2019 Conference of the North American Chapter of the Association for Computational Linguistics: Human Language Technologies, Volume 1 (Long and Short Papers)*, pages 4129–4138.

Ganesh Jawahar, Benoît Sagot, and Djamé Seddah. 2019. What does BERT learn about the structure of language? In *Proceedings of the 57th Annual Meeting of the Association for Computational Linguistics*, pages 3651–3657, Florence, Italy. Association for Computational Linguistics.

Yair Lakretz, German Kruszewski, Theo Desbordes, Dieuwke Hupkes, Stanislas Dehaene, and Marco Baroni. 2019. The emergence of number and syntax units in LSTM language models. In *Proceedings of the 2019 Conference of the North American Chapter of the Association for Computational Linguistics: Human Language Technologies, Volume 1 (Long and Short Papers)*, pages 11–20, Minneapolis, Minnesota. Association for Computational Linguistics.

Tal Linzen and Marco Baroni. 2020. Syntactic structure from deep learning. *CoRR*, abs/2004.10827.

Nelson F Liu, Matt Gardner, Yonatan Belinkov, Matthew E Peters, and Noah A Smith. 2019. Linguistic knowledge and transferability of contextual representations. In *Proceedings of the 2019 Conference of the North American Chapter of the Association for Computational Linguistics: Human Language Technologies, Volume 1 (Long and Short Papers)*, pages 1073–1094.

Alessio Miaschi, Dominique Brunato, Felice Dell'Orletta, and Giulia Venturi. 2020. Linguistic profiling of a neural language model. In *Proceedings of the 28th International Conference on Computational Linguistics*, pages 745–756, Barcelona, Spain (Online). International Committee on Computational Linguistics.

Joakim Nivre, Marie-Catherine De Marneffe, Filip Ginter, Yoav Goldberg, Jan Hajic, Christopher D Manning, Ryan McDonald, Slav Petrov, Sampo Pyysalo, Natalia Silveira, et al. 2016. Universal dependencies v1: A multilingual treebank collection. In *Proceedings of the Tenth International Conference on Language Resources and Evaluation (LREC'16)*, pages 1659–1666.

Matthew Peters, Mark Neumann, Mohit Iyyer, Matt Gardner, Christopher Clark, Kenton Lee, and Luke Zettlemoyer. 2018. Deep contextualized word representations. In *Proceedings of the 2018 Conference of the North American Chapter of the Association for Computational Linguistics: Human Language Technologies, Volume 1 (Long Papers)*, pages 2227–2237.

Peng Qian, Xipeng Qiu, and Xuanjing Huang. 2016. Analyzing linguistic knowledge in sequential model of sentence. In *Proceedings of the 2016 Conference on Empirical Methods in Natural Language Processing*, pages 826–835, Austin, Texas. Association for Computational Linguistics.

Manuela Sanguinetti and Cristina Bosco. 2015. Parttut: The turin university parallel treebank. In *Harmonization and Development of Resources and Tools for Italian Natural Language Processing within the PARLI Project*, pages 51–69. Springer.

Natalia Silveira, Timothy Dozat, Marie-Catherine De Marneffe, Samuel R Bowman, Miriam Connor, John Bauer, and Christopher D Manning. 2014. A gold standard dependency corpus for english. In *LREC*, pages 2897–2904.

Ian Tenney, Dipanjan Das, and Ellie Pavlick. 2019a. BERT rediscovers the classical NLP pipeline. In *Proceedings of the 57th Annual Meeting of the Association for Computational Linguistics*, pages 4593–4601, Florence, Italy. Association for Computational Linguistics.

Ian Tenney, Patrick Xia, Berlin Chen, Alex Wang, Adam Poliak, R Thomas McCoy, Najoung Kim, Benjamin Van Durme, Samuel R Bowman, Dipanjan Das, et al. 2019b. What do you learn from context? probing for sentence structure in contextualized word representations. *arXiv preprint arXiv:1905.06316*.

Robert Tibshirani. 1996. Regression shrinkage and selection via the lasso. *Journal of the Royal Statistical Society: Series B (Methodological)*, 58(1):267–288.

Amir Zeldes. 2017. The GUM corpus: Creating multilayer resources in the classroom. *Language Resources and Evaluation*, 51(3):581–612.

Kelly Zhang and Samuel Bowman. 2018. Language modeling teaches you more than translation does: Lessons learned through auxiliary syntactic task analysis. In *Proceedings of the 2018 EMNLP Workshop BlackboxNLP: Analyzing and Interpreting Neural Networks for NLP*, pages 359–361.

ERNIE-NLI: Analyzing the Impact of Domain-Specific External Knowledge on Enhanced Representations for NLI

Lisa Bauer[1], **Lingjia Deng**[2], **Mohit Bansal**[1]
[1]UNC Chapel Hill [2]Bloomberg
{lbauer6, mbansal}@cs.unc.edu
{ldeng43}@bloomberg.net

Abstract

We examine the effect of domain-specific external knowledge variations on deep large scale language model performance. Recent work in enhancing BERT with external knowledge has been very popular, resulting in models such as ERNIE (Zhang et al., 2019a). Using the ERNIE architecture, we provide a detailed analysis on the types of knowledge that result in a performance increase on the Natural Language Inference (NLI) task, specifically on the Multi-Genre Natural Language Inference Corpus (MNLI). While ERNIE uses general TransE embeddings, we instead train domain-specific knowledge embeddings and insert this knowledge via an information fusion layer in the ERNIE architecture, allowing us to directly control and analyze knowledge input. Using several different knowledge training objectives, sources of knowledge, and knowledge ablations, we find a strong correlation between knowledge and classification labels within the same polarity, illustrating that knowledge polarity is an important feature in predicting entailment. We also perform classification change analysis across different knowledge variations to illustrate the importance of selecting appropriate knowledge input regarding content and polarity, and show representative examples of these changes.

1 Introduction

Recently, the selection and integration of external knowledge into large-scale language models has shown impressive improvements in several Natural Language Understanding (NLU) tasks (Zhang et al., 2019a). Understanding the relation between external knowledge and model performance is fundamental to understanding how best to select and integrate knowledge into NLU tasks. We focus specifically on Natural Language Inference (NLI), which requires understanding sentence semantics with respect to both the content and polarity. NLI is motivated by recognizing textual entailment, or understanding whether a hypothesis entails, contradicts, or is neutral with respect to a premise. For example, given the premise: "Some boys are playing soccer", the hypothesis "Young men are playing a sport" is an entailment whereas the hypothesis "Old men are playing a sport" is a contradiction. Language modeling is a very common and important approach when considering the NLI task.

The NLI state-of-the-art utilizes different language modeling techniques to learn the relations between the hypothesis and the premise. Yoon et al. (2018) used Dynamic Self-Attention (DSA) to learn sentence embeddings, Liu et al. (2019) proposed multi-task deep neural network (MT-DNN) for learning language representations in multiple NLU tasks, and Zhang et al. (2019b) combined semantic role labeling and BERT (Devlin et al., 2019) to explicitly absorb contextual semantics over a BERT framework. However, these approaches limit the source of information available for representing both the premise and hypothesis. Consider the following premise and hypothesis:

People cut their expenses for the Golden years.

People decrease their expenses for retirement.

It is challenging to know that "Golden years" entails "retirement" if we rely only on the context within the two sentences. To illustrate how common this problem is, we conduct a manual analysis of BERT classification errors on the NLI task (specifically on the MNLI corpus (Williams et al., 2018), more details in Section 6), and find that at least 50% of misclassifications require external knowledge, specifically requiring domain-specific knowledge, world knowledge, jargon-based paraphrases, or commonsense knowledge to resolve the entailment. In the above example, a model that learns the relation between "Golden years" and "retirement" from external knowledge can be used to enhance NLI inference.

On the basis of this idea, Chen et al. (2018) and Zhang et al. (2019a) used external knowledge from

Proceedings of Deep Learning Inside Out (DeeLIO): The 2nd Workshop on Knowledge Extraction and Integration for Deep Learning Architectures, pages 58–69
Online, June 10, 2021.

WordNet and TransE (Bordes et al., 2013) and applied it to NLI models. In their work, pre-trained representations of external knowledge from knowledge bases (e.g., TransE) were directly applied; they did not tailor knowledge content or structure specifically to the NLI task and did not improve NLI performance (Zhang et al., 2019a). This finding motivates our investigation on how external knowledge can be efficiently used to improve NLI models. The intention of our work is not to propose a new model that outperforms the state-of-the-art, but instead to focus on building a framework for investigating how different types and representations of external knowledge impact an NLI model's decisions.

Consider our previous examples. We want to represent that the relation between "young men" and "boys" is positive for entailment, and that the relation between "old men" and "boys" is negative for entailment. Similarly, we want to represent that the relation between "Golden years" and "retirement" is positive for entailment. The interplay of external knowledge and entailment gives insight into the power of selecting relevant knowledge with respect to both content and polarity of the knowledge. Here, content indicates the semantic meaning of external knowledge and polarity indicates whether the knowledge relation is positive or negative for entailment. The representation of external knowledge is required to be correct in both aspects for the NLI task. The models learns (1) content via our knowledge extraction phase, by extracting concept edges from knowledge graphs, and (2) polarity via our knowledge training phase, by learning the polarity of the relationships between concepts. We define concepts as words or phrases througout this paper. In this work, we aim to show what type of external knowledge is useful for certain classes of NLI. We examine how different types of knowledge impact neural language model decisions with respect to content and polarity.

To this end, we propose ERNIE-NLI, an NLI model that integrates external knowledge to enhance and probe NLI inference decisions. First, we adapt knowledge content in various sources to our setup: external knowledge relations are mapped to NLI knowledge relations (Section 4.2). In this step, we not only represent external knowledge from different sources in a unified way, but also convert external knowledge content to the NLI task. Second, the polarity is learned (Section 4.3): NLI knowledge embeddings are learned to predict whether they are positive or negative for entailment. In this step, we extend BERT with a knowledge embedding layer and a classification layer. Third, the content and polarity are applied to NLI classification (Section 4.4). All three phases listed above are depicted in Fig. 1. ERNIE-NLI is developed on the basis of ERNIE (Zhang et al., 2019a), which did not improve performance on the NLI task, although it was infused with TransE embeddings. Results show that our model ERNIE-NLI enhanced with adapted knowledge achieves better performance than ERNIE for specific classes depending on knowledge input.

We perform an in-depth analysis to examine how different types of knowledge impact NLI model's decisions with respect to content and polarity. We conduct a series of experiments to investigate why and how the adapted knowledge enhances NLI predictions. From the experiments, we find that:

- Integrating knowledge improves performance for NLI classes that correspond to integrated knowledge with regards to the polarity (e.g., positive knowledge improves entailment classification, etc.).
- Increased amount of knowledge during training improves performance for NLI labels that correspond to increased knowledge with regards to the polarity.
- Presence of knowledge at inference improves performance for NLI labels that correspond to present knowledge with regards to polarity (e.g., a correct entailment prediction with the presence of positive knowledge is observed to occur more often than with the presence of negative knowledge, etc.).
- ERNIE-NLI performance is robust to new knowledge content.

In summary, the proposed NLI model enhanced with adapted external knowledge from various sources achieves better performance for respective classes, allows us to analyze the impact of knowledge type, and is robust when the knowledge at inference time has shifted. We examine this performance with detailed analysis throughout the paper. Overall our contributions are as follows:

- We propose a knowledge analysis framework, ERNIE-NLI, that allow us to directly control and analyze adapted knowledge input, to investigate the characteristics of knowledge that result in a performance increase on the NLI task.

- We present findings that show strong correlations between knowledge polarity and downstream performance, illustrating the knowledge features that are important for increased performance.
- We perform extensive analysis and experimentation to support our findings (e.g., classification change analysis, adding knowledge incrementally, adding unseen knowledge, etc).

2 Related Work

2.1 Natural Language Inference

Early work in Natural Language Inference, also known as Textual Entailment (Dagan et al., 2005), exploited different features including logical rules (Bos and Markert, 2005), dependency parsers (Iftene and Balahur, 2007), and semantics (MacCartney and Manning, 2009), etc. With the development of large human annotated corpus such as the Stanford Natural Language Inference Corpus (Bowman et al., 2015) and the Multi-Genre NLI Corpus (Williams et al., 2018), most recent work has explored various neural models.

Different encoders have been studied to represent sentences, including LSTM (Bowman et al., 2016), tree-based CNN (Mou et al., 2015), TreeLSTM (Choi et al., 2018), etc. Previous work has explored using dynamic self-attention (Yoon et al., 2018), distance-based self-attention (Im and Cho, 2017) and reinforced self-attention (Shen et al., 2018) to enhance sentence encoders. Ensemble methods that combine multiple models have also shown improvements (Wang et al., 2017; Peters et al., 2018; Kim et al., 2019). Sun et al. (2019) improved masked language modeling with knowledge masking strategies, via entity-level and phrase-level masking, which showed improvement on NLI. Sun et al. (2020) then expanded this work to continual pre-training, which incrementally learns pre-training tasks through constant multi-task learning. Peters et al. (2019) investigated embedding knowledge bases into large-scale models in a multitask setup, seeing improvements on relationship extraction, entity typing, and word sense disambiguation.

Using external knowledge to enhance NLI models specifically, Chen et al. (2018) obtained the semantic relations between words from WordNet and calculated the relation embeddings using pre-trained TransE embeddings. Additionally, previous work has explored injecting lexical knowledge into pre-trained models for MNLI (Williams et al., 2018), among other tasks (Lauscher et al., 2020; Levine et al., 2020). Zhang et al. (2019a) adopted a knowledgeable encoder to inject the knowledge information into language representation. However, in contrast to our work, their external knowledge was not trained specifically for the NLI task.

2.2 Knowledge Embeddings

Using knowledge embeddings that represent the relations between entities has been useful in various downstream NLP tasks. Bordes et al. (2013) proposed TransE, a method which modeled relationships by interpreting them as translations operating on the low-dimensional embeddings of the entities. To address the issue of complex relation embeddings, Lin et al. (2015b) proposed CTransR in which the entity pairs are clustered into different groups and where the pairs in the same group share the same relation vector. Xiao et al. (2016) developed TransG, a generative Bayesian non-parametric infinite mixture embedding model, to handle multiple relation semantics of an entity pair. Further, Wang et al. (2019) integrated logic rules into a translation based knowledge graph embedding model. Their method automatically mined logic rules from triples in a knowledge graph.

Previous work has also introduced external knowledge to learn better knowledge embeddings. Lin et al. (2015a) and Luo et al. (2015) utilized relation paths and Guo et al. (2015) integrated additional semantic information and enforced the embedding space to be semantically smooth so that entities in the same semantic category were close to each other in the embedding space. Wang et al. (2014) used entity names and Wikipedia anchors to align the embeddings of entities and words in the same space. In our work, we focus on converting knowledge relations from different knowledge sources to relations that are tailored to the NLI task. We then use this knowledge to illustrate the impact that both knowledge content and representation have on model performance.

2.3 Language Model Challenges

Pre-trained language models face several challenges and previous work has analyzed and illustrated their strenghts and weaknesses. Ettinger (2020) constructed a series of tests for language models and applied these to BERT to study strengths and weakness. Kassner and Schütze

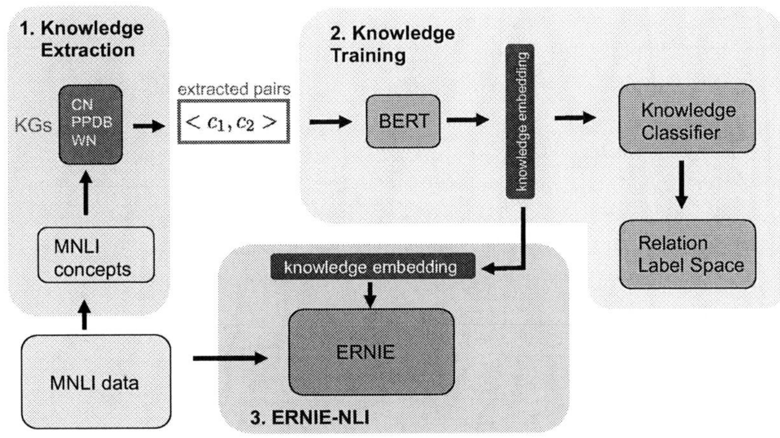

Figure 1: Components of the setup: (1) Knowledge Extraction Phase: Extracts knowledge content from external knowledge sources; (2) Knowledge Training Phase: Learns knowledge embeddings adapted to the NLI task; and (3) ERNIE-NLI: Trains NLI model with the integration of our learned knowledge embeddings.

(2020) added a component that focused on negation to the LAMA (LAnguage Model Analysis) evaluation framework (Petroni et al., 2019), showing that BERT failed on most negated statements. Talmor et al. (2019) designed eight reasoning tasks and illustrated that reasoning abilities are strongly context-dependent. Specific to NLI, Richardson et al. (2019) constructed challenging NLI datasets with new semantic fragments and showed that language models, though trained on NLI benchmark datasets, did not perform well on the new fragments. This previous work has shown that when applying pre-trained language models to a new task, a new domain, or new data variations, these models do not always perform well and additional knowledge may be needed to guide them. We examine how different types of knowledge impact language model decisions with respect to both content and polarity.

3 NLI corpus and External Knowledge

In this section, we introduce the particular NLI corpus and external knowledge sources used throughout this work.

3.1 NLI Corpus

MNLI, the Multi-Genre Natural Language Inference Corpus (Williams et al., 2018), consists of 433k sentence pairs annotated with entailment, contradiction, and neutral labels. The corpus covers various genres of both spoken and written text, and offers a wide range of style, various degrees of formality, and a diverse variety of topics and domains. This dataset is evaluated using standard accuracy.

3.2 External Knowledge Sources

We use several external knowledge sources to learn the relationships between concepts in our task.

ConceptNet (Speer et al., 2017) is a large semantic graph consisting of general knowledge. Concepts are related through predicates such as *IsA*(jazz, genre of music) and *AtLocation*(jazz, new orleans).

PPDB, Paraphrase Database (Ganitkevitch et al., 2013), contains over 220 million paraphrase pairs extracted from bilingual parallel corpora. Each paraphrase pair consists of two concepts that have a similar meaning.

WordNet (Miller, 1995) groups nouns, verbs, adjectives and adverbs into sets of cognitive synonyms (synsets), each expressing a distinct concept. Synsets are linked by different relations including synonym, antonymy, hypernymy, hyponymy, etc.

4 Methods

We introduce our terminology in Section 4.1. Then, we introduce the three steps of ERNIE-NLI: (1) knowledge extraction phase (content): extracting knowledge content from external knowledge sources (Section 4.2), (2) knowledge training phase (polarity): learning knowledge embeddings adapted to the NLI task (Section 4.3), and (3) NLI training phase: training our NLI model with the integration of learned knowledge embeddings (Section 4.4). The three phases are shown in Fig. 1.

4.1 Terminology

We use the following terms throughout the paper. For clarity, we will demonstrate each term given

(A)	*Premise:* I had an additional reason for that belief in the fact that all the cups found contained **sugar**, which Mademoiselle Cynthia never took in her coffee. *Hypothesis:* Mademoiselle Cynthia often took milk or **cream** in her **coffee**. *Label:* neutral *External Knowledge Pair: RelatedTo*(sugar, cream), *AtLocation*(sugar, coffee) *NLI Knowledge Pair:* pos(sugar, cream), pos(sugar, coffee)
(B)	*Premise:* Lalley also is enthused about other bar **efforts** on behalf of the poor, most notably the Legal Assistance Center will operate out of the new courthouse. *Hypothesis:* Lalley is enthusiastic about the bar's **initiative** to help the poor. *Label:* entailment *External Knowledge Pair: ReverseEntailment*(efforts, initiative) *NLI Knowledge Pair:* pos(efforts, initiative)

Table 1: NLI & Knowledge Pair Example.

the example in Table 1, Example (A).

External knowledge pair refers to a pair of two concepts from external knowledge sources, connected by an external knowledge relation, for example *RelatedTo*(sugar, cream). Each concept may be either a single word or a phrase.

External knowledge relation is the relation of the external knowledge pair. Each external knowledge source has a unique set of external knowledge relations. *RelatedTo* is an example of such a relation.

NLI knowledge pair refers to a pair of two concepts from NLI corpus, connected by an NLI knowledge relation, e.g., pos(sugar, cream).

NLI knowledge relation is the relation of the NLI knowledge pair. We define two NLI knowledge relations in Section 4.2: pos() and neg().

NLI pair refers to a pair of sentences, in which one sentence is the premise and the other is the hypothesis, as depicted in Table 1.

NLI label is entailment/neutral/contradiction.

4.2 NLI Knowledge Extraction

To represent external knowledge relations from different sources in a unified way, we define two NLI knowledge relations: pos() and neg(). A rule-based heuristic is developed to map the external knowledge relations to NLI knowledge relations. For example, in Table 1, we see that *RelatedTo* is mapped to pos(). Additionally, an external knowledge relation such as *Antonym* would be mapped to neg(). Each external knowledge relation is mapped to one NLI knowledge relation, where different external knowledge relations may be mapped to the same NLI knowledge relation. The specific mappings are listed in the appendix.

NLI knowledge pairs are extracted from each NLI pair. For the i-th NLI pair, with premise P and hypothesis H, we first identify all the concepts (single word or key phrase) in P and H using Python Keyphrase Extraction (PKE) (Boudin, 2016). We then extract each NLI knowledge pair $y(c_i^1, c_i^2)$ where $c_i^1 \subseteq P$ (a concept in the premise), $c_i^2 \subseteq H$ (a concept in the hypothesis) and where there exists an NLI knowledge relation y between c_i^1 and c_i^2. Considering Example (A) in Table 1, we see that c_i^1 = 'sugar', c_i^2 = 'cream', and y = pos().

There may be multiple NLI knowledge pairs in the i-th NLI pair of premise and hypothesis.

4.3 NLI Knowledge Learning

To learn the NLI knowledge embeddings, we add two additional components to BERT (Devlin et al., 2019). Thus, we learn the embedding of $y\{c_i^1, c_i^2\}$ in the following way. First, the sequence of knowledge tokens {[CLS] c_i^1 [SEP] c_i^2 [SEP]} is passed as input to BERT. Then, we take the subsequent contextual representations from BERT and pass them through a knowledge embedding layer (a linear layer) which casts our BERT representations into a knowledge embedding.

$$\mathbf{o} = \mathrm{BERT}(c_i^1, c_i^2) \quad (1)$$
$$k_i = W_k(\mathbf{o}) + b_k \quad (2)$$

where $\mathbf{o}$ is the contextual representation from BERT, W_k and b_k are weights and bias of the knowledge embedding layer, and k_i is the knowledge embedding. Next, the knowledge embedding k_i is fed into the NLI knowledge relation classification layer for knowledge fine-tuning:

$$l_c = W_c(k_i) + b_c \quad (3)$$
$$y = \mathrm{softmax}(l_c) \quad (4)$$

where W_c and b_c are weights and bias of the classification layer, and y is the NLI knowledge relation prediction. We use cross-entropy loss during training. In this way, we get the knowledge embedding associated with the NLI knowledge relation.

We learn the embeddings for all the NLI knowledge pairs in the i-th NLI pair in the training set such that we have a set of knowledge $K_i = \{k_i^1, \ldots, k_i^m\}$ where m is the length of the knowledge sequence for the i-th NLI pair. We use these embeddings to enhance NLI training described in the next section. The knowledge embeddings are fixed during NLI training. Note that at inference time, we calculate the knowledge embedding of the relation between any two concepts in the premise and hypothesis via Equations 1 and 2, even if the two concepts are not included in the training set. This enables the model to handle unseen concepts and NLI knowledge relations in the inference data.

4.4 NLI Knowledge Enhanced NLI

We propose ERNIE-NLI, built on the ERNIE architecture (Zhang et al., 2019a), to integrate the knowledge embeddings learned in Section 4.3 into the NLI model.

4.4.1 ERNIE

ERNIE (Zhang et al., 2019a) was developed mainly for integrating knowledge graph information into the entity typing and relation extraction tasks. It has two stacked modules: (a) a textual encoder to capture token embeddings and (b) a knowledge encoder to inject the token-oriented knowledge into the textual encoder output. The textual encoder is a multi-layer bidirectional Transformer encoder, similar to BERT. The knowledge encoder concatenates the token embeddings (output from the textual encoder) and entity embeddings (pre-trained TransE embedding).

ERNIE defines two inputs to the model, a token sequence $T = \{w_1, \ldots, w_n\}$ where n is the length of the token sequence, and a entity sequence that aligns to the given tokens as $E = \{e_1, \ldots, e_m\}$ where m is the length of the entity sequence. ERNIE is then defined as:

$$\mathbf{u} = \text{ERNIE}(T, E) \tag{5}$$

For example, consider the following sentence:

Bob Dylan wrote *Blowin' in the Wind.*

To recognize the relation between Bob Dylan and Blowin' in the Wind, ERNIE concatenates the entity embeddings of Bob Dylan and Blowin' in the Wind with the corresponding token embeddings. For more details, please refer to the original paper (Zhang et al., 2019a).

4.4.2 ERNIE-NLI

Though ERNIE is mainly designed for the entity typing and relation extraction tasks, it also reports performance on the MNLI dataset. ERNIE does not show an improvement over BERT, even though it uses the information from the knowledge graph. We speculate that this is because the knowledge type (named entities) is neither the type of knowledge required for the NLI task nor domain-specific to the NLI task. In contrast to ERNIE, which directly uses TransE embeddings (which are not adapted to the NLI task), we propose ERNIE-NLI which uses knowledge embeddings trained on the NLI dataset and tailored for the NLI task.

Similar to ERNIE, two inputs are fed into ERNIE-NLI: a token sequence $T = \{w_1, \ldots, w_n\}$ and a knowledge sequence, aligned to the given tokens, as $K = \{k_1, \ldots, k_m\}$ where m is the length of the knowledge sequence. In contrast to ERNIE, knowledge relations are tailored to the NLI task and knowledge embeddings are trained on the NLI training data. Thus, our model definition becomes:

$$\mathbf{u} = \text{ERNIE}(T, K) \tag{6}$$

where our knowledge embeddings for K are fixed during NLI training, similar to the original setup. However, unlike the original setup, our knowledge embeddings are now adapted to the NLI task.

5 Experiment Setup

As introduced in Section 3, we examine various external knowledge sources. We describe the setups used in this work, all of which are combinations of these sources. The performance of each setup is reported in Section 6.

PC is the basic setup and includes Paraphrase Database (PPDB) and ConceptNet. In this setup, we find that the number of positive NLI knowledge relations is greater than the number of negative NLI knowledge relations. Thus, we design additional setups to balance the ratio of positive and negative relations.

PC&Bal balances the positive and negative NLI knowledge relations to 50%-50% by downsampling positive relations.

PCW adds negative NLI knowledge relations from WordNet to PC.

PCW&Bal balances the positive and negative NLI knowledge relations to 50%-50% on PCW by downsampling positive relations.

6 Results and Analysis

6.1 BERT Error Analysis

Before designing our experiments, we manually analyzed BERT misclassifiations on MNLI, which inspired the decisions regarding content and polarity of knowledge required for improved reasoning and performance. We achieved 83.90% on the MNLI dev set with BERT. We analyzed 40 misclassifications per MNLI domain, and found that across all domains, at least 50% of misclassifications required external knowledge to be resolved. We also found that the combination of ConceptNet and PPDB covered at least 70% of the required concepts for these misclassifications across all domains. Thus, we decided to investigate the impact of external knowledge on NLI models.

6.2 ERNIE-NLI Performance

We run both ERNIE and ERNIE-NLI on the MNLI corpus using our experimental setups. With respect to ERNIE as the baseline, the accuracy changes of ERNIE-NLI are shown in Table 2. As introduced in Section 5, PC&Bal has less positive relations than PC. We can see that in Table 2, PC has better performance on the entailment class than PC&Bal, but has worse performance on neutral and contradiction. Similarly, PCW achieves better performance on entailment than PCW&Bal and worse performance on neutral and contradiction.

PCW has more negative NLI knowledge relations than PC since PCW has additional negative relations from WordNet. As shown in Table 2, PC achieves better performance on the entailment class than PCW and worse performance on the neutral class. Similarly, PC&Bal has better performance on the entailment class than PCW&Bal and worse performance on neutral and contradiction classes.

These results demonstrate a correlation between knowledge polarity and NLI performance, specifically that adding positive knowledge can train an NLI model that is better at making entailment predictions, and that adding negative knowledge can train an NLI model that is better at making neutral and contradiction predictions. As shown in Table 2, the best setup for the entailment class is PC and the best setup for the contradiction and neutral classes is PCW&Bal. The accuracy of the two setups per label and on all labels are included in Table 3 below. Note that in both setups, ERNIE-NLI not only achieves better performance on the particular NLI class, but also achieves better total performance. While ERNIE-NLI achieves better performance in this knowledge-integration setup, for comparison we would like to point out that the state-of-the-art is achieved by T5-11B (Raffel et al., 2020), which achieves 92.2% on the MNLI test set.

Setup	Contra	Neutral	Entail
PC	-0.62	0.13	2.59
PC&Bal	0.22	0.96	-1.06
PCW	-1.00	0.66	1.41
PCW&Bal	0.59	1.47	-0.84

Table 2: ERNIE-NLI improvement over ERNIE in % Accuracy per Contradiction/Neutral/Entailment label.

Model	Contr.	Neut.	Ent.	Total
ERNIE	85.91	83.74	80.84	83.42
ERNIE-NLI E	85.29	83.87	**83.43**	**84.18**
ERNIE-NLI C&N	**86.50**	**85.21**	80.00	83.74

Table 3: % Accuracy per label for ERNIE and ERNIE-NLI using best setup for each label.

6.3 Classification Change Analysis

We further analyze the new errors per label made by ERNIE-NLI compared to ERNIE. Table 4 shows the number of **error** changes grouped by NLI labels, and demonstrates that all the increased error changes from ERNIE to ERNIE-NLI enhanced with PC (i.e., positive numbers in the row of PC) are false entailment classifications. This observation is consistent with the findings in Table 2: with the introduction of more positive than negative knowledge, our model becomes biased towards entailment. Similarly, all of the increased errors changes from ERNIE to ERNIE-NLI enhanced with PCW&Bal (i.e., positive numbers in the row of PCW&Bal) are false neutral predictions. More interestingly, in this PCW&Bal setup where the positive and negative knowledge is balanced, the new errors only occur when the gold label is entailment and all other errors decrease. These results indicate that the model is able to utilize knowledge in a way that reflects an understanding of the NLI label. When the knowledge is balanced,

Gold	Contra		Neutral		Entail	
Prediction	N	E	C	E	C	N
PC	-2	22	-26	24	-9	-81
PCW&Bal	0	-16	-20	-20	-5	117

Table 4: ERNIE-NLI error changes with respect to ERNIE. A positive value indicates that ERNIE-NLI makes more errors than ERNIE on that label and vice versa.

	Contra	Neutral	Entail	Total
0%	86.35	83.93	80.12	83.37
25%	86.25	83.80	80.52	83.44
50%	86.50	85.21	80.00	83.74
78%	84.91	84.40	82.25	83.80
100%	85.29	83.87	83.43	84.18

Table 5: ERNIE-NLI performance with respect to the portion of positive knowledge used during knowledge training.

the model better understands the boundary between entailment and contradiction.

To better understand knowledge effect on ERNIE-NLI, we conduct a series of experiments to answer the following questions:

- Is more knowledge better?
- How does knowledge polarity affect NLI classification?
- How is performance affected if there is new knowledge at inference time?

6.4 Knowledge Portion during Training

To investigate performance gains with respect to the addition of NLI knowledge, we report the NLI performance depending on the portion of positive knowledge used during NLI knowledge learning under the PC setup in Table 5, which shows how the incremental addition of positive knowledge during knowledge embedding training increases the NLI performance for the entailment label. Note that the total accuracy is increased as more positive knowledge is added.

6.5 Knowledge Type during Inference

An NLI contradiction pair may extract positive NLI knowledge relations and an entailment pair may extract negative NLI knowledge relations. We analyze the correlation between the presence of NLI knowledge relations and the prediction results on the dev set. Specifically, we compare the prediction changes from ERNIE to ERNIE-NLI using the PC setup. Table 6 shows these prediction changes. X $\rightarrow$ Y represents the NLI pairs where baseline ERNIE predicts X while ERNIE-NLI predicts Y. We also include the number of correct prediction changes (i.e., where Y is gold).

Label	Pos Rels		Neg Rels		None Rels	
C/N$\rightarrow$E	160	(101)	22	(11)	138	(88)
C/E $\rightarrow$N	156	(96)	24	(16)	140	(57)
N/E $\rightarrow$C	129	(60)	22	(9)	82	(35)

Table 6: ERNIE-NLI classification changes with respect to ERNIE depending on presence of knowledge at inference time. Numbers without parenthesis are the total changes and numbers in the parenthesis are the correct changes.

Since we show results on the PC setup, we focus on the first row and first column in the table. The results in the first row indicate that a correct entailment classification with the presence of positive knowledge is observed to occur more often than with the presence of negative knowledge. The results in the first column indicate that a correct entailment classification with the presence of positive knowledge is observed to occur more often than a correct neutral or contradiction classification with positive knowledge. Thus, we see a strong correlation between the presence of positive knowledge and a correct entailment classification. This is a result of using the PC setup in this analysis, which is tailored for positive relations. Thus, while the correct entailment classification has the strongest correlation, we also see the strong effect of positive relations across all categories.

We would like to note that these findings are not discovered solely by looking at the label accuracies, as other classification shifts in this setting occur. We believe carrying out careful analyses, such as these, enable us to gain a deeper understanding of how knowledge affects the neural model, as we see clear trends in the effect of knowledge presence by polarity via this analysis.

6.6 Unseen Knowledge during Inference

To investigate our model's robustness in a common scenario where there are unseen knowledge relations in the evaluation data, we experiment with using only four external knowledge relations as NLI

Mapping	Contra	Neutral	Entail
Constrained	0.09	0.48	-0.17
Unconstrained	-0.31	0.57	0.63

Table 7: ERNIE-NLI % Accuracy changes for handling unseen relations with respect to ERNIE.

knowledge relations during training. The four relations are: RelatedTo, IsA, Independent, Antonym. During inference, we design two scenarios.

First, we design a constrained scenario in which new relations during inference time are dropped. For example, if an "Entails" relation exists between two concepts according to the knowledge sources, the knowledge is discarded, since it is not included in one of the four relations.

Second, we design an unconstrained scenario that computes the knowledge embedding at inference time. The sequence of the two concepts linked by the "Entails" relation, {[CLS] c_i^1 [SEP] c_i^2 [SEP]}, are fed into the BERT layer in Equation (1) and knowledge embedding layer in Equation (2) to get the knowledge embedding.

We compare the performance of the two scenarios in Table 7. The unconstrained scenario performs better than the constrained scenario, especially on the entailment label, given that there is more positive knowledge. The result shows ERNIE-NLI's capability of utilizing unseen knowledge relations to improve NLI, indicating the robustness of ERNIE-NLI in providing good predictions even if the inference data has shifted.

7 Examples

In this section, we discuss the two examples depicted in Table 1, to show how external knowledge can assist models on the NLI task.

7.1 Introducing World Knowledge

Integrating external knowledge can equip the model with world knowledge it did not have access to before. In Table 1, Example (A), the baseline model without external knowledge predicts contradiction, which is incorrect. Our ERNIE-NLI model with external knowledge predicts neutral, which is correct. The external knowledge used in this example is *RelatedTo*(sugar, cream) and *AtLocation*(sugar, coffee). The baseline model seems to predict this as contradiction mainly because the premise states *never ... in her coffee* while the hypothesis states *in her coffee*. The external knowledge helps correctly align the components: *sugar* and *cream*. Note that although the external knowledge indicates that *sugar* is related to *cream*, it does not necessarily yield an entailment prediction as the context is still being taking into consideration by the model, which understands that *sugar* is the main condition for entailment and that *cream* and *sugar* are not synonymous in this context.

7.2 Emphasizing Phrase Similarity

The model looks for similar words or phrases when it judges whether the hypothesis can be entailed from the premise. In the baseline model, the contextual embeddings alone are not strong enough to drive the prediction. In Table 1, Example (B), the baseline prediction is contradiction, which is wrong. Our ERNIE-NLI model with external knowledge predicts entailment, which is correct. The key knowledge required for this example is *Paraphrase*(efforts, initiative). By adding this paraphrase knowledge, the enhanced model recognizes the entailment relation of the pair.

8 Conclusion

We propose ERNIE-NLI, an NLI model that integrates external knowledge to enhance NLI performance. Our external knowledge representations are tailored to the NLI task and trained to adapt to NLI data requirements. We show that our model enhanced with external knowledge achieves better performance than the previous ERNIE model with non-adapted knowledge depending on the knowledge utilized. We examine these results with several analysis experiments to enable strong conclusions about the correlation between knowledge and NLI classification. Results also demonstrate that the model is able to handle unseen knowledge when the inference data shifts from training data.

Acknowledgments

We thank the reviewers for their useful feedback. This work was performed while Lisa interned at Bloomberg, and was later supported by DARPA MCS Grant N66001-19-2-4031, NSF-CAREER Award 1846185, and an NSF PhD Fellowship. The views are those of the authors and not of the funding agency.

References

Antoine Bordes, Nicolas Usunier, Alberto Garcia-Duran, Jason Weston, and Oksana Yakhnenko. 2013. Translating embeddings for modeling multi-relational data. In *NeurIPS*.

Johan Bos and Katja Markert. 2005. Recognising textual entailment with logical inference. In *HLT-EMNLP*.

Florian Boudin. 2016. pke: an open source python-based keyphrase extraction toolkit. In *COLING*.

Samuel R. Bowman, Gabor Angeli, Christopher Potts, and Christopher D. Manning. 2015. A large annotated corpus for learning natural language inference. In *EMNLP*.

Samuel R. Bowman, Jon Gauthier, Abhinav Rastogi, Raghav Gupta, Christopher D. Manning, and Christopher Potts. 2016. A fast unified model for parsing and sentence understanding. In *ACL*.

Qian Chen, Xiaodan Zhu, Zhen-Hua Ling, Diana Inkpen, and Si Wei. 2018. Neural natural language inference models enhanced with external knowledge. In *ACL*.

Jihun Choi, Kang Min Yoo, and Sang-goo Lee. 2018. Learning to compose task-specific tree structures. In *AAAI*.

Ido Dagan, Oren Glickman, and Bernardo Magnini. 2005. The pascal recognising textual entailment challenge. In *Machine Learning Challenges Workshop*, pages 177–190. Springer.

Jacob Devlin, Ming-Wei Chang, Kenton Lee, and Kristina Toutanova. 2019. Bert: Pre-training of deep bidirectional transformers for language understanding. *NAACL-HLT*.

Allyson Ettinger. 2020. What bert is not: Lessons from a new suite of psycholinguistic diagnostics for language models. *Transactions of the Association for Computational Linguistics*, 8:34–48.

Juri Ganitkevitch, Benjamin Van Durme, and Chris Callison-Burch. 2013. Ppdb: The paraphrase database. In *NAACL-HLT*, pages 758–764.

Shu Guo, Quan Wang, Bin Wang, Lihong Wang, and Li Guo. 2015. Semantically smooth knowledge graph embedding. In *ACL*, pages 84–94, Beijing, China. Association for Computational Linguistics.

Adrian Iftene and Alexandra Balahur. 2007. Hypothesis transformation and semantic variability rules used in recognizing textual entailment. In *ACL-PASCAL Workshop on Textual Entailment and Paraphrasing*.

Jinbae Im and Sungzoon Cho. 2017. Distance-based self-attention network for natural language inference. *arXiv preprint arXiv:1712.02047*.

Nora Kassner and Hinrich Schütze. 2020. Negated and misprimed probes for pretrained language models: Birds can talk, but cannot fly. *ACL*.

Seonhoon Kim, Inho Kang, and Nojun Kwak. 2019. Semantic sentence matching with densely-connected recurrent and co-attentive information. In *AAAI*.

Anne Lauscher, Ivan Vulić, Edoardo Maria Ponti, Anna Korhonen, and Goran Glavaš. 2020. Specializing unsupervised pretraining models for word-level semantic similarity. In *Proceedings of the 28th International Conference on Computational Linguistics*, pages 1371–1383.

Yoav Levine, Barak Lenz, Or Dagan, Ori Ram, Dan Padnos, Or Sharir, Shai Shalev-Shwartz, Amnon Shashua, and Yoav Shoham. 2020. Sensebert: Driving some sense into bert. In *Proceedings of the 58th Annual Meeting of the Association for Computational Linguistics*, pages 4656–4667.

Yankai Lin, Zhiyuan Liu, Huanbo Luan, Maosong Sun, Siwei Rao, and Song Liu. 2015a. Modeling relation paths for representation learning of knowledge bases. In *EMNLP*, pages 705–714, Lisbon, Portugal. Association for Computational Linguistics.

Yankai Lin, Zhiyuan Liu, Maosong Sun, Yang Liu, and Xuan Zhu. 2015b. Learning entity and relation embeddings for knowledge graph completion. In *AAAI*.

Xiaodong Liu, Pengcheng He, Weizhu Chen, and Jianfeng Gao. 2019. Multi-task deep neural networks for natural language understanding. In *ACL*.

Yuanfei Luo, Quan Wang, Bin Wang, and Li Guo. 2015. Context-dependent knowledge graph embedding. In *EMNLP*, pages 1656–1661, Lisbon, Portugal. Association for Computational Linguistics.

Bill MacCartney and Christopher D Manning. 2009. An extended model of natural logic. In *IWCS*.

George A Miller. 1995. Wordnet: a lexical database for english. *Communications of the ACM*, 38(11):39–41.

Lili Mou, Rui Men, Ge Li, Yan Xu, Lu Zhang, Rui Yan, and Zhi Jin. 2015. Natural language inference by tree-based convolution and heuristic matching. In *ACL*.

Matthew E Peters, Mark Neumann, Mohit Iyyer, Matt Gardner, Christopher Clark, Kenton Lee, and Luke Zettlemoyer. 2018. Deep contextualized word representations. In *Proceedings of NAACL-HLT*, pages 2227–2237.

Matthew E Peters, Mark Neumann, Robert Logan, Roy Schwartz, Vidur Joshi, Sameer Singh, and Noah A Smith. 2019. Knowledge enhanced contextual word representations. In *Proceedings of the 2019 Conference on Empirical Methods in Natural Language*

Processing and the 9th International Joint Conference on Natural Language Processing (EMNLP-IJCNLP), pages 43–54.

Fabio Petroni, Tim Rocktäschel, Patrick Lewis, Anton Bakhtin, Yuxiang Wu, Alexander H. Miller, and Sebastian Riedel. 2019. Language models as knowledge bases? In *EMNLP*.

Colin Raffel, Noam Shazeer, Adam Roberts, Katherine Lee, Sharan Narang, Michael Matena, Yanqi Zhou, Wei Li, and Peter J Liu. 2020. Exploring the limits of transfer learning with a unified text-to-text transformer. *Journal of Machine Learning Research*, 21:1–67.

Kyle Richardson, Hai Hu, Lawrence S Moss, and Ashish Sabharwal. 2019. Probing natural language inference models through semantic fragments. *arXiv preprint arXiv:1909.07521*.

Tao Shen, Tianyi Zhou, Guodong Long, Jing Jiang, Sen Wang, and Chengqi Zhang. 2018. Reinforced self-attention network: a hybrid of hard and soft attention for sequence modeling. In *IJCAI*.

Robyn Speer, Joshua Chin, and Catherine Havasi. 2017. Conceptnet 5.5: An open multilingual graph of general knowledge. In *Thirty-First AAAI Conference on Artificial Intelligence*.

Yu Sun, Shuohuan Wang, Yukun Li, Shikun Feng, Xuyi Chen, Han Zhang, Xin Tian, Danxiang Zhu, Hao Tian, and Hua Wu. 2019. Ernie: Enhanced representation through knowledge integration. *ACL*.

Yu Sun, Shuohuan Wang, Yukun Li, Shikun Feng, Hao Tian, Hua Wu, and Haifeng Wang. 2020. Ernie 2.0: A continual pre-training framework for language understanding. *AAAI*.

Alon Talmor, Yanai Elazar, Yoav Goldberg, and Jonathan Berant. 2019. olmpics–on what language model pre-training captures. *arXiv preprint arXiv:1912.13283*.

Pengwei Wang, Dejing Dou, Fangzhao Wu, Nisansa de Silva, and Lianwen Jin. 2019. Logic rules powered knowledge graph embedding. *arXiv preprint arXiv:1903.03772*.

Zhen Wang, Jianwen Zhang, Jianlin Feng, and Zheng Chen. 2014. Knowledge graph and text jointly embedding. In *EMNLP*.

Zhiguo Wang, Wael Hamza, and Radu Florian. 2017. Bilateral multi-perspective matching for natural language sentences. In *IJCAI*.

Adina Williams, Nikita Nangia, and Samuel Bowman. 2018. A broad-coverage challenge corpus for sentence understanding through inference. In *NAACL-HLT*.

Han Xiao, Minlie Huang, and Xiaoyan Zhu. 2016. Transg: A generative model for knowledge graph embedding. In *ACL*, pages 2316–2325.

Deunsol Yoon, Dongbok Lee, and SangKeun Lee. 2018. Dynamic self-attention: Computing attention over words dynamically for sentence embedding. *arXiv preprint arXiv:1808.07383*.

Zhengyan Zhang, Xu Han, Zhiyuan Liu, Xin Jiang, Maosong Sun, and Qun Liu. 2019a. Ernie: Enhanced language representation with informative entities. In *ACL*.

Zhuosheng Zhang, Yuwei Wu, Hai Zhao, Zuchao Li, Shuailiang Zhang, Xi Zhou, and Xiang Zhou. 2019b. Semantics-aware bert for language understanding. *arXiv preprint arXiv:1909.02209*.

A Appendix

A.1 Knowledge Mapping

Table 8 shows the external knowledge relations that are mapped to positive and negative NLI knowledge relations.

A.2 Hyperparameter Settings

For our experiments, we did not tune hyperparameters but rather selected our settings to be consistent with Zhang et al. (2019a). We used batch size 12, learning rate 2e-5, and random seed 42. We did 1 epoch of relation training and 4 epochs of NLI training. We hold these settings constant across all experiments.We built on the framework released by Zhang et al. (2019a), which included a pytorch implementation of ERNIE, and used all versions and infrastructures included in their implementation.

Course Grained	Fine-Grained
Negative	Antonym
	DistinctFrom
	Exclusion
	Unrelated
Positive	IsA
	Synonym
	RelatedTo
	HasFirstSubevent
	MannerOf
	NotCapableOf
	CausesDesire
	MotivatedByGoal
	HasProperty
	Entails
	ForwardEntailment
	CreatedBy
	Equivalence
	DerivedFrom
	dbpedia
	OtherRelated
	Unrelated
	MadeOf
	Desires
	ReceivesAction
	SimilarTo
	EtymologicallyRelatedTo
	HasLastSubevent
	NotHasProperty
	HasSubevent
	DefinedAs
	CausesDesire
	AtLocation
	HasA
	Independent
	ReverseEntailment
	FormOf
	HasContext
	InstanceOf
	PartOf
	NotDesires
	HasPrerequisite
	UsedFor
	CapableOf

Table 8: Fine-grained to course-grained mapping for External Knowledge Relations to NLI Knowledge Relations.

Enhancing Multiple-Choice Question Answering with Causal Knowledge

Dhairya Dalal[1] and **Mihael Arcan**[2] and **Paul Buitelaar**[1,2]
[1]SFI Centre for Research and Training in Artificial Intelligence
[2]Insight SFI Research Centre for Data Analytics
Data Science Institute, National University of Ireland Galway
d.dalal1@nuigalway.ie,
{mihael.arcan,paul.buitelaar}@nuigalway.ie

Abstract

The task of causal question answering aims to reason about causes and effects over a provided real or hypothetical premise. Recent approaches have converged on using transformer-based language models to solve question answering tasks. However, pretrained language models often struggle when external knowledge is not present in the premise or when additional context is required to answer the question. To the best of our knowledge, no prior work has explored the efficacy of augmenting pretrained language models with external causal knowledge for multiple-choice causal question answering. In this paper, we present novel strategies for the representation of causal knowledge. Our empirical results demonstrate the efficacy of augmenting pretrained models with external causal knowledge. We show improved performance on the COPA (Choice of Plausible Alternatives) and WIQA (What If Reasoning Over Procedural Text) benchmark tasks. On the WIQA benchmark, our approach is competitive with the state-of-the-art and exceeds it within the evaluation subcategories of In-Paragraph and Out-of-Paragraph perturbations.

Events

1. Pressure pushes up from inside the volcano.
2. Lava comes out of the volcano.
3. Ash clouds and rocks also come out of some volcanos.
4. The eruption lasts for a long time for some eruptions.
5. The things that come out of the volcano cause disturbances in the environment.
6. The volcano loses the built up pressure.
7. The lava and other debris stop coming out of the volcano.

Question: Suppose ***MORE*** ash clouds forming happens, how will it affect disturbances in the environment.
A. More B. Less C. No Effect

Figure 1: Example question from WIQA. The question poses an perturbation for Event 3 and asks what the implication is on Event 5.

1 Introduction

Recent model-based approaches for question answering tasks have primarily focused on finetuning pretrained transformer-based language models, such as BERT (Devlin et al.) and RoBERTa (Liu et al., 2019c), on task-specific datasets. These language models have been found to contain transferable linguistic knowledge (Liu et al., 2019a) and general knowledge (Petroni et al., 2019) that are effective for most downstream natural language processing (NLP) tasks. For more complex tasks, such as causal reasoning, pretrained language models are often limited as they lack the specific external background knowledge required to effectively reason about causality.

The term causal knowledge has a long history rooted in philosophy, psychology, and many other academic disciplines (Goldman, 1967). In this paper, we will refer to causal facts and causal knowledge interchangeably. Broadly, causal knowledge captures relational knowledge between concepts, which can be useful for reasoning about causality. Causal facts are generally extracted from natural language descriptions. For example, the statement *Global warming is caused primarily by human activities such as coal-burning power plants* would yield the causal fact *factories cause global warming*. These causal facts can also be described explicitly in a knowledge base or expressed formally as triples with an explicit cause-effect relation. For ex-

Proceedings of Deep Learning Inside Out (DeeLIO):
The 2nd Workshop on Knowledge Extraction and Integration for Deep Learning Architectures, pages 70–80
Online, June 10, 2021.

ample, the causal fact *factories cause global warming* would be expressed as the triple (`factory, cause-effect, global warming`). As causal facts are generated from descriptions, the veracity of these facts can be questionable. Ascertaining the verisimilitude of causal knowledge is an open problem and out-of-scope for our experiments. In this paper, we explore if causal knowledge is useful for question answering and present strategies on how to enhance a pretrained language model with causal knowledge.

There is limited work on incorporating external causal knowledge to improve question answering and no prior work on using causal knowledge to improve multiple-choice question answering. The task of causal question answering aims to reason about cause and effects over a provided real or hypothetical premise. Specifically, we explore the multiple-choice formulation of this task in the context of the COPA (*Choice of Plausible Alternatives*) (Gordon et al., 2012b) and WIQA (What If Reasoning over Procedural Text) (Tandon et al., 2019) benchmark tasks. COPA and WIQA are both challenging causal reasoning tasks.

WIQA requires reasoning on hypothetical perturbations to procedural descriptions of events. Consider the example in Figure 1. To answer the hypothetical question about the downstream effect of an increase of *ash and cloud on the environment*, the model must be able to causally link **Event 3** (about *ash clouds*) to **Event 5** (*erupted materials disturb the environment*). If provided a causal fact such as (ash clouds, cause-effect, environmental disturbances), the model could make the causal association and logical leap that the magnitude of the effect is more.

COPA is another multiple-choice causal reasoning task. COPA requires external commonsense causal knowledge to answer questions about the causes and effects for a provided premise. Consider the following example from COPA:

- Premise: Air pollution in the city worsened. What was the CAUSE of this?
- Alternative 1: Factories increased their production.
- Alternative 2: Factories shut down.

Lexically, there is limited information in the premise and alternatives that the model can exploit to answer the question. To successfully answer this question, the model requires both background knowledge about factories and the ability to make causal leaps about the impact of factories on the environment. Causal facts can succinctly capture that knowledge. Consider the following claimed causal fact triples from CauseNet (Heindorf et al., 2020):

- (factory, cause-effect, pollution)
- (factory, cause-effect, air pollution)
- (production, cause-effect, pollution)

If the model was provided these facts apriori, it could reason that factories cause air pollution and the increase of production would worsen the air quality.

This paper presents empirical findings on the efficacy of augmenting pretrained models with causal facts extracted to improve multiple-choice causal question answering. Our contributions can be summarized as follows:

- We present a general method for selecting relevant causal facts from CauseNet for a provided multiple-choice question.
- We present two novel strategies for representing external causal knowledge as embeddings for downstream question answering.
- We present a novel end-to-end neural architecture that augments RoBERTa with external causal knowledge for multiple-choice question answering.

Our experiments demonstrate that augmenting pretrained models with external causal knowledge improves results over the baseline on the COPA and WIQA benchmark tasks. For the WIQA benchmark, we present findings that show causal knowledge improves RoBERTa's performance to nearly match the current state-of-the-art (SOTA) and improve upon the SOTA in specific sub-categories such as in-paragraph and out-of-paragraph reasoning.

2 Related Work

Enhancing language models with external knowledge (in the form of a knowledge graph or knowledge base) remains an open problem. Several promising strategies have emerged for injecting knowledge into large language models as part of the pretraining process. Peters et al. (2019) present the Knowledge Attention and Recontextualization

(KAR) layer which can be inserted into a neural language model architecture and used to train knowledge enhanced contextual embeddings. Liu et al. (2019b) introduce the K-BERT model which learns knowledge enabled representations from sentence trees that consist of inputs augmented with knowledge triples. Sun et al. (2020) introduce the CoLAKE model which jointly learns language and knowledge representations through pretraining on word-knowledge (WK) graphs. To the best of our knowledge, there is no prior work on enhancing language models specifically with causal knowledge.

Next we provide a summary of the question answering tasks which require causal reasoning. The task of binary causal question answering poses questions of cause and effect as yes/no questions (i.e. *Could X cause Y?*). Hassanzadeh et al. evaluate the application of cause-effect pairs extracted from Gigawords corpus for binary question answering. Kayesh et al. (2020) extends this work to automatically learn the yes/no threshold using word embeddings from BERT, RoBERTa, and other transformer-based models. Sharp et al. and Xie and Mu (2019) consider the task of answer reranking for open-ended causal questions. Both papers are evaluated on a set of causal question extracted from the Yahoo! Answers corpus which follows the patterns *What causes ...* and *What is the result of ....* Sharp et al. present three distributional similarity models to model the contextual relationship between cause and effect phrases. Xie and Mu (2019) extend Sharp et al. by proposing methods for building causal embeddings from cause-effect phrase pairs by transferring causal relationships from the phrase-pair level to word-pair level. Our `CausalSkipgram` model for representing causal knowledge expands upon the adapted Skipgram model presented by Sharp et al..

Finally, we summarize the current approaches to causal knowledge extraction and knowledge graph population. Causal relation extraction aims to identify cause and effect phrases in various texts. The extracted cause/effect phrases can be used to populate causal knowledge bases. Recent approaches frame causal relation extraction as a structured sequence classification problem. Dasgupta et al. propose a LSTM architecture that uses word-level embeddings to predict cause and effect tags within a sentence. Li et al. (2021) present SCITE, a BiLSTM-CRF model which uses pretrained Flair embeddings and multi-headed self-attention to extract causal phrases. To date, there are few publicly available causal knowledge bases. CauseNet (Heindorf et al., 2020) is currently the largest publicly available knowledge graph of claimed causal facts. CauseNet consists of about 12 million concepts and 11.5 million relations extracted from Wikipedia and ClueWeb12 [1]. ConceptNet (Speer et al., 2017), a public knowledge graph, consists of 36 relations and includes a *causes* relation. The ATOMIC (Sap et al., 2019) knowledge base consists of 877k textual descriptions of inferential knowledge organized around event prompts and agent-centric activities. ATOMIC describes the social and commonsense knowledge of these events along nine if-then relations which describe the event's causes and effects on other agents/participants. COMET (Bosselut et al., 2019) is a language model adaptation framework that is trained on ATOMIC and ConceptNet to generate novel commonsense facts and construct robust commonsense knowledge bases. This paper uses CauseNet as its primary source for causal knowledge as it contains a broad and deep set of causal facts (including descriptions of physical processes relevant to WIQA).

3 Data

In this section, we describe the datasets used for causal knowledge extraction and our benchmark evaluation. We use CauseNet as the primary source of causal knowledge for our experiments. COPA and WIQA are the benchmark datasets used to evaluate causal knowledge on downstream multiple-choice question answering problems that require causal reasoning.

3.1 CauseNet

CauseNet consists of millions of concepts and causal relations extracted from ClueWeb12 and Wikipedia. ClueWeb12 is comprised of 733,019,372 English web pages crawled between February and March 2012 (Heindorf et al., 2020). Linguistic rules are used to generate candidate sentences that contain causal relations and a BiLSTM-CRF model is used to extract cause and effect concepts from the candidate sentences. Due to the unsupervised methodology used to populate CauseNet, the relations are presented as claimed causal relations. There are two versions of CauseNet, CauseNet-Full and CauseNet-Precision.

[1] https://lemurproject.org/clueweb12/

CauseNet-Precision is a subset of CauseNet-Full where all concepts are manually evaluated and selected to ensure high precision. CauseNet-Full consists of 11,609,890 relations and 12,186,195 concepts.

3.2 COPA (The Choice of Plausible Alternatives)

COPA was first introduced as a SemEval 2012 shared task (Gordon et al., 2012a). COPA consists of a premise and two alternatives. The task is to identify which alternative is most likely the cause or effect of the provided premise. Background commonsense causal knowledge is required to successfully answer questions as there is limited lexical overlap between the premise and alternatives. The COPA dataset consists of 1,000 questions, broken into 500 development and 500 test questions.

Recent pretrained models such as BERT and RoBERTa have seen improved performance on the COPA dataset. However, Kavumba et al. (2019) found that these models exploited superficial cues such as the token frequency in the correct answers. To mitigate this effect, Kavumba et al. expanded the development set to include mirror instances to balance the lexical distribution between correct and incorrect answers. For each set of alternatives, the mirror instance introduces a new premise, where the previous correct alternative is now incorrect. This new dataset, called COPA-Balanced, also categorized the test set into easy and hard groups. The easy group consists of 190 questions where RoBERTa-Large and BERT-Large could answer correctly without the provided premise and the hard group is the remaining 310 questions. We use the COPA-Balanced development set for training and the hard category (which we will refer to as COPA-Balanced Hard) for evaluation.

4 Methodology

In this section, we present our methodologies for causal fact selection and causal representation. Causal facts are extracted from CauseNet using token-based retrieval heuristics. We also present three strategies for representing causal knowledge. The first strategy is input augmentation, where extracted causal facts are converted to causal statements and appended to the plain text input. The second and third strategies involve generating causal embeddings using distributed similarity and knowledge graph embedding approaches.

4.1 Causal Fact Selection

Selecting relevant causal facts for a provided input is an unresolved challenge. We extracted causal facts from CauseNet using a set of retrieval heuristics. Given the large number of concepts and causal relations ($\sim$11.5 million relations and $\sim$12 million concepts), it is computationally expensive to consider all facts during model training. To narrow down the scope of relevant facts, we consider only the question text in WIQA and the premise description in COPA.

First, we extract a list of tokens T from the input question/premise. T consists of unique words as well as unique noun phrases. Each word in the noun phrase is lower-cased and lemmatized. The normalized noun phrase is then converted to a single token by replacing spaces with underscores. Next, we generate a list of potential causal fact candidates. Since we do not know a priori which tokens correspond to causes and effects, we apply a strict filter to ensure that selected causal effects have lexical overlap with the input text. The causal fact table is queried to return all candidate facts where both c and e exist as tokens in T. The causal facts are ranked by frequency and the top five ranked candidates are selected as the final set of relevant causal facts for the input question.

4.2 Causal Knowledge Representation

4.2.1 Distributed Causal Embeddings

In this section, we present our method for modelling causality using a distributional similarity model. `CausalSkipgram` is similar to `cEmbed` presented by Sharp et al.. As mentioned in Section 2, Sharp et al. first proposed adapting the skip-gram word embedding approach (Mikolov et al., 2013) to model causal pairs. Two embeddings are learned for cause and effect concepts respectively. The effect embeddings serve as a context for the cause concepts and the cause embeddings in turn are used as a context for the effect concepts. Sharp et al. consider the cause and effect vectors separately.

`CausalSkipgram` differs from `cEmbed` in three ways. To learn word-level embeddings, `cEmbed` decomposes multi-word phrases and generates word pairs such that each word in the causal phrase is matched with each word in the effect phrase. In contrast, multi-word concepts are converted to a single token during the normalization process for `CausalSkipgram`. Thus,

`CausalSkipgram` learns embeddings for each single token representation of cause and effect concepts. Second, we use Negative Sampling loss (Mikolov et al., 2013) to train `CausalSkipgram`. Finally, Sharp et al. consider the cause and effect vectors as separate features for their question answering application. Instead, we generate a single representation for each causal tuple by mean pooling the cause and effect vectors.

4.2.2 Causal Knowledge Graph Embeddings

In this section, we present `CausalKGE`, which represents causal knowledge as a knowledge graph embedding. We adapt the TransE model presented by Bordes et al. (Bordes et al., 2013). Given a relational triple (consisting of head h, relation r, and tail t), TransE represents entities and relations in a lower-dimensional space such that $h + r \approx t$. TransE treats knowledge graph embeddings as a link prediction problem where the goal is identify what the relation is given two nodes in the graph. TransE treats relations as translations in the embeddings space where adding a the relation vector to the head to should results in a vector that close to the tail vector representation. To model our causal tuples as a knowledge graph, we add the explicit relation "cause-effect" to each tuple. The modeling goal of TransE is thus to predict an effect E, given a cause C and "cause-effect" CR such that $C + CR \approx E$. A causal triple is represented by a single vector which is generated by mean pooling the head, tail, and relation vectors.

5 Experimental Settings

In this section, we describe how we trained our causal representations and the experimental settings for augmenting RoBERTa with causal knowledge for downstream question answering.

5.1 Causal Representation

5.1.1 CausalSkipgram

`CausalSkipgram` generates 256 dimensional embeddings. It takes as input a cause/effect tuple and predicts if the pair is a valid causal fact. We generate five negative examples per causal tuple by randomly matching cause and effect tokens. The samples are filtered to ensure that the generated negative sample does not exist as a valid causal fact. A dataset is generated by first combining the known causal tuples with the negative samples. The dataset is then randomly split into a train, validation, and test set following a standard 70-10-20 split ratio.

The `CausalSkipgram` model is trained for 100 epochs using a batch size of 256 and negative sampling loss (Mikolov et al., 2013). We use the sparse Adam optimizer (Kingma and Ba, 2015) with a learning rate of 0.001 and cosine annealing to learn the learning rate. To extract an embedding for a causal tuple, we extract the hidden cause and effect concept embeddings that comprise the `CausalSkipgram` model. The causal tuple is then represented by a 256-dimensional vector that is generated by mean pooling the cause and effect vectors that comprise the tuple.

5.1.2 CausalKGE

`CausalKGE` produces 100 dimensional TransE embeddings. To train our knowledge graph embedding, we generate a dataset with negative samples following the same process as Section 5.1.1. The key difference is that our dataset consists of causal triples instead of causal tuples. We use the MKB (Sourty et al., 2020) library to train the 100-dimensional TransE embeddings for 25 epochs using the following hyperparameters: gamma value of 6, batch size of 32, negative sample of 5 examples per input. The model is trained to minimize the adversarial loss using the Adam optimizer with a learning rate of 0.001.

5.2 Causality Enhanced RoBERTa for Multiple-Choice Question Answering

In this section, we describe the model architectures and experimental settings for finetuning on the COPA and WIQA tasks.

5.2.1 Baseline

Our baseline multiple-choice question answering model is RoBERTa with a linear head for sequence classification. We use the base RoBERTa implementation and pretrained weights provided by the Huggingface library (Wolf et al.). Two separate baseline models are trained with respect to the COPA and WIQA task definitions.

The input for COPA consists of a premise p, two alternatives a_1, a_2 and a question q, which are all a sequence of tokens. The expected output is a binary value corresponding to either alternative 1 or 2. We format the text input to the RoBERTa models using the convention below, where the separator token is denoted as **<sep>**:

```
<sep>premise<sep>question<sep>
```

Model	COPA Test	COPA-Balanced Hard
RoBERTa baseline	53.00	58.39
+ CausalSkipgram	57.80	58.38
+ CausalKGE	*59.20 (+6.2%/+11.69%)*	62.25
+ InputAugmentation	59.00	*62.29 (+3.9%/+6%)*
Deberta Ensemble - SOTA (He et al., 2020)	**98.40**	N/A

Table 1: Accuracy on the COPA test set and COPA-BALANCED Hard set. CausalKGE improves accuracy over the RoBERTa baseline by 6.2% (absolute) and 11.69% (relative). On the COPA-BALANCED Hard, InputAgumentation improves accuracy by 3.9% (absolute) and 6% (relative) over the baseline.

```
alternative 1<sep>
alternative 2<sep>
```

WIQA entries are similarly formatted and consist of a procedural text P, which comprises of a list of events $e_1 ... e_n$, question q, and answer options $[a_1, a_2, a_3]$. The expected output is the softmax distribution over $[a_1, a_2, a_3]$. The procedural text is flattened into a single string which denote as below context. The WIQA input is formatted as follows:

```
<sep>context<sep>question<sep>
more<sep>less<sep>no effect<sep>
```

The inputs are then encoded using the default byte-pair encoder and passed to the base RoBERTa model. Next the pooled input representation H_1, which consists of the 768 last layer hidden-state representation of the first token of the sequence, is passed to a linear projection classification head. To encourage generalization, dropout with a probability of 0.5 is applied to the classification head as well.

This model is trained to minimize the cross-entropy loss using the AdamW optimizer (Loshchilov and Hutter, 2017) and a learning rate scheduler. We use a learning rate of 0.001 and 500 warmup steps with a weight decay of 0.01 for the scheduler. For both WIQA and COPA we use a batch size of 24 and enable 16-bit floating precision for training. The model is trained for 10 epochs on the WIQA dataset and 50 epochs on the COPA dataset (we use a higher number of epochs as COPA has fewer than 1,000 training examples). We select the checkpoint with the highest validation accuracy and use those weights for evaluation on the provided test sets.

5.2.2 Input Augmentation

The most direct way to incorporate causal information is to append them to the end of text input which we term as `InputAugmentation` method. Relevant causal tuples are converted into causal statements which follow the pattern *C causes E*. Multi-word concepts in the tuples which represented as single tokens are separated back out. For example, the tuple `(human_activity, climate_change)` would be converted into the statement *Human activity causes climate change*.

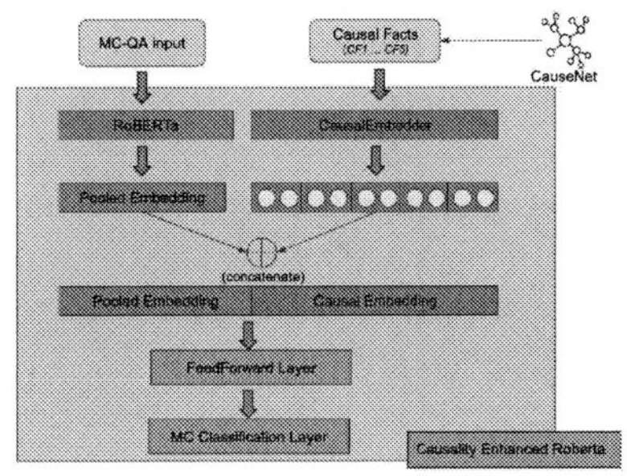

Figure 2: Architecture of Causality Enhanced RoBERTa. The architecture takes as input the multiple-choice question input and relevant causal facts selected from CauseNet.

Inputs for both COPA and WIQA follow the input formatting described in section 5.2.1 with the additional causal facts appended to the input. For example inputs for COPA are formatted using the following convention and RoBERTa specific separator token denoted as **<sep>** below.

```
<sep>premise<sep>alternative 1<sep>
alternative 2<sep>
causal statements 1...5<sep>.
```

The augmented inputs are passed into the base RoBERTa model as presented in section 5.2.1 and trained using the same experimental settings.

5.2.3 Causality Enhanced RoBERTa

To incorporate causal embeddings with RoBERTa, we propose a modified neural architecture (Figure 2). This architecture is used for both `CausalSkipgram` and `CausalKGE`, with the primary difference being the size of the causal em-

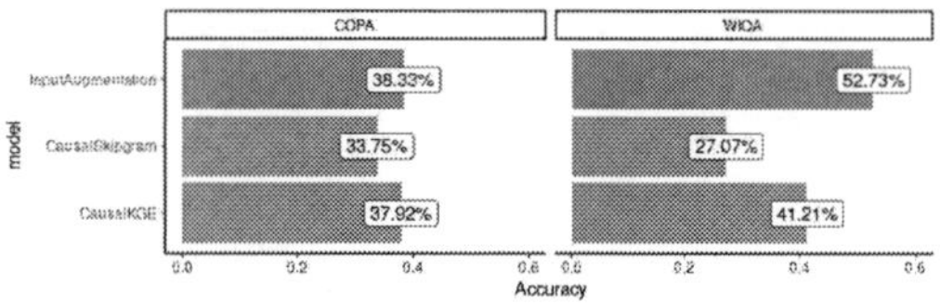

Figure 3: Performance over difficult questions that RoBERTa baseline answered incorrectly.

beddings. The first layer is the causal enhanced input layer which combines the pooled embedding output of RoBERTa with the external causal embeddings. For inputs that have extracted causal facts, a causal embedding vector is generated by concatenating and flattening all the causal embeddings. We extracted up to five causal facts per input. As a result, the combined `CausalSkipgram` embedding input is 1,280 and 500 dimensions for `CausalKGE`. Zero-valued vectors are used if causal facts are missing. The RoBERTa pooled output is then concatenated with causal embeddings. This input is further passed into a FeedForward Network (FFN) with a hidden layer and classifier. The first layer of the FFN has a hidden dimension of 512 and we apply dropout with a probability of 0.5 and ReLU (Agarap, 2018) activation to it. The second layer is the output layer with a softmax activation.

WIQA provides data that has already been split into train, validation, and test sets. We use COPA-Balanced instead of COPA. The balanced set includes mirror instances that make it more difficult for RoBERTa to exploit superficial lexical cues present in the correct answers. We randomly split the COPA-Balanced train set into a train and validation set using an 85 - 15 split.

This model is trained to minimize the cross-entropy loss using the AdamW optimizer and a learning rate scheduler. We use a learning rate of 0.001 and 500 warmup steps with a weight decay of 0.01 for the scheduler. For both WIQA and COPA, we use a batch size of 24 and enable 16-bit floating precision for training. The model is trained for 10 epochs on the WIQA dataset and 50 epochs on the COPA dataset (we use a higher number of epochs as COPA has fewer than 1,000 training examples). We select the checkpoint with the highest validation accuracy and use those weights for evaluation on the provided test sets.

6 Results

In this section, we present the results of our experiments. We find that the inclusion of causal facts improves the performance on both the COPA and WIQA datasets. Additionally, on the WIQA dataset, we observed the Augmented Input method nearly matches the SOTA in overall accuracy and exceeds the SOTA in two of the three subcategories of perturbations.

6.1 COPA Results

We present results on the COPA test set and the COPA-Balanced Hard subset in Table 1. The current state-of-the-art on COPA is DeBERTa-Large, which consists of 3.5 billion parameters. DeBERTa (He et al., 2020) modifies the BERT architecture using the disentangled attention mechanism and an enhanced mask decoder used to predict masked tokens during pretraining. While we are unable to match the performance of DeBERTa, we provide the SOTA as a fair reference for the current benchmark leader. Additionally, our augmentation methodology is not unique to RoBERTa and could be used to augment any language model with external causal information.

We were able to extract causal information from CauseNet for 32% of the questions in the test set, with an average of one causal tuple per question. About 36% of the questions with causal information had two or more extracted causal tuples.

Through the inclusion of external causal information, all three methods outperform the RoBERTa baseline. The `CausalKGE` and `Input Augmentation` have similar performance, improving accuracy by 11.69% and 6% relatively over the RoBERTa baseline on the COPA test set and COPA-Balanced Hard set. In Figure 3, we further evaluate all three methods on the subset of questions that the baseline model was unable to answer. On average, all three methods can answer 36% of questions correctly that the baseline missed, with the Input Augmentation method performing the best.

6.2 WIQA Results

Table 2 provides the results for our experiments on the WIQA dataset. The current SOTA for WIQA is the QUARTET model presented by Rajagopal et al. (Rajagopal et al., 2020). QUARTET modifies the WIQA task to include an explanation structure which identifies the supporting events from

Model	Overall	In-Para.	Out-of-Para.	No Effect
Bert-Baseline (Tandon et al., 2019)	73.80	**79.68**	56.10	89.38
QUARTET - SOTA (Tandon et al., 2019)	**82.07**	73.49	65.65	**95.30**
RoBERTa baseline	67.00	64.0	42.10	92.50
+ CausalSkipgram	65.00	53.96	41.38	92.29
+ CausalKGE	74.00	71.70	55.17	93.78
+ InputAugmentation	80.00	**76.79**	**67.65**	92.43

Table 2: Accuracy of causal augmentation methods on the WIQA dataset. InputAugmentation has the best overall accuracy amongst the augmentation methods. Additionally, it achieves higher accuracy in the In-Paragrah (+3.3%) and Out-of-Paragraph (+2%) sub-categories over the current state-of-the-art QUARTET.

the procedural description that best explain the proposed perturbation. The supporting events come from the explanations influence graph which were selected by human annotators for each question in the WIQA dataset. QUARTET models the explanation task as a multi-task learning problem where the model must predict both the gold relevant supporting sentences and the associated impact of the perturbation for each supporting event. Our approach nearly matches the overall accuracy of QUARTET while outperforming QUARTET in the In-Paragraph and Out-of-Paragraph subcategories.

We were able to select causal information for 55% (1,661) of the questions in the test set, with an average of one causal tuple extracted per question. 37% of questions had two or more extracted causal tuples. The `CausalSkipgram` method was the least successful, performing worse than the RoBERTa baseline across all categories. The `CausalKGE` and `InputAugmentation` methods both improved accuracy upon the RoBERTa baseline in all categories. The `InputAugmentation` method was competitive with the QUARTET method and outperformed it in both the In-Paragraph (+3.3%/+4.5%) and Out-of-Paragraph (+2%/+3%) categories. We do, however, see a -3% decrease in accuracy in the No Effect category. This is likely due to extraneous or irrelevant causal tuples being selected. Future work can explore improving the precision of the causal extraction process.

In Figure 3, we also present the results of the augmentation methods on the questions the baseline RoBERTa model was unable to answer. We find the `InputAugmentation` method can answer 52.73% of the difficult questions that the baseline failed to answer.

7 Conclusion

This paper considers the challenge of enhancing pretrained language with causal knowledge to solve multiple-choice causal question answering problems which require causal reasoning. Specifically, we evaluate our methods on the COPA and WIQA benchmark datasets. We present methods of selecting knowledge from CauseNet and three strategies for representing causal knowledge (`InputAugmentation`, `CausalSkipgram`, and `CausalKGE`). We evaluated the efficacy of enhancing RoBERTa with causal knowledge multiple-choice question answering tasks. We provide results that show improved performance over the RoBERTa baseline on both the COPA and WIQA benchmark tasks. RoBERTa with `CausalKGE` provides a 6.2%/11.69% improvement in accuracy over the baseline. RoBERTa with `Input Augmentation` posts a 3.9%/6% improvement on the COPA-Balanced Hard dataset. We also observed that on average the inclusion of causal knowledge allows RoBERTa to answer 36% of the questions the baseline was unable to answer. On WIQA, our approach is competitive with the SOTA and exceeds SOTA within specific evaluation subcategories. RoBERTa with `InputAugmentation` improves accuracy on the in-paragraph and out-of-paragraph perturbations by (+3.3%/+4.5%) and (+2%/+3%) respectively. On average, the inclusion of causal knowledge allows RoBERTa to answer 40% of the questions that the baseline was unable to answer on the WIQA test set.

Our work demonstrates that causal knowledge is valuable for causal reasoning tasks and that there are many opportunities for future work. Further work can explore improving recall on causal fact selection from CauseNet and more sophisticated techniques to reduce the selection of irrelevant facts. On the language modeling side, future work can explore generalizing the entity-based methods which inject knowledge into the pretraining process to consider explicit causal knowledge. Additionally, further work can evaluate causal knowledge in other reasoning benchmarks such as ROPES and COSMOSQA as well as other causal reasoning tasks.

8 Broader Impact

This paper focused narrowly on the efficacy of causal knowledge for multiple-choice question answering. To the best of our knowledge there are limited societal implications of this research. Broadly improvements to question answering systems have commercial value for information retrieval and other knowledge management commercial use cases. Causal reasoning is one of the outstanding challenges of AI research. We imagine that improvements to causal reasoning can have broader impacts on real-world applications. Models with causal reasoning capacities have the potential to impact applications ranging from medical drug discovery and stock market trading to scientific knowledge mining. There is also a growing interest in the regulatory space for causal systems that can conduct counterfactual reasoning around the allocation of resources to protected groups and audit policy decisions made by automated systems.

9 Acknowledgements

This work was supported by Science Foundation Ireland under grants SFI/18/CRT/6223 (Centre for Research Training in Artificial Intelligence) and SFI/12/RC/2289_P2 (Insight), co-funded by the European Regional Development Fund.

References

Abien Fred Agarap. 2018. Deep learning using rectified linear units (relu). *ArXiv*, abs/1803.08375.

Antoine Bordes, Nicolas Usunier, Alberto Garcia-Duran, Jason Weston, and Oksana Yakhnenko. 2013. Translating embeddings for modeling multi-relational data. In *Advances in Neural Information Processing Systems*, volume 26. Curran Associates, Inc.

Antoine Bosselut, Hannah Rashkin, Maarten Sap, Chaitanya Malaviya, Asli Celikyilmaz, and Yejin Choi. 2019. COMET: commonsense transformers for automatic knowledge graph construction. *CoRR*, abs/1906.05317.

Tirthankar Dasgupta, Rupsa Saha, Lipika Dey, and Abir Naskar. Automatic extraction of causal relations from text using linguistically informed deep neural networks. In *Proceedings of the 19th Annual SIGdial Meeting on Discourse and Dialogue*.

Jacob Devlin, Ming-Wei Chang, Kenton Lee, and Kristina Toutanova. BERT: Pre-training of deep bidirectional transformers for language understanding. In *NAACL 2019 Proceedings: Human Language Technologies, Volume 1 (Long and Short Papers)*. Association for Computational Linguistics.

Alvin I. Goldman. 1967. A causal theory of knowing. *The Journal of Philosophy*, 64(12):357–372.

Andrew Gordon, Zornitsa Kozareva, and Melissa Roemmele. 2012a. SemEval-2012 task 7: Choice of plausible alternatives: An evaluation of commonsense causal reasoning. In **SEM 2012: The First Joint Conference on Lexical and Computational Semantics – Volume 1: Proceedings of the main conference and the shared task, and Volume 2: Proceedings of the Sixth International Workshop on Semantic Evaluation (SemEval 2012)*, Montréal, Canada. Association for Computational Linguistics.

Andrew S. Gordon, Zornitsa Kozareva, and Melissa Roemmele. 2012b. Semeval-2012 task 7: Choice of plausible alternatives: An evaluation of commonsense causal reasoning. In *SemEval@NAACL-HLT*. Association for Computational Linguistics.

Oktie Hassanzadeh, Debarun Bhattacharjya, Mark Feblowitz, Kavitha Srinivas, Michael Perrone, Shirin Sohrabi, and Michael Katz. Answering binary causal questions through large-scale text mining: An evaluation using cause-effect pairs from human experts. In *Proceedings of the Twenty-Eighth International Joint Conference on Artificial Intelligence, IJCAI-19*. International Joint Conferences on Artificial Intelligence Organization.

Pengcheng He, Xiaodong Liu, Jianfeng Gao, and Weizhu Chen. 2020. Deberta: Decoding-enhanced bert with disentangled attention. *ArXiv*, abs/2006.03654.

Stefan Heindorf, Yan Scholten, Henning Wachsmuth, Axel-Cyrille Ngonga Ngomo, and Martin Potthast. 2020. Causenet: Towards a causality graph extracted from the web. In *CIKM*. ACM.

Pride Kavumba, Naoya Inoue, Benjamin Heinzerling, Keshav Singh, Paul Reisert, and Kentaro Inui. 2019. When choosing plausible alternatives, clever hans can be clever. In *Proceedings of the First Workshop on Commonsense Inference in Natural Language Processing*.

H. Kayesh, M. Saiful Islam, J. Wang, S. Anirban, A. S. M. Kayes, and P. Watters. 2020. Answering binary causal questions: A transfer learning based approach. In *2020 International Joint Conference on Neural Networks (IJCNN)*.

Diederik P. Kingma and Jimmy Ba. 2015. Adam: A method for stochastic optimization. *CoRR*, abs/1412.6980.

Zhaoning Li, Qi Li, Xiaotian Zou, and Jiangtao Ren. 2021. Causality extraction based on self-attentive bilstm-crf with transferred embeddings. *Neurocomputing*, 423.

Nelson F. Liu, Matt Gardner, Yonatan Belinkov, Matthew E. Peters, and Noah A. Smith. 2019a. Linguistic knowledge and transferability of contextual representations. In *NAACL-HLT*.

Weijie Liu, Peng Zhou, Zhe Zhao, Zhiruo Wang, Qi Ju, Haotang Deng, and Ping Wang. 2019b. K-BERT: enabling language representation with knowledge graph. *CoRR*, abs/1909.07606.

Yinhan Liu, Myle Ott, Naman Goyal, Jingfei Du, Mandar Joshi, Danqi Chen, Omer Levy, Mike Lewis, Luke Zettlemoyer, and Veselin Stoyanov. 2019c. Roberta: A robustly optimized BERT pretraining approach. *CoRR*, abs/1907.11692.

Ilya Loshchilov and Frank Hutter. 2017. Fixing weight decay regularization in adam. *CoRR*, abs/1711.05101.

Tomas Mikolov, Kai Chen, G. S. Corrado, and J. Dean. 2013. Efficient estimation of word representations in vector space. In *ICLR*.

Matthew E. Peters, Mark Neumann, Robert L. Logan IV, Roy Schwartz, Vidur Joshi, Sameer Singh, and Noah A. Smith. 2019. Knowledge enhanced contextual word representations. *CoRR*, abs/1909.04164.

Fabio Petroni, Tim Rocktäschel, Patrick Lewis, Anton Bakhtin, Yuxiang Wu, Alexander H. Miller, and Sebastian Riedel. 2019. Language models as knowledge bases?

Dheeraj Rajagopal, Niket Tandon, Peter Clark, Bhavana Dalvi, and Eduard Hovy. 2020. What-if I ask you to explain: Explaining the effects of perturbations in procedural text. In *Findings of the Association for Computational Linguistics: EMNLP 2020*. Association for Computational Linguistics.

Maarten Sap, Ronan LeBras, Emily Allaway, Chandra Bhagavatula, Nicholas Lourie, Hannah Rashkin, Brendan Roof, Noah A. Smith, and Yejin Choi. 2019. Atomic: An atlas of machine commonsense for if-then reasoning.

Rebecca Sharp, Mihai Surdeanu, Peter Jansen, Peter Clark, and Michael Hammond. Creating causal embeddings for question answering with minimal supervision. In *ACL 2016 Proceedings of Conference on Empirical Methods in Natural Language Processing*. Association for Computational Linguistics.

Raphaël Sourty, Jose G. Moreno, François-Paul Servant, and Lynda Tamine-Lechani. 2020. Knowledge base embedding by cooperative knowledge distillation. In *Proceedings of the 28th International Conference on Computational Linguistics*. International Committee on Computational Linguistics.

Robyn Speer, Joshua Chin, and Catherine Havasi. 2017. Conceptnet 5.5: An open multilingual graph of general knowledge. In *Proceedings of the Thirty-First AAAI Conference on Artificial Intelligence*. AAAI Press.

Tianxiang Sun, Yunfan Shao, Xipeng Qiu, Qipeng Guo, Yaru Hu, Xuanjing Huang, and Zheng Zhang. 2020. Colake: Contextualized language and knowledge embedding.

Niket Tandon, B. D. Mishra, Keisuke Sakaguchi, Antoine Bosselut, and P. Clark. 2019. Wiqa: A dataset for "what if..." reasoning over procedural text. In *EMNLP/IJCNLP*.

Thomas Wolf, Lysandre Debut, Victor Sanh, Julien Chaumond, Clement Delangue, Anthony Moi, Pierric Cistac, Tim Rault, Rémi Louf, Morgan Funtowicz, Joe Davison, Sam Shleifer, Patrick von Platen, Clara Ma, Yacine Jernite, Julien Plu, Canwen Xu, Teven Le Scao, Sylvain Gugger, Mariama Drame, Quentin Lhoest, and Alexander M. Rush. Transformers: State-of-the-art natural language processing. In *Proceedings of the 2020 Conference on Empirical Methods in Natural Language Processing: System Demonstrations*. Association for Computational Linguistics.

Zhipeng Xie and Feiteng Mu. 2019. Distributed representation of words in cause and effect spaces. In *AAAI*.

A Appendix

A.1 CauseNet Processing Details

Our approach for fact selection is identical for COPA and WIQA. spaCy [2], a python based NLP library, is used for tokenization, lemmatization, and noun-phrase extraction.

CauseNet is formatted as a JSON file where each cause-effect entry consists of relevant concepts, source sentences, and associated linguistic pattern used for causal extraction. Causal facts need to be programmatically extracted and normalized. For simplicity, we define a causal fact as a tuple consisting of cause c and effect e, where $c, e \in Concepts$. $Concepts$ in CauseNet range from single word entities to multi-word expressions (e.g. rising sea levels). We normalize multi-word concepts by first lemmatizing all its constituent words and then joining them into a single token by replacing white spaces with underscores. So the causal concept "rising sea levels" would be normalized to token "rise_sea_level". After iterating through all the entries in CauseNet and normalizing the extracted facts, we store the cause and effect tokens in a two-column causal fact table.

[2]https://spacy.io/

Low Anisotropy Sense Retrofitting (LASeR) : Towards Isotropic and Sense Enriched Representations

Geetanjali Bihani and **Julia Taylor Rayz**
Department of Computer and Information Technology
Purdue University
{gbihani, jtaylor1}@purdue.edu

Abstract

Contextual word representation models have shown massive improvements on a multitude of NLP tasks, yet their word sense disambiguation capabilities remain poorly explained. To address this gap, we assess whether contextual word representations extracted from deep pretrained language models create distinguishable representations for different senses of a given word. We analyze the representation geometry and find that most layers of deep pretrained language models create highly anisotropic representations, pointing towards the existence of representation degeneration problem in contextual word representations. After accounting for anisotropy, our study further reveals that there is variability in sense learning capabilities across different language models. Finally, we propose **LASeR**, a 'Low Anisotropy Sense Retrofitting' approach that renders off-the-shelf representations isotropic and semantically more meaningful, resolving the representation degeneration problem as a post-processing step, and conducting sense-enrichment of contextualized representations extracted from deep neural language models.

1 Introduction

Distributional word representations, developed using large-scale training corpora, form an integral part of the modern NLP methodological paradigm. The advent of deep pre-trained neural language models such as BERT (Devlin et al., 2018) and GPT-2 (Radford et al., 2019) has led the shift towards the development of contextualized word representations. Unlike static word representation models, such as *word2vec* (Mikolov et al., 2013) and *fastText* (Bojanowski et al., 2017), which conflate multiple senses of a word within a single representation, contextual word representation models assign as many representations to a word as the number of contexts it appears in. The preference for contextual word representations can be attributed to the significant improvements they have achieved in a wide variety of NLP tasks including question answering, textual entailment, sentiment analysis (Peters et al., 2018; Devlin et al., 2018) and commonsense reasoning (Da and Kasai, 2019; Sap et al., 2020), to name a few.

To utilize contextual word representations as knowledge resources, it is necessary to determine their ability to mirror the linguistic relations employed in language (Schnabel et al., 2015). There is a growing body of literature that assesses whether contextual representations encode information about word-senses, where each word-sense portrays an aspect of the meaning of a given word in a given context (Jurafsky and Martin, 2019). A recent analysis by Nair et al. (2020) reported that contextual word representations can learn human-like word sense knowledge, where they compared cosine relatedness between homonyms and polysemous word senses against human sense-related judgements. When calculating cosine relatedness, such studies assume the encoded vector space to be isotropic in nature. Geometrically, isotropy in a vector space is defined as vectors being uniformly distributed across all directions, instead of occupying a narrow cone (Ethayarajh, 2019; Mu and Viswanath, 2018). Recent studies point towards anisotropy (lack of isotropy) in contextual word representations (Ethayarajh, 2019; Zhang et al., 2020), which affects prior conclusions regarding word-sense information encoded in vector spaces. For example, in an isotropic vector space, if cosine relatedness between word representations A and B is 0.9, we conclude them to be highly similar. But, if the vector space is anisotropic, where cosine relatedness between randomly sampled words is 0.95, then the representations A and B are deemed less similar than randomly sampled words. This shows that the existence and the extent of anisotropy in the vector space affects conclusions regarding whether representations are actually similar or merely a

Proceedings of Deep Learning Inside Out (DeeLIO): The 2nd Workshop on Knowledge Extraction and Integration for Deep Learning Architectures, pages 81–95
Online, June 10, 2021.

product of representation degeneration. Hence, when evaluating the sense learning capabilities of deep pretrained language models through vector relatedness measures, accounting and adjusting for vector space anisotropy becomes necessary.

In this regard, our work presents three key contributions. First, we analyze and adjust for anisotropy across contextual representations extracted from all layers of four language models (BERT, GPT-2, XLNet and ELECTRA). The representation space for each model encodes anisotropy, varying in terms of number and strength of common directions in model representations. We find that models learning unidirectional context create more anisotropic representations than models learning bidirectional context. Second, we observe that sense information is not equally encoded in all models, where (pseudo) bidirectional models learn to disambiguate word senses better than others. Moreover, sense information is better retained in the lower layers and significantly reduces in the upper model layers due to the representations getting more contextualized. Third, to address these preliminary findings and to contribute towards the creation of sense-coherent representations, we propose **LASeR**, a 'Low Anisotropy Sense Retrofitting' approach, bringing word representations closer to the goal of mirroring lexical semantic relations present in natural language while removing artifacts of representation degeneration from learned representations. Thus, we combine vector space transformation and knowledge-based vector specialization methods to create more isotropic and sense enriched representations, ensuring that we retain the distributional properties learnt during pretraining, while aligning and grounding the representation geometry towards better sense learning.

2 Related Work

Prior works which modify off-the-shelf embeddings to improve their lexical-semantic representation can be divided into two primary categories: (1) Anisotropy treatment methods and (2) Retrofitting methods. Anisotropy treatment methods focus on improving the isotropy of word vectors, promoting uniform distribution of information across all directions (Mu and Viswanath, 2018; Raunak et al., 2019; Wang et al., 2019). Isotropy in contextual vector spaces is regarded valuable, especially when utilizing vector geometry and relatedness measures in downstream analyses (Ethayarajh, 2019). Prior methods that focus on creating more isotropic vector spaces have suggested principle component manipulation (removal, extension) of vector spaces (Mu and Viswanath, 2018; Jo and Choi, 2018). To our knowledge, these methods have been proposed for static word representations, but are yet to be extended to contextual word representations extracted from a wide variety of language models.

On the other hand, retrofitting methods are focused on enhancing the representation geometry, by encoding lexical semantic relations through semantic specialization, a post-processing approach that enforces linguistic constraints on vector spaces by relying on external linguistic knowledge databases (Vulić and Mrkšić, 2018; Faruqui et al., 2015; Jo and Choi, 2018; Vulić, 2018). Semantic specialization as a post processing step (retrofitting) is currently limited to static word representations (Mu and Viswanath, 2018; Vulić and Mrkšić, 2018) where they have yielded impressive performance improvements over raw embeddings (Lauscher et al., 2020a). Existing methods towards semantic specialization of contextual representations primarily focus on retraining the model from scratch (Lauscher et al., 2020b) or post-hoc fine-tuning the model (Zhang et al., 2019; Peters et al., 2019; Wang et al., 2020). These methods are (1) resource-intensive (retraining or fine-tuning) and (2) do not address the representation degeneration problem in vector representations (Gao et al., 2018).

3 Methodology

3.1 Contextual Word Representation Models

In this work, we focus on contextual word representations generated from four transformer-based model architectures, i.e., BERT (Devlin et al., 2018), GPT-2 (Radford et al., 2019), XLNet (Yang et al., 2019) and ELECTRA (Clark et al., 2019). These models have been selected to assess the impact of variation in context learning and pre-training over the quality of generated representations, while keeping the number of hidden layers and dimensionality identical (*layers* = 13 (0 + 12); *dimensions* = 768). BERT and ELECTRA are both bidirectional learners, but they differ in terms of the pre-training objectives used to train the models: BERT uses a masked language modeling objective, limiting its learning to a small subset of word tokens; ELECTRA uses replaced token detection and is able to learn across a wider range of words tokens. On the other hand, GPT-2 and XLNet are both unidirectional learners, where GPT-2 learns only left-to-right context, while XLNet learns over all possible permutations of the given input. A comparison over these models in a uniform setting allows us to relate the behavior of representations to the context learning and pre-training choices of the respective models.

3.2 Data

Contextual word representations for individual words are generated by feeding sentences into the language model. In order to generate representations, we use sense annotated corpora from various SemEval and SenseEval tasks, including SensEval 3 task 1 (`S3-T1`) (Snyder and Palmer, 2004), SensEval 2 all-words task (`S2-TA`) (Edmonds and Cotton, 2001), SemEval 2013 task 12 (`S13-T12`) (Navigli et al., 2013), SemEval 2007 task 7 (`S7-T7`) (Navigli et al., 2007) and SemEval 2015 task 13 (`S15-T13`) (Moro and Navigli, 2015). To ensure that the Wordnet sense keys are unified across corpora, we utilize the Wordnet 3.0 sense annotated data (Vial et al., 2018) and summarized in Table 1. Since we want to evaluate sense-learning, we limit our analyses to multi-sense words, retaining nouns, adjectives and verbs that appear within the corpora as more than one sense.

3.3 Sense Learning Measures

In order to compute how sense information is encoded with the word representations, we define two word-sense specific cosine relatedness measures.

Definition 1 (Sense Similarity). Let w_s be a sense of the word w, appearing in m different contexts. Let v_l be the vector that maps the each word sense occurrence w_{s_i} to the vector space. Then, the average sense similarity between all m instances of the word sense w_s for layer ℓ is

$$SenSim_\ell(w_s) = \frac{1}{m} \sum_j \sum_{k \neq j} \cos(v_\ell(w_{s_j}), v_\ell(w_{s_k})) \quad (1)$$

This metric calculates the average cosine similarity between contextual representations of the same sense of a word.

Corpus	Nouns	Verbs	Adjectives
S3-T1	428	635	166
S2-TA	292	307	344
S13-T12	338	164	46
S7-T7	512	814	380
S15-T13	110	156	127
Total	1680	2076	1063

Table 1: Data Summary.

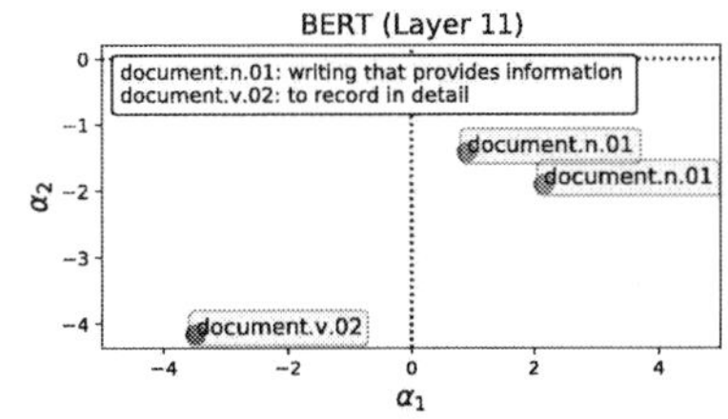

(a) Original Representations

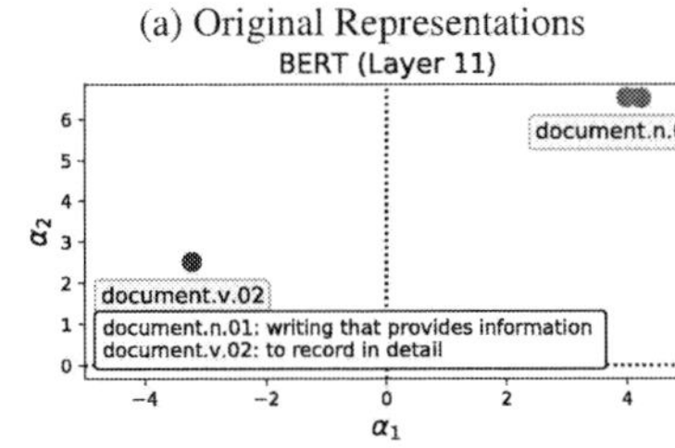

(b) LASeR Representations

Figure 1: Representations of different senses of the word 'document' (BERT Layer 11).

Definition 2 (Inter Sense Similarity). Let the word w have S different word senses, where w_a and w_b are a pair of different senses of w, appearing in m and n different contexts respectively and $a, b \in S$. Let v_l be the vector that maps each word sense occurrence w_{s_i} to the vector space. Then, the average inter sense similarity between the representations of all instances of the word w for layer ℓ is

$$InterSim_\ell(w) = \mathbb{E}_{a,b \in S}\left[\frac{1}{mn} \sum_{j=1}^{m} \sum_{i=1}^{n} \cos(v_\ell(w_{a_i}), v_\ell(w_{b_j}))\right] \quad (2)$$

This metric calculates the average cosine similarity between contextual representations of different senses of a word.

Thus, if a word w has $SenSim_l(w_s) > InterSim_l(w)$, it suggests that the representations for the same sense of a given word lie much closer together within the vector space, as compared to the representations of different senses of the same word. For example, a given word *'document'* can refer to multiple senses. According to WordNet 3.0, two senses of the word *'document'* are: (1) *document.n.01* - writing that provides information and (2) *document.v.02* - to record in detail.

As an example, we have visualized the representations of these two senses as encoded within the vector space of BERT (Layer 11), shown in Figure 1. The 'original' representations, shown in Figure 1(a), of the word sense *document.n.01* lie slightly close to each other, and farther away from the *document.v.02* representation. Thus, if a model is able to encode similar representations for same sense of a word, and distinguishable representations for different senses of a word, we claim that the model encodes sense information.

3.4 Anisotropy Adjusted Sense Similarity

In order to assess whether contextual word representations encode sense information, we measure the sense similarity and inter sense similarity for multi-sense words (polysemes and homonyms) in our datasets, across model layers. Given that contextual word representations encode anisotropy, we calculate anisotropy adjusted sense relatedness measures as follows.

$$B(v_\ell)=\mathbb{E}_{a,b\sim U}[\cos(v_\ell(a),v_\ell(b))] \quad (3)$$

$$SenSim_\ell(w_s)^{*}=SenSim_\ell(w_s)-B(v_\ell) \quad (4)$$

$$InterSim_\ell(w)^{*}=InterSim_\ell(w)-B(v_\ell) \quad (5)$$

This baseline calculation utilizes the theory from prior works examining contextualization in word representations (Ethayarajh, 2019). Here, $B(v_\ell)$ is the average cosine similarlity between n randomly sampled words, U is the set of all word occurrences, and $v_\ell(.)$ maps a word occurrence to the respective word representation in layer ℓ.

3.5 Low Anisotropy Sense Retrofitting

In this subsection, we describe LASeR, a post-processing approach to render off-the-shelf representations more isotropic and sense-enriched. Our approach builds upon the work on anisotropy reduction Mu and Viswanath (2018) and retrofitting Faruqui et al. (2015). Mu and Viswanath (2018) suggests that anisotropy can be reduced by removing primary components to make the representations more distinct and uniformly distributed within the vector space. We extend this to contextual word representations, evaluating the efficacy of removing primary components on anisotropy reduction in contextual representations. Turning towards retrofitting methods, we extend the retrofitting approach proposed by Faruqui et al. (2015), which targets static word representations and brings synonyms closer together in the vector space. Our work extends this retrofitting goal to contextual representations, where we aim to bring representations of same word-senses closer in the vector space, ensuring better sense disambiguation capabilities for representations.

Let $v(w_i)$ be the original contextual representation, $v'(w_i)$ be the *low anisotropy* contextual representation and $\hat{v}(w_i)$ be the *sense enriched* contextual representation of ith occurrence of a word sense w. We simulate an undirected knowledge graph $\Omega(V, E)$, where V represents the vocabulary of word tokens, each word token representing a vertex, and E represents all the edges connecting respective vertices. Finally, Q represent the matrix of post-processed representations $[\hat{v}(w_1), \hat{v}(w_2), \ldots, \hat{v}(w_n)]$. The approach works on achieving dual objectives, described as follows:
Objective 1 (Lower Anisotropy) : Remove top d common directions across all $v(w_i)$, to create $v'(w_i)$, creating more uniformly distributed word vectors and lowering anisotropy in representations.
Objective 2 (Sense Retrofitting) : Learn $\hat{v}(w_i)$ such that same sense representations lie closer together in vector space as well as close to the original embedding

Algorithm 1: LASeR (Low Anisotropy Sense Retrofitting).

Input: Raw word representation $\{v(w_i), w_i \in V\}$

1 Perform mean centering of vector: $\mu \leftarrow \frac{1}{|v|}\Sigma_{w_i \in V} v(w_i); \tilde{v}(w_i) \leftarrow v(w_i) - \mu$

2 Compute the PCA components: $u_{i1}, \ldots, u_{iD} \leftarrow PCA(\{\tilde{v}(w_i), w_i \in \mathcal{V}\})$

3 Remove top d principal components: $v'(w_i) \leftarrow \tilde{v}(w_i) - \Sigma_{j=1}^{d}\left(u_{ij}^{\top} v(w_i)\right) u_{ij}$

4 Apply retrofitting update: $\hat{v}(w_i) = \frac{\sum_{j:(i,j)\in E}\beta_{ij} v(w_j)+\alpha_i v(w_i)}{\sum_{j:(i,j)\in E}\beta_{ij}+\alpha_i}$

Output: Processed word representation $\hat{v}(w_i)$

The algorithm takes the original representations as input. These representations undergo mean centering and removal of dominant primary components (1,2,3) to reduce the anisotropy in the vector space. This is followed by a sense-retrofitting update (4) . Here, for each word token representation $v(w_i)$, we define its neighbours as $v(w_j), \forall j$ where $sense(w_i) = sense(w_j)$, and hyper-parameters β_{ij} and $\alpha_i = 1$ represent the reciprocal of the node degree of the word token w_i and edge weights respectively.

4 Results

We first show anisotropy analysis results (§4.1), further evaluating sense learning in contextual representations (§4.2). Finally, we present improvements in isotropy and lexical-semantic capabilities of the post-processed representations (§4.3).

4.1 Anisotropy Analysis

4.1.1 Similarity between Random Words

We first assess the amount of anisotropy encoded within contextual word vector spaces. We plot the average cosine similarity between 1K randomly sampled words, across different layers of language models, as seen in Figure 2. If a vector space is isotropic, the average cosine similarity between uniformly randomly sampled words would be 0 (Ethayarajh, 2019). Thus, the closer this measure is to 1, the more anisotropic the vector space. It can be seen that anisotropy evolves very differently across different models. Unidirectional language models (XLNet, GPT-2) portray far more anisotropy in word representations as compared to bidirectional language models (BERT, ELECTRA). Thus, language models learning one-directional context (L-to-R or R-to-L) encode more common directions in the representations as compared to those learnt from bidirectional context. Moreover, anisotropy monotonically increases across layers for BERT and XLNet, where both models have been trained on masked language modeling tasks. This shows that anisotropy accumulates in the upper layers of masked language models. The rate of increase in anisotropy in XLNet is higher than BERT representations, showing that permutation language modeling propagates higher amounts of anisotropy than traditional MLM. These results are consistent with the results obtained for all multi-sense words in the corpora (Appendix A).

4.1.2 Analysis of Principal Components

High anisotropy leads to word vectors being distributed within a very narrow cone in the vector space (Mimno and Thompson, 2017), further signifying that the word representations encode common directions (Mu and Viswanath, 2018). We plot the top two dominating directions for word repre-

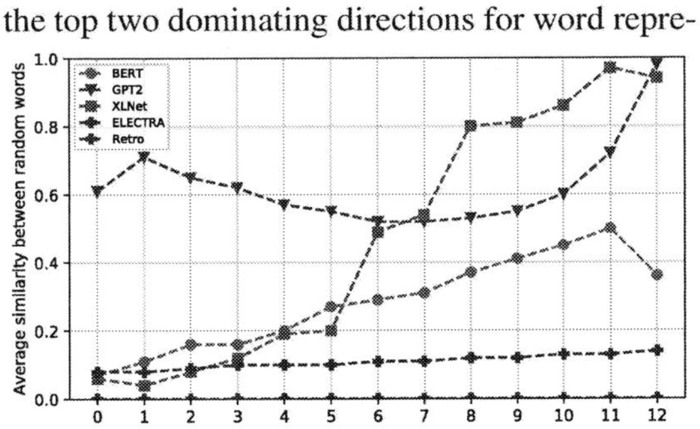

Figure 2: Average similarity between representations of randomly sampled words (1K) across model layers.

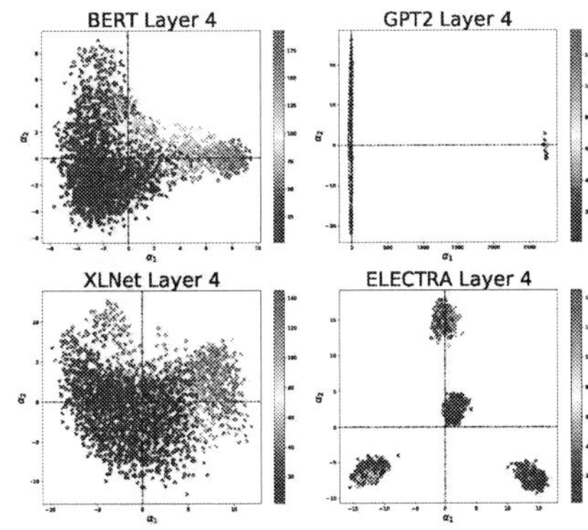

Figure 3: PCA plots of original word representations across top 2 primary components; Blue:Low frequency word tokens, Red:High frequency word tokens.

sentations, across each model's layers, as shown in Figure 3. These plots reveal that contextual word representations extracted from different language models are encoded extremely differently within the vector space. It can be seen that BERT and XLNet embeddings are more spread across the vector space, as compared to GPT-2 and ELECTRA embeddings. Moreover, ELECTRA embeddings form highly concentrated, yet separated regions of anisotropy, thus leading to an overall low score on the average similarity between randomly sampled words. Moreover, GPT-2 embeddings reveal extreme anisotropy, where most of the embeddings encode a singular common direction. The plots in Figure 3 also reveal that word frequency is significantly encoded in the top two principal components of BERT and XLNet embeddings. We cannot claim the same for GPT-2 and ELECTRA embeddings, where all embeddings cluster within highly dense regions of anisotropy.

We also evaluate anisotropy across model layers by assessing the explained variance across common directions encoded across all word representations. We plot the proportion of variance encoded within the top $d = 10$ dominant principal components of the original contextual representations across model layers, shown in Figure 4(a). While bidirectional models such as BERT and ELECTRA encode multiple common directions, unidirectional models like GPT-2 and XLNet embeddings primarily encode a singular common direction. For BERT embeddings, the top 10 primary components only contribute to 17-24% of the explained variance, showing that the embeddings are more uniformly distributed across the vector space, as compared to other models. GPT-2 provides a stark contrast,

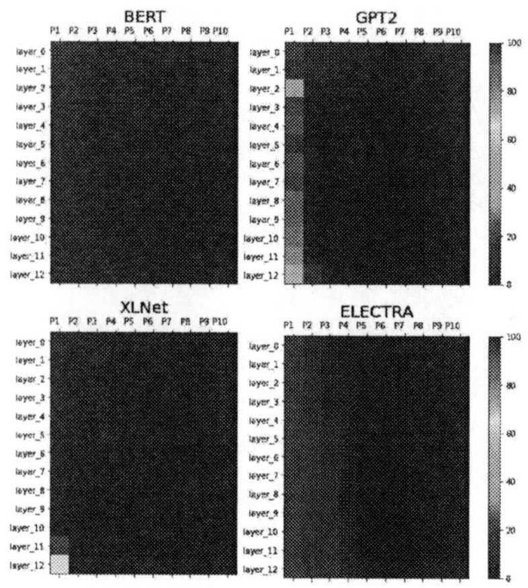

(a) Vanilla Representations.

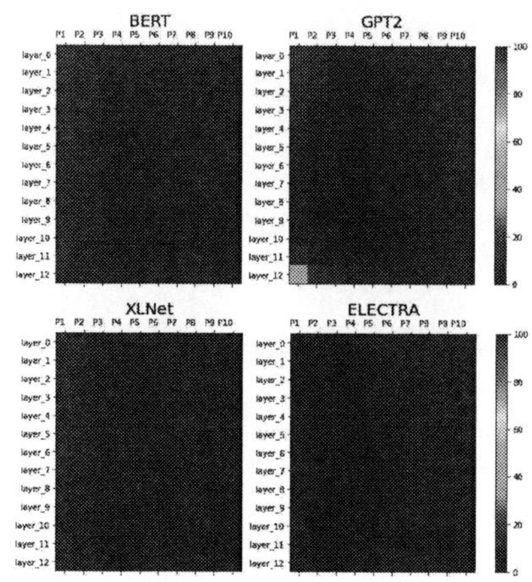

(b) Retrofitted Representations.

Figure 4: Plots of proportion of variance encoded within the top $d = 10$ dominant principal components of the contextual representations across model layers. The horizontal labels (P1-P10) represent each of the ten principal components, and the vertical labels (layer_0 - layer_12) represent each of the 12 model layers.

where the top 10 principal components contribute to up to 97% of the explained variance, highly concentrated within the first principal component, especially for the middle layers (Layer 3-8). XLNet embeddings capture comparatively lower common directions across model layers, apart from the final model layer (Layer 12), where 66.1% of the explained variance is concentrated within the first principal component. Thus, representations learnt through the goal of predicting the next word yields all representations extremely similar.

4.2 Sense Learning in Original Representations

A model differentiates between different word senses if it encodes representations of the same sense of a word to be more similar than the representations of other senses of the same word. We utilize the sense learning measures, defined in (§3.3) to assess whether original representations encode word-sense information. To examine overall learning across model layers, we calculate average sense similarity ($\overline{SenSim_\ell(w)}$) and mean difference between average sense similarity and inter sense similarity for a word token w (Δ).

$$\Delta = \overline{SenSim_\ell(w)} - InterSim_\ell(w); \quad \Delta \in [-1,1] \qquad (6)$$

Ideally, a language model being able to capture distinction between all word senses should have $\overline{SenSim_\ell(w)} = 1$ and $\Delta >> 0$. Here, higher sense similarities correspond to similar senses being encoded closer in the vector space and $\Delta > 0$ shows that on an average, same sense representations are more cohesive and well separated from the representations of other senses.

The evolution of sense learning over different models and their layers is portrayed using sense similarity measures, aggregated in Table 2. The reported vanilla sense similarity scores have been adjusted for anisotropy. Prior to retrofitting, BERT and XLNet embeddings for the same word senses show increasing dissimilarity across model layers, signifying a loss of sense information as the model gets more contextualized. The similarity between same sense word representations from the GPT-2 model is close to 0, showing that GPT-2 captures almost no sense information within the embedding

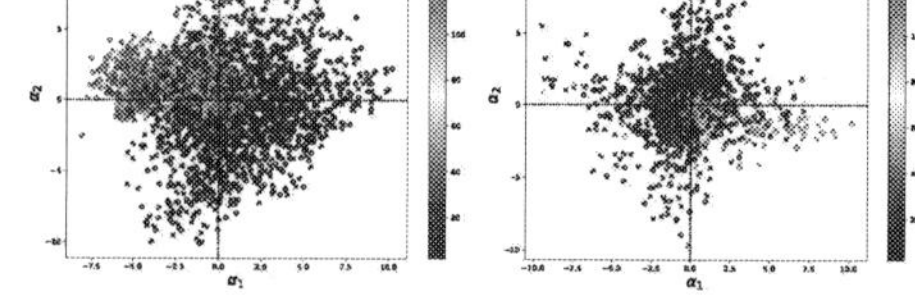

Figure 5: PCA plots of post-processed word representations across top two primary components, for each model.

space. ELECTRA embeddings remain consistent in terms of sense learning, not varying significantly across model layers. Furthermore, $\Delta \sim 0$ across all models shows that the original representations do not significantly distinguish between different senses of a given word. We visualize an example in Figure 1(a), where representations of the word *document* lie close together, regardless of the different senses associated with each occurrence. This finding signifies that the sole reliance on word form to learn representations does not suffice in helping the model distinguish between multiple senses of a given word.

4.3 Low Anisotropy Sense Retrofitting

We evaluate the efficacy of the proposed **LASeR** approach by comparing improvements in vector space isotropy and improved disambiguation of different word senses, as captured by retrofitted word representations.

4.3.1 Improvements in Isotropy

We conduct experiments by removing the most dominant common direction ($d = 1$) across generated embeddings across each model layer. This step yields significantly better isotropy in the resulting representations, where average similarity between randomly sampled words ($k = 1000$) is 0, across all models and model layers. Improvements can also be observed from the reduced proportions of explained variance in Figure 4(b). Overall, most of the anisotropy in the vector space is treated by removing one dominating direction. The retrofitted GPT-2 embeddings still show high anisotropy in the 12th layer, showing that more common directions remain to be addressed and possibly removed. These results show that high anisotropy effects can be reduced by removing the primary common directions across representations. The effect of this step is also visualized in Figure 5, where the representations are significantly less anisotropic and more uniformly spread across the vector space, encoding fewer artifacts of word frequency in the vector space, as compared to the original representations. For visualizations across all model layers, refer to Appendix B. In most cases, removal of the most dominant common direction can yield significant improvements in isotropy, as seen for BERT, XLNet and ELECTRA. In other cases, where representations share more than one significant common directions, such as for GPT-2, we can remove $d > 1$ common directions to treat anisotropy.

4.3.2 Improvements in Sense Representation

The retrofitting update applied to model representations enforces lexical-semantic constraints, bringing same sense representations closer together (increase same-sense cohesion) and pushing different sense representations farther apart (increase inter-sense separation).

Results from Table 2 show the efficacy of our retrofitting update ($\alpha_i = 1$), where average sense similarity between word vectors increases significantly, and similarity between same sense representations is significantly higher than similarity between representations of different senses. This portrays that the retrofitted representations encode same sense representations closer together and different sense representations farther apart. An example of how retrofitting changes the distribution of representations in the vector space is given in Figure 1(b), where inter-sense separation between two different senses of the word *document* increases and same-sense cohesion between representations of the same word sense increases.

Across the model layers, the retrofitting significantly increases sense similarity and Δ. The improved similarity scores can be seen in Figure 6, which show that retrofitting moves same sense representations to be more similar than different sense representations. For BERT embeddings, the improvements are more visible in the upper model layers, as they create more separated different sense representations, and more cohesive same sense representations. The slight drop in cohesion ($SenseSim$) is due to the model's upper layers being more contextualized than the lower layers, also suggested in prior works on contextualization (Ethayarajh, 2019). Retrofitting is extremely effective for GPT-2 embeddings. This can been from the drastic increase in sense similarity ($SenseSim$) and Δ, showing that same sense representations lie closer and different sense representations lie farther apart in the retrofitted vector space.

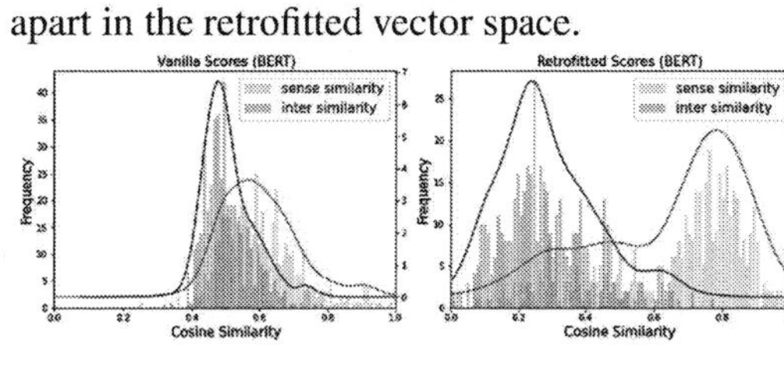

Figure 6: Effect of retrofitting on sense relatedness in contextual embeddings. Here, retrofitted embeddings portray higher same-sense similarity and lower inter-sense similarity.

Layer	BERT		GPT-2		XLNet		ELECTRA	
	vanilla (Δ)	*retro* (Δ)	*vanilla*(Δ)	*retro* (Δ)	*vanilla* (Δ)	*retro* (Δ)	*vanilla* (Δ)	*retro* (Δ)
0	0.82 (0.00)	0.93 (0.04)	0.08 (0.05)	0.49 (0.38)	0.08 (-0.27)	0.85 (-0.02)	0.49 (0.11)	0.64 (0.25)
1	0.74 (0.02)	0.90 (0.08)	0.06 (0.03)	0.51 (0.38)	0.80 (0.02)	0.90 (0.08)	0.50 (0.11)	0.65 (0.26)
2	0.66 (0.05)	0.88 (0.13)	0.06 (0.02)	0.51 (0.38)	0.65 (0.07)	0.83 (0.18)	0.50 (0.12)	0.65 (0.26)
3	0.62 (0.07)	0.85 (0.18)	0.08 (0.04)	0.52 (0.39)	0.58 (0.10)	0.80 (0.23)	0.50 (0.12)	0.65 (0.26)
4	0.54 (0.09)	0.82 (0.23)	0.09 (0.05)	0.53 (0.39)	0.46 (0.09)	0.76 (0.27)	0.51 (0.12)	0.65 (0.26)
5	0.43 (0.10)	0.77 (0.28)	0.09 (0.05)	0.53 (0.39)	0.40 (0.09)	0.72 (0.30)	0.52 (0.13)	0.65 (0.27)
6	0.36 (0.12)	0.72 (0.33)	0.11 (0.06)	0.54 (0.40)	0.23 (0.06)	0.68 (0.31)	0.51 (0.12)	0.65 (0.27)
7	0.31 (0.11)	0.68 (0.35)	0.12 (0.06)	0.55 (0.41)	0.20 (0.06)	0.66 (0.33)	0.52 (0.13)	0.65 (0.27)
8	0.25 (0.10)	0.65 (0.37)	0.11 (0.07)	0.55 (0.41)	0.08 (0.03)	0.64 (0.33)	0.53 (0.13)	0.64 (0.26)
9	0.22 (0.09)	0.63 (0.39)	0.11 (0.07)	0.56 (0.42)	0.07 (0.02)	0.63 (0.34)	0.53 (0.13)	0.64 (0.26)
10	0.22 (0.09)	0.63 (0.38)	0.09 (0.06)	0.56 (0.43)	0.05 (0.01)	0.65 (0.34)	0.53 (0.13)	0.64 (0.27)
11	0.20 (0.07)	0.63 (0.36)	0.08 (0.04)	0.55 (0.43)	0.01 (0.00)	0.65 (0.32)	0.53 (0.13)	0.64 (0.27)
12	0.24 (0.09)	0.62 (0.37)	0.00 (0.01)	0.51 (0.40)	0.02 (0.00)	0.63 (0.32)	0.53 (0.13)	0.64 (0.27)

Table 2: Average sense similarity scores across model layers; $\Delta = SenSim_\ell(w) - InterSim_\ell(w)$.

While originally, the representations were highly anisotropic and held no sense learning, the retrofitted embeddings capture better sense distinction. XLNet embeddings, much like BERT, encode representations of the same word form closer together, especially in lower model layers, regardless of the respective word-sense distinction. Post-retrofitting, XLNet embeddings show higher similarity between same word senses and lower similarity between different word senses, revealing better sense disambiguation. Compared to the other three models, original ELECTRA embeddings are able to capture more distinction between different sense representations and more similarity between same sense representations. Our retrofitting update further improves these lexical-semantic relations in the representation space.

5 Discussion

Recent works have discussed whether contextualized word representations extracted from deep pretrained language models encode word sense knowledge within the representation space. Studies suggest that while lower layer BERT embeddings encode more semantic information (Reif et al., 2019), the upper layer embeddings become increasingly contextual (Ethayarajh, 2019). Works exploring semantic capabilities of representations have also used nearest neighbour classifier probes to assess whether same-sense representations are classified together (Reif et al., 2019; Nair et al., 2020). Since these classifiers show slightly better accuracy than classifying as the most frequent sense, they claim that the representation space encodes sense information. Although our work supports this conclusion, we additionally argue that after accounting for anisotropy, the cohesion between same sense representations and separation between different sense representations is not significant. Here, the principal premise of the removal of anisotropy prior to injecting sense information is based on creating an embedding space geometry where the effects of representation degeneration are reduced. The representation degeneration of embeddings reduces their representational power (Gao et al., 2018). Thus, to improve the representation ability of embeddings, we deem it important to create methods that promote representations that are not only lexico-semantic relation enriched but also isotropic. Our method reveals that the additional step of lowering anisotropy renders improved representation geometry, where word vectors are not constricted within a narrow cone, and are uniformly distributed within the vector space. Further, sense-retrofitting on contextualized word representations render same sense representations more similar and different sense representations more different, increasing the word sense disambiguation capabilities of the encoded representations.

Our work presents a novel intrinsic evaluation of sense information in word embeddings, required to understand the sense geometry encoded by various models. In the future, we will focus on integrating sense information in contextual word representations by extending this approach to words that are unseen to the LASeR model, and further perform extrinsic analyses of the embeddings.

6 Conclusion

In this work, we investigated the geometry of contextual word representations for isotropy and sense disambiguation capabilities. We further proposed a post-processing approach for anisotropy treatment and semantic enrichment of contextual word representations, by transforming the vector space using principal component manipulation and lexical semantic knowledge-based sense-retrofitting. Our method significantly reduced the impact of representation degeneration problem, improving isotropy within the vector space and rendered off-the-shelf contextual word vectors semantically more meaningful. In the future work, we will study the impact of changes in retrofitting hyperparameters and variable removal of primary components on representation quality. Further, we will focus on extrinsic evaluation of the impact of anisotropy removal and sense retrofitting on downstream word-sense disambiguation tasks.

Acknowledgements

This work is partially supported by National Science Foundation grant number 1737591. We would like to thank the three anonymous reviewers for their helpful comments and suggestions. We would also like to thank the members of the AKRaNLU lab at Purdue University for their feedback.

References

Piotr Bojanowski, Edouard Grave, Armand Joulin, and Tomas Mikolov. 2017. Enriching word vectors with subword information. *Transactions of the Association for Computational Linguistics*, 5:135–146.

Kevin Clark, Minh-Thang Luong, Quoc V Le, and Christopher D Manning. 2019. Electra: Pre-training text encoders as discriminators rather than generators. In *International Conference on Learning Representations*.

Jeff Da and Jungo Kasai. 2019. Cracking the contextual commonsense code: Understanding commonsense reasoning aptitude of deep contextual representations. *EMNLP 2019*, page 1.

Jacob Devlin, Ming-Wei Chang, Kenton Lee, and Kristina Toutanova. 2018. Bert: Pre-training of deep bidirectional transformers for language understanding. *arXiv preprint arXiv:1810.04805*.

Philip Edmonds and Scott Cotton. 2001. Senseval-2: overview. In *Proceedings of SENSEVAL-2 Second International Workshop on Evaluating Word Sense Disambiguation Systems*, pages 1–5.

Kawin Ethayarajh. 2019. How contextual are contextualized word representations? comparing the geometry of bert, elmo, and gpt-2 embeddings. *arXiv preprint arXiv:1909.00512*.

Manaal Faruqui, Jesse Dodge, Sujay Kumar Jauhar, Chris Dyer, Eduard Hovy, and Noah A Smith. 2015. Retrofitting word vectors to semantic lexicons. In *Proceedings of the 2015 Conference of the North American Chapter of the Association for Computational Linguistics: Human Language Technologies*, pages 1606–1615.

Jun Gao, Di He, Xu Tan, Tao Qin, Liwei Wang, and Tieyan Liu. 2018. Representation degeneration problem in training natural language generation models. In *International Conference on Learning Representations*.

Hwiyeol Jo and Stanley Jungkyu Choi. 2018. Extrofitting: Enriching word representation and its vector space with semantic lexicons. In *Proceedings of The Third Workshop on Representation Learning for NLP*, pages 24–29.

Dan Jurafsky and James H Martin. 2019. Speech and language processing (3rd draft ed.).

Anne Lauscher, Ivan Vulić, Edoardo Maria Ponti, Anna Korhonen, and Goran Glavaš. 2020a. Specializing unsupervised pretraining models for word-level semantic similarity. In *Proceedings of the 28th International Conference on Computational Linguistics*, pages 1371–1383.

Anne Lauscher, Ivan Vulić, Edoardo Maria Ponti, Anna Korhonen, and Goran Glavaš. 2020b. Specializing unsupervised pretraining models for word-level semantic similarity. In *Proceedings of the 28th International Conference on Computational Linguistics*, pages 1371–1383, Barcelona, Spain (Online). International Committee on Computational Linguistics.

Tomas Mikolov, Kai Chen, Greg Corrado, and Jeffrey Dean. 2013. Efficient estimation of word representations in vector space. *arXiv preprint arXiv:1301.3781*.

David Mimno and Laure Thompson. 2017. The strange geometry of skip-gram with negative sampling. In *Empirical Methods in Natural Language Processing*.

Andrea Moro and Roberto Navigli. 2015. Semeval-2015 task 13: Multilingual all-words sense disambiguation and entity linking. In *Proceedings of the 9th international workshop on semantic evaluation (SemEval 2015)*, pages 288–297.

Jiaqi Mu and Pramod Viswanath. 2018. All-but-the-top: Simple and effective post-processing for word representations. In *6th International Conference on Learning Representations, ICLR 2018*.

Sathvik Nair, Mahesh Srinivasan, and Stephan Meylan. 2020. Contextualized word embeddings encode aspects of human-like word sense knowledge. In *Proceedings of the Workshop on the Cognitive Aspects of the Lexicon*, pages 129–141.

Roberto Navigli, David Jurgens, and Daniele Vannella. 2013. Semeval-2013 task 12: Multilingual word sense disambiguation. In *Second Joint Conference on Lexical and Computational Semantics (* SEM)*,

Volume 2: Proceedings of the Seventh International Workshop on Semantic Evaluation (SemEval 2013), pages 222–231.

Roberto Navigli, Kenneth C Litkowski, and Orin Hargraves. 2007. Semeval-2007 task 07: Coarse-grained english all-words task. In *Proceedings of the Fourth International Workshop on Semantic Evaluations (SemEval-2007)*, pages 30–35.

Matthew E Peters, Mark Neumann, Mohit Iyyer, Matt Gardner, Christopher Clark, Kenton Lee, and Luke Zettlemoyer. 2018. Deep contextualized word representations. *arXiv preprint arXiv:1802.05365*.

Matthew E. Peters, Mark Neumann, Robert Logan, Roy Schwartz, Vidur Joshi, Sameer Singh, and Noah A. Smith. 2019. Knowledge enhanced contextual word representations. In *Proceedings of the 2019 Conference on Empirical Methods in Natural Language Processing and the 9th International Joint Conference on Natural Language Processing (EMNLP-IJCNLP)*, pages 43–54, Hong Kong, China. Association for Computational Linguistics.

Alec Radford, Jeffrey Wu, Rewon Child, David Luan, Dario Amodei, and Ilya Sutskever. 2019. Language models are unsupervised multitask learners. *OpenAI blog*, 1(8):9.

Vikas Raunak, Vivek Gupta, and Florian Metze. 2019. Effective dimensionality reduction for word embeddings. In *Proceedings of the 4th Workshop on Representation Learning for NLP (RepL4NLP-2019)*, pages 235–243.

Emily Reif, Ann Yuan, Martin Wattenberg, Fernanda B Viegas, Andy Coenen, Adam Pearce, and Been Kim. 2019. Visualizing and measuring the geometry of bert. In *Advances in Neural Information Processing Systems*, volume 32. Curran Associates, Inc.

Maarten Sap, Vered Shwartz, Antoine Bosselut, Yejin Choi, and Dan Roth. 2020. Commonsense reasoning for natural language processing. In *Proceedings of the 58th Annual Meeting of the Association for Computational Linguistics: Tutorial Abstracts*, pages 27–33, Online. Association for Computational Linguistics.

Tobias Schnabel, Igor Labutov, David Mimno, and Thorsten Joachims. 2015. Evaluation methods for unsupervised word embeddings. In *Proceedings of the 2015 conference on empirical methods in natural language processing*, pages 298–307.

Benjamin Snyder and Martha Palmer. 2004. The english all-words task. In *Proceedings of SENSEVAL-3, the Third International Workshop on the Evaluation of Systems for the Semantic Analysis of Text*, pages 41–43.

Loïc Vial, Benjamin Lecouteux, and Didier Schwab. 2018. Ufsac: Unification of sense annotated corpora and tools. In *Language Resources and Evaluation Conference (LREC)*.

Ivan Vulić. 2018. Injecting lexical contrast into word vectors by guiding vector space specialisation. In *Proceedings of The Third Workshop on Representation Learning for NLP*, pages 137–143.

Ivan Vulić and Nikola Mrkšić. 2018. Specialising word vectors for lexical entailment. In *Proceedings of the 2018 Conference of the North American Chapter of the Association for Computational Linguistics: Human Language Technologies, Volume 1 (Long Papers)*, pages 1134–1145.

Bin Wang, Angela Wang, Fenxiao Chen, Yuncheng Wang, and C-C Jay Kuo. 2019. Evaluating word embedding models: Methods and experimental results. *APSIPA transactions on signal and information processing*, 8.

Ruize Wang, Duyu Tang, Nan Duan, Zhongyu Wei, Xuanjing Huang, Cuihong Cao, Daxin Jiang, Ming Zhou, et al. 2020. K-adapter: Infusing knowledge into pre-trained models with adapters. *arXiv preprint arXiv:2002.01808*.

Zhilin Yang, Zihang Dai, Yiming Yang, Jaime Carbonell, Russ R Salakhutdinov, and Quoc V Le. 2019. Xlnet: Generalized autoregressive pretraining for language understanding. In *Advances in neural information processing systems*, pages 5753–5763.

Zhengyan Zhang, Xu Han, Zhiyuan Liu, Xin Jiang, Maosong Sun, and Qun Liu. 2019. ERNIE: Enhanced language representation with informative entities. In *Proceedings of the 57th Annual Meeting of the Association for Computational Linguistics*, pages 1441–1451, Florence, Italy. Association for Computational Linguistics.

Zhong Zhang, Chongming Gao, Cong Xu, Rui Miao, Qinli Yang, and Junming Shao. 2020. Revisiting representation degeneration problem in language modeling. In *Proceedings of the 2020 Conference on Empirical Methods in Natural Language Processing: Findings*, pages 518–527.

A Anisotropy Across All Words

We plot the average similarity between all words (multi-sense nouns, verbs and adjectives) extracted from the annotated corpora, across model layers, as shown in Figure 7.

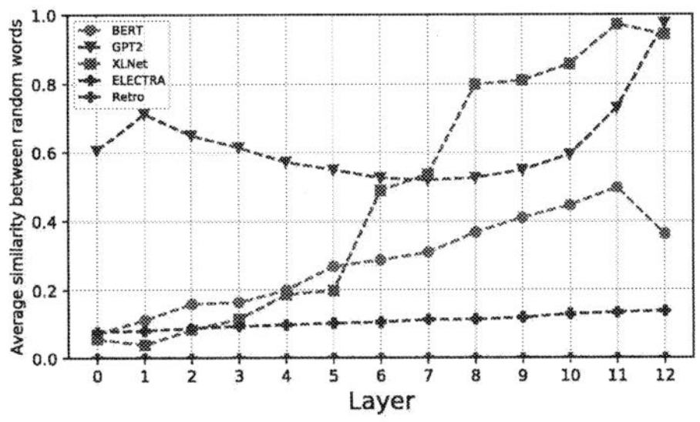

Figure 7: Average similarity between representations of randomly sampled words across model layers.

B PCA Plots of Word Representations

We plot distribution of word representations across the vector space, for all models across their layers. To assess whether word frequency is encoded within vector dimensions, we color code representations ranging from low frequency words (Blue) to high frequency words (Red). The plots are given in Figure 8 (BERT), Figure 9 (GPT-2), Figure 10 (XLNet) and Figure 11 (ELECTRA). We see that using LASeR post-processing ($d = 1$ and hyperparameters mentioned in the main text), anisotropy in vector space is significantly treated. For extremely anisotropic models such as GPT2 and ELECTRA, remove of the first primary component yields more uniformly spread word representations.

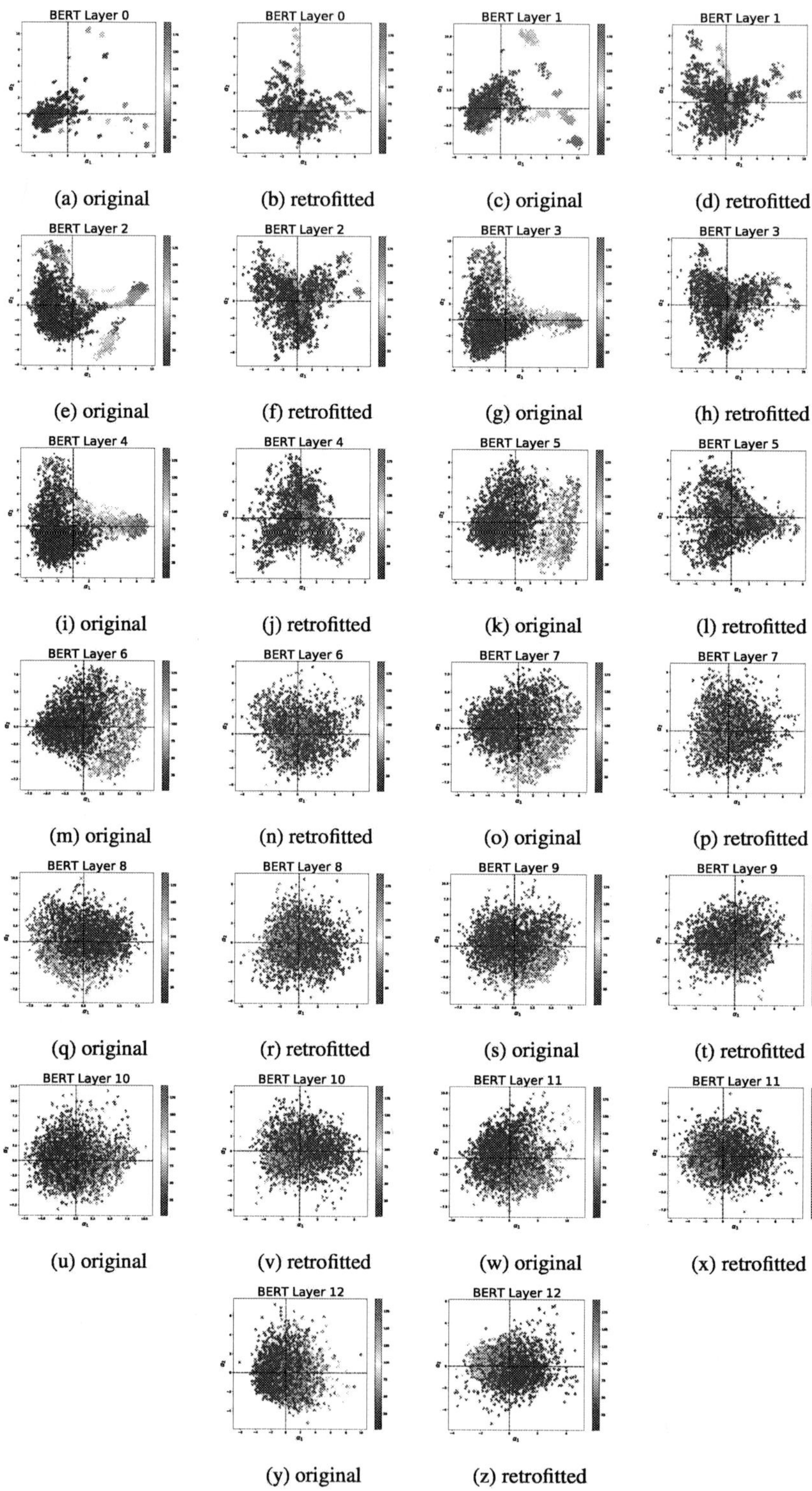

(a) original (b) retrofitted (c) original (d) retrofitted
(e) original (f) retrofitted (g) original (h) retrofitted
(i) original (j) retrofitted (k) original (l) retrofitted
(m) original (n) retrofitted (o) original (p) retrofitted
(q) original (r) retrofitted (s) original (t) retrofitted
(u) original (v) retrofitted (w) original (x) retrofitted
(y) original (z) retrofitted

Figure 8: PCA Plots of BERT Word Representations.

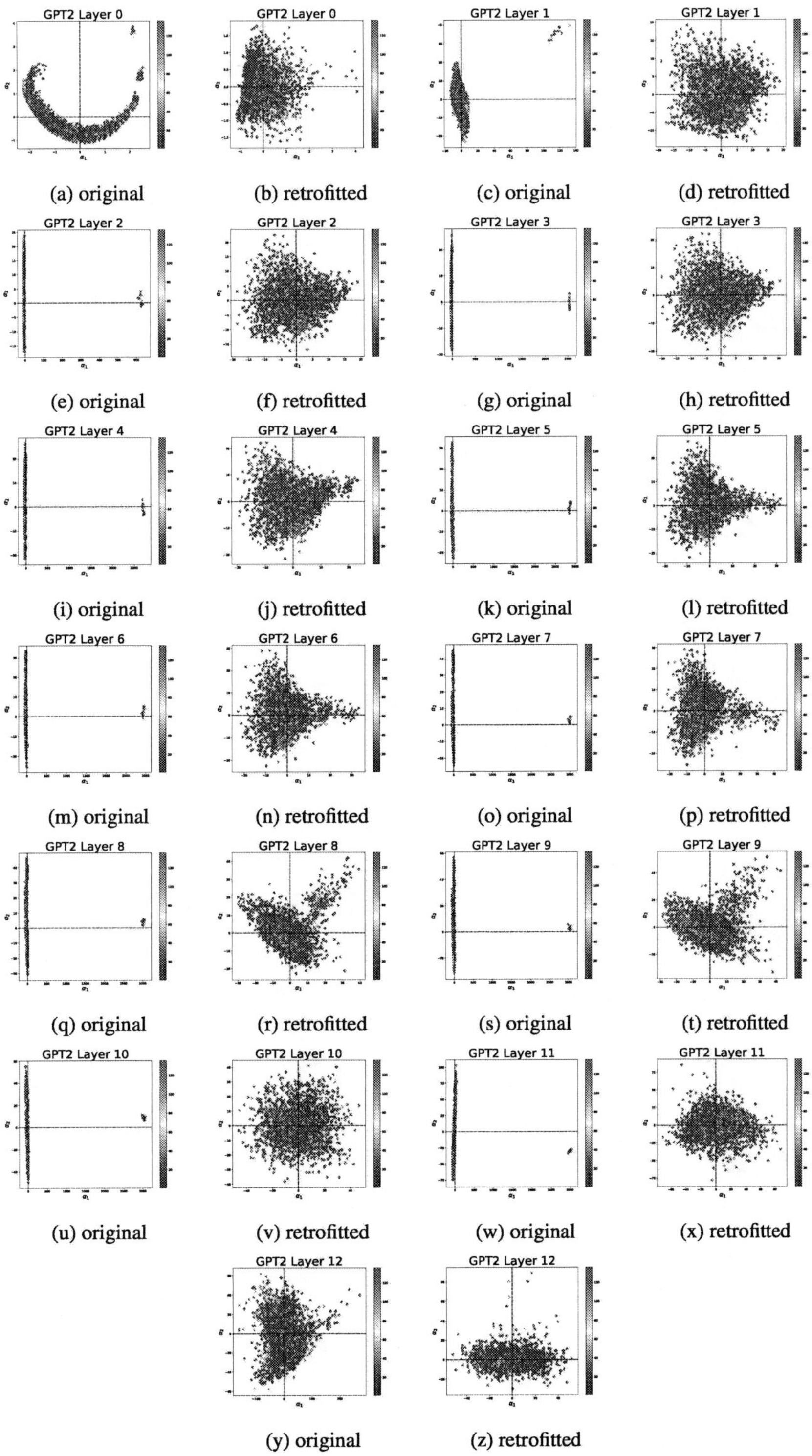

(a) original (b) retrofitted (c) original (d) retrofitted
(e) original (f) retrofitted (g) original (h) retrofitted
(i) original (j) retrofitted (k) original (l) retrofitted
(m) original (n) retrofitted (o) original (p) retrofitted
(q) original (r) retrofitted (s) original (t) retrofitted
(u) original (v) retrofitted (w) original (x) retrofitted
(y) original (z) retrofitted

Figure 9: PCA Plots of GPT2 Word Representations.

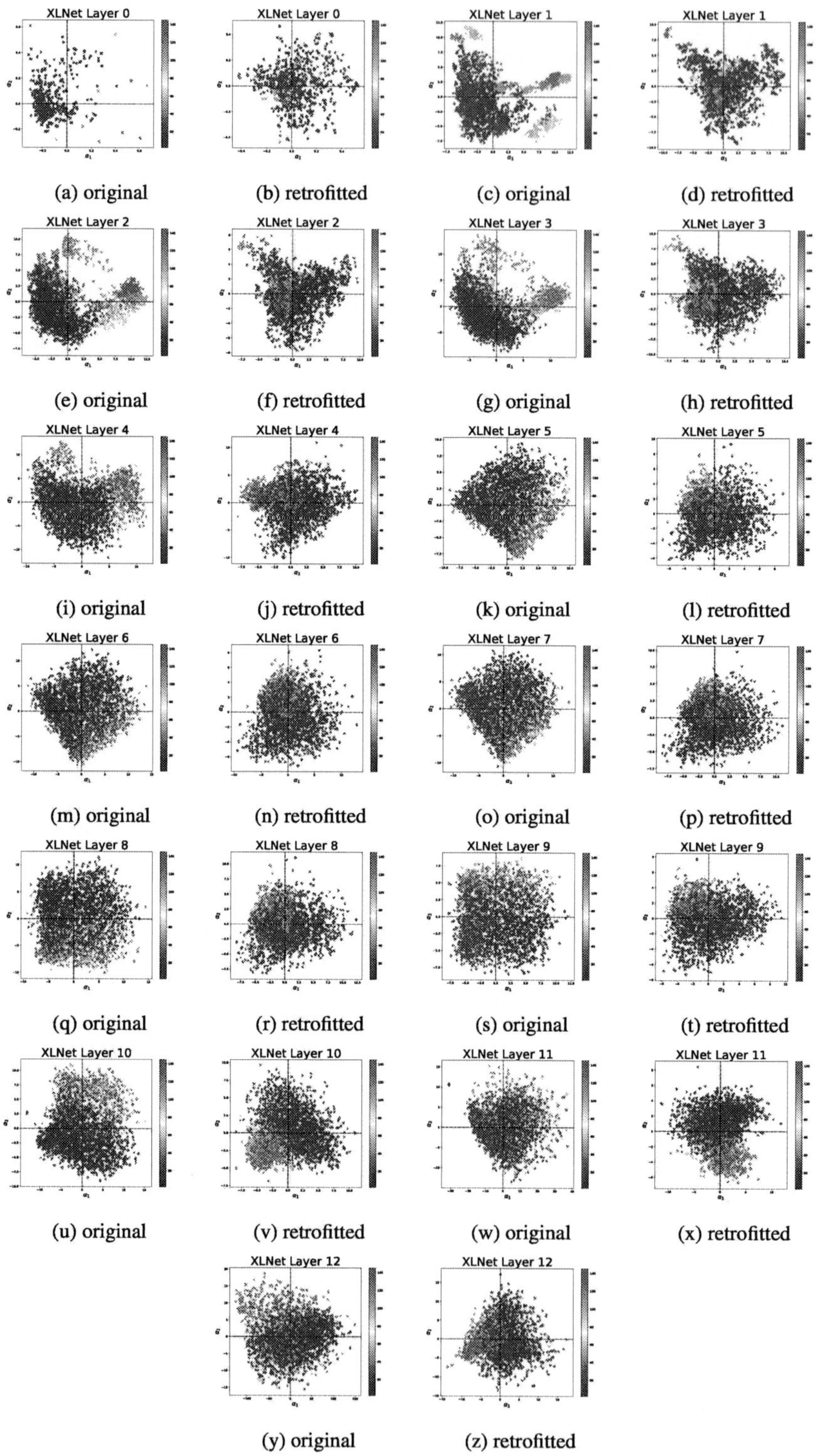

(a) original (b) retrofitted (c) original (d) retrofitted

(e) original (f) retrofitted (g) original (h) retrofitted

(i) original (j) retrofitted (k) original (l) retrofitted

(m) original (n) retrofitted (o) original (p) retrofitted

(q) original (r) retrofitted (s) original (t) retrofitted

(u) original (v) retrofitted (w) original (x) retrofitted

(y) original (z) retrofitted

Figure 10: PCA Plots of XLNet Word Representations.

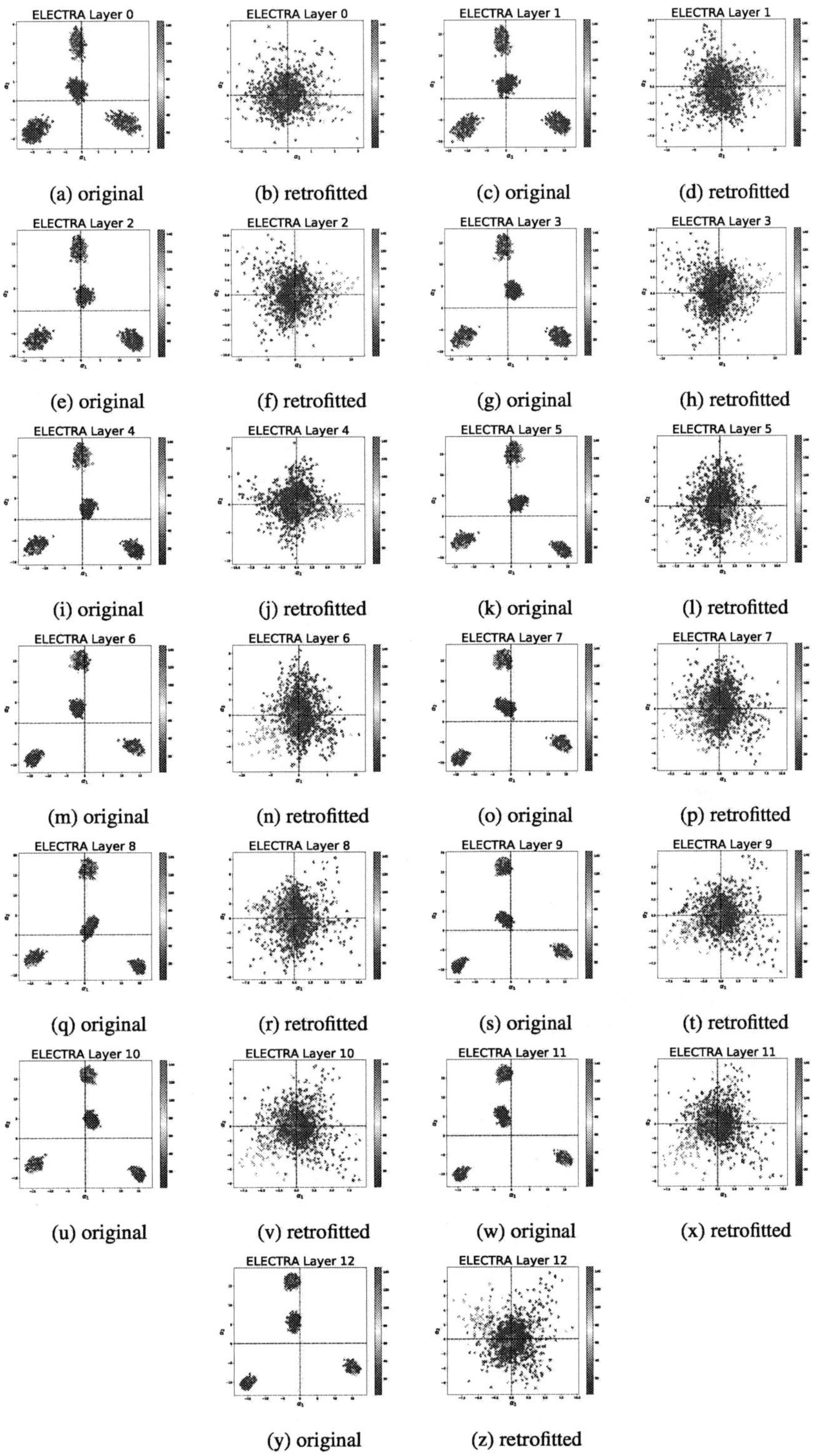

(a) original (b) retrofitted (c) original (d) retrofitted

(e) original (f) retrofitted (g) original (h) retrofitted

(i) original (j) retrofitted (k) original (l) retrofitted

(m) original (n) retrofitted (o) original (p) retrofitted

(q) original (r) retrofitted (s) original (t) retrofitted

(u) original (v) retrofitted (w) original (x) retrofitted

(y) original (z) retrofitted

Figure 11: PCA Plots of ELECTRA Word Representations.

KW-ATTN: Knowledge Infused Attention for Accurate and Interpretable Text Classification

Hyeju Jang[1, 2], Seojin Bang[3], Wen Xiao[1], Giuseppe Carenini[1], Raymond Ng[1], Young Ji Lee[4]
[1]Department of Computer Science, University of British Columbia
[2]British Columbia Centre for Disease Control
[3]School of Computer Science, Carnegie Mellon University
[4]School of Nursing, University of Pittsburgh
{hyejuj, xiaowen3, carenini, rng}@cs.ubc.ca
seojinb@cs.cmu.edu, leeyoung@pitt.edu

Abstract

Text classification has wide-ranging applications in various domains. While neural network approaches have drastically advanced performance in text classification, they tend to be powered by a large amount of training data, and interpretability is often an issue. As a step towards better accuracy and interpretability especially on small data, in this paper we present a new knowledge-infused attention mechanism, called KW-ATTN (KnoWledge-infused ATTentioN) to incorporate high-level concepts from external knowledge bases into Neural Network models. We show that KW-ATTN outperforms baseline models using only words as well as other approaches using concepts by classification accuracy, which indicates that high-level concepts help model prediction. Furthermore, crowdsourced human evaluation suggests that additional concept information helps interpretability of the model.

1 Introduction

Text classification is a fundamental Natural Language Processing (NLP) task which has wide-ranging applications such as topic classification (Lee et al., 2011), fake news detection (Shu et al., 2017), and medical text classification (Botsis et al., 2011). The current state-of-the-art approaches for text classification use Neural Network (NN) models. When these techniques are applied to real data in various domains, there are two problems. First, neural approaches tend to require large training data, but it is often the case that large training data or pretrained embeddings are not available in domain-specific applications. Second, when text classification is applied in real life, not only the accuracy, but also the interpretability or explainability of the model is important.

As a way to improve interpretability as well as accuracy, incorporating high-level concept information can be useful. High-level concepts could help interpretation of model results because concepts summarize individual words. The concept "*medication*" would be not only easier to interpret than the words "*ibuprofen*" or "*topiramate*" but also contributes to understanding the words better. In addition, higher-level concepts can make raw words with low frequency more predictive. For instance, the words "*hockey*" and "*archery*" might not occur in a corpus frequently enough to be considered important by a model, but knowing that they belong to the concept "*athletics*" could give more predictive power to the less frequent individual words depending on the task, because the frequency of the concept "*athletics*" would be higher than individual words.

In this paper we present a new approach that incorporates high-level concept information from external knowledge sources into NN models. We devise a novel attention mechanism, KW-ATTN, that allows the network to separately and flexibly attend to the words and/or concepts occurring in a text, so that attended concepts can offer information for predictions in addition to the information a model learns from texts or a pretrained model. We test KW-ATTN on two different tasks: patient need detection in the healthcare domain and topic classification in general domains. Data is annotated with high level concepts from external knowledge bases: BabelNet (Navigli and Ponzetto, 2012) and UMLS (Unified Medical Language System) (Lindberg, 1990). We also conduct experiments and analyses to evaluate how high-level concept information helps with interpretability of resultant classifications as well as accuracy. Our results indicate that KW-ATTN improves both classification accuracy and interpretability.

Our contribution is threefold: (1) We propose a novel attention mechanism that exploits high-level concept information from external knowledge bases, designed for providing an additional layer of interpretation using attention. This attention

Proceedings of Deep Learning Inside Out (DeeLIO): The 2nd Workshop on Knowledge Extraction and Integration for Deep Learning Architectures, pages 96–107
Online, June 10, 2021.

mechanism can be plugged in different architectures and applied in any domain for which we have a knowledge resource and a corresponding tagger. (2) Experiments show KW-ATTN makes statistically significant gains over a widely used attention mechanism plugged in RNN models and other approaches using concepts. We also show that the attention mechanism can help prediction accuracy when added on top of the pretrained BERT model. Additionally, our attention analysis on patient need data annotated with BabelNet and UMLS indicates that choice of external knowledge impacts the model's performance. (3) Lastly, our human evaluation using crowdsourcing suggests our model improves interpretability.

Section 2 relates prior work to ours. Section 3 explains our method. Section 4 evaluates our model on two different tasks in terms of classification accuracy. Section 5 describes our human evaluation on interpretability. Section 6 concludes.

2 Related Work

2.1 Knowledge-infused Neural Networks

There has been a growing interest in incorporation of external semantic knowledge into neural models for text classification. Wang et al. (2017) proposed a framework based on convolutional neural networks that combines explicit and implicit representations of short text for classification by conceptualizing a short text as a set of relevant concepts using a large taxonomy knowledge base. Yang and Mitchell (2017) proposed KBLSTM, a RNN model that uses continuous representations of knowledge bases for machine reading. Xu et al. (2017) incorporated background knowledge with the format of entity-attribute for conversation modeling. Stanovsky et al. (2017) overrided word embeddings with DBpedia concept embeddings, and used RNNs for recognizing mentions of adverse drug reaction in social media.

More advanced neural architectures such as transformers has been also benefited by external knowledge. (Zhong et al., 2019) proposed a Knowledge Enriched Transformer (KET), where contextual utterances are interpreted using hierarchical self-attention and external commonsense knowledge is dynamically leveraged using a context-aware affective graph attention mechanism. ERNIE (Zhang et al., 2019) integrated entity embeddings pretrained on a knowledge graph with corresponding entity mentions in the text to augment the text representation. KnowBERT (Peters et al., 2019) trained BERT for entity linkers and language modeling in a multitask setting to incorporate entity representation. K-BERT (Liu et al., 2020) injected triples from knowledge graphs into a sentence to obtain an extended tree-form input for BERT.

Although all these prior models incorporated external knowledge into advanced neural architectures to improve model performance, they didn't pay much attention to interpretability benefits. There have been a few knowledge-infused models that considered interpretability. Kumar et al. (2018) proposed a two-level attention network for sentiment analysis using knowledge graph embedding generated using WordNet (Fellbaum, 2012) and top-k similar words. Although this work mentions interpretability, it did not show whether/how the model can help interpretability. Margatina et al. (2019) incorporated existing psycho-linguistic and affective knowledge from human experts for sentiment related tasks. This work only showed attention heatmap for an example.

Our work is distinguished from others in that KW-ATTN is designed in consideration of not only accuracy but also interpretability of the model. For this reason, KW-ATTN allows separately and flexibly attending to the words and/or concepts so that important concepts for prediction can be included in prediction explanations, adding an extra layer of interpretation. We also perform human evaluation to see the effect of incorporating high-level concepts on interpretation rather than just showing a few visualization examples.

2.2 Interpretability

Interpretability is the ability to explain or present a model in an understandable way to humans (Doshi-Velez and Kim, 2017). This interpretability is beneficial for developers to understand the model, help identify and possibly fix issues with the model, or to enhance the model. It is crucial for application end users because knowing explanations or justifications behind a model's prediction can further assist in decision making or the task at hand.

To provide interpretability, researchers have used inherently interpretable models such as sparse linear regression models, decision trees, or rule sets. These models are generally useful for simple prediction tasks, yet it is difficult to apply them to complicated tasks. To interpret complex models used for complex tasks, one can examine how prediction changes between two different inputs (Shrikumar et al., 2017; Lundberg and Lee, 2017) or by locally perturbing an input (Ribeiro et al., 2016). However, a recent and popular method in NLP has been the use of an attention mechanism, which was found to be effective in helping interpret complex models by highlighting which inputs are informative to prediction (Wang et al., 2016; Lin et al., 2017; Ghaeini et al., 2018; Seo et al., 2016).

Along the lines of work using attention for interpretation, our model improves attention-based interpretability by using high-level concept information. To our knowledge, no prior work used external high-level concept information for better interpretability.

3 Our Approach

3.1 External Knowledge Bases

We automatically annotate data with high-level concepts from two knowledge bases: BabelNet and UMLS.

3.1.1 BabelNet

BabelNet (Navigli and Ponzetto, 2012) is a constantly growing semantic network which connects concepts and named entities in a large network of semantic relations, currently made up of about 16 million entries, called Babel synsets. In our study, we use the hypernyms of Babel synsets as additional higher-level concept information for the raw words or phrases in text. We first map texts with concepts in Babel synsets using an entity linking toolkit, Babelfy (Moro et al., 2014), and then retrieve hypernyms, high-level concepts, of the concepts using BabelNet APIs. Table 1 shows example annotations for the sentence "My mom was diagnosed with stage 3 ovarian cancer."

Expression	BabelNet Concepts
"Mom"	*mother*
"diagnosed"	*analyze*
"state"	*state*
"ovarian cancer"	*disease*

Table 1: Babelfy annotations for BabelNet concepts

3.1.2 Unified Medical Language System (UMLS)

We also exploit an external medical ontology, the UMLS (Lindberg, 1990), for a comparison with BabelNet for the patient need task. The UMLS is a high-level ontology for organizing a great number of concepts in the biomedical domain, which provides unified access to many different biomedical resources. On top of the UMLS, the UMLS semantic network (McCray, 2003) implements an upper-level conceptual layer for all UMLS concepts. This semantic network categorizes all concepts in the UMLS into 134 semantic types and provides 54 links between the semantic types to represent relationships in the biomedical domain.

We use the semantic types of the UMLS semantic network as additional higher-level concepts because it can abstract more fine clinical concepts that exist across much larger medical ontologies such as UMLS, SNOMED (Benson, 2010), and ICT-10(Organization et al., 2017). To obtain the semantic types, we annotate raw text by using MetaMap. Table 2 shows an example from MetaMap. Note that the automatic annotation can be noisy (e.g., incorrect semantic types for "mom" in the example).

Expression	UMLS Semantic Type
"Mom"	*Quantitative Concept*
"Diagnosed"	*Diagnostic Procedure*
"Stage 3 ovarian cancer"	*Neoplastic Process*

Table 2: MetaMap annotations for UMLS concepts

3.2 Incorporating High-Level Concepts

To incorporate high-level concept information into a NN model, we design a new attention mechanism, KW-ATTN, which allows giving separate but complementary attentions to a word and its corresponding concept. To test KW-ATTN, we choose a one-level RNN architecture with an attention mechanism (1L), a hierarchical RNN architecture with an attention mechanism (2L) as in Hierarchical Attention Network (HAN) (Yang et al., 2016), and a pretrained BERT (Devlin et al., 2018). Our 2L model architecture is shown in Figure 1. The whole architecture begins with words in each sentence as input. They are embedded and encoded using a word encoder, and then the resulting hidden representations move forward to a word-concept attention layer after being concatenated with the corresponding concept embeddings. This part is different from common RNN architectures for text classification, where only the hidden representations from the word encoder are used for a word-level attention layer. Then, the output of this attention layer is used in the next phase, a sentence encoder in case of 2L, and a final layer in case of

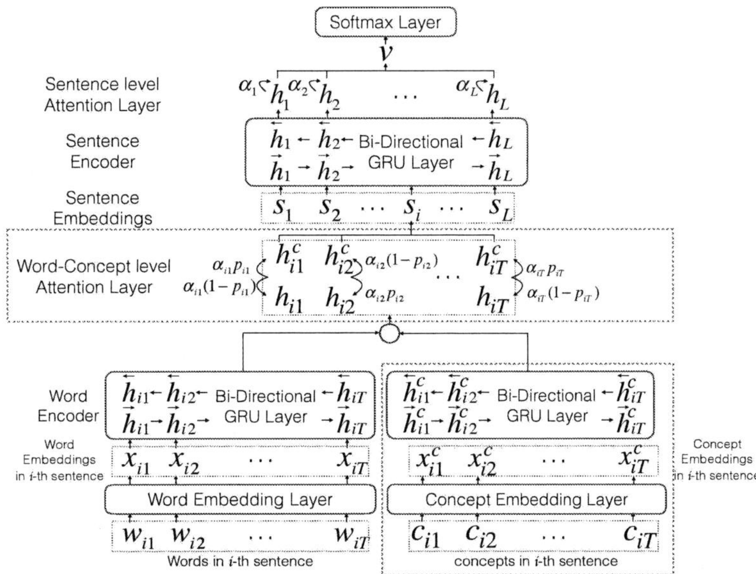

Figure 1: Overview of KW-ATTN (in red) when plugged in HAN (2L). KW-ATTN 1L does not have the sentence embeddings, sentence encoder, and sentence level attention layers. KW-BERT replaces the word encoder with a pretrained BERT model.

1L. When KW-ATTN is applied to BERT (KW-BERT), the word encoder using RNN is replaced with BERT and then the output of KW-ATTN is feed to the final layer as in 1L.

Word and Concept Embeddings: Each word w_{it} (a one-hot vector, where $t \in \{1, \cdots, T\}$ and T_i is the number of words in the i-th sentence) is mapped to a real-valued vector x_{it} through an embedding matrix W_e by $x_{it} = W_e w_{it}$. To use high-level concepts, each concept c_{it} (a one-hot vector) corresponding to word w_{it} is also mapped to x^c_{it} through an embedding matrix W_{ec} by $x^c_{it} = W_{ec} c_{it}$. When a word is not mapped into a concept, we map the concept vector to a *no-concept* vector.

Word and Concept Encoders: We encode T words in each sentence i using a word encoder. The corresponding T concepts are also encoded using a concept encoder. We use a bi-directional GRU (Cho et al., 2014) to build a representation for the t-th word and concept in the sentence i, denoted as h_{it} and h^c_{it} as follows:

$$\overrightarrow{h}_{it} = \overrightarrow{GRU}(x_{it}),\ \overleftarrow{h}_{it} = \overleftarrow{GRU}(x_{it}),$$
$$h_{it} = [\overrightarrow{h}_{it}, \overleftarrow{h}_{it}],$$
$$\overrightarrow{h}^c_{it} = \overrightarrow{GRU}(x^c_{it}),\ \overleftarrow{h}^c_{it} = \overleftarrow{GRU}(x^c_{it}),$$
$$h^c_{it} = [\overrightarrow{h}^c_{it}, \overleftarrow{h}^c_{it}].$$

where $t \in \{1, \cdots, T\}$, and T_i is the number of words in the i-th sentence. Note that we obtain a representation that summarizes the information of the whole sentence around the t-th word w_{it} by concatenating the forward hidden state $\overrightarrow{h}_{it}$ and the backward hidden state $\overleftarrow{h}_{it}$.

Word-Concept Attention: In this stage, the output from the word encoder h_{it} and the corresponding concept output h^c_{it} are combined by going through a word-concept level attention layer. This layer consists of two attention levels. One is an attention vector α_{it} that tracks the importance of a combined word-concept, which we call "combined" attention. The other attention vector we call "balancing" attention p_{it} is for flexibly incorporating concept information into the model. The balancing attention is introduced to give attention complementarily to both word and concept because the importance of a word or concept can differ at times. For example, when "football" is attended, we don't know if "football" itself is important for the prediction, or "football", "tennis", and all others together are important. Additionally, this balancing attention helps the model to be more robust to noisy concepts that may be caused by automatic annotation.

In detail, each position in a sentence includes a word and its corresponding concept. For each position, combined attention α is assigned, which represents attention to the position (both word and concept). Within each position, balancing attention p is assigned to a concept and its complement $1-p$ is assigned to the corresponding word. As seen in Figure 1, α_{it} represents the contribution of the position t (both the t-th word and its concept) to the meaning of the sentence i in the sentence, while $1 - p_{it}$ represents a weight on the word and p_{it} represents a weight on the word's concept. Hence, $\alpha_{it}(1-p_{it})$ and $\alpha_{it}p_{it}$ represent the contribution of the t-th word and concept to the sentence i, respectively. This attention mechanism using combined and balancing attentions enables us to give separate but complementary attentions to the word and concept. In addition, we set p_{it} as 0 when a word does not have a corresponding concept because in this case the model should attend only the word. The new attention mechanism is as follows:

$$\begin{aligned} u_{it} &= \tanh(W_\alpha[h_{it}, h_{it}^c] + b_\alpha) \\ p_{it} &= \text{sigmoid}(w_p[h_{it}, h_{it}^c] + b_p) \\ \alpha_{it} &= \frac{\exp\left(u_{it}^T u_\alpha\right)}{\sum_t \exp\left(u_{it}^T u_\alpha\right)} \\ s_i &= \sum_t \alpha_{it}\left((1-p_{it})h_{it} + p_{it}h_{it}^c\right) \end{aligned}$$

where W_α, b_α, w_p, b_p and u_α are the model parameters. s_i is a representation for the i-th sentence.

s_i is used as an input to the next layer, the sentence encoder in case of 2L (HAN). Then, the sentence representations h_i go through the sentence level attention layer, and build a document vector v, as shown in Figure 1. In case of a 1L model or a BERT model, all the words in the document are treated as one single sentence. Then, there is a single representation s_1, which is equivalent to the document vector v in the 2L case.

Finally, based on this vector v, classification probability for each class is computed in the final layer.

4 Experiments

KW-ATTN is evaluated on two different datasets for patient need detection (need dataset) (Jang et al., 2019) and topic classification (Yahoo answers) (Zhang et al., 2015). We use different tasks to more broadly demonstrate the benefits of our approach.

4.1 Data

Patient need detection: This dataset is for detecting patient need in posts from an online cancer discussion forum. We use the health information need data for binary classification (450 positive samples out of 853). Although this dataset is quite small, we choose to use it because RNN approaches showed effectiveness (Jang et al., 2019) and it is a dataset we can compare the effect of general knowledge graph and domain-specific medical ontology. We build two different concept annotations with BabelNet and UMLS.

Yahoo answers: This dataset is for topic classification. It incluldes 10 different topics such as Society & Culture and Sports. To generate a dataset that is still small but one order of magnitude bigger than the need dataset, we randomly select 10,000 instances of the dataset enforcing a balanced dataset (1,000 instances per topic), and annotate them with BabelNet concepts.

The data statistics of our concept annotated datasets are summarized in Table 3. The ratios of words that match concepts are 6.6%(the need dataset with BabelNet), 36.3%(the need dataset with UMLS), and 8.9%(Yahoo answers). In all our experiments, we perform 10-fold cross-validation ten times. For each run, we use 80% of data for training, 10% for development, and 10% for test.

4.2 Experiment Settings

We compare our KW-ATTN 1L and 2L with a widely used attention mechanism leveraging only words (Yang et al., 2016; Ying et al., 2018). We call it **ATTN**. In addition, we use other proven approaches that leverage concept information: **Concept-replace** uses input documents where raw words are replaced with the corresponding BabelNet/UMLS high-level concepts when the mappings are available, as in (Stanovsky et al., 2017; Magumba et al., 2018). **Concept-concat** uses concatenation to combine word and concept embeddings, as in (Wang et al., 2017; Zhou et al., 2018). **Attn-concat** uses concatenation to combine a concept embedding and a hidden representation of word and use ATTN. **Attn-gating** uses a gate mechanism to select salient features of a hidden word representation, conditioned on the concept information. Both Attn-concat and Attn-gating are state-of-the-art presented by Margatina et al. (2019). All these methods are tested in 1L and 2L settings.

The parameters for RNN models are tuned on

Data	Classes	#D	#S	#W	#C(D)	#C(S)	Voca(W)	Voca(C)
Need-BN	2	853	19.2	11.0	13.9	0.7	12,484	629
Need-UMLS	2	853	19.2	11.0	75.6	6.15	12,484	118
Yahoo answers	10	10,000	7.9	12.9	10.1	1.3	65,003	3,816

Table 3: Data summary statistics. Need-BN: need dataset with BabelNet concepts, Need-UMLS: need dataset with UMLS concepts, #D: # of documents, #S: average # of sentences per document, #W: # of words per sentence, #C(D): # of annotated concepts per document, #C(S): # of annotated concepts per sentence, Voca(W): word vocabulary size, Voca(C): concept vocabulary size.

	Yahoo answers		Need BN		Need UMLS	
Model	1L	2L	1L	2L	1L	2L
ATTN	.557	.574	.706	.684	.706	.684
Concept-replace	.560	.563	.698	.671	.699	.676
Concept-concat	.569	.571	.664	.602	.702	.661
Attn-concat (Margatina et al., 2019)	.585	.577	.669	.669	.709	.681
Attn-gating (Margatina et al., 2019)	.593	.577	.712	.587	.679	.631
KW-ATTN	**.605***	**.597***	**.721***	**.692***	**.727***	**.703***

Table 4: Comparison of KW-ATTN against baselines for 1-level (1L) and 2-level (2L) networks, in terms of F1 macro scores. *: indicates statistically significant improvement over the next best model via t-test ($p < 0.05$).

development data in the following ranges: word embedding dimension: 25, 50, 100, 200, GRU size: 10, 25, 50, learning rate: 0.1, 0.05, 0.01, 0.005, 0.001, 0.0005, and 0.0001. The word embeddings are initialized randomly, and concept embeddings are initialized using pretrained concept embeddings trained on English web data and BabelNet semantic network, SW2V (Mancini et al., 2016).[1] We randomly initialize word embeddings rather than using pretrained embeddings because our model often uses phrases recognized by knowledge resources, and they are usually not part of pretrained embeddings. We optimize parameters using Adam (Kingma and Ba, 2014) with epsilon 1e-08, decay 0.0, a mini-batch size of 32, and the loss function of negative log-likelihood loss. We use early-stopping.

In addition, we also conduct experiments with pre-trained BERT Word Encoder (**KW-BERT**) to see if injecting concept also helps the model trained on large-scale corpora. We use the 'bert-base-uncased' model, and the dimension of Concept bi-GRU is 384, making the concept representation the same dimension of BERT word representations. We show both the results from frozen models and fine-tuned models.The frozen models do not update parameters of pretrained models, i.e., they use pre-trained contextualized embeddings without fine-tuning. In contrast, fine-tuned BERT or KW-BERT are adapted to the target task. The learning rates for learning frozen models and fined-tuned models are 2e-3 and 1e-6, respectively.

4.3 Experiment Results

The results are shown in Table 4. First, we observe that 2L models do not perform better than 1L models. This could be because 2L models are too large for the data sizes, especially for the need data. It could indicate that the document itself is not too long to put in one RNN, and the sentence boundary might not be necessary for the classification. Second, using concept information alone does not perform well in general, which indicates that concept information alone is not sufficient. Using word and concept information together (concept-concat) also do not always result in a gain of performance. Third, Attn- models generally perform better than simpler Concept- models. However, KW-ATTN significantly improves over all other models for both tasks, indicating the effeteness of our mechanism.

In addition, Table 4 shows that for the need task, while both types of concepts help the prediction, UMLS concepts help slightly more. This suggests that choosing the right knowledge resource, especially for domain specific tasks, is critical for prediction performance.

To see the effect of data size on the model, we

[1] We also tried SW2V Wiki, SensEmbed (Iacobacci et al., 2015) and SENSEMBERT (Scarlini et al., 2020) pretrained embeddings, but SW2V WEB slightly outperformed others (no statistical significance).

compare KW-ATTN and ATTN across different data sizes of Yahoo reviews (Table 5). KW-ATTN models significantly outperform ATTN models consistently. However, as the data size becomes larger, performance gains, while still significant, diminish, showing that, in this domain, our method is more effective when the data is smaller.

	1L		2L	
Data size	ATTN	KW-ATTN	ATTN	KW-ATTN
2,500	.460	**.523*** (+.063)	.479	**.516*** (+.037)
5,000	.527	**.561*** (+.034)	.539	**.555*** (+.016)
10,000	.557	**.605*** (+.048)	.574	**.585*** (+.011)
20,000	.611	**.634*** (+.023)	.618	**.621*** (+.003)
30,000	.624	**.645*** (+.021)	.631	**.635*** (+.004)

Table 5: F1 macro scores by data size in Yahoo answers. * indicates statistically significant improvement over corresponding ATTN model via t-test ($p < 0.05$).

Table 6 shows the comparison between BERT and KW-BERT. We can see that additional concept information substantially improves the performances on both datasets in case of frozen models whereas it only improves the performance on the need dataset when fine-tuned. The results from the frozen models indicate that the encoded concepts provide complementary information to BERT. However, when fine-tuned, KW-BERT outperforms BERT only on the Need dataset. This could be because a BERT model itself is learnt on Wikipedia, which may lack knowledge on medicine. Although BERT learns task-specific knowledge during finetuning, but the data is small and additional high-level concept information still helps. This may suggest that KW-BERT could be more beneficial for small data problems in domains that require more expert knowledge than Wikipedia can provide.

We can also notice that the frozen models poorly perform on the Need dataset compared with RNN models (Table 4) whereas they drastically outperform on the Yahoo dataset. This could be because the documents in the Need dataset are conversational coming from an online forum, which are markedly different from the Wikipedia dataset on which BERT is trained. We can see that when fine-tuned, both BERT and KW-BERT beat RNN models, which suggests that finetuning allows learning task/domain specific information.

Attention Analysis: To better understand why UMLS concepts help more on the need dataset, we draw the distributions of concept attentions in models with both annotations in Figure 2. Interestingly, for the average attention of each concept,

	Yahoo answers		Need UMLS	
Model	Frozen	Finetuned	Frozen	Finetuned
BERT	.652	**.698**	.585	.735
KW-BERT	**.701***	.695	**.652***	**.744***

Table 6: Comparison of BERT baseline and BERT with KW-ATTN (KW-BERT), in terms of F1 macro scores. *: indicates statistically significant improvement over the corresponding BERT baseline via t-test ($p < 0.05$).

the attention for the model using BabelNet annotations is greater than the model using UMLS annotations. However, the max attention of each concept is greater for UMLS annotations than for BabelNet annotations, which indicates that UMLS concepts are more actively used. Additionally, attentions from the model using UMLS concepts show lower variance. This result indicates that the model using UMLS concepts assigns a similar attention to each concept whereas the model using BabelNet concepts sometimes assigns small or large attentions to concept. In other words, the model using UMLS concepts consistently select a concept to attend whereas the model using BabelNet concepts is less consistent. Intuitively, this makes sense as the UMLS concepts are domain specific to the task of health information need detection.

5 Human Evaluation on Interpretability

We use human evaluation to see whether additional high-level concept information given by KW-ATTN can be beneficial for interpretation. We compare top-ranked attended words/concepts by KW-ATTN with top-ranked attended words by ATTN. We use Amazon Mechanical Turk (MTurk). Since we use crowdsourcing, we conduct evaluation only on the Yahoo reviews dataset for topic classification, which covers general domains.

5.1 Experiment Design

For each Human Intelligence Task (HIT) in MTurk, we provide a prediction and its explanation for a text, generated from either KW-ATTN 1L or ATTN 1L.[2] We use 1L because one attention layer is simpler to interpret. Then, we ask whether MTurkers would assign the given topic to the text based on the given explanation. Only one explanation is randomly given, and which model the explanations is from is not shown to MTurkers. Additionally, we ask them to rate their confidence in their answer.

[2]The screenshot of the MTurk user interface can be found in the Appendix.

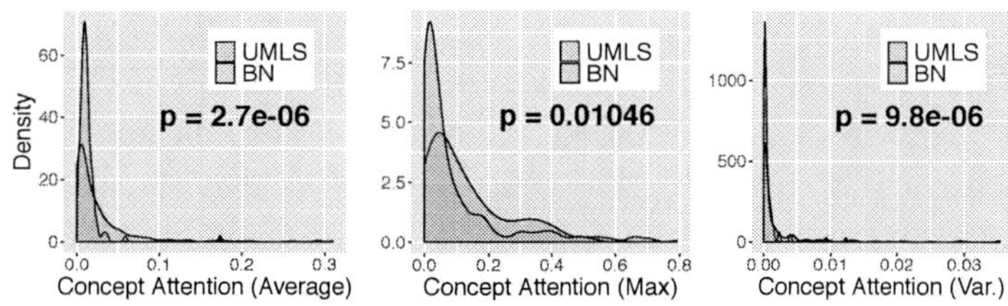

Figure 2: Distributions of concept attentions for the two annotations for patient need detection: UMLS and BabelNet (BN). For each concept, average (left), maximum (middle), variance (right) of attention values from all occurrences are used.

Explanation Type	Example
No concept	"java, yields, best, language, results, built"
KW same number	"java as a(n) object-oriented_programming_language, ide as a(n) application, php as a(n) free_software, swing, best, looking"
KW same length	"java as a(n) object-oriented_programming_language, ide as a(n) application, php as a(n) free_software"
KW replacement	"object-oriented_programming_language, application, free_software, swing, best, looking"

Table 7: Examples of different types of explanations used for human evaluation.

We assume that attention can be used for prediction explanations based on (Wiegreffe and Pinter, 2019; Serrano and Smith, 2019). We choose to ask about the validity of a given prediction unlike prior work that asked to guess a model's prediction based on an explanation (Nguyen, 2018; Chen et al., 2020). Although we acknowledge that the model's prediction may bias the annotators, we choose this approach since humans have high-level concepts as background knowledge. Humans do not require external additional concept information for guessing a correct topic label among multiple topic options especially when the given topic options are distinct from each other. For example, although the high-level concept "athletics" is not given for the word "baseball" in an explanation, humans would not have a problem with classifying it into the *sports* category when given topic options are *sports* and *music*. However, high-level concepts may help users to have more confidence when interpreting the explanation for a given topic. Therefore, we evaluate users' trusts about the system indirectly by requesting them to assess a given topic based on an explanation and rate their confidence.

The top 6 ranked features (words and concepts) with the highest attention weights are selected as an explanation. The high-level concept of a word is included in the explanation as the format of "[word] as a(n) [concept]" only when the balancing weight, p, for the concept is non-zero (See Section 3.2). We remove stopwords and punctuations from explanations.

Four different types of explanations are given to MTurkers and compared in our analysis as shown in Table 7. A **no-concept** explanation consists of 6 words. A **KW-same-number** explanation also contains 6 words and their corresponding concepts if they exist. A **KW-same-length** is composed of 3 words and their corresponding concepts if they exist. A **KW-replacement** consists of 6 words or concept. When a word has a lower attention value than its corresponding concept according to the p attention value, it is replaced by its concept in the explanation. Note that **KW-** explanations are all from the same model using KW-ATTN, and **no-concept** explanations are from a model using ATTN.

We randomly pick 200 samples that have correct predicted labels made by both systems. To make the 200 samples, we draw 100 samples with the prediction probability higher than .90 for their predicted labels, and 100 samples with the prediction probability between .80 and .90. To balance topics, we pick equal number of samples for each topic. We do not perform the same MTurk task for incorrectly predicted samples because when a system makes an incorrect prediction, assessing interpretability is not straightfoward. There can be multiple different reasons about the wrong prediction.

For MTurk, each HIT asks questions about an explanation generated by a system for one sample, as shown in Figure 3. For each HIT, 5 MTurkers participate. We hire North American Master MTurkers with HIT acceptance rates above 98% in order to ensure high quality of the evaluation. We pay \$0.03–\$0.05 for each HIT.

5.2 Human Evaluation Results

As shown in Table 8, KW-same-number and KW-same-length explanations resulted in a significantly higher confidence in assigning given topics to explanations compared to no-concept explanations. This indicates that the additional high-level concept information from KW-ATTN is beneficial for improving interpretability. We can also observe that KW-replacement explanations improve confidence although the gain is not significant.

Explanation Type	Pred	Conf	Time
No-concept	4.70	4.15	11.31
KW-same-number	4.82	4.40*	11.64
KW-same-length	4.77	4.31*	11.37
KW-replacement	4.74	4.22	12.34

Table 8: Human evaluation results on interpretation. Pred: average # of "yes" on predicted topics, Conf: average confidence score, Time: average time taken for each HIT, *: indicates statistically significant difference over no-concept via t-test ($p < 0.05$).

It is important to note that KW-same-length and KW-replacement explanations both improve interpretability over no-concept explanations as well as KW-same-number. While KW-same-number explanations provide more information (12 at maximum in total including both words and concepts), KW-same-length and KW-replacement give the same or less amount of information compare to no-concept (6 at maximum in total). This indicates that the high-level concept information really helps.

6 Conclusion

We presented a new attention mechanism, KW-ATTN, which extends a NN model by incorporating high-level concepts. Our experiments showed that using high-level concept information improves predictive power by helping the data sparseness problem in small data. Furthermore, in our crowdsourcing experiments, we found significant improvement on the confidence of human evaluators on predictions, suggesting that our new attention mechanism provides benefits in explaining the predictions. High-level concepts provide an additional layer of information above raw words that can assist in understanding predictions. Additionally, our attention mechanism can distinguish between the importance of words vs. concepts, providing further information. We are optimistic that KW-ATTN can be applied widely.

References

Tim Benson. 2010. Snomed ct. In *Principles of Health Interoperability HL7 and SNOMED*, pages 189–215. Springer.

Taxiarchis Botsis, Michael D Nguyen, Emily Jane Woo, Marianthi Markatou, and Robert Ball. 2011. Text mining for the vaccine adverse event reporting system: medical text classification using informative feature selection. *Journal of the American Medical Informatics Association*, 18(5):631–638.

Hanjie Chen, Guangtao Zheng, and Yangfeng Ji. 2020. Generating hierarchical explanations on text classification via feature interaction detection. *arXiv preprint arXiv:2004.02015*.

Kyunghyun Cho, Bart Van Merriënboer, Dzmitry Bahdanau, and Yoshua Bengio. 2014. On the properties of neural machine translation: Encoder-decoder approaches. *arXiv preprint arXiv:1409.1259*.

Jacob Devlin, Ming-Wei Chang, Kenton Lee, and Kristina Toutanova. 2018. Bert: Pre-training of deep bidirectional transformers for language understanding. *arXiv preprint arXiv:1810.04805*.

Finale Doshi-Velez and Been Kim. 2017. Towards a rigorous science of interpretable machine learning. *arXiv preprint arXiv:1702.08608*.

Christiane Fellbaum. 2012. Wordnet. the encyclopedia of applied linguistics.

Reza Ghaeini, Xiaoli Z Fern, and Prasad Tadepalli. 2018. Interpreting recurrent and attention-based neural models: a case study on natural language inference. *arXiv preprint arXiv:1808.03894*.

Ignacio Iacobacci, Mohammad Taher Pilehvar, and Roberto Navigli. 2015. Sensembed: Learning sense embeddings for word and relational similarity. In *Proceedings of the 53rd Annual Meeting of the Association for Computational Linguistics and the 7th International Joint Conference on Natural Language Processing (Volume 1: Long Papers)*, pages 95–105.

Hyeju Jang, Young Ji Lee, Giuseppe Carenini, Raymond Ng, Grace Campbell, and Kendall Ho. 2019. Neural prediction of patient needs in an ovarian cancer online discussion forum. In *Canadian Conference on Artificial Intelligence*, pages 492–497. Springer.

Diederik P Kingma and Jimmy Ba. 2014. Adam: A method for stochastic optimization. *arXiv preprint arXiv:1412.6980*.

Abhishek Kumar, Daisuke Kawahara, and Sadao Kurohashi. 2018. Knowledge-enriched two-layered attention network for sentiment analysis. In *Proceedings of the 2018 Conference of the North American Chapter of the Association for Computational Linguistics: Human Language Technologies, Volume 2 (Short Papers)*, pages 253–258.

Kathy Lee, Diana Palsetia, Ramanathan Narayanan, Md Mostofa Ali Patwary, Ankit Agrawal, and Alok Choudhary. 2011. Twitter trending topic classification. In *2011 IEEE 11th International Conference on Data Mining Workshops*, pages 251–258. IEEE.

Zhouhan Lin, Minwei Feng, Cicero Nogueira dos Santos, Mo Yu, Bing Xiang, Bowen Zhou, and Yoshua Bengio. 2017. A structured self-attentive sentence embedding. *arXiv preprint arXiv:1703.03130*.

C Lindberg. 1990. The unified medical language system (umls) of the national library of medicine. *Journal (American Medical Record Association)*, 61(5):40–42.

Weijie Liu, Peng Zhou, Zhe Zhao, Zhiruo Wang, Qi Ju, Haotang Deng, and Ping Wang. 2020. K-bert: Enabling language representation with knowledge graph. In *AAAI*, pages 2901–2908.

Scott M Lundberg and Su-In Lee. 2017. A unified approach to interpreting model predictions. In *Advances in Neural Information Processing Systems*, pages 4765–4774.

Mark Abraham Magumba, Peter Nabende, and Ernest Mwebaze. 2018. Ontology boosted deep learning for disease name extraction from twitter messages. *Journal of Big Data*, 5(1):31.

Massimiliano Mancini, Jose Camacho-Collados, Ignacio Iacobacci, and Roberto Navigli. 2016. Embedding words and senses together via joint knowledge-enhanced training. *arXiv preprint arXiv:1612.02703*.

Katerina Margatina, Christos Baziotis, and Alexandros Potamianos. 2019. Attention-based conditioning methods for external knowledge integration. In *Proceedings of the 57th Annual Meeting of the Association for Computational Linguistics*, pages 3944–3951.

Alexa T McCray. 2003. An upper-level ontology for the biomedical domain. *International Journal of Genomics*, 4(1):80–84.

Andrea Moro, Alessandro Raganato, and Roberto Navigli. 2014. Entity Linking meets Word Sense Disambiguation: a Unified Approach. *Transactions of the Association for Computational Linguistics (TACL)*, 2:231–244.

Roberto Navigli and Simone Paolo Ponzetto. 2012. BabelNet: The automatic construction, evaluation and application of a wide-coverage multilingual semantic network. *Artificial Intelligence*, 193:217–250.

Dong Nguyen. 2018. Comparing automatic and human evaluation of local explanations for text classification. In *Proceedings of the 2018 Conference of the North American Chapter of the Association for Computational Linguistics: Human Language Technologies, Volume 1 (Long Papers)*, pages 1069–1078.

World Health Organization et al. 2017. International classification of diseases (icd) information sheet. 2017.

Matthew E Peters, Mark Neumann, Robert L Logan IV, Roy Schwartz, Vidur Joshi, Sameer Singh, and Noah A Smith. 2019. Knowledge enhanced contextual word representations. *arXiv preprint arXiv:1909.04164*.

Marco Tulio Ribeiro, Sameer Singh, and Carlos Guestrin. 2016. Why should i trust you?: Explaining the predictions of any classifier. In *Proceedings of the 22nd ACM SIGKDD international conference on knowledge discovery and data mining*, pages 1135–1144. ACM.

Bianca Scarlini, Tommaso Pasini, and Roberto Navigli. 2020. Sensembert: Context-enhanced sense embeddings for multilingual word sense disambiguation. In *AAAI*, pages 8758–8765.

Minjoon Seo, Aniruddha Kembhavi, Ali Farhadi, and Hannaneh Hajishirzi. 2016. Bidirectional attention flow for machine comprehension. *arXiv preprint arXiv:1611.01603*.

Sofia Serrano and Noah A Smith. 2019. Is attention interpretable? *arXiv preprint arXiv:1906.03731*.

Avanti Shrikumar, Peyton Greenside, and Anshul Kundaje. 2017. Learning important features through propagating activation differences. *arXiv preprint arXiv:1704.02685*.

Kai Shu, Amy Sliva, Suhang Wang, Jiliang Tang, and Huan Liu. 2017. Fake news detection on social media: A data mining perspective. *ACM SIGKDD Explorations Newsletter*, 19(1):22–36.

Gabriel Stanovsky, Daniel Gruhl, and Pablo Mendes. 2017. Recognizing mentions of adverse drug reaction in social media using knowledge-infused recurrent models. In *Proceedings of the 15th Conference of the European Chapter of the Association for Computational Linguistics: Volume 1, Long Papers*, pages 142–151.

Jin Wang, Zhongyuan Wang, Dawei Zhang, and Jun Yan. 2017. Combining knowledge with deep convolutional neural networks for short text classification. In *IJCAI*, pages 2915–2921.

Yequan Wang, Minlie Huang, Xiaoyan Zhu, and Li Zhao. 2016. Attention-based lstm for aspect-level sentiment classification. In *Proceedings of the 2016 conference on empirical methods in natural language processing*, pages 606–615.

Sarah Wiegreffe and Yuval Pinter. 2019. Attention is not not explanation. In *Proceedings of the 2019 Conference on Empirical Methods in Natural Language Processing and the 9th International Joint Conference on Natural Language Processing (EMNLP-IJCNLP)*, pages 11–20.

Zhen Xu, Bingquan Liu, Baoxun Wang, Chengjie Sun, and Xiaolong Wang. 2017. Incorporating loose-structured knowledge into conversation modeling via recall-gate lstm. In *2017 International Joint Conference on Neural Networks (IJCNN)*, pages 3506–3513. IEEE.

Bishan Yang and Tom Mitchell. 2017. Leveraging knowledge bases in lstms for improving machine reading. In *Proceedings of the 55th Annual Meeting of the Association for Computational Linguistics (Volume 1: Long Papers)*, pages 1436–1446.

Zichao Yang, Diyi Yang, Chris Dyer, Xiaodong He, Alex Smola, and Eduard Hovy. 2016. Hierarchical attention networks for document classification. In *Proceedings of the 2016 Conference of the North American Chapter of the Association for Computational Linguistics: Human Language Technologies*, pages 1480–1489.

Haochao Ying, Fuzhen Zhuang, Fuzheng Zhang, Yanchi Liu, Guandong Xu, Xing Xie, Hui Xiong, and Jian Wu. 2018. Sequential recommender system based on hierarchical attention network. In *IJCAI International Joint Conference on Artificial Intelligence*.

Xiang Zhang, Junbo Zhao, and Yann LeCun. 2015. Character-level convolutional networks for text classification. In *Advances in neural information processing systems*, pages 649–657.

Zhengyan Zhang, Xu Han, Zhiyuan Liu, Xin Jiang, Maosong Sun, and Qun Liu. 2019. Ernie: Enhanced language representation with informative entities. *arXiv preprint arXiv:1905.07129*.

Peixiang Zhong, Di Wang, and Chunyan Miao. 2019. Knowledge-enriched transformer for emotion detection in textual conversations. *arXiv preprint arXiv:1909.10681*.

Hao Zhou, Tom Young, Minlie Huang, Haizhou Zhao, Jingfang Xu, and Xiaoyan Zhu. 2018. Commonsense knowledge aware conversation generation with graph attention. In *IJCAI*, pages 4623–4629.

A Appendices

Figure 3 shows a screenshot of the Amazon Mechanical Turk user interface in our human evaluation.

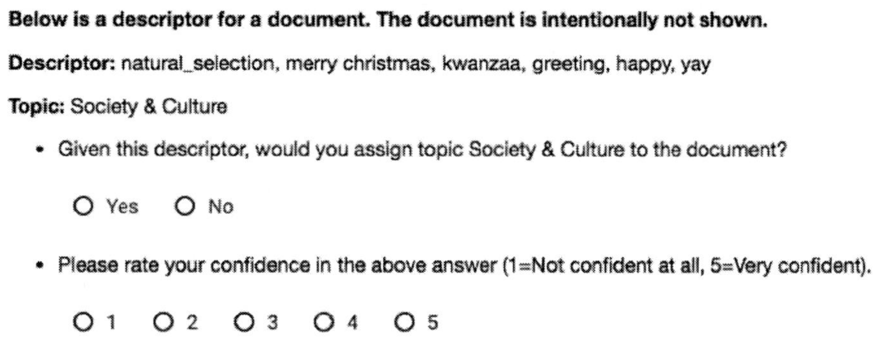

Below is a descriptor for a document. The document is intentionally not shown.

Descriptor: natural_selection, merry christmas, kwanzaa, greeting, happy, yay

Topic: Society & Culture

- Given this descriptor, would you assign topic Society & Culture to the document?

  ○ Yes ○ No

- Please rate your confidence in the above answer (1=Not confident at all, 5=Very confident).

  ○ 1 ○ 2 ○ 3 ○ 4 ○ 5

Figure 3: Our MTurk interface for human evaluation about interpretability.

Multi-input Recurrent Independent Mechanisms for leveraging knowledge sources: Case studies on sentiment analysis and health text mining

Parsa Bagherzadeh and Sabine Bergler
CLaC Labs, Concordia University
Montréal, Canada
{p_bagher, bergler}@cse.concordia.ca

Abstract

This paper presents a way to inject and leverage existing knowledge from external sources in a Deep Learning environment, extending the recently proposed Recurrent Independent Mechnisms (RIMs) architecture, which comprises a set of interacting yet independent modules. We show that this extension of the RIMs architecture is an effective framework with lower parameter implications compared to purely fine-tuned systems.

1 Introduction

Deep neural networks have been successfully applied to a variety of natural language processing tasks such as text classification, sequence labeling, sequence generation, etc. Deep architectures are often non-modular, homogeneous systems and trained end-to-end. End-to-end training is performed with the hope that the structure of a networks is sufficient to direct gradient descent from a random initial state to a highly non-trivial solution (Glasmachers, 2017).

An important issue with the end-to-end training is that throughout the training of a system composed of several layers, valuable information contained in a problem decomposition that resulted in a specific network design is ignored (Glasmachers, 2017). In non-modular systems, explicit decomposition of high level tasks into distinct subprocesses is not possible and necessary complexity has to be induced through the complexity of the input stimulus. This results in large systems whith the required number of training samples becoming intractable. Interpretation of these black box systems is difficult (Miikkulainen and Dyer, 1991).

In compositional systems, in contrast, smaller modules encode specialized expertise which is known to impact one aspect of the task at hand. The aggregation of the modules acts synergistically to address the overall task. In a modular system, the components act largely independently but communicate occasionally. Module autonomy is crucial because in the case of distributional shifts (significant changes in some modules), other modules should remain robust (Schölkopf et al., 2012), (Goyal et al., 2019). Modules also need to interact occasionally to achieve compositional behavior (Bengio, 2017).

Many current neural modular systems, such as EntNet (Henaff et al., 2017) and IndRNN (Li et al., 2018), offer only module independence, but no module communication. The recently proposed Recurrent Independent Mechanisms (RIMs) (Goyal et al., 2019), however, suggest to model a complex system by dividing the overall model into M communicative recurrent modules.

Deep architectures often rely solely on raw data in large quantities with a requirement of representativeness regarding task requirements. This becomes problematic for tasks with a specialized, low-frequency terminology, where high quality knowledge sources for NLP and AI are often available and have proven their effectiveness. Embedding expert knowledge in extended pre-trained word embeddings is costly. We present untied inedpendent modules to embed knowledge from different sources onto systems input. Knowledge sources, as independent experts, provide different annotations (abstractions) for the input, combining various classifications for solving the task.

For instance, providing sentiment lexica for sentiment analysis reduces the demand for training data by expanding the limited training vocabulary with an extended set of annotated terms. Precompiled word embeddings are to be considered knowledge sources in the same spirit and we demonstrate that they inter-operate with a variety of other knowledge sources such as gazetteers and POS encoding.

Consider Example 1 from the Stanford Sentiment Treebank (SST-2) (Socher et al., 2013).

(1) *This is an absurd comedy about alienation, separation and loss.*

Proceedings of Deep Learning Inside Out (DeeLIO): The 2nd Workshop on Knowledge Extraction and Integration for Deep Learning Architectures, pages 108–118
Online, June 10, 2021.

Figure 1 shows annotations from different knowledge sources for Example 1, such as tokenization (from the ANNIE tokenizer), POS tags (from the Stanford POS tagger), and sentiment annotations from three sentiment lexica (AFINN (Nielsen, 2011), MPQA (Wilson et al., 2005), and NRC (Mohammad et al., 2013)).

	x_t^1	x_t^2	x_t^3	x_t^4	x_t^5
t	Token	POS	AFINN	MPQA	NRC
1	This	DT	0	Neutral	-0.19
2	is	VBZ	0	Neutral	0.00
3	an	DT	0	Neutral	0.08
4	absurd	JJ	0	Neg.	-1.56
5	comedy	NN	+1	Neg.	0.27
6	about	IN	0	Neutral	-0.34
7	alienation	NN	-2	Neg.	0.00
8	,	,	0	Neutral	0.27
9	separation	NN	0	Neutral	-0.29
10	and	CC	0	Neutral	0.41
11	loss	NN	-3	Neg.	-0.51
12	.	.	0	Neutral	-0.06

Figure 1: Various annotations for Example 1

The annotations of the different sentiment lexica in Figure 1 vary substantially: *comedy* is classified as positive (+1) in AFINN, as negative in MPQA, and almost neutral in NRC. (Özdemir and Bergler, 2015a) showed that this variance in judgements is not prohibitive, in fact (Özdemir and Bergler, 2015b) showed that combining 5 sentiment lexica outperformed all other combinations. These differences are in fact advantageous in an ensemble setting and reflect diversity among experts. The differences cannot be exploited, when a single embedding is used for tokens, but may be retained, when different lexica are embedded independently in different modules.

We add input independence to the RIMs architecture, providing different language annotations as inputs to a set of independent, but interacting modules. The resulting system is a flexible modular architecture for leveraging token-level knowledge in form of different annotation embeddings, which will be given different weights for the task at hand dependeing on their usefulness during training (see Figure 11). The system is evaluated on tasks such as sentiment analysis and analysis of health-related tweets for different health concerns.

Our experiments demonstrate that leveraging knowledge sources under a modular framework consistently improves performance with little increase in parameter space. Additionally, when frozen language models are supplemented with knowledge sources, the drop in performance is minimal, making this technique particularly beneficial for users that do not have access to powerful computational resources. Lastly, the modular nature of the system allows to visualize the models functionality.

2 Methods

2.1 RIMs

Recurrent independent mechanisms (RIMs) is a modular architecture that models a dynamic system by dividing it into M recurrent modules (Goyal et al., 2019). At time-step t, each module R_m ($m = 1, \ldots, M$) has a hidden state $h_t^m \in \mathbb{R}^{d_h}$.

Input selection Each module R_m gets the augmented input $X_t = x_t \oplus \mathbf{0}$, where $\mathbf{0}$ is an all-zero vector and $\oplus$ is the row-level concatenation. Then, using an attention mechanism, module R_m selects input:

$$A_t^m = softmax(\frac{h_{t-1}^m W_m^{query} (X_t W^{key})^T}{\sqrt{d}}) X_t W^{val} \quad (1)$$

where $h_{t-1}^m W_m^{query}$ is the *query*, $X_t W^{key}$ is the *key*, and $X_t W^{val}$ is the *value* in the attention mechanism (Vaswani et al., 2017). The matrices $W_m^{query} \in \mathbb{R}^{d_h \times d_{in}^{query}}$, $W^{key} \in \mathbb{R}^{d_{in} \times d_{in}^{key}}$, and $W^{val} \in \mathbb{R}^{d_{in} \times d_{in}^{val}}$ are linear transformations for constructing query, key, and value for the input selection attention.[1]

If the input x_t is considered relevant to module R_m, the attention mechanism in Equation 1 assigns more weight to it (selects it), otherwise more weight will be assigned to the null input (Goyal et al., 2019).

The $softmax$ values of Equation 1 determine a set S_t of top m_{Active} modules.[2] Among M modules, those with the least attention on the null input are the active modules. The selected input A_t^m determines a temporary hidden state $\tilde{h}_t^m$ for the active modules:

$$\tilde{h}_t^m = R_m(h_{t-1}^m, A_t^m) \quad m \in S_t \quad (2)$$

where $R_m(h_{t-1}^m, A_t^m)$ denotes one iteration of updating the recurrent module R_m based on previous state h_{t-1}^m and current input A_t^m. The hidden states

[1] d_{in}^{query}, d_{in}^{key}, and d_{in}^{val} are dimensionalities of query, key, and value respectively (for the input selection attention)

[2] The cardinality $|S_t| = m_{Active}$ is currently a fixed hyperparameter, that can ultimately be determined based on the target task.

of the inactive modules R_m ($m \notin S_t$) remain unchanged:

$$h_t^m = h_{t-1}^m \quad m \notin S_t \tag{3}$$

Module communication To obtain the actual hidden states h_t^m, the active modules communicate using an attention mechanism:

$$h_t^m = softmax(\frac{Q_{t,m}(K_{t,:})^T}{\sqrt{d_h}})V_{t,:} + \tilde{h}_t^m \quad m \in S_t \tag{4}$$

where

$$Q_{t,m} = \tilde{h}_t^m \tilde{W}_m^{query}$$

$K_{t,:}$ is the row-level concatenation of all $K_{t,m}$ ($m = 1, \ldots, M$) defined as:

$$K_{t,m} = \tilde{h}_t^m \tilde{W}_m^{key}$$

and $V_{t,:}$ is the row-level concatenation of all $V_{t,m}$ ($m = 1, \ldots, M$) defined as:

$$V_{t,m} = \tilde{h}_t^m \tilde{W}_m^{val}$$

The matrices $\tilde{W}_m^{query} \in \mathbb{R}^{d_h \times d_{com}^{query}}$, $\tilde{W}_m^{key} \in \mathbb{R}^{d_h \times d_{com}^{key}}$ and $\tilde{W}_m^{val} \in \mathbb{R}^{d_h \times d_{com}^{val}}$ are used for constructing query, key, and value for the *communication* attention.[3]

Note that both the key $K_{t,:}$ and the value $V_{t,:}$ depend on the temporary hidden states of all modules, therefore h_t^m in Equation 4 is determined by attending to all modules. The overall hidden state of the RIMs model at time-step t can be defined as $h_t = [h_t^1, \ldots, h_t^M]$ which is the concatenation of the hidden states of all modules.

Classification We choose a simple attention layer together with a classifier to obtain the appropriate vector representation of a given sample. Attention (Bahdanau et al., 2015) determines importance scores $e_t = w_{att}^T h_t$ using a latent context vector w_{att}. The score is then normalized using $\alpha_t = \frac{exp(e_t)}{\sum_j e_j}$ for a weighted sum $H = \sum_t \alpha_t * h_t$, which is the input for a classifier.

2.2 Multi-input RIMs

We extend this architecture to so-called *multi-input RIMs*, which consist of a set of M modules, similar to the standard RIMs. The standard RIMs model assumes the same input sequence for all modules (X_t in Equation 1), which share the same linear transformation matrices W^{key} and W^{val} for constructing the keys and values for the attention mechanism.

[3] d_{com}^{query}, d_{com}^{key}, and d_{com}^{val} are dimensions of query, key, and value respectively (for the *communication* attention)

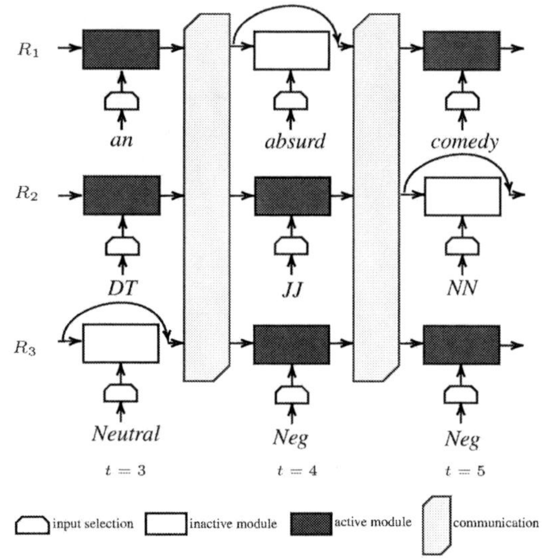

Figure 2: A 3 module multi-input RIMs for Example 1 at $t = 3, ..., 5$. The dynamics of each module is independent of the others and active modules communicate at each time-step

In contrast, we untie the input attention mechanism and consider dedicated linear transformations W_m^{key} and W_m^{val} for module R_m. Untying the attention mechanism allows modules to have different inputs X_t^m ($m = 1, \ldots, M$) each potentially with a different dimensionality. This supports our use of each module to encode a different knowledge source, one being word embeddings, one being a gazetteer list, etc. The input selection mechanism of Equation 1 then expands to Equation 5:

$$A_t^m = softmax(\frac{h_{t-1}^m W_m^{query}(X_t^m W_m^{key})^T}{\sqrt{d_h}})X_t^m W_m^{val} \tag{5}$$

where $X_t^m = x_t^m \oplus \mathbf{0}$.

In Equation 5, the $softmax$ produces two attention scores, i.e. how much the module R_m attends to the input x_t^m and the null input $\mathbf{0}$. The top m_{active} modules with least attention scores to the null input form a set S_t. The temporary hidden state for active modules is determined by Equation 2 and modules communicate according to Equation 4, identical to standard RIMs. An illustration of the multi-input RIMs model is provided in Figure 2.

3 Tasks

We explore the potential of multi-input RIMs by ablation on different tasks that are each very specific in their description and do not have large training datasets, namely three sentiment analysis tasks and two health-related tweet classification tasks.

3.1 Sentiment analysis

Here we consider three sentiment benchmark datasets with their respective tasks:

SST-2 Stanford sentiment tree-bank for the task of binary sentiment classification of movie reviews (Socher et al., 2013). The models are trained on the data provided by the GLUE benchmark[4] (Wang et al., 2018).

SE17-4A SemEval 2017 task 4 subtask A is a 3-class problem for sentiment classification of tweets (Rosenthal et al., 2017). The tweets are classified as *Negative*, *Neutral*, and *Positive*. The performance for this task is measured by the macro-average of recall scores for positive, negative, and neutral classes and evaluated by the TweetEval benchmark (Barbieri et al., 2020)[5].

SE15-11 SemEval 2015 task 11 is a pilot task of sentiment analysis for figurative language tweets. The training set comprises a collection of sarcastic, ironic, and metaphoric tweets (4490 tweets) annotated on an 11 point scale ($-5, \ldots, +5$) (Ghosh et al., 2015). The performance is measured by *Cosine* similarity between the gold standard labels and predictions.

We use the following sentiment lexica as knowledge sources:

1. *AFINN*: A manually compiled lexicon of 2500 words, rated for valence scores with an integer between -5 and 5 together with their prior polarities (Nielsen, 2011).

2. *MPQA*: A manually compiled lexicon of 8000 words, distinguishing positive, negative, and neutral sentiment scores (Wilson et al., 2005).

3. *NRC HashTag sentiment*: An automatically compiled resource, that uses seed hashtags (Mohammad et al., 2013). The polarity of the seed hashtag is used to calculate PMI-based[6] scores (Church and Hanks, 1990).

[4]http://gluebenchmark.com

[5]https://github.com/cardiffnlp/tweeteval

[6]point-wise mutual information

The training set SE15-11 has been released as tweet IDs and part of the training set is not available anymore[7], therefore we randomly select 20% of the available tweets as test set and use the remaining for training.

3.2 Health experience classification of tweets

Personal experiences gleaned from social media can enhance awareness of the state of public health. Here we focus on two tasks:

SM18-2 The task of medication intake report detection was introduced as SMM4H 2018 Task 2 (Weissenbacher et al., 2018) as a 3-way classification task. Tweets in which the user clearly expresses a personal medication intake/consumption are considered Class 1. Tweets where the user may have taken some medication are labeled as Class 2. Class 3 tweets mention medication names but do not indicate personal intake. The total number of samples in the training set is 17700.

SM20-5 Birth defect mention detection concerning a child is a 3-class problem, where Class 1 tweets indicate that the user's child has a birth defect. Class 2 tweets are unclear as to whether the poster speaks of birth defects of their child. Class 3 tweets merely mention birth defects but not with respect to the poster's child (Klein et al., 2020). The training set includes 18382 samples.

Both, SM18-2 and SM20-5 benefit from specialized gazetters of relevant medical terms, in particular:

1. *Drugs*: A gazetteer list of drug names compiled from Drug Bank (Wishart et al., 2018).

2. *Diseases*: A list of terms for *infections, wounds, injuries, pain, etc.*, compiled from subtree C in MeSH[8] (Lipscomb, 2000). Disease mentions are important evidence for medication intake classification, since drugs are usually consumed to treat a disease.

3. *Birth Defect*: Congenital, hereditary, and neonatal diseases and abnormalities (from MeSH C16).

[7]about 33% of the tweets are not available

[8]https://meshb.nlm.nih.gov/treeView

4. *Pregnancy*: Pregnancy complication terms (from MeSH C13.703)

For SM18-2, the gold labels of the competition set have not been disclosed, therefore we randomly hold out a test set (20% of the original training data). For SM18-2 and SM20-5 the performances are measured in terms of micro-F1 scores for 0 and 1 class.

4 Implementation

Preprocessing We preprocess the data using a GATE pipeline (Cunningham et al., 2002) with the ANNIE English Tokenizer (for SST-2 task) and ANNIE tweet tokenizer as well as the hashtag tokenizer (for the tweet tasks).

Embeddings Each annotation type provides a sequence (see Figure 1) which is used as input for a dedicated module in multi-input RIMs. Therefore, each sequence has to be properly embedded. The annotation types can be embedded either using pretrained embeddings or using randomly initialized embeddings that are learned during the training.

Tokens are embedded using ELMo (Peters et al., 2018) or RoBERTa (Liu et al., 2019) pretrained models. For ELMo, we use the pretrained model provided by AllenNLP[9] and for RoBERTa, the model provided by Hugging Face[10].

POS tags following (Bagherzadeh and Bergler, 2021), we apply Word2Vec on POS tag sequences instead of token sequences. The POS embeddings are trained using the Gensim package (Rehurek and Sojka, 2010) with a window size of 5 and dimensionality 20. The pretraining is performed on combined training data of all tasks introduced in Section 3.

AFINN and NRC matches do not require an embedding, since the lexica quantify the sentiment scores numerically.

MPQA matches for *Negative*, *Neutral*, and *Positive* polarities are encoded numerically by -1, 0, and 1 respectively.

Medical Gazetteer matches are embedded using a learnable embedding matrix $B \in \mathbb{R}^{5\times 20}$. The 5 rows in B correspond to 4 medical resources[11] plus one row to indicate no annotation.

[9] https://allennlp.org/

[10] https://huggingface.co/

The multi-input RIMs model is a flexible architecture and the modules can be of any recurrent type. Here, we use LSTMs for complex inputs, such as *Token* or *POS*, and RNNs for annotations with simpler encodings, such as gazetteers.

Module	d_{in}	d_h	d_{in}^{quer}	d_{in}^{key}	d_{in}^{val}	d_{com}^{quer}	d_{com}^{key}	d_{com}^{val}
Token	1024	256	512	512	1024	64	64	256
POS	50	256	100	100	50	64	64	256
Senti[1]	1	256	16	16	1	64	64	256
Medic[2]	20	256	100	100	20	64	64	256

1: AFIIN, MPQA, NRC
2: Drug, Preg, BirthDef, Disease

Figure 3: Hyper-parameters used in the experiments.

Figure 3 summarizes the hyper-parameters used for multi-input RIMs. We use the learning rates of $lr = 0.5e - 2$ and $lr = 0.5e - 4$ for ELMo- and RoBERTa-based models respectively. The hyper-parameters are tuned based on a grid-search approach. The multi-input RIMs model itself (excluding the language models) has 4M learnable parameters.

To calculate classification loss we use cross-entropy loss and we optimize the models using the Adam optimizer (Kingma and Ba, 2015). The models are implemented using PyTorch (Paszke et al., 2017).

5 Numerical results

We present a set of ablation studies to evaluate the effectiveness and contribution of different knowledge sources.

All modules active Figures 4–6 report results for the multi-input RIMs model when the modules are provided with different annotation types and all modules are kept active ($M = m_{Active}$). For the runs where the *Token* annotation is the only input ($M = 1$), the model is reduced to a simple LSTM with ELMo or RoBERTa embeddings, which we consider to form baselines.

Figure 4 shows that all sentiment tasks benefit from the sentiment lexica. For SST-2, *AFINN* and *MPQA* add more to the task than *NRC*. On the other hand, *NRC* yields considerable performance improvements for the tweet sentiment data sets of

[11] Drug, Disease, Birth defect, and Pregnancy

M	Annotations	SST-2 (Acc %)		SE17-4A (mac-Rec %)		SE15-11 (Cosine)	
		ELMo	RoBERTa	ELMo	RoBERTa	ELMo	RoBERTa
1	Token	88.5	96.4	64.1	70.2	78.1	82.2
2	Token + AFINN	91.2	96.7	66.8	71.6	80.1	83.0
2	Token + MPQA	90.3	96.5	65.9	71.2	80.0	83.2
2	Token + NRC	89.7	96.4	67.1	71.5	82.1	83.9
2	Token + POS	89.2	96.4	65.2	70.8	78.9	82.2
3	Token + POS + AFINN	91.8	97.1	68.3	72.0	81.4	83.3
3	Token + POS + MPQA	90.7	96.9	67.2	71.8	81.1	83.3
3	Token + POS + NRC	90.5	96.5	68.9	72.4	82.6	84.4
5	Token + POS + AFINN + MPQA + NRC	**92.3**	**97.3**	**70.4**	**73.3**	**83.2**	**85.0**
1	Token$^{\mathcal{F}}$	83.2	94.1	61.1	68.2	75.3	80.3
5	Token$^{\mathcal{F}}$ + POS + AFINN + MPQA + NRC	89.1	95.4	68.2	71.6	81.4	84.1

$\mathcal{F}$: Frozen language model

Figure 4: Multi-input RIMs on sentiment tasks with knowledge sources. Each annotation is the input of a dedicated module. In each run, all modules are kept active ($m_{Active} = M$)

SE17-4a and SE15-11. We surmise the greater effectiveness of the *NRC* lexicon for the tweet sentiment tasks is due to the fact that it is constructed from tweet corpora.

POS constitutes general linguistic knowledge and demonstrates consistent yet small improvements for the sentiment tasks. However, *POS* improves performance for the health concerns data of SM18-2 (Figure 5) and SM20-5 (Figure 6). Note that both tasks concern detection of personal experience mentions, for which categories such as pronouns (both personal and possessive) and verbs in past tense are important, which carry distinctive POS tags.

POS constitutes general linguistic knowledge and demonstrates consistent yet small improvements for the sentiment tasks. However, *POS* improves performance for the health concerns data of SM18-2 (Figure 5) and SM20-5 (Figure 6). Note that both tasks concern detection of personal experience mentions, for which categories such as pronouns (both personal and possessive) and verbs in past tense are important, which carry distinctive POS tags.

Improvements from medical knowledge gazetteers are also compelling. Figure 5 shows that the *Disease* gazetteer enhances the performance for the medication intake task, corroborating the hypothesis that disease mentions are strong evi-

M	Annotations	ELMo	RoBERTa
1	Token	68.2	72.0
2	Token + Drug	71.3	73.9
2	Token + Disease	70.5	73.0
2	Token + POS	71.5	74.1
3	Token + POS + Drug	73.6	74.8
3	Token + POS + Disease	72.7	74.5
4	Token + POS + Drug + Disease	**74.8**	**76.4**
1	Token$^{\mathcal{F}}$	64.2	70.0
4	Token$^{\mathcal{F}}$ + POS + Drug + Disease	71.6	73.8

Figure 5: Multi-input RIMs for SM18-2, personal drug intake. All modules are active

M	Annotations	ELMo	RoBERTa
1	Token	62.6	68.2
2	Token + BirthDef	65.3	70.4
2	Token + Preg	63.8	69.1
2	Token + POS	65.0	69.9
3	Token + POS + BirthDef	67.5	72.2
3	Token + POS + Preg	67.0	71.0
4	Token + POS + BirthDef + Preg	**69.3**	**73.6**
1	Token$^{\mathcal{F}}$	60.3	65.4
4	Token$^{\mathcal{F}}$ + POS + BirthDef + Preg	66.5	69.6

Figure 6: Multi-input RIMs for SM20-5, birth defect in a child. All modules are active

dence for medication intake. Similarly, Figure 6 shows that the *Pregnancy* gazetteer, as a complementary knowledge source, provides effective support for birth defect mention detection.

Some modules active We next evaluate performance when limiting the number of active modules ($m_{Active} < M$). Figures 7-9 show experiments for multi-input RIMs with each annotation as input to different modules. Interestingly, for most tasks, limiting the number of modules yields better performance, corroborating observations made by (Goyal et al., 2019).

This confirms the importance of forcing the annotations into competition mode for the moderate to small datasets: if $m_{Active} < M$, the modules compete for activation. As argued by (Goyal et al., 2019) and (Parascandolo et al., 2018) the competition between modules for representational resources (here the annotations) potentially leads to independence among learned mechanisms, making each module specialize on a simpler sub-problem, which prevents individual RIMs from dominating (Bengio et al., 2020).

Freezing language model vs fine-tuning We are interested in the behaviour of multi-RIMs when the language models are frozen. Freezing models such as BERT has recently demonstrated improvements (including speed-up) in the Adapters framework (Houlsby et al., 2019) and (Pfeiffer et al., 2020). The Adapters rely on injecting new trainable layers (modules) as intermediate layers within a frozen language model. The trainable layers are then expected to learn task specific representations.

Here, we investigate task adaptation using multi-input RIMs, combining trainable modules with complementary task specific resources/representations to compensate for possible losses in learning capacity of the model.

The last two rows in Figures 4-6 report performance when the language model is frozen (no fine-tuning). The fully-featured versions of all frozen systems still outperform the token-only baseline for all tasks for ELMo and almost all tasks for RoBERTa.

All of runs were executed on an Intel® Core i7 2.20GHz CPU. When we fine tune our RoBERTa-based models, the average time for a forward pass and back-propagation for one sample is 1.71sec compared to 0.63sec when the language model is frozen.

This significant reduction in training overhead when freezing language models is helpful for users whose access to computational resources is limited. The reported experiments suggest that appropriate knowledge sources can compensate for losses when freezing heavy language models such as ELMo or RoBERTa.

Comparison with SOTA The SST-2, SE17-4A, SM20-5 tasks have been deployed on GLUE, TweetEval, and Codalab benchmarks respectively, therefore, the state of the art (SOTA) results are available. Current SOTA performances on SST-2 are obtained by (Sun et al., 2019) and (Raffel et al., 2020) (tied), SOTA for SE17-4A is reported by (Barbieri et al., 2020), and SOTA for SM20-5 is reported by (Bai and Zhou, 2020) as shown in Figure 10.

For other tasks however, we replicated the reported SOTA system for each task. For SM18-2 the SOTA performance is reported for (Xherija, 2018), which is a two-layer stacked bi-LSTM with attention. The SOTA results for SE15-11 are reported by *CRNN-RoBERTa* (Potamias et al., 2020) for a RoBERTa-based model in which a bi-LSTM layer is stacked on top of the RoBERTa model, together with a pooling operation for its last layer. The model is replicated here based on hyper-paramters provided in (Potamias et al., 2020).

Figure 10 shows that multi-input RIMs perform at or above SOTA for all benchmarks with greater performance gains for tasks with comparatively smaller datasets and more complex linguistic requirements (SM18-2, SM20-5, SE15-11).

6 Module activation patterns

An advantage of a modular system is the possibility of module inspection. The functionality of each module during the course of processing has to be transparent for assessment.

Figure 11 provides the activation patterns of two multi-input RIMs when applied to two inputs from SST-2 (Figure 11a) and SM20-5 (Figure 11b) to assess whether they give insight into the functionality of the modules.

In Figure 11a, the modules that operate on sentiment knowledge sources (*AFINN*, *MPQA*, and *NRC*) are active only when an annotation is available and are idle (inactive) otherwise. The sentiment modules also compete with one another. Consider *Beautifully* at $t = 1$. For this token, both AFINN and MPQA provide annotations (AFINN:

M	m_{Active}	SST-2 (Acc %) ELMo	SST-2 (Acc %) RoBERTa	SE17-4A (mac-Rec %) ELMo	SE17-4A (mac-Rec %) RoBERTa	SE15-11 (Cosine) ELMo	SE15-11 (Cosine) RoBERTa
	1	89.6	95.5	65.4	71.0	80.4	82.8
	2	91.7	96.7	67.2	71.9	82.6	84.0
5	3	**92.8**	96.9	69.7	**74.5**	84.0	84.8
	4	91.9	**97.5**	**71.3**	73.9	82.9	**85.6**
	5	92.3	97.3	70.4	74.3	**83.2**	85.0

Figure 7: Multi-input RIMs with 5 modules for the sentiment tasks. The number of active modules varies.

M	m_{Active}	ELMo	RoBERTa
	1	73.1	74.5
4	2	75.0	**77.2**
	3	**75.3**	77.0
	4	74.8	76.4

Figure 8: (μF1) of multi-input RIMs with 4 modules (Token + POS + Drug + Disease) on SM18-2. The number of active modules varies.

M	m_{Active}	ELMo	RoBERTa
	1	68.0	70.4
4	2	70.0	73.2
	3	**70.6**	73.3
	4	69.3	**73.6**

Figure 9: (μF1) of multi-input RIMs with 4 modules (Token + POS + BirthDef + Preg) on SM20-5. The number of active modules varies.

+3, MPQA: Pos.), but the AFINN module wins the competition and is active while the MPQA module is inactive. The larger NRC lexicon provides more annotations for the input leading to more activity for the NRC module compared to the other sentiment modules for this sentence.

Inactivity of token modules at certain time steps is particularly interesting, indicating that the model has chosen to attend to a external knowledge source. We find that 63% of the time, when the sentiment lexia provide consistent sentiment polarities, the token module is inactive.

The activation patterns in Figure 11b show the *Birth Defect* and *Pregnancy* gazetteer modules are active only, when an annotation is available. The tokens *CHD* ($t = 9$) and *T18* ($t = 15$) are matched by the *Birth Defect* gazetteer and the token *stillbirth* ($t = 20$) is matched by the *Pregnancy* gazetteer.

Task	SOTA	RIMs
SST-2 (Acc)	**97.5** (1,2)	**97.5**
SE17-4A (mac-Rec)	72.6 (3)	**74.5**
SE15-11 (Cosine)	82.2 (4)	**85.6**
SM18-2 (μF1)	69.2 (5)	**77.2**
SM20-5 (μF1)	69.0 (6)	**73.6**

Figure 10: Comparison of the state of the art systems with multi-input RIMs. 1: Ernie (Sun et al., 2019), 2: T5 (Raffel et al., 2020), 3: RoBERTa-RT (Barbieri et al., 2020) 4: CRNN-RoBERTa (Potamias et al., 2020), 5: (Xherija, 2018), 6: (Bai and Zhou, 2020)

The activity patterns are the result of the input selection mechanism (attention). Multi-input RIMs modules are free to select an input signal or ignore it, which allows each module to potentially focus on a specific part of the input. The input selection mechanism prevents the modules from getting updated with spurious inputs (here the input at steps, where no annotation is available). Additionally, this allows the system to develop different modules to select complementary input signals, biasing the behavior away from combining redundant encodings.

We believe that the activation patterns can be useful for model explanation. Nevertheless, the activation patterns have to be studied under a variety of NLP tasks and different, richer annotations, which demands a dedicated study and is beyond the scope of this paper.

7 Conclusion

This paper presents proof of concept for a modular system for leveraging different knowledge sources. Under the proposed model, various annotations with different encodings are used as inputs for a set of independent, decoupled, but interacting modules, a novel extension of the RIMs architecture.

Deploying several readily available knowledge sources (gazetteer lists and part-of-speech information), our experiments report on different sentiment tasks and data sets, as well as two health-related tasks and datasets. The results suggest that the modules successfully interoperate for addressing different target tasks and multiple datasets with drastically reduced parameter space (and processing resources).

In addition to the transfer potential of RIMs, we probed their transparency. The activation patterns of the modules in multi-input RIMs showed inter-

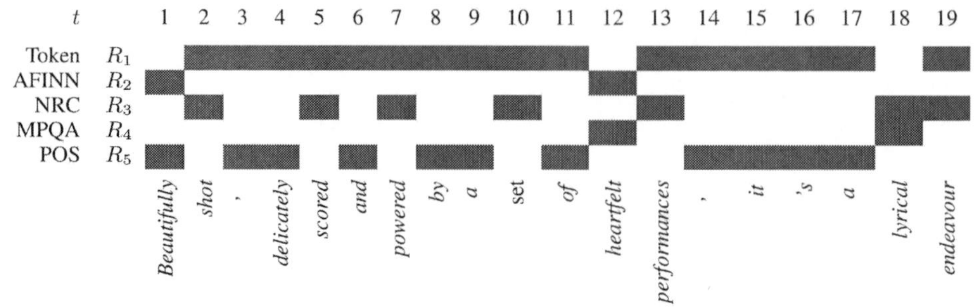

a – Input: *"Beautifully shot, delicately scored and powered by a set of heartfelt performances, it's a lyrical endeavour"*

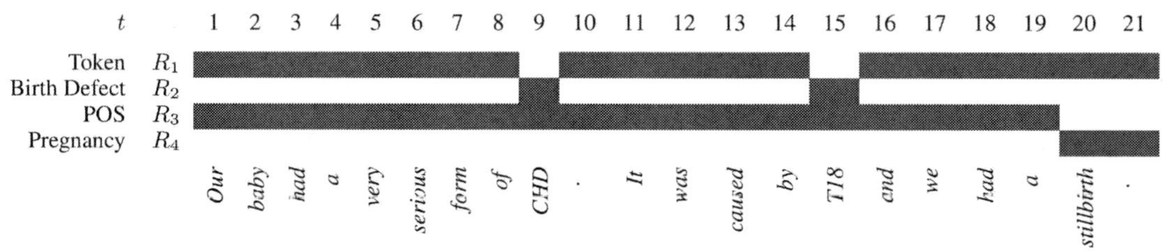

b – Input: *"Our baby had a very serious form of CHD. It was caused by T18 and we had a stillbirth."*

Figure 11: Activation patterns of the modules of RIMs (ELMo as token embedding) for two samples: (a) SST-2 with $M = 5$ and $m_{Active} = 2$, (b) SM20-5 with $M = 4$ and $m_{Active} = 2$. The gray squares indicate active modules and the white regions indicate inactivity.

estingly differentiated motifs. In particular, the activation patterns show that modules are active only when their input annotation is relevant for the target task. To interpret the functionality of different modules in multi-input RIMs architectures, we plan a detailed analysis of the module activation patterns under different NLP tasks in the future.

References

Parsa Bagherzadeh and Sabine Bergler. 2021. Leveraging knowledge sources for detecting self-reports of particular health issues on social media. In *Proceedings of the 12th International Workshop on Health Text Mining and Information Analysis*, pages 38–48, online.

Dzmitry Bahdanau, Kyunghyun Cho, and Yoshua Bengio. 2015. Neural machine translation by jointly learning to align and translate. In *Proceedings of the 3rd International Conference on Learning Representations, ICLR'15*.

Yang Bai and Xiaobing Zhou. 2020. Automatic Detecting for Health-related Twitter Data with BioBERT. In *SMM4H 2020*.

Francesco Barbieri, Jose Camacho-Collados, Luis Espinosa Anke, and Leonardo Neves. 2020. TweetEval: Unified benchmark and comparative evaluation for tweet classification. In *Findings of the Association for Computational Linguistics: EMNLP 2020*, pages 1644–1650, Online.

Yoshua Bengio. 2017. The consciousness prior. *arXiv preprint arXiv:1709.08568*.

Yoshua Bengio, Tristan Deleu, Nasim Rahaman, Rosemary Ke, Sébastien Lachapelle, Olexa Bilaniuk, Anirudh Goyal, and Christopher Pal. 2020. A meta-transfer objective for learning to disentangle causal mechanisms. In *Proceedings of the 8th International Conference on Learning Representations, ICLR'20*.

Kenneth Church and Patrick Hanks. 1990. Word association norms, mutual information, and lexicography. *Computational linguistics*, 16(1):22–29.

Hamish Cunningham, Diana Maynard, Kalina Bontcheva, and Valentin Tablan. 2002. GATE: A Framework and Graphical Development Environment for Robust NLP tools and applications. In *Proceedings of the 40th Anniversary Meeting of the Association for Computational Linguistics (ACL'02)*.

Aniruddha Ghosh, Guofu Li, Tony Veale, Paolo Rosso, Ekaterina Shutova, John Barnden, and Antonio Reyes. 2015. SemEval 2015 Task 11: Sentiment analysis of figurative language in Twitter. In *Proceedings of the 9th international workshop on semantic evaluation (SemEval 2015)*, pages 470–478.

Tobias Glasmachers. 2017. Limits of end-to-end learning. In *Asian Conference on Machine Learning*, pages 17–32.

Anirudh Goyal, Alex Lamb, Jordan Hoffmann, Shagun Sodhani, Sergey Levine, Yoshua Bengio, and Bernhard Schölkopf. 2019. Recurrent independent mechanisms. *arXiv preprint arXiv:1909.10893*.

Mikael Henaff, Jason Weston, Arthur Szlam, Antoine Bordes, and Yann LeCun. 2017. Tracking the world state with recurrent entity networks. In *Proceedings of the 5th International Conference on Learning Representations, ICLR'17*.

Neil Houlsby, Andrei Giurgiu, Stanislaw Jastrzebski, Bruna Morrone, Quentin De Laroussilhe, Andrea Gesmundo, Mona Attariyan, and Sylvain Gelly. 2019. Parameter-efficient transfer learning for NLP. In *International Conference on Machine Learning*, pages 2790–2799. PMLR.

Diederik P Kingma and Jimmy Ba. 2015. Adam: A method for stochastic optimization. In *Proceedings of the 3rd International Conference on Learning Representations, ICLR'15*.

Ari Z. Klein, Ivan Flores, Arjun Magge, Anne-Lyse Minard, Karen O'Connor, Abeed Sarker, Elena Tutubalina, Davy Weissenbacher, and Graciela Gonzalez-Hernandez. 2020. Overview of the fifth Social Media Mining for Health Applications (SMM4H) Shared Tasks at COLING 2020. In *Proceedings of the Fifth Social Media Mining for Health Applications (SMM4H) Workshop & Shared Task*.

Shuai Li, Wanqing Li, Chris Cook, Ce Zhu, and Yanbo Gao. 2018. Independently recurrent neural network (IndRNN): Building a longer and deeper RNN. In *Proceedings of the IEEE Conference on Computer Vision and Pattern Recognition*, pages 5457–5466.

Carolyn E Lipscomb. 2000. Medical subject headings (MeSH). *Bulletin of the Medical Library Association*, 88(3).

Yinhan Liu, Myle Ott, Naman Goyal, Jingfei Du, Mandar Joshi, Danqi Chen, Omer Levy, Mike Lewis, Luke Zettlemoyer, and Veselin Stoyanov. 2019. RoBERTa: A robustly optimized BERT pretraining approach. *arXiv preprint arXiv:1907.11692*.

Risto Miikkulainen and Michael G Dyer. 1991. Natural language processing with modular PDP networks and distributed lexicon. *Cognitive Science*, 15(3):343–399.

Saif Mohammad, Svetlana Kiritchenko, and Xiaodan Zhu. 2013. NRC-Canada: Building the state-of-the-art in sentiment analysis of tweets. In *Second Joint Conference on Lexical and Computational Semantics (* SEM), Volume 2: Proceedings of the Seventh International Workshop on Semantic Evaluation (SemEval 2013)*, pages 321–327.

Finn Årup Nielsen. 2011. A new ANEW: Evaluation of a word list for sentiment analysis in microblogs. In *Workshop on 'Making Sense of Microposts: Big things come in small packages'*, pages 93–98.

Canberk Özdemir and Sabine Bergler. 2015a. CLaC-SentiPipe: SemEval2015 Subtasks 10 b,e, and Task 11. In *Proceedings of SemEval 2015 at NAACL/HLT*.

Canberk Özdemir and Sabine Bergler. 2015b. A comparative study of different sentiment lexica for sentiment analysis of tweets. In *Proceedings of the International Conference on Recent Advances in Natural Language Processing (RANLP 2015)*.

Giambattista Parascandolo, Niki Kilbertus, Mateo Rojas-Carulla, and Bernhard Schölkopf. 2018. Learning independent causal mechanisms. In *International Conference on Machine Learning (ICML)*, pages 4036–4044.

Adam Paszke, Sam Gross, Soumith Chintala, Gregory Chanan, Edward Yang, Zachary DeVito, Zeming Lin, Alban Desmaison, Luca Antiga, and Adam Lerer. 2017. Automatic differentiation in PyTorch. In *Advances in Neural Information Processing Systems 2017*.

Matthew E Peters, Mark Neumann, Mohit Iyyer, Matt Gardner, Christopher Clark, Kenton Lee, and Luke Zettlemoyer. 2018. Deep contextualized word representations. In *Proceedings of NAACL-HLT*, pages 2227–2237.

Jonas Pfeiffer, Andreas Rücklé, Clifton Poth, Aishwarya Kamath, Ivan Vulić, Sebastian Ruder, Kyunghyun Cho, and Iryna Gurevych. 2020. AdapterHub: A framework for adapting transformers. In *Proceedings of the 2020 Conference on Empirical Methods in Natural Language Processing: System Demonstrations*, pages 46–54, Online.

Rolandos Alexandros Potamias, Georgios Siolas, and Andreas-Georgios Stafylopatis. 2020. A transformer-based approach to irony and sarcasm detection. *Neural Computing and Applications*, pages 1–12.

Colin Raffel, Noam Shazeer, Adam Roberts, Katherine Lee, Sharan Narang, Michael Matena, Yanqi Zhou, Wei Li, and Peter J. Liu. 2020. Exploring the limits of transfer learning with a unified text-to-text transformer. *Journal of Machine Learning Research*, 21(140):1–67.

Radim Rehurek and Petr Sojka. 2010. Software framework for topic modelling with large corpora. In *In Proceedings of the LREC 2010 Workshop on New Challenges for NLP Frameworks*.

Sara Rosenthal, Noura Farra, and Preslav Nakov. 2017. SemEval-2017 Task 4: Sentiment analysis in Twitter. In *Proceedings of the 11th International Workshop on Semantic Evaluation (SemEval-2017)*, pages 502–518.

Bernhard Schölkopf, Dominik Janzing, Jonas Peters, Eleni Sgouritsa, Kun Zhang, and Joris Mooij. 2012. On causal and anticausal learning. In *Proceedings of the 29th International Conference on Machine Learning (ICML 2012)*, pages 1255–1262.

Richard Socher, Alex Perelygin, Jean Wu, Jason Chuang, Christopher D Manning, Andrew Ng, and Christopher Potts. 2013. Recursive deep models for semantic compositionality over a sentiment treebank. In *Proceedings of the 2013 Conference on Empirical Methods in Natural Language Processing*, pages 1631–1642.

Yu Sun, Shuohuan Wang, Yukun Li, Shikun Feng, Xuyi Chen, Han Zhang, Xin Tian, Danxiang Zhu, Hao Tian, and Hua Wu. 2019. Ernie: Enhanced representation through knowledge integration. In *Proceedings of the 57th Annual Meeting of the Association for Computational Linguistics*, page 1441–1451.

Ashish Vaswani, Noam Shazeer, Niki Parmar, Jakob Uszkoreit, Llion Jones, Aidan N Gomez, Łukasz Kaiser, and Illia Polosukhin. 2017. Attention is all you need. In *Advances in Neural Information Processing Systems*, pages 5998–6008.

Alex Wang, Amanpreet Singh, Julian Michael, Felix Hill, Omer Levy, and Samuel Bowman. 2018. GLUE: A multi-task benchmark and analysis platform for natural language understanding. In *Proceedings of the 2018 EMNLP Workshop BlackboxNLP: Analyzing and Interpreting Neural Networks for NLP*, pages 353–355, Brussels, Belgium.

Davy Weissenbacher, Abeed Sarker, Michael J. Paul, and Graciela Gonzalez-Hernandez. 2018. Overview of the third Social Media Mining for Health (SMM4H) Shared Tasks at EMNLP 2018. In *Proceedings of the 2018 EMNLP Workshop SMM4H: The 3rd Social Media Mining for Health Applications Workshop & Shared Task.*

Theresa Wilson, Janyce Wiebe, and Paul Hoffmann. 2005. Recognizing contextual polarity in phrase-level sentiment analysis. In *Proceedings of Human Language Technology Conference and Conference on Empirical Methods in Natural Language Processing*, pages 347–354.

David S Wishart, Yannick D Feunang, An C Guo, Elvis J Lo, Ana Marcu, Jason R Grant, Tanvir Sajed, Daniel Johnson, Carin Li, Zinat Sayeeda, et al. 2018. Drugbank 5.0: a major update to the drugbank database for 2018. *Nucleic acids research*, 46(D1):D1074–D1082.

Orest Xherija. 2018. Classification of medication-related tweets using stacked bidirectional LSTMs with context-aware attention. In *Proceedings of the 3rd Social Media Mining for Health Applications (SMM4H) Workshop & Shared Task at EMNLP.*

What BERTs and GPTs know about your brand? Probing contextual language models for affect associations

Vivek Srivastava*, **Stephen Pilli***, **Savita Bhat***, **Niranjan Pedanekar**†, **Shirish Karande**
TCS Research, Pune, India
{srivastava.vivek2, stephen.pilli, savita.bhat, n.pedanekar, shirish.karande}@tcs.com

Abstract

Investigating brand perception is fundamental to marketing strategies. In this regard, brand image, defined by a set of attributes (Aaker, 1997), is recognized as a key element in indicating how a brand is perceived by various stakeholders such as consumers and competitors. Traditional approaches (e.g., surveys) to monitor brand perceptions are time-consuming and inefficient. In the era of digital marketing, both brand managers and consumers engage with a vast amount of digital marketing content. The exponential growth of digital content has propelled the emergence of pre-trained language models such as BERT and GPT as essential tools in solving myriads of challenges with textual data. This paper seeks to investigate the extent of brand perceptions (i.e., brand and image attribute associations) these language models encode. We believe that any kind of bias for a brand and attribute pair may influence customer-centric downstream tasks such as recommender systems, sentiment analysis, and question-answering, e.g., suggesting a specific brand consistently when queried for '*innovative*' products. We use synthetic data and real-life data and report comparison results for five contextual LMs, viz. BERT, RoBERTa, DistilBERT, ALBERT and BART.

1 Introduction

Brands play a vital role in marketing strategies. They are essential to company positioning, marketing campaigns, customer relationships, and profits (Lovett et al., 2014). A brand persona is broadly defined by a set of attributes or dimensions; for instance, '*Mountain Dew*' may be recognized by attributes such as '*adventurous*' and '*rugged*'. While Aaker's dimensions (Aaker, 1997) are widely used to define a brand persona, more fine-grained attributes are documented in Lovett et al. (2014). Furthermore, evaluating a brand persona, i.e., how a brand is perceived by various stakeholders such as consumers, competitors, and market analysts has been an active area of research (Culotta and Cutler, 2016; Davies et al., 2018). Following the widespread success of pre-trained word representations, alternatively called Language Models (LMs), consumer-specific downstream tasks such as recommender systems, dialogues systems, and information retrieval engines look to make use of brand persona along with these representations to better fulfill consumer requirements.

Accordingly, we formulate our first research question (**RQ1**) as *Do LMs store implicit associations between brands and brand image attributes?*. To answer this, we look specifically at brands and brand image defined as affect attributes. Since LMs are trained on real-world data; we believe that these representations may be useful in understanding correlations between a brand and its persona attributes. While numerous studies have investigated unintended biases in Natural Language Processing systems (Dev et al., 2020; Dixon et al., 2018; Bolukbasi et al., 2016; Kiritchenko and Mohammad, 2018; Hutchinson et al., 2020), this is probably the first work that explores brand and affect attributes associations in pre-trained LMs.

These LMs are trained in an unsupervised manner on large-scale corpora. The training corpora generally comprise a variety of textual data such as common web crawl, Wikipedia dump, and book corpora. They are optimized to statistical properties of the training data from which they pick up and amplify real-world trends and associations along with biases such as gender and race (Kurita et al., 2019). Some of these biases may be beneficial for downstream applications (e.g., filtering out mature content for non-adult viewers) while some can be inappropriate (e.g., resume sorting system believing men are more qualified programmers than women (Bolukbasi et al., 2016; Kiritchenko and

* equal contribution
† corresponding author

Proceedings of Deep Learning Inside Out (DeeLIO): The 2nd Workshop on Knowledge Extraction and Integration for Deep Learning Architectures, pages 119–128
Online, June 10, 2021.

Mohammad, 2018). Marketing applications such as recommender systems and sentiment analysis can also perpetuate and highlight unfair biases, such as consistently showing popular brands as recommendations and not considering uncommon brands with less positive sentiment. With this in mind, we formulate our second research question (**RQ2**) as *Do the associations embedded in LMs signify any bias?* We also investigate *whether these associations are consistent across all LMs* as **RQ3**.

Brand personas are alternatively characterized as brand archetypes in Bechter's work (Bechter et al., 2016). Brand archetypes are widely used as effective branding and marketing strategy. According to Jung (Jung, 1954), archetypes are defined as inherent images within the collective human unconsciousness having universal meaning across cultures and generations. When successfully used, archetypal branding provides a narrative to connect with consumers. We formulate the following research questions: **RQ4** as *Do LMs capture brand personality intended by a brand?* and **RQ5** as *Do LMs capture brand personality as perceived by consumers?* We propose to use brand-attribute associations to understand brand archetypes perceived by LMs.

In this work, we probe five different LMs (BERT (Devlin et al., 2018), ALBERT (Lan et al., 2019), RoBERTa (Liu et al., 2019), DistilBERT (Sanh et al., 2019) and BART (Lewis et al., 2019)) on affect associations by using Masked Language Model (MLM) head. The choice of LMs was guided by three factors: 1) availability of MLM head, 2) variety in model architectures and 3) type and size of training data used while pre-training. Table 1 summarizes all the five LMs based on the pre-training data and the architecture. We believe that diversity in architectures and training data can influence the affective associations stored in representations. We propose to evaluate word representations based on following dimensions: 1) contextual similarity (Ethayarajh, 2019), 2) statistical implicit association tests (Kurita et al., 2019; Ethayarajh et al., 2019), 3) controlled probing tasks (Talmor et al., 2019) and 4) brand archetypes (Bechter et al., 2016). We observe that LMs do encode affective associations between brands and image attributes (**RQ1**). Some of these associations are consistently observed across multiple LMs (**RQ3**) and are shown to be further enhanced by finetuning thus implying certain bias (**RQ2**). We find that brand images or personality captured by LMs do not concur with either intended or consumer perceived brand personality. We believe that appropriate dataset and more rigor is needed to address **RQ4** and **RQ5**.

LM	Pre-training Data	Architecture
BERT	BookCorpus (800M words), English Wikipedia (2,500M words)	L=24, H=1024, A=16, T=340M
RoBERTa	BookCorpus (800M words), CC-NEWS (63M articles), OpenWebText (8M documents), Stories	L=24, H=1024, A=16, T=355M
DistilBERT	BookCorpus (800M words), English Wikipedia (2,500M words)	L=6, H=768, A=12, T=66M
ALBERT	BookCorpus (800M words), English Wikipedia (2,500M words)	L=24, H=1024, A=12, T=66M
BART	BookCorpus (800M words), CC-NEWS (63M articles), OpenWebText (8M documents), Stories	L=12, H=1024, A=16

Table 1: Variants of LMs. L–total layers, H–hidden size, A–self-attention heads, T–total parameters. We mention the architecture of the *large* version of all the LMs.

2 Related Work

The success of pre-trained word embeddings in achieving state-of-the-art results has sparked widespread interest in investigating information captured in these representations. Typically defined as '*probing task*', a wide variety of analyses have been proposed. For instance, (Hewitt and Manning, 2019) proposes a structural probe to test whether syntax trees are embedded in word representation space. Experiments in (Wallace et al., 2019) are aimed to investigate the numerical reasoning capabilities of an LM. Similarly, (Petroni et al., 2019) presents an in-depth analysis of relational knowledge present in pre-trained LMs. Penha and Hauff (2020) probe the contextual LMs (BERT and RoBERTa) for the conversational recommendation of books, movies, and music. Our work seeks to apply the idea of probing to a relatively unexplored area of affect analysis. To the best of our knowledge, this is the first work that presents a multi-pronged investigation of brands and subjective knowledge like affect attributes represented in contextual representation. Field and Tsvetkov (2019) is the most relevant prior work in terms of affect analysis. They present an entity-centric affective analysis with the use of contextual representations, where they find that meaningful affect information is captured in contextualize word representations but these representations are heavily biased towards their training data.

A significant effort has been seen in investigating the intrinsic bias in word embeddings. These representations are trained in an unsupervised manner using a large amount of training data typically consisting of common web crawls. As a result, all kinds of biases like gender, race, demography along with trends and preferences get encoded in LMs. Works in (Kurita et al., 2019; Dev et al., 2020; Ethayarajh et al., 2019) propose methodologies to measure and mitigate bias in word representations. Our work is targeted at finding trends and preferences that certain entities have by using a combination of old and new such measures.

3 Dataset

In this work, we evaluate affect information captured in the LMs for different brands. Accordingly, the selected brands should have large volumes of online data to get significant representation in the LMs. We choose 697 major US national brands reported in (Lovett et al., 2014). These brands are categorized into 16 different product categories. To analyze affect associations, we refer to surveys conducted by Young and Rubicam (Y&R) (Lovett et al., 2014) to measure a broad array of perceptions and attributes for a large number of brands. We choose 40 affect attributes listed as a part of '*Brand Image*' in (Lovett et al., 2014). We also manually map (see Table 8 in supplementary material and Bechter et al. (2016)) these attributes to one of the five Aaker's dimensions of brand personality. We restrict our analysis only to positive affect attributes since '*Arrogant*' and '*Unapproachable*' were the only two negative affect attributes observed in Y&R surveys. We understand the analysis with negative attributes is essential to explore the complete brand perception and we intend to pursue this in future. We consider three different data sources for our experiments as tabulated in Table 2. We choose appropriate datasets based on experiments' requirements. We describe the datasets in detail in supplementary material.

4 Experimental Setup

We outline our approach for exploring answers to the research questions stated above.

- **RQ1, RQ3**: Understanding brand and attribute word association at different layers of the LMs (see contextual geometry in Section 4.1).
- **RQ1, RQ2, RQ3, RQ4, RQ5**: Analyzing closeness between the brand and attribute words using statistical tests (see implicit association test in Section 4.2).
- **RQ1**: Probing for the association as well as the influence of brand name and the surrounding context on the attribute word (see probing task in Section 4.3).
- **RQ4**: Examining brand perceptions in terms of archetypes and affect attributes (see brand archetype in Section 4.4).

4.1 Contextual Geometry

Taking inspiration from (Ethayarajh, 2019), we use geometrical analysis to understand associations between brands and brand image attributes. Ethayarajh (2019) analyzes geometry of contextual representations across different layers. We follow the same approach to specifically analyze representations for brands and affect attributes. We use two metrics introduced in (Ethayarajh, 2019): *self-similarity* and *intra-sentence similarity*. Additionally, we use a similar methodology to define associations among brand words and affect words. We consider Ads. Dataset data for these experiments.

Let *bw* be a *brand word* and *aw* be an *attribute* or *affect word* appearing in sentences $\{s_1, s_2, ..., s_n\}$ at positions $\{i_1, i_2, .., i_n\}$ and $\{j_1, j_2, .., j_n\}$ respectively. Accordingly, $bw = s_1[i_1] = s_2[i_2] = .. = s_n[i_n]$ and $aw = s_1[j_1] = s_2[j_2] = .. = s_n[j_n]$ with i_k and j_k representing positions in sentence s_k. In other words, a brand word *bw* is the i_1^{th} word in sentence s_1 and attribute word *aw* is the j_1^{th} word in sentence s_1. Let $f_l(s, i)$ be a function that maps $s[i]$ to its representation in layer *l* of language model *f* (Ethayarajh, 2019). Then,

4.1.1 *affect-similarity*

The *affect-similarity* between *bw* and *aw* in layer *l* is defined as the average cosine similarity between contextualized representations of brand and attribute across *n* unique contexts.

$$AffSim_l(bw, aw) = \frac{1}{n}\sum_k cos(f_l(s_k, i_k), f_l(s_k, j_k))$$

Dataset	Data	Example	Brand	Attribute
Ads. Dataset (Hussain et al., 2017)	35k Action Reason pairs	"I should buy Converse shoes because they are stylish."	Converse	stylish
BCD (Roy et al., 2019)	1962 sentences from webpages containing both brand and affect attributes	"Verizon is a global leader delivering innovative communications solutions."	Verizon	innovative
Synthetic (Table 16 in Supplementary Material)	40 hand crafted sentences	"Apple is a trendy brand."	Apple	trendy

Table 2: Representative examples from three different datasets.

4.1.2 *intra-brand similarity*

The *intra-brand similarity* between a pair of brand words in layer l is

$$IntraBrandSim_l(bw_i, bw_j) = \frac{1}{n(n-1)} \sum_k \sum_{p \neq k} cos(f_l(s_k, i_k), f_l(s_p, j_p))$$

In other words, the *intra-brand similarity* provides average cosine similarity between representations of two brands across n different contexts. This measure captures how close the two brands are in the vector space.

4.1.3 *intra-attribute similarity*

Similarly, we define the *intra-attribute similarity* between a pair of attributes in layer l as the average cosine similarity between two attributes across n different contexts. This measure helps us understand the association between different affect words in the vector space and can be used while defining and analyzing brand persona.

4.2 Implicit Association Tests

The Implicit Association Test (IAT) (Greenwald et al., 1998) in its purest form measures association between two target concepts with respect to an attribute. This test has enabled the examination of unconscious thought processes and implicit biases among people in different contexts (Sleek, 2018). We believe that a variety of implicit biases and associations may be encoded in LMs. We use two interpretations of IAT (viz. WEAT and RIPA) to investigate brand and attribute associations in LMs.

The *Word Embedding Association Test* (WEAT) (Caliskan et al., 2017) for non-contextual word embeddings shows implicit biases captured in these representations. May et al. (2019) extend this test to sentence embeddings for contextual LMs. Since our focus is on words; we follow the approach used in (Kurita et al., 2019) to adapt WEAT for words. We also consider the new measure, *log-probability bias score*, introduced in (Kurita et al., 2019). This test follows a similar approach to WEAT except for the cosine similarity computation between target word and attributes is replaced by log-probability.

The work in (Ethayarajh et al., 2019) proves that any embedding model that implicitly does matrix factorization, subspace projection under certain conditions, can be considered as debiasing the embedding vectors. Accordingly, they propose a new method of the association called *relational inner product association* (RIPA) that uses the subspace projection method. We adapt RIPA measure for brands and attribute words.

Both *log-probability* and *RIPA* have been proposed as an alternative to the basic WEAT association test. We detail the experimental structure for these tests below.

4.2.1 WEAT

The WEAT test simulates the human implicit association test for word embeddings, measuring the association between two equal-sized sets of target concepts and two sets of attributes (May et al., 2019). Specifically, in our case, we consider high-level brand categories as target concept sets and Aaker's dimensions as attribute sets. Specific details about test statistics along with permutation test and effect size can be found in (Caliskan et al., 2017; May et al., 2019; Kurita et al., 2019).

4.2.2 Log-probability score

We consider the same set of broad categories for brands and Aaker's dimensions for attributes as target and attribute sets respectively for finding log-probability score. Similar to (Kurita et al., 2019), we compute the mean log probability bias score for each attribute and permute the attributes to measure statistical significance with the permutation test.

For both *WEAT* and *log-probability* test, we use synthetic data generated by appropriate handcrafted templates. We apply these tests to all combinations of brand categories and Aaker's dimensions. We apply these tests on combinations of all brand categories except '*Food and Dining*' and 5 Aaker's

LM	Brand pair		Attribute pair		Brand-attribute pair	
	MS	LS	MS	LS	MS	LS
BERT	Chrysler-Jeep	ESPN-Wilson	Safe-Secure	Innovative-Reasonable	Disney-Magical	Toyota-Reasonable
RoBERTa	Dodge-Jeep	BBC-Sonic	Bright-Vibrant	Tough-Responsible	Disney-Magical	Target-Kind
DistilBERT	Chrysler-Volkswagen	Fox-Honda	Nice-Wonderful	Fun-Robust	IBM-Innovate	Microsoft-Popular
ALBERT	Honda-Toyota	Sprint-IBM	Lovely-Charming	Funny-Bright	Volkswagen-Excellent	Samsung-Best
BART	Dodge-Lincoln	Intel-Nokia	Strong-Efficient	Friendly-Lovely	Jeep-Simple	Intel-Efficient

Table 3: Affect associations across different LMs for least similar (LS) and most similar (MS) brands and attributes.

affect dimensions. We use the pairwise ranking to rank these combinations.

4.2.3 RIPA

For our affect analysis formulation, we define RIPA as the projection of the affect word vector i.e. attribute onto the bias subspace defined by a pair of brands. We use handcrafted templates to generate sentences corresponding to 40 attributes combined with brand words. Thus, we get 40 representations for every brand and 697 representations for every attribute. Final brand and attribute vectors are computed by taking an average of corresponding vector sets. RIPA score between each attribute word and a pair of brand words is then calculated by taking the inner product of the first principal component of the subspace defined by the pair of brand words and attribute word. For a brand pair (x,y) and an attribute word w, a positive RIPA score suggests the relatively more association of w with the brand x and vice-versa.

4.3 Probing Tasks

A large body of research comprising of probing tasks is dedicated to exploring what is captured by contextual LMs. We define two probing tasks that are essentially cloze tasks to analyze brand and affect attributes associations. In the simplest form, we consider MLM setup: given a sentence with brand and masked attribute word, we use pre-trained LM with MLM head to predict words at the masked position. If a model predicts the correct attribute in the top-5 position, then we infer that the model representations have captured the corresponding affect association. Additionally, to understand the behavior after fine-tuning, we introduce MLP with a 1-hidden layer to the MLM setup to train the LMs as discussed in (Talmor et al., 2019); we call this setup MLP-MLM.

To further analyze sensitivity to context, we define perturbed language control, where we introduce nonsensical words into the sentences. We observe if there is any effect of nonsense words to affect associations. MLM setup is used to experiment on all LMs using Ads. Dataset and BCD datasets, whereas MLP-MLM uses only Ads. Dataset and is experimented on all the LMs except BART.

4.4 Brand Archetypes

Brand archetypes provide a relatable connection between brands and consumers. We consider implicit and explicit perceptions of archetypes. We use Lovett's data (Lovett et al., 2014) to understand people's tacit perceptions about brand archetypes in terms of affect attributes. We believe that training data used for pre-training LMs may record impressions about the brand in the wild. Accordingly, we consider pre-trained LMs to investigate the explicit perceptions for archetypes. We consider 12 archetypes (Jung, 1954) for this analysis. We manually map every archetype to a set of affect attributes from Lovett's attributes (Lovett et al., 2014) with the help from (Bechter et al., 2016) (see Table 8 and 10 in Supplementary Material).

To understand the brand archetype information captured in the LMs, we take the intersection of the top attributes obtained using the brand-attribute affect similarity and the attributes for a given archetype (obtained after manual mapping). First, we identify the top-5 attributes for a given brand using the affect similarity score and then we take the percentage overlap with the list of attributes corresponding to each of the archetypes. The percentage overlap suggests the degree of brand archetype-related knowledge instilled in the LMs. To better evaluate our results qualitatively we choose five brands (*Adidas*, *Apple*, *GAP*, *Pepsi*, and *Porsche*) from different brand categories.

5 Discussion

We present a battery of analyses aimed at finding how much knowledge do the off-the-shelf LMs capture about brands and affect attributes.

5.1 Affect Association

We believe that *brand persona* can be succinctly defined by a set of affect words, namely attributes.

We make use of *intra-attribute similarity* to understand which of the attributes are closer to each other in embedding space. Using *intra-brand similarity*, we also examine how the brands of a category are positioned in the vector space. Additionally, the *affect similarity* helps us find the correlation between brand and affect words. We argue that a brand persona can be identified by combining results from these three measures. It should be noted that some of these associations of brands and attributes are indeed consistent across all LMs (**RQ1, RQ3**). Table 3 reports some of the most similar and least similar associations. By far, brands of category '*Cars*' are seen to have high similarity among themselves consistently across all LMs. In some instances, brands of categories '*Technology*' and '*Telecommunication*' are found to have a close association. Similarly, *cliques* of attributes are observed such as *elegant, lovely, fashionable, popular* in BERT and *reliable, efficient, helpful, convenient* in DistilBERT. These clusters of attributes can further be beneficial in defining a brand persona. Using the *affect-similarity*, we found interesting associations between brands and attributes. For instance, brand '*Disney*' is associated most with attributes , '*magical*' and '*fun*' across all LMs whereas brand '*IBM*' is highly associated with '*innovative*' and '*intelligent*'. These positive associations help understand the brand persona. We also observe the least similar relations across all LMs. There are some surprising results, such as brands '*Intel*' and '*Samsung*' not being '*efficient*' and '*Best*' respectively. Such associations may not be what brand marketing teams would want to portray for their brands. We believe that these negative associations are also important in identifying the perception of a brand.

5.2 Contextual Representation

The *self-similarity* metric provides a measure to evaluate the contextualization of a word. Following (Ethayarajh, 2019), lower self-similarity is observed when the representations are more contextualized. We compare the average self-similarity of a representative brand and attribute words for each layer of selected LMs. For all five models, self-similarity is lower in upper layers or final layers i.e. the word representations are more context-specific. Out of five LMs, RoBERTa representations have the lowest self-similarity. Furthermore, it should be noted that different words have different levels of context specificity in different LMs.

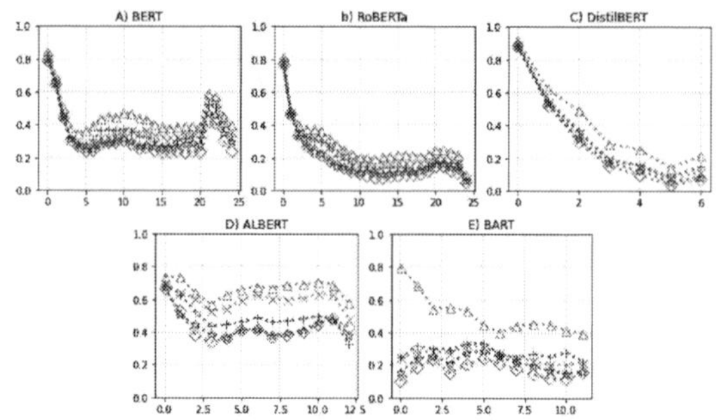

Figure 1: *Self-Similarity* for brand and attribute words '*Google*' ($+$), '*Gymboree*' ($\triangle$), '*good*' ($*$) , '*exceptional*' (x) and '*bad*' ($\diamond$).

Ethayarajh (2019) observes that the variety of context is important for having variations in representation and common words or popular words like '*the*', '*of*' and '*to*' generally have larger variation in their representations. We believe that popular brands have the diverse contexts in the training data used for pre-training the LMs and hence are more contextualized. As can be seen in Figure 1, representations for *Google* are more context-specific as compared to those for *Gymboree*. Affect words '*good*','*bad*' and '*exceptional* also have different context specificity implying a certain kind of inequality in the encoded knowledge corresponding to different words. This pattern is observed across all LMs implying that variation in representations is consistent irrespective of the amount of training data used while pre-training.

5.3 Implicit Association Tests

In WEAT as well as in Log Probability, the null hypothesis is that there is no significant difference between the two sets of brand categories in terms of their relative similarity to the two sets of Aaker's dimensions. The polarity of the effect size indi-

LM	Brand Category	Aaker's Dimensions	WEAT	LOG PROB
BERT	Sports/Health	sincerity/ ruggedness	-0.5244	-1.1856
RoBERTa	Media/Finance	excitement/ sincerity	0.63615	0.6602
DistilBERT	Childrens/ Dept. Stores	competence/ excitement	-0.9681	-1.1161
ALBERT	Tech./Beauty	sophistication/ competence	0.3396	-0.6067

Table 4: Effect-size of *WEAT* and *Log Probability* (at p-value < 0.01)

LM	Media & entertainment		Technology product & stores		Cars	
	Fun	**Original**	**Original**	**Reasonable**	**Traditional**	**Worthy**
BERT	Disney	HBO	Sony	Microsoft	Volvo	Volvo
RoBERTa	YouTube	CNBC	IBM	Apple	GM	GM
DistilBERT	YouTube	MTV	Apple	Samsung	GM	Jaguar
ALBERT	YouTube	MTV	Pioneer	Sharp	Buick	Buick

Table 5: Top brand and attribute associations for three different brand categories using RIPA association test.

cates that the categories and dimensions are directly or inversely related. For example, consider, the *Sports/Health* in brand category and *sincerity/ruggedness* in Aaker's Dimensions from Table 4 the polarity of effect size indicates that they are inversely related, which means *'Sports'* is more associated with *'ruggedness'* similarly *'Health'* is to the *'sincerity'* (**RQ2**). Since we are considering the permutation test, the p-value indicates the significance of their association. Most of these associations are consistently observed across all LMs (**RQ1, RQ3**). This has intrigued us to further examine which LM is better at capturing brand personality as perceived by consumers. The pairwise ranking is applied to all the combinations of brand categories and Aaker's dimensions (Aaker, 1997). The resultant ranked dimensions of all the categories are assessed against the ground truth values/ consumers perception (please refer Table 9 in Supplementary Material) in Lovett's data (Lovett et al., 2014). Using the same procedure, all the LMs are ranked independently for each brand category (refer to Table 15 in Supplementary Material). We observe that BERT has better agreement with consumers' perceptions of brand personality amongst all the language models in both WEAT and Log Probability (**RQ5**). Though RoBERTa did follow, other LMs agree equally likely in Log Probability. Furthermore, DistilBERT has a consistently poor agreement in Log Probability. One interesting observation is that WEAT and Log Probability give the same ranking for all LMs in the *'Cars'* brand category.

RIPA test measures the word embedding association using the subspace projection method (Ethayarajh et al., 2019). A positive score suggests that brand x is more associated with attribute word w than brand y for a given brand pair (x,y) and attribute word w. We combine this score for a brand with all attributes to compute a preference score for a brand. Based on this preference score, we found the most associated brands for every attribute word. Representative results are presented in Table 5. We observe that the predictions across different LMs for a given category are occasionally consistent (e.g., YouTube being associated as a fun brand in RoBERTa, DistilBERT, and ALBERT) (**RQ3**). This could be attributed to the perception of brands being captured by the various LMs. Also, we see the diversity in the predictions for different attribute words (e.g., BERT and RoBERTa has different brand association across different categories) which also signifies that the brand associations being captured by the LMs vary with the context (**RQ1**).

5.4 Impact of fine-tuning

Comparing the LMs off-the-shelf gives us an idea of how affect-related attributes are represented in LMs. From Table 6, we find that BART and RoBERTa have the better brand and attribute associations amongst the LMs on the Ads. Dataset and the BCD datasets (**RQ1**). Further, to understand the impact of fine-tuning, we employ techniques proposed by (Talmor et al., 2019) to measure the language mismatch. In this exercise, we fine-tune the LM with examples from Ads. Dataset; high performance indicates that the LM was able to overcome the language mismatch with a very small number of samples. Trends in the Figure 2 conveys that BERT and RoBERTa achieve high performance with a limited number of samples, in turn indicating that their internal representations are well suited for any downstream tasks related to brand personality. On the other hand, ALBERT has the least performance improvement of 8.08%, meaning ALBERT has poor internal representation and needs more samples to overcome the language mismatch. BERT outperforms all LMs with 22.28% improvement followed by RoBERTa with 20.06%.

5.5 Sensitivity to context

To understand the context-dependency of the attributes related to affect, we employ perturbed language control as discussed by (Talmor et al., 2019). This control task gives us an idea of how well the pre-trained representation of the words in context can influence the affect association. For exam-

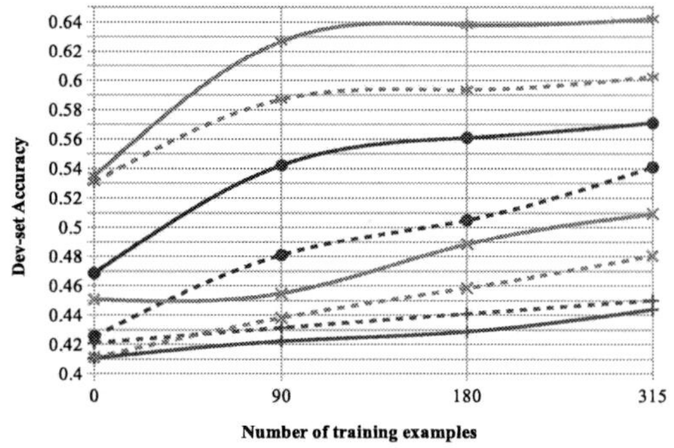

Figure 2: MLP-MLM with (- -) and without perturbation (–) for different LMs- BERT (•), ALBERT (+), DistilBERT (x), RoBERTa (*)

ple, consider the statement *"I should play Nintendo because it is [MASK] ."* and its perturbed version *"I snap play Nintendo ya it is [MASK] ."*. If *'fun'* from the set of attributes is persistently perceived to be in top-5 predictions irrespective of perturbation, we say that context doesn't influence attributes. In either of the setups discussed in ***Controlled probing task***, the drop in accuracy after perturbation indicates that the affect attributes are context-dependent. Our observations on *MLM* setup (Table 6) and *MLP-MLM* setup (Figure 2) indicate that the attributes are moderately influenced by the context. We need more samples to comment on ALBERT.

LM	Zero-shot		Perturbed	
	Ads. Dataset	BCD	Ads. Dataset	BCD
BERT	0.51	0.66	0.47	0.64
RoBERTa	0.58	0.77	0.51	0.77
DistilBERT	0.46	0.55	0.45	0.54
ALBERT	0.42	0.55	0.41	0.53
BART	0.65	0.61	0.59	0.61

Table 6: MLM setup with and without perturbation on the Ads. Dataset and BCD datasets.

LM	Top archetype(s) based on the attribute overlap
BERT	Creator, Jester, Outlaw, Magician, Hero, Sage, Explorer, Innocent
RoBERTa	Creator, Jester, Outlaw, Magician, Hero, Sage, Explorer, Innocent
DistilBERT	Ruler, Everyman, Magician, Sage, Innocent
ALBERT	Creator, Jester, Outlaw, Magician, Hero, Sage, Explorer, Innocent
BART	Ruler, Everyman, Magician, Sage, Innocent

Table 7: Archetype information extracted from the LMs for the brand *Adidas*.

5.6 Archetypes

We investigate implicit perceptions about brands using data collected in a survey (Lovett et al., 2014). Table 7 shows the result of the top archetype(s) extracted from the various LMs for the brand *Adidas*. The actual archetype of *Adidas* is Creator[1]. We make three major observations about the brand archetype extracted from different LMs (**RQ4**). First, we observe the same prediction of the top archetype across various LMs. For instance, we get the same set of top archetype(s) prediction with BERT, RoBERTa, and ALBERT for the brand *Adidas*. This behavior could be attributed to the absence of explicit brand archetype-related information in the LMs. Next, we observe multiple top archetypes with the same degree of attribute overlap which suggests that LMs does not capture the brand archetype information distinctly. Lastly, we observe that the degree of attribute overlap for the top archetypes is consistently very low (i.e., an overlap of only one out of five attributes) for all the five brands across all the five LMs. This low degree of attribute overlap is also suggestive of the absence of archetype-related information in the LMs. The actual archetype of a brand can not be distinguished in any of the LMs. We make similar observations for other brands as well (see Table 11 to 14 in Supplementary Material). The current observation that the LMs do not reflect the expected perception of the brand's archetype needs to be investigated further with archetype-specific datasets.

6 Conclusion

In this paper, we presented a series of exploration setups to address research questions pertaining to associations between brands and brand image attributes.

Our analyses were able to tease out varied responses even from the models having identical training data and pre-training learning objectives. We observed that there exists a definite association between brands and attribute affect words across all LMs (**RQ1**). This impression is observed across a range of abstraction i.e. from individual brands and broader categories to attributes and Aaker's dimensions.

In all our experiments, some categories such

[1]https://report.adidas-group.com/2019/en/group-management-report-our-company/corporate-strategy/adidas-brand-strategy.html

as '*Cars*' and '*Technology product & stores*' and brands such as '*Disney*' and '*Intel*' are found to have consistent associations across all LMs (**RQ3**). However, it is interesting to note that these biases do not concur with both consumer perceptions and intended perceptions of the brand (**RQ4** and **RQ5**).

Lastly, it is seen that perturbations in sentence moderately influences the association between brands and affect words. Improved performance in fine-tuning implies that affect associations are enhanced (**RQ2**). Since we do not have enough data, it remains to be seen how additional training data changes the landscape.

This work documents an initial investigation of brand and attribute associations in different LMs. With enough task-specific data, we plan to evaluate how the affect associations are enhanced. We also intend to use these observations in further defining brand-persona and brand-archetype definitions. These impressions can help understand perceptions about a brand. Furthermore, this can be extended in investigating impressions about iconic entities such as sports teams, celebrities, and politicians.

References

Jennifer L Aaker. 1997. Dimensions of brand personality. *Journal of marketing research*, 34(3):347–356.

Clemens Bechter, Giorgio Farinelli, Rolf-Dieter Daniel, and Michael Frey. 2016. Advertising between archetype and brand personality. *Administrative Sciences*, 6(2):5.

Tolga Bolukbasi, Kai-Wei Chang, James Zou, Venkatesh Saligrama, and Adam Kalai. 2016. Quantifying and reducing stereotypes in word embeddings. *arXiv preprint arXiv:1606.06121*.

Aylin Caliskan, Joanna J Bryson, and Arvind Narayanan. 2017. Semantics derived automatically from language corpora contain human-like biases. *Science*, 356(6334):183–186.

Aron Culotta and Jennifer Cutler. 2016. Mining brand perceptions from twitter social networks. *Marketing science*, 35(3):343–362.

Gary Davies, José I Rojas-Méndez, Susan Whelan, Melisa Mete, and Theresa Loo. 2018. Brand personality: theory and dimensionality. *Journal of product & brand management*.

Sunipa Dev, Tao Li, Jeff M Phillips, and Vivek Srikumar. 2020. On measuring and mitigating biased inferences of word embeddings. In *Proceedings of the AAAI Conference on Artificial Intelligence*, volume 34, pages 7659–7666.

Jacob Devlin, Ming-Wei Chang, Kenton Lee, and Kristina Toutanova. 2018. Bert: Pre-training of deep bidirectional transformers for language understanding. *arXiv preprint arXiv:1810.04805*.

Lucas Dixon, John Li, Jeffrey Sorensen, Nithum Thain, and Lucy Vasserman. 2018. Measuring and mitigating unintended bias in text classification. In *Proceedings of the 2018 AAAI/ACM Conference on AI, Ethics, and Society*, pages 67–73.

Kawin Ethayarajh. 2019. How contextual are contextualized word representations? comparing the geometry of bert, elmo, and gpt-2 embeddings. *arXiv preprint arXiv:1909.00512*.

Kawin Ethayarajh, David Duvenaud, and Graeme Hirst. 2019. Understanding undesirable word embedding associations. *arXiv preprint arXiv:1908.06361*.

Anjalie Field and Yulia Tsvetkov. 2019. Entity-centric contextual affective analysis. *arXiv preprint arXiv:1906.01762*.

Anthony G Greenwald, Debbie E McGhee, and Jordan LK Schwartz. 1998. Measuring individual differences in implicit cognition: the implicit association test. *Journal of personality and social psychology*, 74(6):1464.

John Hewitt and Christopher D Manning. 2019. A structural probe for finding syntax in word representations. In *Proceedings of the 2019 Conference of the North American Chapter of the Association for Computational Linguistics: Human Language Technologies, Volume 1 (Long and Short Papers)*, pages 4129–4138.

Zaeem Hussain, Mingda Zhang, Xiaozhong Zhang, Keren Ye, Christopher Thomas, Zuha Agha, Nathan Ong, and Adriana Kovashka. 2017. Automatic understanding of image and video advertisements. In *Proceedings of the IEEE Conference on Computer Vision and Pattern Recognition*, pages 1705–1715.

Ben Hutchinson, Vinodkumar Prabhakaran, Emily Denton, Kellie Webster, Yu Zhong, and Stephen Denuyl. 2020. Social biases in nlp models as barriers for persons with disabilities. *arXiv preprint arXiv:2005.00813*.

CG Jung. 1954. Psychological aspects of the mother archetype. collected works 9/1.

Svetlana Kiritchenko and Saif M Mohammad. 2018. Examining gender and race bias in two hundred sentiment analysis systems. *arXiv preprint arXiv:1805.04508*.

Keita Kurita, Nidhi Vyas, Ayush Pareek, Alan W Black, and Yulia Tsvetkov. 2019. Measuring bias in contextualized word representations. *arXiv preprint arXiv:1906.07337*.

Zhenzhong Lan, Mingda Chen, Sebastian Goodman, Kevin Gimpel, Piyush Sharma, and Radu Soricut. 2019. Albert: A lite bert for self-supervised learning of language representations. *arXiv preprint arXiv:1909.11942*.

Mike Lewis, Yinhan Liu, Naman Goyal, Marjan Ghazvininejad, Abdelrahman Mohamed, Omer Levy, Ves Stoyanov, and Luke Zettlemoyer. 2019. Bart: Denoising sequence-to-sequence pre-training for natural language generation, translation, and comprehension. *arXiv preprint arXiv:1910.13461*.

Yinhan Liu, Myle Ott, Naman Goyal, Jingfei Du, Mandar Joshi, Danqi Chen, Omer Levy, Mike Lewis, Luke Zettlemoyer, and Veselin Stoyanov. 2019. Roberta: A robustly optimized bert pretraining approach. *arXiv preprint arXiv:1907.11692*.

Mitchell Lovett, Renana Peres, and Ron Shachar. 2014. A data set of brands and their characteristics. *Marketing Science*, 33(4):609–617.

Chandler May, Alex Wang, Shikha Bordia, Samuel R. Bowman, and Rachel Rudinger. 2019. On measuring social biases in sentence encoders. In *Proceedings of the 2019 Conference of the North American Chapter of the Association for Computational Linguistics: Human Language Technologies, Volume 1 (Long and Short Papers)*, pages 622–628.

Gustavo Penha and Claudia Hauff. 2020. What does bert know about books, movies and music? probing bert for conversational recommendation. In *Fourteenth ACM Conference on Recommender Systems*, pages 388–397.

Fabio Petroni, Tim Rocktäschel, Patrick Lewis, Anton Bakhtin, Yuxiang Wu, Alexander H Miller, and Sebastian Riedel. 2019. Language models as knowledge bases? *arXiv preprint arXiv:1909.01066*.

Soumyadeep Roy, Niloy Ganguly, Shamik Sural, Niyati Chhaya, and Anandhavelu Natarajan. 2019. Understanding brand consistency from web content. In *Proceedings of the 10th ACM Conference on Web Science*, pages 245–253.

Victor Sanh, Lysandre Debut, Julien Chaumond, and Thomas Wolf. 2019. Distilbert, a distilled version of bert: smaller, faster, cheaper and lighter. *arXiv preprint arXiv:1910.01108*.

Scott Sleek. 2018. The bias beneath: Two decades of measuring implicit associations. *APS Observer*, 31(2).

Alon Talmor, Yanai Elazar, Yoav Goldberg, and Jonathan Berant. 2019. olmpics–on what language model pre-training captures. *arXiv preprint arXiv:1912.13283*.

Eric Wallace, Yizhong Wang, Sujian Li, Sameer Singh, and Matt Gardner. 2019. Do nlp models know numbers? probing numeracy in embeddings. *arXiv preprint arXiv:1909.07940*.

Attention vs non-attention for a Shapley-based explanation method

Tom Kersten
University of Amsterdam
t.kersten@uva.nl

Hugh Mee Wong
University of Amsterdam
h.m.wong@uva.nl

Jaap Jumelet
ILLC, University of Amsterdam
j.w.d.jumelet@uva.nl

Dieuwke Hupkes
Facebook AI Research
dieuwkehupkes@fb.com

Abstract

The field of explainable AI has recently seen an explosion in the number of explanation methods for highly non-linear deep neural networks. The extent to which such methods – that are often proposed and tested in the domain of computer vision – are appropriate to address the explainability challenges in NLP is yet relatively unexplored. In this work, we consider *Contextual Decomposition* (CD) – a Shapley-based input feature attribution method that has been shown to work well for recurrent NLP models – and we test the extent to which it is useful for models that contain attention operations. To this end, we extend CD to cover the operations necessary for attention-based models. We then compare how long distance subject-verb relationships are processed by models with and without attention, considering a number of different syntactic structures in two different languages: English and Dutch. Our experiments confirm that CD can successfully be applied for attention-based models as well, providing an alternative Shapley-based attribution method for modern neural networks. In particular, using CD, we show that the English and Dutch models demonstrate similar processing behaviour, but that under the hood there are consistent differences between our attention and non-attention models.

1 Introduction

Machine learning models using deep neural architectures have seen tremendous performance improvements over the last few years. The advent of models such as LSTMs (Hochreiter and Schmidhuber, 1997) and, more recently, attention-based models such as Transformers (Vaswani et al., 2017) have allowed some language technologies to reach near human levels of performance. However, this performance has come at the cost of the interpretability of these models: high levels of non-linearity make it a near impossible task for a human to comprehend how these models operate.

Understanding how non-interpretable black box models make their predictions has become an active area of research in recent years (Hupkes et al., 2018; Jumelet and Hupkes, 2018; Samek et al., 2019; Linzen et al., 2019; Tenney et al., 2019; Ettinger, 2020, i.a.). One popular interpretability approach makes use of *feature attribution methods*, that explain a model prediction in terms of the *contributions* of the input features. For instance, a feature attribution method for a sentiment analysis task can tell the modeller how much each of the input words contributed to the decision of a particular sentence.

Multiple methods of assigning contributions to the input feature approaches exist. Some are based on local model approximations (Ribeiro et al., 2016), others on gradient-based information (Simonyan et al., 2014; Sundararajan et al., 2017) and yet others consider perturbation-based methods (Lundberg and Lee, 2017) that leverage concepts from game theory such as Shapley values (Shapley, 1953). Out of these approaches the Shapley-based attribution methods are computationally the most expensive, but they are better able at explaining more complex model dynamics involving feature interactions. This makes these methods well-suited for explaining the behaviour of current NLP models on a more linguistic level.

In this work, we therefore focus our efforts on that last category of attribution methods, focusing in particular on a method known as Contextual Decomposition (CD, Murdoch et al., 2018), which provides a polynomial approach towards approximating Shapley values. This method has been shown to work well on recurrent models without attention (Jumelet et al., 2019; Saphra and Lopez, 2020), but has not yet been used to provide insights into the linguistic capacities of attention-based models. Here, to investigate the extent to which this method is also applicable for attention

Proceedings of Deep Learning Inside Out (DeeLIO): The 2nd Workshop on Knowledge Extraction and Integration for Deep Learning Architectures, pages 129–139
Online, June 10, 2021.

based models, we extend the method to include the operations required to deal with attention-based models and we compare two different recurrent models: a multi-layered LSTM model (similar to Jumelet et al., 2019), and a Single Headed Attention RNN (SHA-RNN, Merity, 2019). We focus on the task of *language modelling* and aim to discover simultaneously whether attribution methods like CD are applicable when attention is used, as well as how the attention mechanism influence the resulting feature attributions, focusing in particular on whether these attributions are in line with human intuitions. Following, i.a. Jumelet et al. (2019), Lakretz et al. (2019) and Giulianelli et al. (2018), we focus on how the models process long-distance subject verb relationships across a number of different syntactic constructions. To broaden our scope, we include two different languages: English and Dutch.

Through our experiments we find that, while both English and Dutch language models produce similar results, our attention and non-attention models behave differently. These differences manifest in incorrect attributions for the subjects in sentences with a plural subject-verb pair, where we find that a higher attribution is given to a plural subject when a singular verb is used compared to a singular subject.

Our main contributions to the field thus lie in two dimensions: on the one hand, we compare attention and non-attention models with regards to their explainability. On the other hand, we perform our analysis in two languages, namely Dutch and English, to see if patterns hold in different languages.

2 Background

In this section we first discuss the model architectures that we consider. Following this, we explain the attribution method that we use to explain the different models. Finally, we consider the task which we use to extract explanations.

2.1 Model architectures

To examine the differences between attention and non-attention models, we look at one instance of each kind of model. For the attention model, we consider the Single Headed Attention RNN (SHA-RNN, Merity, 2019), and for our non-attention model a multi-layered LSTM (Gulordava et al., 2018). Since both models use an LSTM at their core, we hope to capture and isolate the influence of the attention mechanism on the behaviour of the model. Using a Transformer architecture instead would have made this comparison far more challenging, given that these kinds of models differ in multiple significant aspects from LSTMs with regards to their processing mechanism. Below, we give a brief overview of the SHA-RNN architecture.

SHA-RNN The attention model we consider is the Single Headed Attention RNN, or SHA-RNN, proposed by Merity (2019). The SHA-RNN was designed to be a reasonable alternative to the comparatively much larger Transformer models. Merity argues that while larger models can bring better performance, this often comes at the cost of training and inference time. As such, the author proposed this smaller model, which achieves results comparable to earlier Transformer models, without hyperparameter tuning.

The SHA-RNN consists of a block structure with three modules: an LSTM, a pointer-based attention layer and a feed-forward Boom layer (we provide a graphical overview in Figure 1). These blocks can be stacked to create a similar setup to that of an encoder Transformer. Layer normalisation is applied at several points in the model.

The attention layer in the SHA-RNN uses only a single attention head, creating a similar mechanism to Grave et al. (2017) and Merity et al. (2017). This is in contrast to most other Transformer (and thus attention) models, which utilise multiple attention heads. However, recent work, like Michel et al. (2019), has shown that using only a single attention head may in some cases provide similar performance to a multi-headed approach, while significantly reducing the computational cost. Importantly, when using multiple blocks of the SHA-RNN, the attention layer is only applied in the second to last block.

The Boom layer represents the feed-forward layers commonly found in Transformer models (Vaswani et al., 2017). In his work, Merity uses a single feed-forward layer with a GELU activation (Hendrycks and Gimpel, 2016), followed by summation over the output to reduce the dimension of the resulting vector to that before applying the feed-forward layer.

2.2 Contextual Decomposition

The interpretability method that we use and extend in this paper is Contextual Decomposition (CD

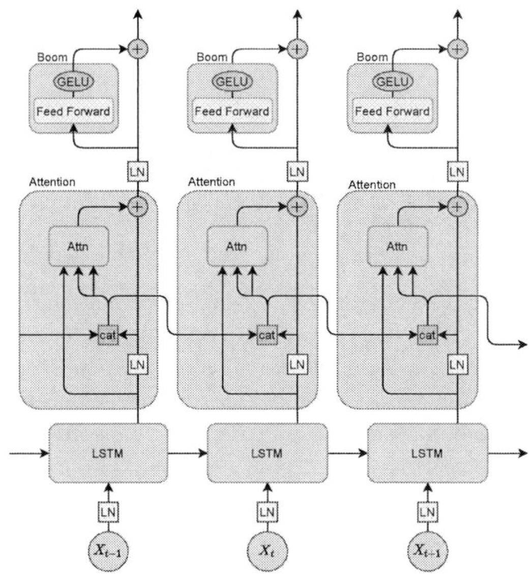

Figure 1: A schematic overview of a block in the SHA-RNN. A block in the SHA-RNN is composed of an LSTM, a single headed attention layer and a Boom feed-forward layer. Throughout the model, layer normalisation is used. Hidden states are passed between subsequent steps in the model. The memory state is concatenated with previous memory states, and passed on as well.

Murdoch et al., 2018), a feature attribution method for explaining individual predictions made by an LSTM. CD decomposes the output into a sum of two contribution types $\beta + \gamma$: one part resulting from a specific "relevant" token or phrase (β), and one part resulting from all other input to the model (γ), which is said to be "irrelevant". The token or phrase of interest is provided as an additional parameter to the model.

CD performs a modified forward pass through the model for each individual token in the input sentence. The $\beta + \gamma$ decomposition is achieved by splitting up the hidden and cell state of the LSTM into two parts as well:

$$h_t = \beta_t + \gamma_t \tag{1}$$

$$c_t = \beta_t^c + \gamma_t^c \tag{2}$$

This decomposition is constructed such that β corresponds to contributions made solely by elements in the relevant phrase, while γ represents all other contributions. Fundamental to CD is the role of interactions between β and γ terms that arrive from operations such as (point-wise) multiplications. CD resolves this by "factorizing" the outcome of a non-linear activation function into a sum of components, based on an approximation of the Shapley value of the activation function (Shapley, 1953).

For example, the forget gate update of the cell state in an LSTM is defined as

$$c_t' = c_{t-1} \odot \sigma(W_f x_t + V_f h_{t-1} + b_f) \tag{3}$$

where $W_f \in \mathbb{R}^{d_x \times d_h}$, $V_f \in \mathbb{R}^{d_h \times d_h}$ and $b_f \in \mathbb{R}^{d_h}$. CD decomposes both c_{t-1} and h_{t-1} into a sum of β and γ terms:

$$\begin{aligned} c_t' = & (\beta_{t-1}^c + \gamma_{t-1}^c) \\ & \odot \sigma(W_f x_t + V_f(\beta_{t-1} + \gamma_{t-1}) + b_f) \end{aligned} \tag{4}$$

The forget gate is then decomposed into a sum of four components (x, β, γ & b_f), based on their Shapley values, which leads to a cross product between the terms in the decomposed cell state, and the decomposed forget gate. The $\beta + \gamma$ decomposition of the new cell state c_t is formed by determining which specific interactions between β and γ components should be assigned to the new β_t^c and γ_t^c terms.

In this work, we consider the generalisation of the CD method proposed by Jumelet et al. (2019), namely Generalized Contextual Decomposition (GCD). They alter the way that β and γ interactions are divided over these terms. As such, this method provides a more complete picture of the interactions within the model. For a more detailed explanation of the procedure we refer to the original papers.

2.3 Number Agreement Task

To test our models, we consider the Number Agreement (NA) task, a linguistic task that has stood central in various works in the interpretability literature (Lakretz et al., 2019; Linzen et al., 2016; Gulordava et al., 2018; Wolf, 2019; Goldberg, 2019). In this task, a model is evaluated by how well it is able to track the subject-verb relations over long distances, as assessed by the percentage of cases in which the model is able to match the form of the verb to the number of the subject. The challenge in the NA task lies in the presence of one or more attractor nouns between the subject and the verb that competes with the subject. For instance in the sentence "The boys at the car greet", "car" forms the attractor noun, and is a different number than the boys, thereby possibly confusing the model to predict a singular verb, "greets".

Several earlier studies preceded us in considering number agreement as a means to investigate language models. Linzen et al. laid the groundwork for this task, using it to assess the ability of LSTMs to learn syntax-sensitive dependencies. In their work, they only considered the English language. Gulordava et al. (2018) extended the task to the Italian, Hebrew and Russian languages. Moreover, they provided a more in-depth study of the Italian model, comparing it to human subjects. Lakretz et al. (2019) provided a detailed look at the underlying mechanisms of LSTMs by which they are able to model grammatical structure. To this end, they performed an ablation study and discovered which units were mainly responsible for this mechanism. Finally, further research into the Italian version of the NA task in Lakretz et al. (2020) investigated how emergent mechanisms in language models relate to linguistic processing in humans.

Number agreement has also been explored before in the context of attribution methods. Due to the clear dependency between a subject and a verb, it is a useful task to evaluate whether a model based its prediction of the verb on the number information of the subject. Poerner et al. (2018) provide a large suite of evaluation tasks for attribution methods including number agreement, and show that attribution methods can sometimes yield unexpected contribution patterns. Jumelet et al. (2019) employ Contextual Decomposition to investigate the behaviour of an LSTM LM on a number agreement task, and demonstrate that their model employs a *default reasoning* heuristic when resolving the task, with a strong bias for singular verbs. Hao (2020) investigates an attribution method on a range of number agreement constructions containing relative clauses, showing that LMs possess a robust notion of number information.

3 Method

In this section, we first look at extending Contextual Decomposition for the SHA-RNN. Following this, we outline the models which we will use for our experiments. Finally, we explain how we extended the Number Agreement task and how we applied Contextual Decomposition to the NA task, forming the Subject Attribution task.

3.1 Contextual Decomposition for the SHA-RNN

The original Contextual Decomposition paper (Murdoch et al., 2018) only defines the decomposition for an LSTM model. The SHA-RNN also contains several operations that have not previously been covered by these two papers. As such, we have defined the decompositions for the following two operations: Layer Normalization (Ba et al., 2016) and the Softmax operation in the Single Headed Attention layer (Merity, 2019). Based on these new decompositions, we leverage the implementation of Contextual Decomposition in the `diagNNose` library of Jumelet (2020) to also cover our SHA-RNN.

Layer Normalization Layer Normalization estimates the normalization statistics over the summed inputs to the neurons in a hidden layer. A definition of the Layer Normalization operation can be found in Eq. (5).

$$\begin{aligned} \mu &= \frac{1}{n}\sum_{i=1}^{n} a_i, \\ \sigma &= \sqrt{\frac{1}{n}\sum_{i=1}^{n}(a_i-\mu)^2}, \\ \mathrm{LN}(a) &= \alpha\frac{a-\mu}{\sigma}+\delta, \end{aligned} \tag{5}$$

where a represents the inputs to the hidden layer, n the number of hidden units and α and δ are learnable parameters.

Because it looks at all inputs in a layer, both β and γ might interact within this layer. As such, we must define how we handle the decomposition of this operation, which we show in Eq. (6).

$$\begin{aligned} \beta^{l+1} &= \mathrm{LN}(\beta^l)-\delta, \\ \gamma^{l+1} &= \mathrm{LN}(\beta^l+\gamma^l)-\mathrm{LN}(\beta^l)+\delta \\ \mathrm{LN}(a) &= \mathrm{LN}(\beta^l+\gamma^l)=\beta^{l+1}+\gamma^{l+1} \end{aligned} \tag{6}$$

Our decomposition strictly separates the γ contributions from the β contributions, which means that no information from γ may be captured in β.

Softmax Similar to our treatment of the Layer Normalization operation, we strictly separate γ from the β components, as can be observed in Eq. (7).

$$\begin{aligned} \beta^{l+1} &= \mathrm{Softmax}(\beta^l), \\ \gamma^{l+1} &= \mathrm{Softmax}(\beta^l+\gamma^l)-\beta^{l+1} \end{aligned} \tag{7}$$

3.2 Models

For our experiments we consider two types of models: the attention SHA-RNN model and the non-attention LSTM model. Below, we will outline the specific architectures used and training hyperparameters chosen to build and train these models.

3.2.1 Architectures

LSTM model The LSTM model we use is similar to the one used by Gulordava et al. (2018). The model is a stacked two layer LSTM, each with 650 hidden units. Word embeddings are trained alongside the model and the weights of the embedding layer are tied to the decoder layer (Inan et al., 2017).

SHA-RNN model For our SHA-RNN we use two blocks (see Fig. 1), each with an LSTM with 650 hidden units. Furthermore, our model also utilises a trained word embedding layer with tied weights, similar to our non-attention model. Finally, our Boom layer does not increase our dimension size, but keeps it at 650. This means our Boom layer reduces to a feed-forward layer with GELU activations.

3.2.2 Training

We trained four models to conduct our experiments on. For both the attention (SHA-RNN) and non-attention (LSTM) model architectures, a model was trained on a Dutch and English corpus. Both corpora are based on wikipedia text. Following Gulordava et al. (2018), only the 50.000 most common words were retained in the vocabulary for both corpora, replacing all other words with `<unk>` tokens. The corpora were split into a training, validation and test set.

The training of the models is split up in two phases: first, the model is trained for thirty epochs with a learning rate of 0.02 and a batch size of 64. Then, we fine-tune the model for an additional five epochs with the learning rate halved to 0.01 and a batch size of 16. During training, we set dropout to 0.1. We use the LAMB optimizer (You et al., 2019) following Merity (2019).

3.3 Extending Number Agreement

In this work, we extend the Number Agreement (NA) task to the Dutch language. We do so by applying the same procedure that was used in Lakretz et al. (2019), namely by creating a synthetic dataset. This is different from the works of Linzen et al. (2016) and Gulordava et al. (2018), which derived their sentences directly from corpora.

Our version of the NA task contains a total of five different templates. First of all, we use a simple template called Simple in which the verb immediately follows the subject. We then extend this by adding a prepositional phrase which modifies the subject between the subject and the verb, either by having a prepositional phrase containing a noun (NounPP) or containing a proper noun (NamePP). We then have the sentence conjunction (SConj) task, which consists of two Simple templates separated by a conjunction. The challenge of the SConj task is correctly predicting the number of the verb in the second sentence. Finally, we have the ThatNounPP template, which contains a declarative content clause which incorporates a second subject-verb dependency with a noun modifying prepositional phrase in its that-clause. An overview of the templates including example sentences can be found in Table 1.

We create our final NA-task by obtaining frequent words from our corpus to populate these sentence templates. This process is done for both the Dutch and the English corpora, such that we can more easily compare the results.

3.4 Subject Attribution Task

We propose a new task for input feature attribution methods based on the Number Agreement task: Subject Attribution. The goal of the task to produce explanations in such a way that congruent subject-verb relations gain higher attributions than non-congruent ones.

In context of the NA task this means that we compare the attribution scores of the subject of the sentence in the case where it is and is not congruent with the number of the verb. In our evaluation we consider a higher attribution for the congruent noun compared to the non-congruent noun to be correct, as this would be in line with human intuition. A schematic overview of this task can be found in Fig. 2.

In this work, we use the task in the following way: we apply our attribution method on each sentence within our dataset, generating input feature attributions. We then compare the subject attributions of these sentences to find in which percentage of the sentences the attributions for the subject were higher for the congruent verb than the non congruent one.

NA-task	Template	Example
Simple	DET N V	De jongen groet The boy greets
NounPP	DET N PREP DET N V	De jongens bij de auto groeten The boys at the car greet
NamePP	DET N PREP NAME V	De jongens bij Pat groeten The boys at Pat greet
SConj	DET N V en/and DET N V	De jongen groet en de moeders missen The boy greets and the mothers miss
ThatNounPP	DET N V dat/that DET N PREP DET N V	De jongen denkt dat de moeders bij de auto missen The boy thinks that the mothers at the car miss

Table 1: Overview of the templates for the NA-tasks. DET is a determiner, N a noun, NAME a name of a person, V a verb and PREP a preposition. The underlined noun in the template signifies the subject belonging to the relevant verb.

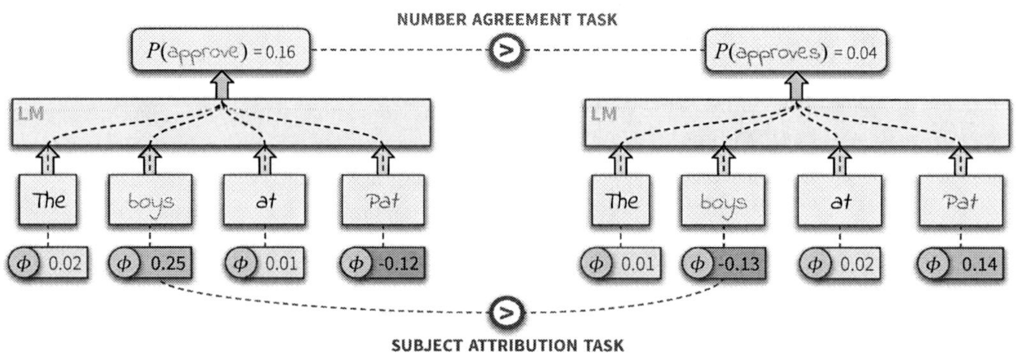

Figure 2: Schematic overview of the default **number agreement task** that compares the output probabilities of the LM, and the **subject attribution task** that compares the attribution scores of the subject to the correct and incorrect form of the verb. We hypothesise that for a model with a sophisticated understanding of number agreement, the subject's contribution to the correct verb form is greater than to the incorrect form.

4 Results and analysis

In our work, we have considered several experiments. Firstly, we evaluate the ability of our models to handle the data itself by comparing the model perplexities. Following this, we look at the Number Agreement and Subject Attribution tasks to evaluate the differences between our models.

4.1 Model Perplexities

To establish the adequacy of our models on the data, we calculate the perplexity for each model over the held-out test set (Table 2). Due to the different data sets used for the two languages, direct comparisons between the perplexity scores for the English and Dutch models are not feasible. We do observe that for both languages, the SHA-RNN yields a perplexity score that is 5% lower than the score of the LSTM counterpart.

Model	Perplexity
LSTM (English)	56.24
LSTM (Dutch)	34.24
SHA-RNN (English)	53.25
SHA-RNN (Dutch)	32.54

Table 2: Model perplexities

4.2 Number Agreement

To assess the performance of the different language models, we consider the different sentence structures presented in Table 1. For each sentence structure, we evaluate the predictive performance of the model on matching the form of the verb to the number of the relevant subject. For example, given a singular subject, we evaluate $p(\text{VERB}_\text{S}|\text{SUBJ}_\text{S}) > p(\text{VERB}_\text{P}|\text{SUBJ}_\text{S})$. The same sentence templates have been used for the Subject Attribution task. We apply Contextual Decomposition to the sentences to investigate the behavioural differences between the models.

We examine the results of our experiments along two axes: language and attention. First, we compare the Dutch and English language models. Following this, we analyse the differences between the attention and non-attention models.

4.2.1 Language axis

Across the board, the Dutch models perform slightly better on the NA tasks than the English models. This could be due to the data sets used, as the Dutch data set was larger than the English one, giving the Dutch model more opportunities to learn. We do find similar patterns between the Dutch models (Table 3a) and the English models (Table 3b): between the two languages, the models generally share the tasks and conditions that they perform well on. There are exceptions to this, as in the case of the Simple NA task for the LSTM, with Dutch models performing better on the singular condition while their English counterparts achieve higher scores on the plural condition.

When we compare the results of the models on the Subject Attribution task in Tables 3a and 3b, we find more substantial differences between the models across the languages. In case of the English models, the SHA-RNN performed rather poorly on the plural conditions of the Subject Attribution task. This is remarkable, given that the Dutch SHA-RNN yields significantly higher scores on these conditions.

We observe that for the English SHA-RNN, contextual decomposition consistently yields attribution scores that are lower for the plural conditions than those for the singular conditions (see Fig. 3 for an example). In the Dutch SHA-RNN, this behaviour is only apparent for the Simple, NounPP and NamePP tasks.

Jumelet et al. (2019) encountered similar behaviours when applying CD to an LSTM language model. They attributed the lower attributions to a bias towards singular verbs in the model, which resulted in a form of default reasoning. However, our accuracy results do not indicate a similar bias, as we found all our models performing well on both plural and singular subjects. This raises the question as to what is causing this behaviour, which we leave for future work.

Overall, these results do not demonstrate any significant differences between the Dutch and English models. While we have shown that differences occur across conditions, we find that for most conditions, both models behave similarly, with the two LSTM models displaying more similarities than the SHA-RNN models.

4.2.2 Attention axis

To compare the attention models (SHA-RNNs) to the non-attention model (the LSTMs), we again first consider the accuracy scores in Tables 3a and 3b. A comparison between the SHA-RNN and the LSTM shows that the SHA-RNN performs slightly worse than the LSTM by a small margin. There are some cases where this difference is more pronounced, such as for the English ThatNounPP task (see Table 3b), where we observe large differences for the singular subject conditions. This behaviour goes against the perplexity results in Table 2, which indicate a better performing SHA-RNN. This is in line with the results found by Nikoulina et al. (2021), who demonstrate that perplexity is not always directly correlated to performance on downstream tasks, as appears to be the case for our Number Agreement task.

Looking at the model explanations in Tables 3a and 3b we see that across the board the LSTM performs better on the Subject Attribution task. We find that both SHA-RNN models generally do not produce the expected attributions for the plural subject conditions, while there are very few instances of the LSTM performing under 50%, only failing by a large margin for the English LSTM on the Simple P̲ and NamePP P̲ conditions (see Table 3a).

From our observations, the attention and non-attention models behave differently both in terms of accuracy scores on the NA task and the explanations from the Subject Attribution task. We find that the difference between the architectures of the SHA-RNN and the LSTM leads to significant variations in general performance as well as behavioural patterns.

5 Conclusion

In this paper, we compared both attention (SHA-RNN) and non-attention (LSTM) language models across two languages, namely Dutch and English. To test these models, we extended the Number Agreement task from Lakretz et al. (2019) to the Dutch language, which allows us to compare these models across both languages. In addition to this, we extended a feature attribution method called Contextual Decomposition (Murdoch et al., 2018) to the SHA-RNN model. We applied Contextual

NA-task	Singular Subject			Plural Subject		
	Condition	SHA-RNN	LSTM	Condition	SHA-RNN	LSTM
Simple	S	92.1 (77.8)	99.2 (65.4)	P	94.0 (25.9)	94.4 (58.6)
NounPP	SS	99.0 (83.3)	94.7 (56.1)	PS	91.5 (20.7)	98.5 (70.0)
NounPP	SP	95.2 (82.0)	94.7 (48.3)	PP	96.8 (21.3)	98.7 (71.2)
NamePP	S	59.3 (58.3)	81.8 (57.2)	P	83.8 (43.3)	75.3 (48.8)
SConj	SS	95.8 (77.0)	96.0 (90.3)	SP	88.7 (43.8)	89.3 (63.0)
SConj	PS	42.8 (67.0)	89.5 (89.3)	PP	94.0 (50.2)	95.5 (42.8)
ThatNounPP	SSS	98.3 (72.2)	96.7 (80.7)	SPS	99.3 (61.8)	100.0 (89.3)
ThatNounPP	SSP	99.0 (65.5)	94.7 (75.2)	SPP	99.2 (66.2)	100.0 (91.8)
ThatNounPP	PSS	97.8 (70.7)	96.8 (83.5)	PPS	99.7 (62.2)	100.0 (89.3)
ThatNounPP	PSP	98.2 (62.0)	91.3 (78.0)	PPP	99.5 (65.8)	100.0 (91.7)

(a) Results for the **Dutch** language models.

NA-task	Singular Subject			Plural Subject		
	Condition	SHA-RNN	LSTM	Condition	SHA-RNN	LSTM
Simple	S	94.0 (93.3)	92.7 (93.3)	P	99.3 (11.7)	96.3 (35.7)
NounPP	SS	86.0 (92.3)	78.3 (95.5)	PS	82.5 (8.8)	93.3 (54.6)
NounPP	SP	83.8 (93.5)	54.8 (94.0)	PP	97.0 (9.0)	96.8 (59.5)
NamePP	S	68.0 (89.3)	86.7 (96.5)	P	66.2 (14.5)	52.3 (12.5)
SConj	SS	93.8 (93.0)	94.3 (90.5)	SP	99.3 (15.7)	96.3 (87.2)
SConj	PS	82.3 (93.5)	94.3 (94.3)	PP	99.3 (10.7)	98.8 (90.5)
ThatNounPP	SSS	91.8 (100.0)	70.7 (92.0)	SPS	92.3 (5.0)	95.8 (51.3)
ThatNounPP	SSP	85.2 (100.0)	43.7 (94.0)	SPP	98.7 (4.2)	100.0 (65.7)
ThatNounPP	PSS	86.2 (99.8)	69.7 (92.3)	PPS	92.0 (4.3)	97.0 (55.7)
ThatNounPP	PSP	81.2 (100.0)	46.3 (92.3)	PPP	98.2 (2.3)	99.5 (68.0)

(b) Results for the **English** language models.

Table 3: Overview of prediction accuracy scores (the numbers outside the brackets) and subject attribution behaviour (in brackets) on the Number Agreement tasks for the Dutch and English language models. For each task, the noun inflections are given in the condition column, with S indicating singular and P indicating plural. The underlined letter in the condition indicates the noun belonging to the verb that is predicted. The numbers in brackets denote the performance on the subject attribution task: the percentage of cases in which the attributions of the subjects were higher to the congruent verb than to the non-congruent ones. The colour coding of the table cells follows the performance on this subject attribution task along a colour gradient from green (high performance) to red (low performance).

Decomposition to the Number Agreement task to obtain interpretable explanations and compared the different models from a feature attribution standpoint.

We found that both the Dutch and English models behaved similarly in terms of accuracy. While general performance differed between the two languages, we did find that similar behavioural patterns emerged from the models. This partially held for the explanations obtained through Contextual Decomposition, where we did uncover differences. These differences were centred around the SHA-RNN, which we found behaved as if it applied default reasoning similar to the work of Jumelet et al. (2019).

Comparing our attention and non-attention models, we found immediate differences, both when comparing the performance on the Number Agreement task as when looking into the attributions. Both models performed differently on the same tasks and feature attributions varied between them. We found that our LSTM performed better on the attribution task.

Our current results suggest that attention and non-attention models behave differently according to Contextual Decomposition. More specifically, we find that the attention models have more difficulty producing correct attributions for plural sentences. A logical next step would then be to compare our current results by those obtained through different attribution methods such as SHAP (Lundberg and Lee, 2017) and Integrated Gradients (Sundararajan et al., 2017). Should we find that Contextual Decomposition holds up well to these other

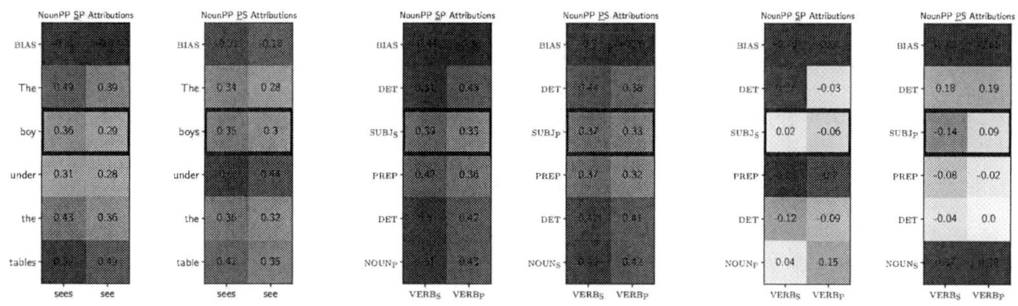

(a) Example SHA-RNN attributions (b) Aggregated SHA-RNN attributions (c) Aggregated LSTM attributions

Figure 3: Contextual Decomposition attributions for the English models (SHA-RNN and LSTM) on the SP and PS conditions of the NounPP task. Fig. 3a shows the attributions of two individial sentences, while Figs. 3b and 3c show aggregated attributions over all sentences of that condition. Note that in Fig. 3b the attribution for the subject under the singular verb is both higher in the SP condition as well as in PS condition, while in Fig. 3c the attribution is higher for the subject matching the verb form.

methods, it could then prove to be a valuable method for approximating Shapley values in polynomial time. Moreover, it is worth looking into the application of Contextual Decomposition in Transformer architectures, which rely more heavily on these kinds of attention mechanisms.

An alternative line of research that we would like to explore is the attention mechanism itself. Even though it has been shown that attention does not provide guarantees for explainability (Jain and Wallace, 2019), it would still be worthwhile to investigate the attention patterns that are employed by the SHA-RNN.

References

Lei Jimmy Ba, Jamie Ryan Kiros, and Geoffrey E. Hinton. 2016. Layer normalization. *CoRR*, abs/1607.06450.

Allyson Ettinger. 2020. What bert is not: Lessons from a new suite of psycholinguistic diagnostics for language models. *Transactions of the Association for Computational Linguistics*, 8:34–48.

Mario Giulianelli, Jack Harding, Florian Mohnert, Dieuwke Hupkes, and Willem Zuidema. 2018. Under the hood: Using diagnostic classifiers to investigate and improve how language models track agreement information. In *Proceedings of the 2018 EMNLP Workshop BlackboxNLP: Analyzing and Interpreting Neural Networks for NLP*, pages 240–248, Brussels, Belgium. Association for Computational Linguistics.

Yoav Goldberg. 2019. Assessing BERT's Syntactic Abilities. page 4.

Edouard Grave, Armand Joulin, and Nicolas Usunier. 2017. Improving neural language models with a continuous cache. In *5th International Conference on Learning Representations, ICLR 2017, Toulon, France, April 24-26, 2017, Conference Track Proceedings*. OpenReview.net.

Kristina Gulordava, Piotr Bojanowski, Edouard Grave, Tal Linzen, and Marco Baroni. 2018. Colorless green recurrent networks dream hierarchically. In *Proceedings of the 2018 Conference of the North American Chapter of the Association for Computational Linguistics: Human Language Technologies, NAACL-HLT 2018, New Orleans, Louisiana, USA, June 1-6, 2018, Volume 1 (Long Papers)*, pages 1195–1205. Association for Computational Linguistics.

Yiding Hao. 2020. Attribution analysis of grammatical dependencies in lstms. *CoRR*, abs/2005.00062.

Dan Hendrycks and Kevin Gimpel. 2016. Bridging nonlinearities and stochastic regularizers with gaussian error linear units. *CoRR*, abs/1606.08415.

Sepp Hochreiter and Jürgen Schmidhuber. 1997. Long Short-Term Memory. *Neural Computation*, 9(8):1735–1780.

Dieuwke Hupkes, Sara Veldhoen, and Willem Zuidema. 2018. Visualisation and 'diagnostic classifiers' reveal how recurrent and recursive neural networks process hierarchical structure. *Journal of Artificial Intelligence Research*, 61:907–926.

Hakan Inan, Khashayar Khosravi, and Richard Socher. 2017. Tying word vectors and word classifiers: A loss framework for language modeling. In *5th International Conference on Learning Representations, ICLR 2017, Toulon, France, April 24-26, 2017, Conference Track Proceedings*. OpenReview.net.

Sarthak Jain and Byron C Wallace. 2019. Attention is not explanation. In *Proceedings of the 2019 Conference of the North American Chapter of the Association for Computational Linguistics: Human Language Technologies, Volume 1 (Long and Short Papers)*, pages 3543–3556.

Jaap Jumelet. 2020. diagnnose: A library for neural activation analysis. In *Proceedings of the Third BlackboxNLP Workshop on Analyzing and Interpreting Neural Networks for NLP*, pages 342–350.

Jaap Jumelet and Dieuwke Hupkes. 2018. Do language models understand anything? on the ability of LSTMs to understand negative polarity items. In *Proceedings of the 2018 EMNLP Workshop BlackboxNLP: Analyzing and Interpreting Neural Networks for NLP*, pages 222–231, Brussels, Belgium. Association for Computational Linguistics.

Jaap Jumelet, Willem Zuidema, and Dieuwke Hupkes. 2019. Analysing neural language models: Contextual decomposition reveals default reasoning in number and gender assignment. In *Proceedings of the 23rd Conference on Computational Natural Language Learning (CoNLL)*, pages 1–11, Hong Kong, China. Association for Computational Linguistics.

Yair Lakretz, Dieuwke Hupkes, Alessandra Vergallito, Marco Marelli, Marco Baroni, and Stanislas Dehaene. 2020. Exploring processing of nested dependencies in neural-network language models and humans. *CoRR*, abs/2006.11098.

Yair Lakretz, German Kruszewski, Theo Desbordes, Dieuwke Hupkes, Stanislas Dehaene, and Marco Baroni. 2019. The emergence of number and syntax units in LSTM language models. In *Proceedings of the 2019 Conference of the North American Chapter of the Association for Computational Linguistics: Human Language Technologies, Volume 1 (Long and Short Papers)*, pages 11–20, Minneapolis, Minnesota. Association for Computational Linguistics.

Tal Linzen, Grzegorz Chrupała, Yonatan Belinkov, and Dieuwke Hupkes, editors. 2019. *Proceedings of the 2019 ACL Workshop BlackboxNLP: Analyzing and Interpreting Neural Networks for NLP*. Association for Computational Linguistics, Florence, Italy.

Tal Linzen, Emmanuel Dupoux, and Yoav Goldberg. 2016. Assessing the ability of lstms to learn syntax-sensitive dependencies. *Trans. Assoc. Comput. Linguistics*, 4:521–535.

Scott M. Lundberg and Su-In Lee. 2017. A unified approach to interpreting model predictions. In *Advances in Neural Information Processing Systems 30: Annual Conference on Neural Information Processing Systems 2017, December 4-9, 2017, Long Beach, CA, USA*, pages 4765–4774.

Stephen Merity. 2019. Single headed attention RNN: stop thinking with your head. *CoRR*, abs/1911.11423.

Stephen Merity, Caiming Xiong, James Bradbury, and Richard Socher. 2017. Pointer sentinel mixture models. In *5th International Conference on Learning Representations, ICLR 2017, Toulon, France, April 24-26, 2017, Conference Track Proceedings*. OpenReview.net.

Paul Michel, Omer Levy, and Graham Neubig. 2019. Are sixteen heads really better than one? In *Advances in Neural Information Processing Systems 32: Annual Conference on Neural Information Processing Systems 2019, NeurIPS 2019, December 8-14, 2019, Vancouver, BC, Canada*, pages 14014–14024.

W. James Murdoch, Peter J. Liu, and Bin Yu. 2018. Beyond word importance: Contextual decomposition to extract interactions from lstms. In *6th International Conference on Learning Representations, ICLR 2018, Vancouver, BC, Canada, April 30 - May 3, 2018, Conference Track Proceedings*. OpenReview.net.

Vassilina Nikoulina, Maxat Tezekbayev, Nuradil Kozhakhmet, Madina Babazhanova, Matthias Gallé, and Zhenisbek Assylbekov. 2021. The rediscovery hypothesis: Language models need to meet linguistics. *CoRR*, abs/2103.01819.

Nina Poerner, Hinrich Schütze, and Benjamin Roth. 2018. Evaluating neural network explanation methods using hybrid documents and morphosyntactic agreement. In *Proceedings of the 56th Annual Meeting of the Association for Computational Linguistics (Volume 1: Long Papers)*, pages 340–350.

Marco Túlio Ribeiro, Sameer Singh, and Carlos Guestrin. 2016. "why should I trust you?": Explaining the predictions of any classifier. In *Proceedings of the Demonstrations Session, NAACL HLT 2016, The 2016 Conference of the North American Chapter of the Association for Computational Linguistics: Human Language Technologies, San Diego California, USA, June 12-17, 2016*, pages 97–101. The Association for Computational Linguistics.

Wojciech Samek, Grégoire Montavon, Andrea Vedaldi, Lars Kai Hansen, and Klaus-Robert Müller. 2019. *Explainable AI: interpreting, explaining and visualizing deep learning*, volume 11700. Springer Nature.

Naomi Saphra and Adam Lopez. 2020. Lstms compose—and learn—bottom-up. In *Proceedings of the 2020 Conference on Empirical Methods in Natural Language Processing: Findings*, pages 2797–2809.

Lloyd S Shapley. 1953. A value for n-person games. *Contributions to the Theory of Games*, 2(28):307–317.

Karen Simonyan, Andrea Vedaldi, and Andrew Zisserman. 2014. Deep inside convolutional networks: Visualising image classification models and saliency maps. In *2nd International Conference on Learning Representations, ICLR 2014, Banff, AB, Canada, April 14-16, 2014, Workshop Track Proceedings*.

Mukund Sundararajan, Ankur Taly, and Qiqi Yan. 2017. Axiomatic attribution for deep networks. In *Proceedings of the 34th International Conference on Machine Learning, ICML 2017, Sydney, NSW, Australia, 6-11 August 2017*, volume 70 of *Proceedings of Machine Learning Research*, pages 3319–3328. PMLR.

Ian Tenney, Dipanjan Das, and Ellie Pavlick. 2019. Bert rediscovers the classical nlp pipeline. In *Proceedings of the 57th Annual Meeting of the Association for Computational Linguistics*, pages 4593–4601.

Ashish Vaswani, Noam Shazeer, Niki Parmar, Jakob Uszkoreit, Llion Jones, Aidan N. Gomez, Lukasz Kaiser, and Illia Polosukhin. 2017. Attention is all you need. In *Advances in Neural Information Processing Systems 30: Annual Conference on Neural Information Processing Systems 2017, December 4-9, 2017, Long Beach, CA, USA*, pages 5998–6008.

Thomas Wolf. 2019. Some additional experiments extending the tech report "Assessing BERT's Syntactic Abilities" by Yoav Goldberg. page 7.

Yang You, Jing Li, Jonathan Hseu, Xiaodan Song, James Demmel, and Cho-Jui Hsieh. 2019. Reducing BERT pre-training time from 3 days to 76 minutes. *CoRR*, abs/1904.00962.

Predicting Numerals in Natural Language Text Using a Language Model Considering the Quantitative Aspects of Numerals

Taku Sakamoto[1] and **Akiko Aizawa**[2,1]
[1]The University of Tokyo, 7-3-1 Hongo, Bunkyo-ku, Tokyo, Japan
[2]National Institute of Informatics, 2-1-2 Hitotsubashi, Chiyoda-ku, Tokyo, Japan
{t_sakamoto, aizawa}@nii.ac.jp

Abstract

Numerical common sense (NCS) is necessary to fully understand natural language text that includes numerals. NCS is knowledge about the numerical features of objects in text, such as size, weight, or color. Existing neural language models treat numerals in a text as string tokens in the same way as other words. Therefore, they cannot reflect the quantitative aspects of numerals in the training process, making it difficult to learn NCS. In this paper, we measure the NCS acquired by existing neural language models using a masked numeral prediction task as an evaluation task. In this task, we use two evaluation metrics to evaluate the language models in terms of the symbolic and quantitative aspects of the numerals, respectively. We also propose methods to reflect not only the symbolic aspect but also the quantitative aspect of numerals in the training of language models, using a loss function that depends on the magnitudes of the numerals and a regression model for the masked numeral prediction task. Finally, we quantitatively evaluate our proposed approaches on four datasets with different properties using the two metrics. Compared with methods that use existing language models, the proposed methods reduce numerical absolute errors, although exact match accuracy was reduced. This result confirms that the proposed methods, which use the magnitudes of the numerals for model training, are an effective way for models to capture NCS.

1 Introduction

Numerical common sense (NCS) is knowledge about the numerical features of objects in the real world, such as size, weight, or color, each of which has its own range and probability distribution (Yamane et al., 2020). Consider the following example sentence.

"John is 200 *cm tall."*

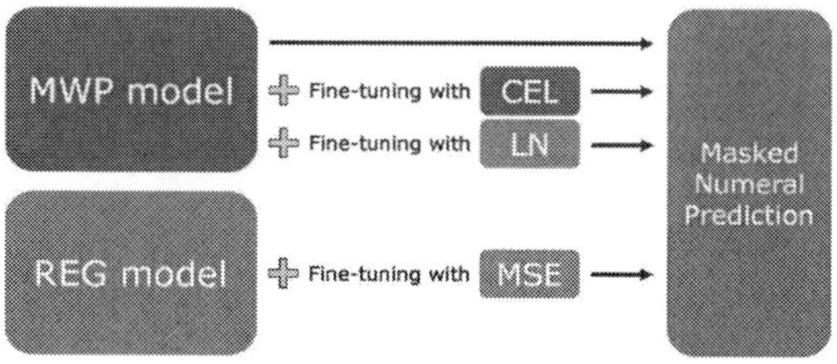

Figure 1 An overview of our proposed approaches for the masked numeral prediction task. We propose to use a new loss function $Loss_{\mathrm{NUM}}$ (LN) that is based on the magnitudes of numerals for fine tuning masked word prediction (MWP) model and a regression (REG) model that treats the masked numeral prediction as a regression task.

When we read this sentence, we can infer from it not only that John's height is *200 cm* but that John is a tall person. However, this kind of inference cannot be achieved by a system that does not have NCS about how tall people generally are. Therefore, it is essential to have knowledge about real-world numerical features for a deep understanding of natural language text containing numerals.

In recent years, BERT, GPT-3, and other neural language models have achieved a level of performance on par with or better than human performance in many natural language processing tasks (Devlin et al., 2019; Liu et al., 2019; Lan et al., 2020; Brown et al., 2020). Moreover, several studies have recently been conducted to investigate whether pre-trained neural language models have commonsense knowledge, and these studies often conclude that the language models have been successful in acquiring some commonsense knowledge (Petroni et al., 2019; Davison et al., 2019; Bouraoui et al., 2019; Zhou et al., 2019; Talmor et al., 2020).

However, it has also been reported that current neural language models still perform poorly in natural language processing tasks that require NCS and a deep understanding of numerals, such as numerical reasoning, numerical question answer-

Proceedings of Deep Learning Inside Out (DeeLIO): The 2nd Workshop on Knowledge Extraction and Integration for Deep Learning Architectures, pages 140–150
Online, June 10, 2021.

ing, and numerical error detection/correction (Dua et al., 2019; Chen et al., 2019). Numerals appear frequently in various forms, such as dates, numbers of people, percentages, and so on, regardless of the domain of passages. Hence, the acquisition of numerical common sense by neural language models and the analysis of the acquired numerical common sense are essential research topics to support systems for reasoning on text containing numerals and smooth conversation with humans at a high level.

One of the major problems that make it difficult for language models to understand the meaning of numerals and to acquire NCS is that naive language models treat numerals in text as string tokens, just like any other word (Spithourakis and Riedel, 2018). This makes it difficult to obtain a mapping between the string tokens and the magnitudes of the numerals, which is needed to capture NCS.

In this study, we use the masked numeral prediction task (Spithourakis and Riedel, 2018; Lin et al., 2020) to evaluate and verify the NCS acquired by neural language models. The task requires models to predict masked numerals in an input passage from their context. We use two types of evaluation metrics: hit@k accuracy (Lin et al., 2020) and MdAE and MdAPE (Spithourakis and Riedel, 2018) for this task. Hit@k accuracy calculates the percentage of predictions in which the groundtruth numeral is within the top k predicted numerals, and we can say that they evaluate language models in terms of the **symbolic** aspect of numerals. MdAE and MdAPE are calculated from the difference between the groundtruth numerals and the predicted numerals, and we can say that they evaluate language models in terms of the **quantitative** aspect of numerals.

To perform this task, we investigate the following two approaches to reflect the magnitudes of the numerals for fine-tuning language models on the masked numeral prediction task (Figure 1).

1. A masked word prediction model with a new loss function $Loss_{\text{NUM}}$ that is based on the differences between the groundtruth numerals and predicted numerals;

2. A masked word prediction model, called the REG model, structured with an additional output layer to predict a numeral from an input passage containing a masked numeral.

We use the BERT-based masked word prediction model as a baseline and conducted experiments on four datasets, which differ from each other in the length and domain of the passages as well as the distribution and characteristics of the numerals appearing in the datasets. We compare the results and investigate the relationship between the characteristics of the numerals in the datasets and the performance of each method. Although fine-tuning with $Loss_{\text{NUM}}$ causes a decrease in the exact match accuracy, we found that it reduces numerical absolute errors, which indicates the effectiveness of $Loss_{\text{NUM}}$. The results of the REG model show the difficulty of predicting numerals in natural language text with the regression model. However, there were some numerals that the REG model predicted better than the existing language model, indicating that the REG model and existing language models are good at predicting numerals with different characteristics.

In our experiments, to eliminate the negative effects of the sub-word approach, we do not split the numerals into sub-words. The sub-word approach splits words into shorter tokens called sub-words. It has the advantage that even low-frequency words can be represented by a combination of sub-words that appear in a text more frequently. However, unlike the case of words, sub-words derived from numerals often have little relationship to the meaning of the original numerals, which can make it difficult to understand the meaning of numerals (Wallace et al., 2019). All other words are separated into sub-words in our experiments.

To summarize, in this work, we tackle the problem of dealing with numerals in naive language models on the masked numeral prediction task. Our contributions are as follows:

- We use two evaluation metrics (exact match accuracy and numerical absolute errors) for the masked numeral prediction task to evaluate the language models in terms of the symbolic and quantitative aspects of the numerals, respectively.

- We propose a new loss function to reflect not only the symbolic aspect but also the quantitative aspect of numerals in the training of language models. For the masked numeral prediction task, we also employ a regression model, which predicts numerals as quantities.

- We quantitatively evaluate our proposed approaches on four datasets with different properties using the two metrics. The reduction in the numerical absolute errors of the predictions confirms the effectiveness of our proposed approaches.

2 Related Work

2.1 Masked Numeral Prediction

Masked numeral prediction is the task of predicting a masked numeral in an input passage from the context (e.g., "The movie I saw yesterday was [MASK] minutes long.") It can be used as an indicator to evaluate the NCS acquired by language models.

Lin et al. (2020) analyzed NCS captured by current language models using a masked numeral prediction task in which masked numerals were limited to numerals that could be uniquely determined, such as "A car usually has [MASK] wheels." They showed that even the current best pre-trained language models still perform poorly compared to humans on the task, which requires NCS. They also found that even though pre-trained language models seemingly make the correct predictions, the models are often unable to maintain the correct answer under even small changes, for instance, if the above target sentence changes to "A car usually has [MASK] *round* wheels."

Spithourakis and Riedel (2018) examined numeracy of neural language models using the masked numeral prediction task. Numeracy refers to the ability to understand the meanings of numerals and to deal with them properly. They conducted their experiments on scientific paper and clinical text datasets that include many numerals that represent the quantities of something. To improve the prediction accuracy for such numerals, they proposed a method that uses character-level recurrent neural networks (Graves, 2013; Sutskever et al., 2011) for prediction, a method that predicts the distribution of the numerals as a mixture of Gaussian distributions, and an ensemble method of these methods. They showed that the accuracy of the prediction of quantity-like numerals can be improved by methods that consider the magnitudes of the numerals.

2.2 Natural Language Processing Tasks That Involve Numerals

2.2.1 Machine Reading Comprehension Requiring NCS

Dua et al. (2019) created a machine reading comprehension dataset called DROP that contains questions requiring numerical operations such as addition, subtraction, and sorting to answer correctly. They used the DROP dataset to evaluate current machine reading comprehension models and showed that many questions requiring only simple numerical operations easily solved by humans cannot be answered correctly by current models. To improve the performance of the models on the DROP dataset, Hu et al. (2019) built a specialized architecture for numerical operations and achieved a significant improvement in accuracy, although not to human level. In contrast, Geva et al. (2020) showed that even if they use a generative model that is not specialized for numerical operations, they can improve the performance on DROP using additional data for numerical operation training. In our experiments, we use the passages in the DROP dataset for the masked numeral prediction task.

2.2.2 Numerical Error Detection

Numerical error detection is the task of determining whether or not numerals in input passages are errors (Chen et al., 2019; Spithourakis et al., 2016). To determine if a target numeral is an error, it is necessary to have knowledge of the range of values that the numeral can and cannot take. For example, to notice numerical errors in sentences with dates (for example, "Her birthday is December -3." or "Her birthday is December 20.5."), it is necessary to know that the range of possible values for numerals representing dates is generally an integer between 1 and 31. Therefore, the accuracy of numerical error detection can be used to quantitatively evaluate the NCS of the detection models. Chen et al. (2019) experimented with the BiGRU model to detect numerals multiplied by a random factor in Numeracy-600K, which is a dataset of market comments. They showed that the BiGRU model was able to detect numerical errors with less than 60% accuracy even with small numeral changes of approximately 10%. Moreover, it achieved an accuracy of only 76% even with large numeral changes of approximately 90%. In our experiments, we use the article titles from this dataset as one of the datasets for the masked numeral prediction task.

2.2.3 Numeral Type Prediction

Numeral type prediction is the task of classifying numerals in text into one of several fixed categories. Prediction models are required to classify numerals using their numerical values and contexts. Chen et al. (2018) aimed to understand the meanings of numerals in financial tweets for crowd-based

Token-type NCS	• Spiders have **8** legs. • A week has **7** days.
Quantity-type NCS	• The adult male is approximately **170** cm tall. • The length of movies is about **120** minutes.

Table 1 Two types of NCS.

forecasting, providing the dataset FinNum, which contains financial tweets in which numerals are annotated with their categories. Their categories include "Monetary," "Percentage," "Temporal" (date and time), and so on. They used a convolutional neural network (CNN), long short-term memory (LSTM), and bidirectional LSTM in experiments and concluded that character-level CNN performed the best. We use the FinNum dataset in our experiments for the masked numeral prediction task.

3 NCS

3.1 Two Types of NCS

NCS is the knowledge about numerical features of objects in the real world, such as size, weight, and price. NCS is required to understand natural language text that includes numerals or that refers to the real-world numerical features of some objects. We focus on the fact that numerals have two aspects, symbolic and quantitative, and hypothesize that there are two types of NCS: token type and quantity type (Table 1).

Token-type NCS refers to numerical knowledge involving numerals that can be appropriately understood as string tokens. This knowledge is definition-like or rule-like knowledge that cannot use other numerals instead, like "A week has 7 days." (Table 1). This kind of NCS is relatively easy to learn, even with conventional language models that treat numerals as string tokens in the same way as other words. Related work on the evaluation and analysis of token-type NCS acquired by current neural language models was reviewed in Section 2.1.

Quantity-type NCS refers to knowledge of numerical properties that have some kind of distribution or range, like "The adult male is approximately 170 cm tall." (Table 1). To acquire this kind of NCS, it is necessary to understand numerals as not only string tokens, but also quantities. Quantity-type NCS is more important for numerical error detection/correction and numerical reasoning than the token-type NCS. In recent years, there has been an increasing amount of research on the acquisition of quantity-type NCS, including the creation of datasets that collect the distributions of some attributes such as weight, length, and price of common objects as well as the verification of such NCS acquired by neural language models using these datasets (Elazar et al., 2019; Zhang et al., 2020; Yamane et al., 2020). In this paper, we aimed to acquire quantity-type NCS as well as token-type NCS with language models, focusing on the fact that there are these two types of NCS.

3.2 Masked Numeral Prediction

3.2.1 Task Description

Masked numeral prediction is the task of predicting a masked numeral in an input natural language text from the words around the masked numeral (e.g., "The movie I saw yesterday was [MASK] minutes long.") (Spithourakis and Riedel, 2018; Lin et al., 2020). In this paper, we use this task as an indicator to evaluate the NCS acquired by language models.

The masked numeral prediction task is defined as follows:

Input : A passage containing exactly one target numeral masked with a special token "[MASK]"

Output : A ranking of predicted numerals

Language models take a passage that contains exactly one masked numeral as input, predict the numerals that could replace the mask token from the context words, and return the predicted numerals in the form of a ranking. The aim of the language models is to predict numerals that are closer to the groundtruth numerals. In the task considered in this paper, the target numerals are limited to numerals in arithmetic form such as "3.14" and "1,000," and numerical words such as "five" or "twenty" are not considered. For negative numerals, only the parts excluding signs were treated as target numerals; the signs were treated as context words (for example, in the case of the negative numeral "-10," only "10" was masked as the target numeral). For fractions, the denominator and numerator were treated as two different numerals in training and evaluation (e.g., the fraction "2/3" was masked in two ways: "[MASK]/3" and "2/[MASK]").

3.2.2 Evaluation Metrics

Exact Match Accuracy A masked numeral prediction model generates a probability distribution over its vocabulary of numeral tokens using a softmax function and returns a ranking of them for each mask. *Hit@k accuracy* calculates the percentage of predictions in which the groundtruth numeral is within the top k predicted numerals from the generated ranking (Lin et al., 2020). In our experiments, we used $k = 1, 3$, and 10 for evaluation.

Numerical Absolute Error The hit@k accuracy metric simply evaluates whether the groundtruth numerals are included in the top k predictions. It does not take into account how close the predicted numerals are to the groundtruth numerals. However, in the masked numeral prediction task, a prediction for a mask that is closer to the groundtruth numeral is generally considered to be a better prediction, even if it is incorrect, so we need an additional evaluation metric to evaluate language models in terms of the magnitude of the difference between the groundtruth numeral and the predicted numeral.

Therefore, in the evaluation in this paper, following a previous work (Spithourakis and Riedel, 2018), we use the *median absolute error* (MdAE) and *median absolute percentage error* (MdAPE). MdAE and MdAPE are commonly used to evaluate regression models. They evaluate closeness on the number line between groundtruth numerals and predicted numerals (Spithourakis and Riedel, 2018). We can say that they evaluate language models in terms of the quantitative aspects of numerals. MdAE and MdAPE are calculated as follows:

$$\mathrm{MdAE} = \mathrm{median}\{|\mathrm{ans}_i - \mathrm{pred}_i|\} \quad (1)$$

$$\mathrm{MdAPE} = \mathrm{median}\left\{\left|\frac{\mathrm{ans}_i - \mathrm{pred}_i}{\mathrm{ans}_i}\right|\right\} \quad (2)$$

where ans_i is the magnitude of a groundtruth numeral, pred_i is the magnitude of a predicted numeral, and N is the number of masked numerals.

4 Approach

4.1 $Loss_{\mathrm{NUM}}$

Naive masked word prediction (MWP) models return a probability distribution over their vocabulary (only numeric words) and they are trained using the cross entropy loss between their outputs and the distribution of the correct answers as a loss function. The usual cross entropy loss treats each token in the vocabulary except for the correct answer equally. However, in the case of the masked numeral prediction task, we are motivated to train language models with a loss function that yields a smaller error for predictions that are numerically closer to the groundtruth numeral and a larger error for predictions that are further away. This is because it is generally considered that a prediction of "9" is better than a prediction of "1" for a mask for which the correct answer is "10." Therefore, in this paper, we propose a loss function $Loss_{\mathrm{NUM}}$, that depends on the magnitudes of the numerals for fine-tuning MWP models.

$Loss_{\mathrm{NUM}}$ is defined as follows:

$$Loss_{\mathrm{NUM}} = \sum_{i=1}^{N} \{(\log(\mathrm{ans}_i) - \log(\mathrm{pred}_i))^2 \times \mathrm{CEL}_i\} \quad (3)$$

where ans_i is the numerical magnitude of a groundtruth numeral, pred_i is the magnitude of the initial numeral predicted by the MWP model, N is the number of masked numerals, and CEL_i is the cross entropy loss calculated for the i-th masked numeral. $Loss_{\mathrm{NUM}}$ is computed using the logarithmic differences between the groundtruth numerals and predicted numerals following the treatment of numerical errors in a previous study (Geva et al., 2020). This is because the logarithmic difference gives more weight to off-by-one errors in small numerals, which are considered to be more fatal than off-by-one errors in large numerals. These differences are then multiplied by the usual cross entropy loss to obtain the $Loss_{\mathrm{NUM}}$. If it is used when fine-tuning pre-trained language models, we expect that the models will be fine-tuned to return numeral tokens that are numerically closer to the groundtruth numerals.

4.2 REG Model

The approach described in Section 4.1 uses ordinary MWP models and the proposed loss, which reflects the magnitudes of the predicted and groundtruth numerals as the loss function during fine tuning. In this section, we propose to use a regression (REG) model for the masked numeral prediction task.

The REG model is structured with an additional numeric output layer as the final layer of BERT. The output layer generates a single numeral between 0 and MAX_NUM from an input passage processed by BERT, where MAX_NUM is the largest numeral occurring in training data. The mean squared error between groundtruth numerals and predicted numerals, which is often used as a loss function and an evaluation metric in regression tasks, is adopted as the loss function ($Loss_{\mathrm{MSE}}$) for fine-tuning the REG model on the masked numeral prediction task. Similarly to the calculation of $Loss_{\mathrm{NUM}}$, $Loss_{\mathrm{MSE}}$ is calculated using the logarithmic values of both the groundtruth numerals and predicted numerals to give more weight to off-by-one errors in small numerals, which are considered to be more fatal than off-by-one errors in large numerals.

$$Loss_{\mathrm{MSE}} = \sum_{i=1}^{N} (\log(\mathrm{ans}_i) - \log(\mathrm{pred}_i))^2 \quad (4)$$

where ans_i is the numerical magnitude of a groundtruth numeral, pred_i is the magnitude of the initial numeral predicted by the REG model, and N is the number of masked numerals. For the evaluation, which includes exact match accuracy, the final output numeral is rounded to the nearest integer and is used as the initial predicted numeral. Next, the integers closest to the first predicted numeral are used as the second predicted numeral, the third predicted numeral, and so on, in order of closeness.

Statistic	WP	SP	FT	AT
Number of passages	4,329	14,821	3,992	420,000
Ave. passage len [tokens]	281.8	278.2	36.7	12.9
Number of numerals	65,783	120,105	10,312	537,214
% of integers	96.4%	80.0%	86.7%	98.5%
% of one-time numerals	2.93%	3.69%	9.74%	0.36%
Variety of numerals	3,667	7,944	1,503	4,204
Numeral duplication	25,269	57,372	1,354	22,555
Mean	1.57e6	5.55e16	2.02e15	2.98e7
Median	24.0	5.0	20.0	17.0

Table 2 Dataset statistics across different four datasets (training set).

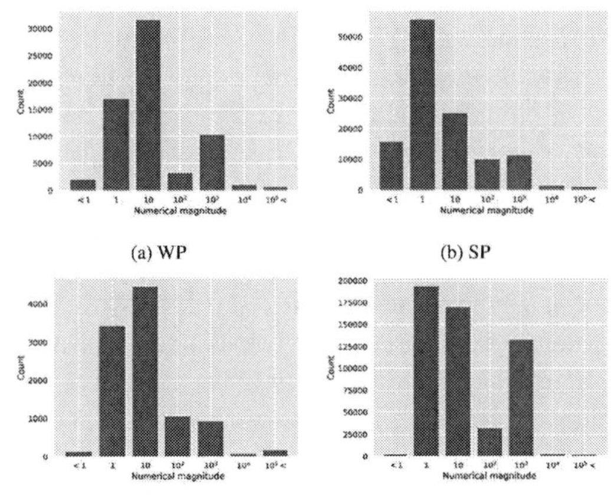

(a) WP (b) SP (c) FT (d) AT

Figure 2 Distribution of the numerals in the training data.

5 Experiments

5.1 Dataset

In our experiments, we used four datasets, DROP (Wikipedia) (Dua et al., 2019), arXiv (Science Papers) (Spithourakis and Riedel, 2018), FinNum (Financial Tweets) (Chen et al., 2018), and Numeracy-600K (Article Titles) (Chen et al., 2019). The data in these datasets differ in passage length, the domain of the passages, and the distribution of the numerals that appear in the datasets. These datasets were created and used for different numerical tasks such as numerical machine reading comprehension and numeral type prediction (Section 2). We use them for the masked numeral prediction in this work. We denote these datasets as "WP," "SP," "FT," and "AT," respectively.

Statistics about the passages and numerals in these four datasets are listed in Table 2. The percentage of numerals that appear only in each dataset ("% of one-time numerals"), the number of different numerals that appear in a dataset ("Variety of numerals"), and the number of numerals that appear more than once in the same passage ("Numeral duplication") are given. Every passage in all four datasets contains one or more numerals.

WP and SP have relatively long passages, and prediction models can make predictions based on hints from unmasked numerals around the masked numeral. In contrast, FT and AT have shorter passages, so there are fewer unmasked numerals in the same passage. In addition, WP and AT tend to contain more token-type numerals such as dates, years, and game scores, whereas SP and FT tend to contain more quantity-type numerals such as the scores of experimental results and stock prices.

The distribution of the numerals in each dataset is shown in Figure 2. The x-axis of each figure shows, from left to right, the counts of numerals less than 1, numerals between 1 and 10, ..., numerals between 10,000 and 100,000, and numerals greater than 100,000. We can see from this figure that WP and AT certainly contain many years, and thus the proportion of four-digit numerals in WP and AT is higher than in the other datasets, and FT has more numerals with six or more digits to represent high amounts of money.

5.2 Experimental Setup

In the experiments, we used the BERT-based MWP model as the baseline model. It consists of the BERT model with an additional softmax layer as the final layer. Given an input passage processed by BERT, the softmax layer outputs the probability distribution over the model's vocabulary of numeric words. Each mask in a passage can be filled with a single numeric word, and the numeric vocabulary contains not numerals expressed in English words such as "ten" and "twenty-four" but numerals expressed in arithmetic characters such as "10," "2021," and "10,000."

In this experiment, we used the Adam optimizer with a learning rate of 5×10^{-5}. The batch size for fine-tuning and evaluation was 32 and the max-grad-norm was 1.0. All tokens except the numerals in the passages were tokenized by the BERT tokenizer and passages were truncated to sequences no longer than 512 tokens.

In this evaluation, we did not split numerals into sub-words using BERT but treated them as single words using our own additional rules. By treating numerals as single words, we believe that it becomes easier to learn mappings between strings of numerals and their corresponding numerical magnitudes, which is difficult to learn from sub-word segmented numerals. The single word segmentation of numerals also eliminates the need to use encoder–decoder models or other methods to predict sub-word sequences for masks when predicting numerals, which has the advantage of making the masked numeral prediction task easier to handle, even for naive MWP models.

6 Result and Discussion

6.1 $Loss_{\mathrm{NUM}}$

Table 3 shows the result of the naive BERT-based MWP model with pre-training but without fine-tuning (MWP), fine-tuned MWP with cross entropy loss (Ft. MWP w/ CEL), and fine-tuned MWP with $Loss_{\mathrm{NUM}}$ (3) (Ft. MWP w/ LN). Each dataset is divided into three parts: training set, validation set, and test set. Each fine-tuned model is fine-tuned first on the training set and then on the validation set of the corresponding dataset, and then it is evaluated on the test set of the same dataset.

First, comparing MWP and Ft. MWP w/ CEL, we can see that the scores of all metrics have been improved by fine-tuning for all datasets. Moreover, the increases in the scores obtained on FT and AT are substantially larger than those obtained on WP and SP. This is probably because the average passage lengths of WP and SP are longer than those of FT and AT, and the language models succeeded

Dataset	Approach	hit@1↑	hit@3↑	hit@10↑	MdAE↓	MdAPE↓
WP	MWP	23.8	32.1	45.0	7.0	42.9
	Ft.MWP w/ CEL	**28.5**	36.6	49.0	**5.4**	**25.0**
	Ft.MWP w/ LN	**28.5**	**37.2**	**50.2**	6.0	28.6
SP	MWP	40.1	50.2	63.1	2.0	50.0
	Ft.MWP w/ CEL	45.5	55.5	67.7	**1.0**	33.3
	Ft.MWP w/ LN	**48.4**	**57.6**	**69.2**	**1.0**	**25.5**
FT	MWP	19.9	27.8	43.2	10.0	85.1
	Ft.MWP w/ CEL	**40.5**	**49.1**	**60.0**	**3.0**	50.0
	Ft.MWP w/ LN	40.0	48.2	59.4	**3.0**	**46.7**
AT	MWP	20.1	32.7	54.7	7.0	80.0
	Ft.MWP w/ CEL	**56.3**	**69.1**	**80.4**	**1.0**	**0.0994**
	Ft.MWP w/ LN	55.7	68.5	80.0	**1.0**	0.0995

Table 3 Hit@k accuracy (%), MdAE, and MdAPE (%) of the BERT-based MWP models on the four datasets.

in predicting masked numerals in WP and SP to some extent from context words and surrounding unmasked numerals without fine-tuning (Table 2).

Next, we compare Ft.MWP w/ CEL and Ft. MWP w/ LN. Focusing on the MdAE and MdAPE scores, it is confirmed that the reduction in the numerical absolute errors of the predictions, which is the objective of the proposed loss function $Loss_{\mathrm{NUM}}$, is achieved on the SP and FT datasets. In contrast, the MdAE and MdAPE scores of the WP and AT datasets increased. This may be due to the different nature of the numerals in these datasets. Because of the nature of the domains of these datasets, the WP and AT datasets contain many numerals that are better understood as string tokens, such as years, dates, and football game scores. Hence, fine-tuning with $Loss_{\mathrm{NUM}}$ does not improve the accuracy of masked numeral prediction in these datasets. In contrast, the SP and FT datasets contain more numerals that are better understood as quantities, such as the numerals representing scores of experimental results or detailed amounts of money, and it is thought that reflecting the magnitudes of these numerals in model training improves the prediction accuracy in SP and FT.[1] The proposed loss function $Loss_{\mathrm{NUM}}$, which is intended to help language models understand the magnitudes of the numerals and reduce the numerical absolute errors, also leads to a small but significant improvement in the hit@k accuracies on some datasets.

Passages **a)** and **b)** in Table 4 are examples where the MWP model fine-tuned with the cross entropy loss made largely incorrect predictions. Passage **a)** shows predictions in a context where it can be

[1]The percentage of integers in the dataset and the distribution of the numerals can also reveal the trend of the numerals in the dataset (Table 2, Figure 2).

inferred that the masked numeral is greater than 1724 and not much larger than 1724. The MWP model fine-tuned with the cross entropy loss returned "1925," which is numerically far from the groundtruth numeral, although it is considered to be a numeral representing a year. In contrast, the MWP model fine-tuned with $Loss_{\mathrm{NUM}}$ returned "1727," which is not correct, but is above 1724 and not far from 1724. Note that "1925" and "1727" do not appear in the context passage, and the models chose these numerals out of their respective vocabularies. In passage **b)**, the context suggests that the masked numeral is considered to be a numeral representing a percentage between 0 and 100 (more specifically, between 75.6 and 100) from its context. However, for this mask, the MWP model fine-tuned with the cross entropy loss predicted "50,000," which substantially exceeds 100. In contrast, the MWP model fine-tuned with $Loss_{\mathrm{NUM}}$ successfully predicted a numeral less than 100, although it should be greater than 75.6. These are successful examples where language models were fine-tuned to predict numerals that are numerically close to the groundtruth numerals by fine-tuning them with $Loss_{\mathrm{NUM}}$, which imposes large penalties on numerically large errors. In some cases, fine-tuning language models with $Loss_{\mathrm{NUM}}$ caused them to fail to predict numerals that the models fine-tuned with the cross entropy loss predicted correctly. This could also cause them to predict numerals that were rather far from the groundtruth numerals.

6.2 REG Model

In this section, we compare and analyze prediction results of the naive BERT-based MWP model fine-tuned with the cross entropy loss and the REG model fine-tuned with $Loss_{\mathrm{MSE}}$ (4). We used the WP dataset to train and evaluate them.

The results of the fine-tuned MWP model with the cross entropy loss (Ft. MWP w/ CEL) and the fine-tuned REG model with $Loss_{\mathrm{MSE}}$ (Ft. REG w/ MSE) listed in Table 5 reveal that the REG model is substantially inferior to the MWP model with respect to prediction accuracy. [2] However, the REG model can predict large numerals better and has fewer large errors, indicating that the two models are good at predicting numerals with different characteristics (Figure 3). Figure 3 shows heat maps representing confusion matrices of the groundtruth numerals and the numerals predicted by the two models. The numerals are classified by the number of digits. In both heat maps, the y axis is the number of digits of the groundtruth numerals and the x-axis is that of predicted numerals. The darker the blue, the higher the percentage of numerals belonging to the corresponding cell in each row.

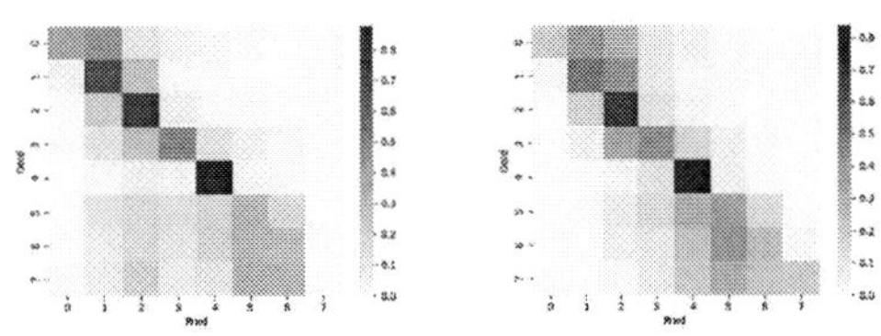

(a) Fine-tuned MWP model (b) Fine-tuned REG model

Figure 3 Confusion matrices of the digits of the groundtruth numerals and the predicted numerals from the two models.

The percentage of substantially incorrect predictions that differ by more than one, two, and three digits from the groundtruth numerals are respectively 8.5%, 3.4%, and 1.5% for the MWP model, whereas they are significantly lower, that is, 7.7%, 1.8%, and 0.4% for the REG model (Table 6). This indicates that the overall prediction accuracies of the REG model are quite low, and for many numerals, the MWP model can provide better predictions. However, there are certain numerals that the REG model can predict more accurately than the MWP model. Moreover, the confusion matrices also indicate that the REG model is more suitable for predicting large numerals than the MWP model, suggesting that the MWP and REG models are good at predicting different types of numerals.

Table 4 shows examples of incorrect predictions made by the MWP models and the REG model. Passage **c)** is an example where the REG model made better predictions for a large numeral than did the MWP models. The reason why the MWP models predicted "94.7" and "10.7" is that the context in which the word "census" appears in the training data has many occurrences of numerals that represent percentages (including "94.7" and "10.7"), such as the percentage of population by age. From these results, it can be seen that the MWP models basically do not understand the magnitude of the numerals and learn relationships between numerals as string tokens and context words. Passage **d)** shows that the MWP models are effective in predicting a masked numeral where the groundtruth numeral also appears elsewhere in the passage.

[2] Note that the difference between the scores of "Ft. MWP w/ CEL" in WP on Table 3 and the scores of "Ft. MWP w/ CEL" on Table 5 is because the models in Table 5 are trained on half of the Wikipedia dataset.

Passage	Ans	CEL	LN	REG
a) Captain John Lovewell made three expeditions against the Indians. On the first expedition in December **1724**, he and his militia company of **30** men left Dunstable, ... On December **10**, **1724**, they and a company of rangers killed two Abenakis. In February **[MASK]**, Lovewell made a second expedition to the Lake Winnipesaukee area. ...	1725	1925	1727	762.0
b) Houston is considered an Automobile dependency city, with an estimated **[MASK]**% of commuters driving alone to work in **2016**, up from **71.7**% in **1990** and **75.6**% in **2009**. ...	77.2	50,000	11	12.0
c) As of the census of **2010**, there were **[MASK]** people, **140,602** households, and **114,350** families residing in the county. ...	516,564	94.7	10.7	118523.0
d) In September **1941**, Partisans organized sabotage at the General Post Office in Zagreb. ... In November **[MASK]**, German troops attacked and reoccupied this territory, with the majority of Partisan forces escaping towards Bosnia. ...	1941	1941	1941	1287.0

Table 4 Examples of incorrect predictions in the WP dataset. We list the context passages containing one masked numerals ("Passage"), the groundtruth numerals ("Ans") and the numerals predicted by the MWP model fine-tuned with the cross entropy loss ("CEL"), by the MWP model fine-tuned with $Loss_{\mathrm{NUM}}$ ("LN"), and by the REG model fine-tuned with $Loss_{\mathrm{MSE}}$ ("REG").

Model	hit@1↑	hit@3↑	hit@10↑	MdAE↓	MdAPE↓
Ft.MWP w/ CEL	27.4	35.8	48.6	6.0	28.6
Ft.REG w/ MSE	4.19	7.52	15.2	54.0	60.0

Table 5 Hit@k accuracy (%), MdAE, and MdAPE (%) of two approaches on the WP dataset.

Model	±2~ digits	±3~ digits	±4~ digits
Ft.MWP w/ CEL	8.5%	3.4%	1.5%
Ft.REG w/ MSE	**7.7%**	**1.8%**	**0.4%**

Table 6 Percentages of substantially incorrect predictions of the MWP and REG model.

6.3 Future Work

MdAE, which uses the numerical absolute errors between predicted numerals and groundtruth numerals, is sensitive to the scale of the data and is easily affected by the prediction accuracy for large numerals in a dataset that contains numerals of different scales and types. MdAPE, which evaluates absolute percentage errors, imposes large penalties on the overestimation of masked numerals. For example, a prediction of "1" for "31" in a sentence "Today is October 31." and a prediction of "31" for "1" in a sentence "Today is October 1." should both be equally wrong, but the former results in an error of approximately $\frac{|31-1|}{31} \times 100 \approx 100\%$, whereas the latter results in an error of $\frac{|1-31|}{1} \times 100 = 3000\%$. Because of these problems, there is room for consideration of the appropriate evaluation metrics for the masked numeral prediction task.

Although the REG model has a lower prediction accuracy than existing language models, there are certain numerals that the REG model can predict more accurately than the MWP model. This implies that the overall prediction accuracy can be improved by using the MWP model and the REG model differently depending on the target numerals. Such a combination method is also one task for future work.

7 Conclusion

In this paper, we used the exact match accuracy and numerical absolute errors metrics to evaluate the masked numerical prediction task, focusing on the fact that numerals have two aspects: symbolic and quantitative. Based on this fact, we proposed two methods to reflect the two aspects of numerals in the training of language models. Although the proposed loss function, $Loss_{\mathrm{NUM}}$, decreased the exact match accuracy slightly, it also reduced the numerical absolute errors on the masked numeral prediction task, indicating the effectiveness of $Loss_{\mathrm{NUM}}$. Furthermore, we analyzed the relationship between the properties of numerals in datasets and the performances of different prediction methods on four datasets with different properties. As a result, it was found that the types of numerals that are likely to be mistakenly predicted depend on which method is used.

Acknowledgements

The authors would like to thank the anonymous reviewers for their helpful comments. This work was supported by JSPS KAKENHI Grant Number 21H03502 and SIP2 NEDO Program "Big-data and AI-enabled Cyberspace Technologies."

References

Zied Bouraoui, José Camacho-Collados, and Steven Schockaert. 2019. Inducing relational knowledge from BERT. *CoRR*, abs/1911.12753.

Tom B. Brown, Benjamin Mann, Nick Ryder, Melanie Subbiah, Jared Kaplan, Prafulla Dhariwal, Arvind Neelakantan, Pranav Shyam, Girish Sastry, Amanda Askell, Sandhini Agarwal, Ariel Herbert-Voss, Gretchen Krueger, Tom Henighan, Rewon Child, Aditya Ramesh, Daniel M. Ziegler, Jeffrey Wu, Clemens Winter, Christopher Hesse, Mark Chen, Eric Sigler, Mateusz Litwin, Scott Gray, Benjamin Chess, Jack Clark, Christopher Berner, Sam McCandlish, Alec Radford, Ilya Sutskever, and Dario Amodei. 2020. Language models are few-shot learners.

Chung-Chi Chen, Hen-Hsen Huang, Yow-Ting Shiue, and Hsin-Hsi Chen. 2018. Numeral understanding in financial tweets for fine-grained crowd-based forecasting. *CoRR*, abs/1809.05356.

Chung-Chi Chen, Hen-Hsen Huang, Hiroya Takamura, and Hsin-Hsi Chen. 2019. Numeracy-600K: Learning numeracy for detecting exaggerated information in market comments. In *Proceedings of the 57th Annual Meeting of the Association for Computational Linguistics*, pages 6307–6313, Florence, Italy. Association for Computational Linguistics.

Joe Davison, Joshua Feldman, and Alexander Rush. 2019. Commonsense knowledge mining from pretrained models. In *Proceedings of the 2019 Conference on Empirical Methods in Natural Language Processing and the 9th International Joint Conference on Natural Language Processing (EMNLP-IJCNLP)*, pages 1173–1178, Hong Kong, China. Association for Computational Linguistics.

Jacob Devlin, Ming-Wei Chang, Kenton Lee, and Kristina Toutanova. 2019. BERT: Pre-training of deep bidirectional transformers for language understanding. In *Proceedings of the 2019 Conference of the North American Chapter of the Association for Computational Linguistics: Human Language Technologies, Volume 1 (Long and Short Papers)*, pages 4171–4186, Minneapolis, Minnesota. Association for Computational Linguistics.

Dheeru Dua, Yizhong Wang, Pradeep Dasigi, Gabriel Stanovsky, Sameer Singh, and Matt Gardner. 2019. DROP: A reading comprehension benchmark requiring discrete reasoning over paragraphs. In *Proceedings of the 2019 Conference of the North American Chapter of the Association for Computational Linguistics: Human Language Technologies, Volume 1 (Long and Short Papers)*, pages 2368–2378, Minneapolis, Minnesota. Association for Computational Linguistics.

Yanai Elazar, Abhijit Mahabal, Deepak Ramachandran, Tania Bedrax-Weiss, and Dan Roth. 2019. How large are lions? inducing distributions over quantitative attributes. In *Proceedings of the 57th Annual Meeting of the Association for Computational Linguistics*, pages 3973–3983, Florence, Italy. Association for Computational Linguistics.

Mor Geva, Ankit Gupta, and Jonathan Berant. 2020. Injecting numerical reasoning skills into language models. In *Proceedings of the 58th Annual Meeting of the Association for Computational Linguistics*, pages 946–958, Online. Association for Computational Linguistics.

Alex Graves. 2013. Generating sequences with recurrent neural networks. *CoRR*, abs/1308.0850.

Minghao Hu, Yuxing Peng, Zhen Huang, and Dongsheng Li. 2019. A multi-type multi-span network for reading comprehension that requires discrete reasoning. In *Proceedings of the 2019 Conference on Empirical Methods in Natural Language Processing and the 9th International Joint Conference on Natural Language Processing (EMNLP-IJCNLP)*, pages 1596–1606, Hong Kong, China. Association for Computational Linguistics.

Zhenzhong Lan, Mingda Chen, Sebastian Goodman, Kevin Gimpel, Piyush Sharma, and Radu Soricut. 2020. Albert: A lite bert for self-supervised learning of language representations.

Bill Yuchen Lin, Seyeon Lee, Rahul Khanna, and Xiang Ren. 2020. Birds have four legs?! NumerSense: Probing Numerical Commonsense Knowledge of Pre-Trained Language Models. In *Proceedings of the 2020 Conference on Empirical Methods in Natural Language Processing (EMNLP)*, pages 6862–6868, Online. Association for Computational Linguistics.

Yinhan Liu, Myle Ott, Naman Goyal, Jingfei Du, Mandar Joshi, Danqi Chen, Omer Levy, Mike Lewis, Luke Zettlemoyer, and Veselin Stoyanov. 2019. Roberta: A robustly optimized bert pretraining approach.

Fabio Petroni, Tim Rocktäschel, Sebastian Riedel, Patrick Lewis, Anton Bakhtin, Yuxiang Wu, and Alexander Miller. 2019. Language models as knowledge bases? In *Proceedings of the 2019 Conference on Empirical Methods in Natural Language Processing and the 9th International Joint Conference on Natural Language Processing (EMNLP-IJCNLP)*, pages 2463–2473, Hong Kong, China. Association for Computational Linguistics.

Georgios Spithourakis, Isabelle Augenstein, and Sebastian Riedel. 2016. Numerically grounded language models for semantic error correction. In *Proceedings of the 2016 Conference on Empirical Methods in Natural Language Processing*, pages 987–992, Austin, Texas. Association for Computational Linguistics.

Georgios Spithourakis and Sebastian Riedel. 2018. Numeracy for language models: Evaluating and improving their ability to predict numbers. In *Proceedings of the 56th Annual Meeting of the Association for Computational Linguistics (Volume 1: Long Papers)*, pages 2104–2115, Melbourne, Australia. Association for Computational Linguistics.

Ilya Sutskever, James Martens, and Geoffrey Hinton. 2011. Generating text with recurrent neural networks. In *Proceedings of the 28th International Conference on International Conference on Machine Learning*, ICML'11, pages 1017–1024, USA. Omnipress.

Alon Talmor, Yanai Elazar, Yoav Goldberg, and Jonathan Berant. 2020. oLMpics-on what language model pre-training captures. *Transactions of the Association for Computational Linguistics*, 8:743–758.

Eric Wallace, Yizhong Wang, Sujian Li, Sameer Singh, and Matt Gardner. 2019. Do NLP models know numbers? probing numeracy in embeddings. In *Proceedings of the 2019 Conference on Empirical Methods in Natural Language Processing and the 9th International Joint Conference on Natural Language Processing (EMNLP-IJCNLP)*, pages 5307–5315, Hong Kong, China. Association for Computational Linguistics.

Hiroaki Yamane, Chin-Yew Lin, and Tatsuya Harada. 2020. Measuring numerical common sense: Is a word embedding approach effective?

Xikun Zhang, Deepak Ramachandran, Ian Tenney, Yanai Elazar, and Dan Roth. 2020. Do language embeddings capture scales? In *Findings of the Association for Computational Linguistics: EMNLP 2020*, pages 4889–4896, Online. Association for Computational Linguistics.

Xuhui Zhou, Yue Zhang, Leyang Cui, and Dandan Huang. 2019. Evaluating commonsense in pretrained language models. *CoRR*, abs/1911.11931.

Author Index

Aizawa, Akiko, 140
Arcan, Mihael, 70

Bagherzadeh, Parsa, 108
Balachandran, Vidhisha, 25
Bang, Seojin, 96
Bansal, Mohit, 58
Bauer, Lisa, 58
Becker, Maria, 11
Bergler, Sabine, 108
Bhat, Savita, 119
Bihani, Geetanjali, 81
Brunato, Dominique, 40
Buitelaar, Paul, 70

Carenini, Giuseppe, 96
Chen, Yubei, 1
Cohen, William, 25
Collins, Michael, 25

Dalal, Dhairya, 70
Dell'Orletta, Felice, 40, 48
Deng, Lingjia, 58
Dhingra, Bhuwan, 25

Frank, Anette, 11

Hupkes, Dieuwke, 129

Jang, Hyeju, 96
Jumelet, Jaap, 129

Karande, Shirish, 119
Kersten, Tom, 129

LeCun, Yann, 1
Lee, Young ji, 96
Liang, Siting, 11

Miaschi, Alessio, 40, 48

Ng, Raymond, 96

Olshausen, Bruno, 1

Pedanekar, Niranjan, 119
Pilli, Stephen, 119
Puccetti, Giovanni, 48

Rayz, Julia, 81

Sakamoto, Taku, 140
Srivastava, Vivek, 119
Sun, Haitian, 25

Venturi, Giulia, 40

Wong, Hugh Mee, 129
Wu, Junjie, 31

Xiao, Wen, 96

Yun, Zeyu, 1

Zhou, Hao, 31

Association for Computational Linguistics
209 N. Eighth Street
Stroudsburg, Pennsylvania 18360

ISBN 978-1-7138-3022-1

9 781713 830221

CURRAN ASSOCIATES INC.
proceedings.com